Bible
Dictionary

Bible Facts at Your Fingertips

CONTRIBUTING WRITERS:
CECIL MURPHEY
GARY HUFFMAN
LYNN JAMES
JUNE EATON
BARBARA ROBERTS PINE

CONSULTANT:
GARY BURGE, PH.D.

PUBLICATIONS INTERNATIONAL, LTD.

Cecil Murphey, M.A., M.Div., is the author of 66 books, including the *Dictionary of Biblical Literacy* and *Invading the Privacy of God*. He also co-wrote the biography *Gifted Hands* with Dr. Ben Carson.

Gary W. Huffman, a graduate of Princeton Theological Seminary, is a pastor of The First Presbyterian Church. He is also a master practitioner in Neuro-Linguistics.

Rev. Lynn James, L.C.P.C., is an ordained minister and co-pastor with a M.Div. from Christian Theological Seminary. In addition, she is a licensed clinical counselor in private practice, specializing in work with survivors of interpersonal violence.

June Eaton is a teacher and freelance writer with an M.A. from Northwestern University. Her published work includes Sunday school curriculum, stories and articles in more than 50 Christian publications, and contributions to eight books.

Barbara Roberts Pine is an author and speaker who holds an M.A. in Theology from Fuller Theological Seminary. She has lectured at religious retreats and leadership seminars, and her published writing includes the book *Life with a Capital "L"*.

Picture credits:
Front cover: **Scala/Art Resource**

Archive Photos: 42, 60, 163, 291, 461; **Art Resource:** Alinari: 59, 247, 250, 264, 276; Foto Marburg: 50; Giraudon: 79, 112; Erich Lessing: 127, 173, 267; Joseph Parnell/Jewish Museum, New York: 234; The Pierpont Morgan Library, New York: 296 (m.652,f.103v.); Scala: 74, 325; **Corbis-Bettmann:** 11, 33, 34, 39, 80, 89, 128, 141, 178, 211, 220, 230, 243, 298, 397, 432; UPI: 261; **Richard T. Nowitz:** 97, 118, 189, 254, 262, 297, 337, 345, 360, 382, 438, 487; Abe A. Nowitz: 174; **Richard T. Nowitz/FPG International:** 481; **Z. Radovan, Jerusalem:** 8, 57, 92, 107, 113, 123, 146 (bottom), 149, 160, 165, 225, 271, 285, 301, 327, 333, 338, 352, 357, 379, 386, 411, 416, 420, 469, 492, 494, 511; **Ann Ronan at Image Select:** 26, 47, 197, 202, 280; **SuperStock:** 119, 347, 370, 388, 471, 505; Avignon, France/Silvio Fiore: 23; Bearsted Collection, Upton House near Banbury: 500; Christie's Images: 299; Correr Civic Museum, Venice/ET Archive, London: 206; Explorer, Paris: 142 (left); Jewish Museum, New York: 401; Musee Du Louvre, Paris: 146 (top); St. Anne's Museum, Lubeck: 142 (right).

Louis Weber, C.E.O.
Publications International, Ltd.
7373 North Cicero Avenue
Lincolnwood, Illinois 60646

Permission is never granted for commercial purposes.

Manufactured in U.S.A.

8 7 6 5 4 3 2 1

ISBN: 0-7853-3765-2

spelling are also furnished, to show you how the entry words should sound.

More than 150 sidebar articles provide extra material to enhance your enjoyment and understanding of the Bible, its times and events, and the people who march across its pages. These are also intended to enrich your knowledge about the lives of biblical personalities so that you can more easily draw parallels in your own life.

The New Revised Standard Version of the Bible is the main source for quotations in this volume, though many references are made to the Apocrypha as well as to other versions and translations of Scripture. (A guide to the abbreviations used in the references appears on page 6.) Some of the information has been derived from historical and other ancient nonbiblical writings, but all facts are supported by the Bible texts themselves.

The information gathered for this book covers many different subject areas, including biographical data, archaeology, everyday life, food, clothing, shelter, geography, flora and fauna, religion, history, travel, business, education, and a host of other categories. It can provide answers to such intriguing questions as: Who was Deborah, and what made her unique as a woman? What did the denarius, shekel, and drachma have in common? How are sheep portrayed in the Old Testament versus the New Testament? Why was rain so important to the Israelites? Where did the crucifixion take place?

The Bible: A to Z will not only answer your questions; it will also help you identify people and incidents, clarify concepts, and furnish background information to make your study of the Bible a rich and fulfilling experience.

THE BOOKS OF THE BIBLE

THE OLD TESTAMENT

BOOK	ABBREVIATION
Genesis	Gen
Exodus	Ex
Leviticus	Lev
Numbers	Nu
Deuteronomy	Dt
Joshua	Jos
Judges	Jdg
Ruth	Ru
1 Samuel	1Sa
2 Samuel	2Sa
1 Kings	1Ki
2 Kings	2Ki
1 Chronicles	1Ch
2 Chronicles	2Ch
Ezra	Ezr
Nehemiah	Ne
Esther	Est
Job	Job
Psalms	Ps
Proverbs	Pr
Ecclesiastes	Eccl
Song of Solomon	SS
Isaiah	Isa
Jeremiah	Jer
Lamentations	Lam
Ezekiel	Eze
Daniel	Da
Hosea	Hos
Joel	Joel
Amos	Am
Obadiah	Ob
Jonah	Jon
Micah	Mic
Nahum	Nah
Habakkuk	Ha
Zephaniah	Zeph
Haggai	Hag
Zechariah	Zech
Malachi	Mal

THE NEW TESTAMENT

BOOK	ABBREVIATION
Matthew	Mt
Mark	Mk
Luke	Lk
John	Jn
Acts of the Apostles	Ac
Romans	Ro
1 Corinthians	1Co
2 Corinthians	2Co
Galatians	Gal
Ephesians	Eph
Philippians	Php
Colossians	Col
1 Thessalonians	1Thess
2 Thessalonians	2Thess
1 Timothy	1Ti
2 Timothy	2Ti
Titus	Tit
Philemon	Phm
Hebrews	He
James	Jas
1 Peter	1Pe
2 Peter	2Pe
1 John	1Jn
2 John	2Jn
3 John	3Jn
Jude	Jude
Revelation	Rev

APOCRYPHAL BOOKS

BOOK	ABBREVIATION
Tobit	Tob
Judith	Jdt
Additions to Esther	AddEst
Wisdom of Solomon	Wis
Sirach (Ecclesiasticus)	Sir
Baruch	Bar
1 Esdras	1Esd
2 Esdras	2Esd
Letter of Jeremiah	Let Jer
Prayer of Azariah and the Song of the Three Jews	Song of Thr
Susanna	Sus
Bel and the Dragon	Bel
1 Maccabees	1Mac
2 Maccabees	2Mac
3 Maccabees	3Mac
4 Maccabees	4Mac
Prayer of Manasseh	Pr Man
Psalm 151	Ps

AARONIC BLESSING—The priestly blessing pronounced by Aaron (Nu 6:22–27): "The Lord bless you and keep you, the Lord make his face to shine upon you, and be gracious to you. The Lord lift up his countenance upon you, and give you peace."

ABANA *(uh BAN uh)*—A major river of Damascus. When Elisha told the Syrian commander Naaman to wash seven times in the Jordan River to cure his leprosy, Naaman insisted that the waters of the Abana were better (2Ki 5:12).

ABARIM *(uh BAR im)*—A mountainous region near the Dead Sea. The Israelites camped there during their wilderness wanderings (Nu 21:10–20, 33:44). *See* **IYE-ABARIM.**

ABBA *(AH buh; "daddy" or "poppa")*—Jesus and Paul used this informal term to affectionately address God. The word occurs three times in the New Testament, always in prayer (Mk 14:36; Ro 8:15; Gal 4:6).

ABEDNEGO *(uh BED neh goh; "servant of [the deity] Nego")*—The Babylonian name given to one of Daniel's friends. When offered rich food, Abednego—and two other men—refused, choosing to live on vegetables and water. They became exceptional in learning and wisdom (Da 1:7–17).

¹ABEL *(AY buhl)*—The second son of Adam and Eve (Gen 4:1–2). His animal offering was more acceptable to God than his brother Cain's offering of grain. Jealous and angry, Cain murdered Abel.

AARON

The older brother of Moses, Aaron accompanied Moses in leading the Israelites out of Egypt (Ex 12:31) and on the journey through the wilderness (Ex 16).

For Israel to win the battle against Amalek, Moses needed to keep his staff raised over his head. When his arms wearied, Aaron and Hur supported his hands (Ex 17:12).

Aaron became Israel's first high priest (Ex 6:20, 7:7; Nu 26:59; Lev 8:6). Despite being a strong spiritual leader, he occasionally disobeyed God. When Moses was on the mountain receiving the tables of law, Aaron made a golden calf for the people to worship (Ex 32:1–6). Later, he and his sister Miriam criticized Moses and insisted that he was not the only prophet of God.

Although Miriam alone was punished with leprosy, Aaron appealed to Moses for mercy on behalf of them both (Nu 12:1–12). Because of the times he had shown a lack of trust in God, Aaron was not allowed to enter the Promised Land (Nu 20:22–29).

²ABEL *(AY buhl)*—The site, located near Beth-Shemesh, where the Philistines returned the ark of the covenant after it was taken from Israel in battle (1Sa 6:18).

ABEL-BETH-MAACAH *(AY buhl beth MA uh kuh)*—A

city in northern Israel where Sheba fled after he revolted in Israel (2Sa 20:14–15).

ABIATHAR *(uh BYE uh thar)*—A descendant of Eli the high priest, Abiathar was the only survivor when his brothers and his father Ahimelech were slain under the orders of King Saul (1Sa 22:20–22).

ABIB *(A bib)*—The first Hebrew month (March–April), during which the Israelites celebrated the Passover and the Feast of Unleavened Bread.(Dt 16:1).

ABIEL *(AY bee el; "my father is God")*—**1.** The grandfather of King Saul (1Sa 9:1). **2.** One of David's mighty men (1Ch 11:32).

ABIEZER *(AY bih EE zur; "my father is help")*—**1.** A descendant of Manasseh (1Ch 7:18). **2.** One of David's mighty men from the tribe of Benjamin (2Sa 23:27).

ABIGAIL *(AB ih gayl; "my father rejoices")*—**1.** Nabal's wife. She befriended David and later married him after Nabal's death (1Sa 25:3). **2.** A sister of David (1Ch 2:16).

ABIHAIL *(AB ih hayl; "my father is strength")*—**1.** A Levite of the family of Merari (Nu 3:35). **2.** The wife of Abishur of Judah (1Ch 2:29). **3.** A man from the tribe of Gad who fathered seven sons (1Ch 5:14). **4.** A niece of King David (2Ch 11:18). **5.** The father of Queen Esther (Est 2:15).

ABIHU *(uh BYE hoo; "my father is he")*—A priest and son of Aaron. He and his brother Nadab offered unauthorized fire to God. They both died for that profane act (Lev 10:1–3).

ABIJAH *(uh BYE jah; "my father is the Lord")*—**1.** The head of the priestly division at the time of David (1Ch 24:10). **2.** Grandson of King Saul (1Ch 7:8). **3.** A corrupt judge and son of

Samuel (1Sa 8:1–5). **4.** Son of King Jeroboam I (1Ki 14:1). **5.** Son and successor of King Rehoboam (2Ch 12:16). **6.** Mother of King Hezekiah (2Ch 29:1). **7.** The head of a family of priests after the Exile (Ne 12:1). **8.** Hezron's wife (1Ch 2:24). **9.** One of the priests who signed a renewed covenant with God (Ne 10:7).

ABIMELECH (*uh BIM e lek; "my father is king"*)—**1.** King of the Philistines and a contemporary of Abraham (Gen 20:1). **2.** King of the Philistines, likely the son of Abimelech 1 (Gen 26:1–6). **3.** A son of Gideon who killed 69 of his 70 brothers (Jdg 8:31–9:6). **4.** Another name for King Achish, in whose presence David feigned madness (1Sa 21:10–15).

ABIRAM (*uh BYE ruhm; "my father is exalted"*)—**1.** A Reubenite who, with his brother Dathan, rebelled against Moses (Nu 16). **2.** The firstborn son of Hiel. At the cost of his Abiram's life, Ahab rebuilt Jericho (1Ki 16:34).

ABISHAG (*AB ih shag*)—A beautiful virgin chosen to lie against David to give him warmth (1Ki 1:1–4).

ABISHAI (*AB ih shy*)—David's nephew. A courageous follower of David, he single-handedly killed 300 enemies.

ABNER (*AB nur; "father is a lamp"*)—Uncle of King Saul. He became the commander of Saul's army (1Sa 14:50–51).

ABOMINATION—Anything that offends the spiritual or moral sense. In the Old Testament, abominations included carved images of pagan gods (Dt 7:25–26), sexual transgressions (Lev 18), and the practice of magic or witchcraft (Dt 18:9–12).

ABRAHAM'S BOSOM—A synonym for the life hereafter.

ABRAHAM

The first great patriarch of Israel, Abraham was the primary model of faithfulness.

He was born as Abram and lived in Haran. When he was 75, God called him to go to Canaan. Although childless, God promised him and his wife Sarai a son, through whom he would be the father of a great nation. When he was 99, God changed Abram's name to Abraham (and Sarai became Sarah). The following year, Sarah gave birth to Isaac.

Abraham and an angel at the sacrifice of Isaac

Some years later, God tested Abraham by telling him to sacrifice Isaac. Obediently, he bound the boy and raised a knife to kill him. At the last moment, God intervened, showing Abraham a ram entangled in the bushes for him to sacrifice instead.

After Sarah died, Abraham purchased the Cave of Machpelah in which to bury her. Abraham then married Keturah, and their sons became ancestors of the tribes of Dedan and Midian. He died at age 175. The story of Abraham marks the beginning of the nation of Israel and their commitment to monotheism.

In the Old Testament, people who died were believed to reunite with their ancestors (Gen 15:15). Because Abraham was regarded as the father of the Jews, the deceased would join him in the afterlife. (Lk 16: 19–31).

ABRAM—The original name of Abraham.

ABSALOM *(AB suh luhm)*— A son of David who took the kingship from his father by force. David escaped, and Absalom became king (2Sa 19:19). Later, he was killed in battle against David's forces.

ABSTINENCE—The voluntary, self-imposed, and deliberate denial of certain pleasures, such as food, drink, or sex. As a noun, the term appears only in Acts 27:21. As a verb, it appears six times in the New Testament.

ABYSS *(uh BISS)*—A bottomless pit. Originally, the word meant a deep mass of waters, but the Bible frequently used it to refer to the place of the dead (Lk 8:31).

ACACIA *(uh KAY shuh)*—A large, thorny tree with rough, gnarled bark. Its heavy, durable wood was used to build the ark of the covenant and the first tabernacle (Ex 36:20).

ACCAD—*See* **AKKAD.**

ACCEPTANCE—To receive or treat with favor. The Bible mentions individuals being accepted by God, but the word also applies to offerings God accepted when given according to divine instructions.

ACCESS—A relationship in which believers have confidence they are acceptable to God. This relationship is possible because Jesus opened "the new and living way" to God (Heb 10:20).

ACCO *(ACK co)*—A major port on the Mediterranean coast north of Mount Carmel. In New Testament times, it was called Ptolemais. On his third missionary journey, Paul disembarked there to visit its church (Ac 21:7).

ACELDAMA—*See* **AKELDAMA**.

ACHAIA *(uh KAY yah)*—The name for Greece, given when the Romans conquered Corinth in 146 B.C.. Paul passed through Achaia on his way to Jerusalem (Ac 19:21) and appeared before Gallio on false charges (Ac 18:12–27).

ACHAICUS *(uh KAY kuhs)*—A Christian from Corinth whom the Corinthian church sent to Paul in Ephesus (1Co 16:17).

ACHAN *(AY kuhn; "troubler" or "troubled")*—A wealthy man who, after the destruction of Jericho, disobeyed Joshua's instructions and stole goods (Jos 7:1). For this, the Israelites suffered defeat when they attacked the small village of Ai (Jos 7:2–5). As pun-

ishment, Joshua and the elders stoned him to death.

ACHISH *(AY kish)*—1. Ruler of Gath. He protected David when he fled from King Saul. (1Sa 21:10). 2. Ruler of Gath, possibly Achish 1 (1Ki 2:39).

ACHOR *(AY kor; "trouble")*—A valley near Jericho where Achan and his family were stoned to death (Jos 7:24–26).

ACHSAH *(AK suh; "anklet" or "ornament")*—The only daughter of Caleb. She was promised in marriage to anyone who could capture Kiriath-sepher (Debir); Othniel won that honor (Jos 15:16–17).

ACTS OF THE APOSTLES—The fifth book of the New Testament. Written by Luke as a sequel to his account of Jesus, Acts traces the development of the Church from Jerusalem to the ends of the Earth (Ac 1:8). The book recounts two major conflicts: Jews who rejected the message about Jesus (Ac 4:1–31) and early followers who believed that no one could become a follower of Jesus without first becoming a Jew.

ACTS, BOOK OF THE—*See* **ACTS OF THE APOSTLES.**

ADAH *(AY duh; "adorned")*—**1.** The wife of Lamech, mother of Jabal and Jubal (Gen 4:19–21, 23). **2.** The wife of Esau, mother of Eliphaz (Gen 36:2, 4).

ADAM *(AD uhm; "humanity" or "human being")*—The first human, he was created by God on the sixth day of creation and placed in the Garden of Eden. Adam and his wife disobeyed the Lord by eating from a forbidden tree and were cast out of the garden. In the New Testament, Paul compared the spiritual relationship between Adam and Jesus: Adam was an example of disobedience and death, while Christ—the second Adam—was the ultimate example of obedience (Ro 5:12–21; 1Co 15:20–49).

ADAR, ADDAR *(uh DAR)*—The 12th month of the Jewish year (February–March). The Feast of Purim is celebrated during Adar.

ADMAH *(AD muh)*—A city destroyed along with Sodom and Gomorrah because of its wickedness (Dt 29:23).

ADONAI *(uh DOH nye)*—A divine name, generally translated as "the Lord." In the late post-exilic period, it became a substitute to Jews for Yahweh (YHWH), the unspeakable name of God. Adonai is also interpreted as "to rule" and "God is the Almighty Ruler." In earliest times, it was a common name for God.

ADONI-BEZEK *(uh DOH nye BEH zek; "lord of Bezek")*—The king of Bezek. He was defeated by Israel and severely mutilated because of the cruel treatment he had inflicted on 70 kings (Jdg 1:5–7).

ADONIJAH (*AD oh NIGH juh; "the Lord is my Lord"*)—**1.** Son of David. He tried to seize the throne, but David appointed Solomon instead (2Sa 3:4). **2.** A Levite chosen by King Jehoshaphat to teach the people (2Ch 17:8). **3.** A family leader who set his seal upon the renewed covenant with God under Nehemiah (Ne 10:16).

ADONI-ZEDEK (*uh DOH nye ZEH dek; "lord of righteousness"*)—An Amorite king who fought against Joshua (Jos 10:1–27). Joshua had him killed and his body hung on a tree until sunset.

ADONIRAM (*ad uh NYE ruhm; "my lord is exalted"*)—A taskmaster who supervised the forced labor under David, Solomon, and Rehoboam (1Ki 4:6; 5:14). Rehoboam sent him to the dissatisfied tribes of Israel, and the people stoned him to death.

ADOPTION—An important means of ensuring succession within families and of providing for transmission of property. Abraham adopted his slave Eliezer as his heir. Moses was adopted by the daughter of Pharaoh (Ex 2:10). In the New Testament, the word appears five times and refers to God's grace by which individuals become children of God.

ADRAMYTTIUM (*add rah MITT ee um*)—An important seaport on the west coast of Asia Minor. When Paul was a prisoner on his way to Rome, he boarded a ship there (Ac 27:1–6).

ADRIA, SEA OF (*AY dree uh*)—Part of the Mediterranean Sea south of Italy and Greece and between Crete and Malta. The ship carrying Paul and other prisoners drifted there before landing on Malta (Ac 27:27).

ADULLAM *(uh DULL um)*—
1. A city assigned to Judah after the Israelite conquest (Jos 15:35). **2.** A large cave near the city of Adullam where David sought shelter during his flight from Saul (1Sa 22:1).

ADULTERY—The seventh commandment forbade sexual relations outside of marriage. In the Old Testament, adultery referred to sexual relations between a married (or betrothed) woman and any man not her husband. Adultery was only recognized when it was committed against the husband. In the New Testament, Jesus declared that a husband could also be held responsible for committing adultery against his wife (Mt 5:27). The Old Testament also applied the term figuratively to Israel's spiritual straying from its covenant with God.

ADVENT *("coming")*—A season immediately preceding Christmas that celebrates the Incarnation of Christ. In the western Church it is observed during the four Sundays prior to Christmas; in the eastern churches it begins in mid-November.

ADVOCATE—A term derived from the Greek word *parakletos* ("one called alongside [a person]"). John used this title to refer to Jesus (1Jn 2:1). Jesus called the Holy Spirit an advocate (Jn 14:16).

AENON *(EE nuhn)*—A place near Salim where John the Baptist performed his baptisms during the early part of Jesus' ministry (Jn 3:23).

AFRICA—Although it is not specifically named in the Bible, various places and people from Africa are mentioned. In the Old Testament, Egypt was a powerful adversary. In the New Testament, Jesus and his family took refuge in Egypt (Mt 2:13); Simon, who bore Jesus' cross (Mk 15:21), came from Cyrene;

and Philip the evangelist instructed a eunuch of the Ethiopian court (Ac 8: 26–39).

AGABUS (*AG uh buhs; "he loved" or "locust"*)—A New Testament prophet who foretold a great famine that would extend over the entire Roman Empire (Ac 11:27–30). Agabus also prophesied about Paul's imprisonment at Jerusalem (Ac 21:10–11).

AGAG (*AY gag; "warlike"*)— 1. An Amalekite king whose life King Saul spared (1Sa 15:1–9). 2. A name mentioned in the Book of Numbers (Nu 24:7) that may be a title that symbolized the enemies of God.

AGAGITES (*AY guh gytes*)— Descendants of Agag, an Amalekite king defeated by Saul (1Sa 15:7–9). Haman, an enemy of the Jews, was an Agagite.

AGAPE (*ah GAH pay*)—A Greek word for love used in the New Testament. It often refers to the un-merited love God shows to humanity in sending Jesus. When used in association with human love, it means selfless love.

AGORA (*ah GO ruh*)—The center of the lower part of a town (Ac 16:19). In the early phases of Greek city development, the agora was a natural open space near the main entrance to the acropolis. At the agora in Athens, Paul shared his faith with the people (Ac 17:17).

AGRIPPA—See **HEROD**.

AHAB (*AY hab; "father is brother"*)—1. A wicked king of Israel (1Ki 16:30). Under the influence of his wife Jezebel, Ahab built a temple to Baal and opposed the worship of Israel's God, destroying the altars and killing the prophets. He reigned 20 years (873–853 B.C.). 2. The son of Koliah. He was a false prophet who preached

AGRICULTURE

Archaeologists have discovered that farming had been practiced in Bible lands from the earliest times. No human activity is as prevalent as agriculture, and it was important enough for the Law of Moses to regulate it (Lev 19:9).

Biblical farmers depended heavily on rainfall for the success of their crops. A five-month dry season (mid-May to mid-October) left the land baked hard, and it was not until after the "early rains" (late October to November) that the ground could be prepared. Most of the water was provided by winter rains, but the "latter rains" (March-April) were necessary to bring the crops to harvest. The best conditions for growing grain were located in the hotter and more easily irrigated Jordan Valley, which had a shorter growing season than other areas. The most important crops were wheat, barley, grapes, and olives.

during the time of Jeremiah (Jer 29:21–23).

AHASUERUS (*uh HAZ yoo EAR uhs*)—**1.** King of Persia. Also called Xerxes I, he married Esther (Est 2:17). **2.** Father of Darius the Mede (Da 9:1).

AHAVA (*uh HAY vuh*)—A river in Babylon along whose banks Ezra assembled exiles returning to Jerusalem to fast and pray for a safe journey (Ezr 8:15, 21, 31).

AHAZ (*AY haz; "he grasped" or "he possessed"*)—**1.** Son and successor of King Jotham of Judah. Ahaz observed pagan practices and sacrificed his son as a burnt offering. During his reign, the Assyrian Empire forced Judah to pay tribute.

2. Son of Micah (the great-grandson of Saul) (1Ch 8:35–36).

AHAZIAH *(AY huh ZIGH uh; "the Lord sustains")*—**1.** Son of Ahab and Jezebel. He succeeded his father as king of Samaria (1Ki 22:51). Ahaziah continued the evil religious practices of his parents and worshiped Baal. **2.** The sixth king of Judah. He was the son and successor of Joram (2Ki 8:24).

AHIJAH, AHIAH *(uh HIGH juh, uh HIGH uh; "the Lord is my brother")*—**1.** Son of Ahitub. A priest at the time of Saul, he was in charge of the ark of the covenant. Ahijah was possibly the same person as Ahimelech 2 (1Sa 21:22). **2.** A prophet who told Jeroboam that God would tear 10 northern tribes from the Solomonic kingdom and give them to Jeroboam (1Ki 11:29–39). **3.** The father of Baasha, evil king of Israel (1Ki 15:27, 33). **4.** Son of

Jerahmeel of Judah (1Ch 2:25). **5.** Son of Bela of Benjamin (1Ch 8:7). **6.** One of David's mighty men (1Ch 11:36). **7.** A Levite during the days of King David. He was in charge of treasures in the house of God (1Ch 26:20). **8.** A secretary for Solomon (1Ki 4:3). **9.** Father of Ahitub and possibly an ancestor of Ezra (2Esd 1:1).

AHIKAM *(uh HIGH kuhm; "my brother has risen")*—An official of King Josiah. He was sent to the prophetess Huldah to ask guidance (2Ch 34:14, 20). Later, he protected Jeremiah against King Jehoiakim (Jer 26:24).

AHIMAAZ *(uh HIM ayaz; "brother of wrath")*—**1.** Father of Saul's wife Ahinoam (1Sa 14:50). **2.** A priest who kept David informed of the progress of Absalom's rebellion (2Sa 15:27, 36; 17:20). **3.** Solomon's commissary officer assigned to Naphtali (1Ki 4:15).

AHIMELECH (*uh HIM eh lek; "my brother is king"*) — **1.** A priest who innocently helped David flee from King Saul. He was killed for that action (1Sa 21). **2.** Son of Abiathar. During David's reign, he shared an important priestly role with Zadok (2Sa 8:17). **3.** A Hittite who befriended David when he hid from King Saul in the wilderness (1Sa 26:6).

AHITHOPHEL (*uh HITH oh fel; "brother of foolishness"*) — David's counselor (2Sa 15:12). When Absalom rebelled against David, Ahithophel defected. He advised Absalom to pursue David, who had fled to Jerusalem. When Absalom did not heed his advice and the rebellion faltered, Ahithophel committed suicide rather than face treason charges.

AHITUB (*uh HIGH tub; "brother is good"*) — **1.** A priest and grandson of Eli. He was the father of Ahimelech (1Sa 14:3, 9). **2.** The father of Zadok the priest (2Sa 8:17). He was appointed as high priest by King Saul. **3.** A temple official, descendant of Ahitub 2 (1Ch 9:11).

AHLAB (*AH lub*) — A town in the territory of Asher from which the Israelites were unable to drive out the Canaanites (Jdg 1:31). Its location is unknown.

AI (*AY eye*) — **1.** A city in the territory of Ephraim where Abraham pitched his tent (Gen 12:8). After Joshua conquered Jericho, his forces attempted to take Ai—but they were defeated. Later, Israel captured the city (Jos 7–8). **2.** A city in Ammon of unknown location (Jer 49:3).

AIJALON, AJALON (*AY juh lon; "place of the deer"*) — **1.** A Levitical city in the tribal territory of Dan (Jos 19:42). When fighting the Amorites at Aijalon, Joshua commanded the sun to stand still until the Israelites won (Jos 10:12–14). **2.** A city in the tribal territory of Zebulun where Elon the judge was buried (Jdg 12:12).

AIN KAREM (*ayn KA rem*)—A village in the hill country west of Jerusalem, traditionally accepted as the home of Elizabeth and Zechariah and birthplace of their son, John the Baptist.

AKELDAMA, ACELDAMA (*uh kell DA mah*)—A field outside the walls of Jerusalem where Judas committed suicide after he betrayed Jesus. Because it was bought with money paid for the betrayal, it was called "Field of Blood." (Mt 27:3–10; Ac 1:18–19).

AKIBA (*uh KI ba*)—A Jewish rabbi (c. A.D. 50–136) who classified the teachings of the great rabbis and influenced the Mishnah.

AKKAD (*ACK kad; "fortress"*)—**1.** One of four ancient Mesopotamian cities built by Nimrod (Gen 10:10). **2.** A region between the Tigris and Euphrates rivers, near modern Baghdad. It came to designate the northern part of Babylonia.

AKKADIAN (*uh KAY de uhn*)—A name applied to various Semitic dialects, particularly Assyrian and Babylonian. Akkadian was written from left to right and contained approximately 600 cuneiform signs (combinations of wedges).

AKRABBIM (*ack RAB im*)—A mountain pass on the southern border of Canaan (Nu 34:4). Judas Maccabeus defeated the Idumeans in that region (1Mac 5:3).

ALABASTER (*al uh BAS ter*)—A soft, light, creamy stone, often carved into vases. In such a container the woman who anointed Jesus at Bethany carried the expensive ointment (Mt 26:7).

21

ALALAH *(uh LAH luh)*—A Syrian city-state of the second millennium B.C., located in the plain of Antioch. Excavated in 1936–49, the site has yielded an abundance of texts that shed light on that period.

ALEPH *(AH lef)*—The first letter of the Hebrew alphabet. It also has the numerical value of one.

ALEXANDER—1. Alexander Balas, also called Alexander Epiphanes (1Mac 10:1). He was ruler of Seleucid Syria (150–145 B.C.). 2. Alexander Jannaeus, son of John Hyrcanus and successor of King Aristobulus I of the house of the Maccabees. 3. Son of Simon of Cyrene, the North African who carried Jesus' cross (Mk 15:21); possibly the brother of Rufus (Ro 16:13). 4. A relative of the high priest Annas, who was present when the apostles Peter and John were examined by the Sanhedrin for healing a lame man at the gate of the temple. 5. A Jew who tried to speak in Paul's defense at Ephesus (Ac 19:33–34). 6. A heretical teacher at Ephesus mentioned by Paul (1Ti 1:19–20). 7. A coppersmith who opposed Paul (2Ti 4:14–15). He may be the same person as Alexander 5 or 6, or the person identified as a hostile witness at Paul's trial.

ALEXANDRA—Wife of the Hasmonean king Alexander Jannaeus. After her husband's death, she ruled over the Jewish state (76–69 B.C.). She kept peace among the various Jewish factions.

ALEXANDRIA—A major Egyptian shipping port founded by Alexander the Great (331 B.C.) in an effort to unite the ancient kingdom of the pharaohs with his envisioned Hellenistic world empire. The city's population of nearly a million included the largest

ALEXANDER THE GREAT

Though he is not mentioned in the Bible, Alexander the Great was the founder of the Hellenistic (Greek) Empire and one of the greatest leaders of all time.

The Son of Philip II (King of Macedon), Alexander III was advised by Aristotle

that he could rule the world if he could make people adopt Greek culture. In 334 B.C., Alexander began his conquest in three phases: First (334–330 B.C.), the conquest of the Persian Empire; then (330–327 B.C.) he put down nationalist uprisings in the empire. During this period, he founded a number of cities called Alexandria. One of them was in North Africa, where Jewish scholars made a Greek translation of the Old Testament called the Septuagint.

Finally, in 327 B.C., he undertook his famous march through Afghanistan into India. His eastward progress stopped when his troops refused to go farther. But by then Alexander had extended his empire east from Greece, around the Mediterranean Sea to Egypt, and then to the borders of India.

During the final 18 months of his life, his empire began to unravel from within. He died in Babylon in 323 B.C. at the age of 33. Because Alexander left no heir, his three generals divided his kingdom.

number of Jews who lived outside Israel.

ALIEN—A foreigner, sojourner, or stranger from a country other than Israel. Aliens did not enjoy the rights of the citizens of Israel (Dt 14:21). To the Jews, an alien was a Gentile or non-Israelite.

ALLEGORY *(AL eh gor ee)*—A figure of speech, often an extended metaphor, frequently used in the Bible. It is a symbolic representation of a truth about human conduct or experience. Some consider the story of Jonah and the Song of Solomon allegories. In Galatians 4:21–31, Paul presents an allegory of two women. Hagar and her son Ishmael represent the law, while Sarah and her son Isaac represent spiritual freedom.

ALMIGHTY—The first Greek translation of the Bible—the Septuagint—translated the Hebrew term "El Shaddai" as "Almighty." This term occurs 31 times in the Book of Job—and only 17 times elsewhere in the Old Testament (Gen 17:1). In the New Testament, the term appears in 2Co 6:18 and nine times in the Book of Revelation—mostly as divine self-designations or ascriptions of praise.

ALMOND—A large tree resembling the peach tree in size and fruit. The nuts were eaten or used for making oil and medicine. Its Hebrew name, *shaqued*, means "awakening," because it is the first to bloom in the spring. The almond's pinkish-white blossoms appear before its leaves.

ALMS, ALMSGIVING *(ahlmz)*—Gifts to the needy. In the Old Testament, people were commanded to care for the poor (Dt 15:11). God promised blessings to those generous with the poor (Pr 14:21). The New Testament stressed alms-

ALPHABET

Alpha and *beta* are the first two letters of the Greek alphabet, a term that refers to a system of signs representing single sounds of speech. The alphabet was devised to provide a writing system for a language. It was an improvement over the Egyptian and Mesopotamian systems, which consisted of hundreds of symbols indicating specific words or syllabic values.

Ancient surfaces, such as animal skins and stone, were the first writing materials in early biblical times. The earliest writings were made on clay tablets (Ex 32:16) using an engraving tool or chisel. Throughout the ancient world, other writing surfaces—such as ivory, leaves, bark, wood, metals, linen, baked clay, wax, or pottery fragments—were also used.

The three main materials on which the Bible texts were written were skins, papyrus, and vellum (parchment made from animal skin). The New Testament was written in Greek using all capital letters (called *uncial letters*) without spaces between words.

giving as a mark of righteousness, and Jesus emphasized giving sincerely (Mt 6:1–4).

ALOES (*AL ohs*)—**1.** A general name for the aromatic wood of various plants. Most biblical references are to eaglewood or sandalwood, which were valued as sources for incense and perfume. **2.** Aloes brought by Nicodemus to wrap the body of Jesus (Jn 19:39). This is the only New Testament reference to the true aloe, a member of the lily family.

ALPHA AND OMEGA *(AL fuh, oh MAY guh)*—The first and last letters of the Greek alphabet. They were mentioned together to signify "the beginning and the end" (Rev 21:6) or to indicate completeness. John used the term to describe God (Rev 1:8, 21:6). In the Old Testament, the same idea occurs when God blesses Israel "from aleph to tau" (the first and last letters of the Hebrew alphabet) (Lev 26:3–13). Alpha and omega are common in early Christian art and writings, generally with reference to Christ.

ALPHAEUS *(al FEE uhs; "leader of a thousand")*—1. Father of the Apostle James (Mt 10:3). Tradition says he was the same person as Cleopas, the husband of Mary and father of James and Joseph (Mt 27:56). 2. Father of Levi, who later became the Apostle Matthew and wrote the first Gospel (Mt 9:9).

ALTAR—A table, platform, or elevated place on which a priest placed an offering to God. The altar was the focus of the Israelite sanctuary (Ex 20:24).

Cain slaying Abel at the altar

AMALEK *(AM uh lek; "warlike")*—A grandson of Esau. Eventually, the word became the name for a region in the territory of Ephraim (Jdg 5:14).

AMALEKITES *(uh MAL uh kites)*—Descendants of Esau, this tribe attacked Israel when they started into Canaan. The two groups remained enemies during the period of the Judges. King Saul defeated their armies, and David raided them. The final biblical reference to Amalekites says that the last of the tribe were destroyed (1Ch 4:42–43).

AMARNA LETTERS *(uh MAR nuh)*—In 1887, a peasant woman discovered some tablets in the ruins of the ancient capital of Egypt (c.1375–1358 B.C.). Archaeologists then uncovered fragments of 350 documents written in a wedge-shaped cuneiform script that was popular in ancient Mesopotamia.

AMASA *(uh MAS uh; "burden-bearer")*—1. King David's nephew (1Ch 2:17) and a captain in his army (2Sa 17:25). When David's son Absalom rebelled and claimed his father's throne, Amasa was named commander of David's militia. After Absalom's defeat (2Sa 18:14),

David named Amasa commander of the royal army (2Sa 19:13). 2. An Israelite from Ephraim who opposed the enslavement of captives from the tribe of Judah (2Ch 28:12–15).

AMAZIAH *(AM uh ZYE uh; "the Lord is mighty" or "strength of the Lord")*—1. A king of Judah (son of King Joash). He was 25 when he began his 29-year reign. The Old Testament declares that he did "what was right" in God's eyes (2Ki 14:3). 2. A man from the tribe of Simeon (1Ch 4:34). 3. A Levite and temple singer appointed by King David (1Ch 6:45). 4. A priest who reported to Jeroboam II that Amos had conspired against the king (Am 7:10–11).

AMBASSADOR—An official representative of rulers (1Ki 5:1). If an ambassador was rudely treated, it was considered an insult to the ruler and could lead to war (2Sa 19:4–6). In the

New Testament, Paul called himself Christ's ambassador (Eph 6:20) and applied that term to all Christians (2Co 5:20).

AMEN—A Hebrew word that means certainty, truthfulness, and faithfulness. Both the Old and New Testament used it as a liturgical response at the end of psalms and doxologies in which the congregation affirms what has been prayed. In the Gospels,

AMULETS

Amulets—small objects that were believed to have supernatural powers to protect the wearer against enchantments—were common in all periods of antiquity. They derived their efficacy from close physical contact with a holy person or object.

Amulets supposedly protected their owner from sickness, disease, accidents, witchcraft, evil spirits, and demons. They also were thought to serve as aids to success. They assumed many shapes, with animal and human figurines especially popular. The crescents worn by the two Midian kings and their camels (Jdg 8:21,26) and by women as ornaments (Isa 3:20) were fundamentally of this nature, as possibly were the earrings from which Aaron formed the golden calf (Ex 32:2).

Phylacteries (or frontlets), which were small square leather boxes or cases that contained quotations from the Old Testament, can also be regarded as amulets (Dt 6:8; Mt 23:5). Many early Christians wore amulets marked with a fish (as a symbol of Christ). The Church later spoke against the use of amulets and declared them a heathen superstition.

Jesus often prefaced his teachings with "amen," which was translated as "for truly I tell you" (Mt 5:18).

AMMONITES (*AM oh nights*)—Descendants of Lot's son (Ben-ammi) by his younger daughter (Gen 19:38). Throughout much of the Old Testament record, they are enemies of Israel. During the days of the Exodus, God instructed the Israelites not to associate with the Ammonites (Dt 23:3).

AMNON (*AM nahn; "faithful"*)—1. The oldest son of David (2Sa 3:2). Amnon raped his half-sister Tamar and incurred the wrath of Absalom, Tamar's full brother. After waiting two years, Absalom had Amnon (who was heir to David's throne) murdered. 2. Son of Shimon, and a distant relative of Judah (1Ch 4:20).

AMON (*AM muhn; "trustworthy"*)—1. Egyptian god of the wind (Jer 46:25); as Amon-Re he was the supreme god of the Egyptians. 2. An idolatrous king of Judah who ruled 642–640 B.C. (2Ki 2: 19–24). 3. Governor of Samaria. When Micaiah, a court prophet, predicted death for King Ahab of Judah, the king sent him to Amon for imprisonment (1Ki 22:26). 4. An Israelite who returned after the Exile (Ne 7:59).

AMORITES (*AM or ites*)—Inhabitants of the land west of the Euphrates River. The Amorites were a major tribe in Canaan, and the Old Testament frequently uses Amorites as a synonym for all Canaanites. Israelite tradition depicts the Amorites as evil (Jdg 6:10).

AMOS (*AY muhs; "burden-bearer"*)—1. A shepherd-prophet of the eighth century B.C. Amos denounced the people of the northern kingdom of

Israel for their idol worship and oppression of the poor. His prophecies and the few facts about his life are found in the Book of Amos. **2.** An ancestor of Jesus (Mt 1:10).

AMOS, BOOK OF *(AY muhs)*—The third book of the Minor Prophets (chronologically, the first of the writing prophets), filled with denunciations of the northern kingdom during a time of idol worship. The nine chapters of the book emphasize one central theme: The people of Israel have broken their covenant with God, and punishment will be severe.

AMRAM *(AM ram; "the kinsman is exalted")*—**1.** Father of Moses, Aaron, and Miriam (Ex 6:18–20). He lived 137 years and was the father of the Levitical family that served in the wilderness tabernacle (Nu 3:27). **2.** One of the returned exiles who married a foreign wife. He was com-manded by Ezra to divorce her (Ezr 10:34).

AMRAPHEL *(AM rah fel; "powerful people")*—The king of Shinar at the time of Abraham. He helped defeat the kings of Sodom and Gomorrah (Gen 14:1, 9).

ANAK *(AY nak; "long-necked")*—The father of three sons whose descendants were giants. (Jos 21:11; Jdg 1:20). The name is also taken as a tribal designation equivalent to the Anakim.

ANAKIM, ANAKITES *(AY nuhk im, AY nuh kites)*—A race of giants (Dt 1:28), descended from Anak. Spies sent out by Moses considered themselves grasshoppers when compared to them (Nu 13:33). Moses prophesied that once the Israelites crossed the Jordan they would be victorious over them (Dt 9:2–3). Goliath of Gath (1Sa 17:4) was probably the last Anakim.

ANANIAS *(an uh NYE us; "protected by the Lord" or "the Lord is gracious")*—1. A member of the church at Jerusalem who, with his wife Sapphira, sold land and pretended to donate the entire amount to the church (Ac 5:1–10). They fell dead, a sign of God's punishment for hypocrisy. 2. A disciple in Damascus who assisted the blinded Saul (later Paul) in recovering his eyesight (Ac 9:10–18). 3. A high priest appointed by Herod Agrippa II (c. A.D. 48). He ordered Paul brought before him (Ac 22:30).

ANATHEMA *(ah NATH eh mah)*—A strong expression of destruction and moral unworthiness. For the sake of fellow Jews, Paul was willing to be anathema (Ro 9:3)—not only prepared to die, but to endure the moral degradation of an outcast from God.

ANATHOTH *(AN uh thoth)*—A Levitical town in the territory of Benjamin (Jos 21:18); the birthplace of Jeremiah (Jer 1:1). Although Jeremiah predicted the city's destruction, he bought his cousin's field there because he believed God would bring the people back (Jer 32:7–9). Destroyed by the Babylonians, it was re-settled after the Exile (Ne 11:32).

ANATOLIA *(an uh TOL yuh)*—A peninsula—also called Asia Minor—situated in the western part of the continent of Asia. It is roughly identified with modern Turkey. In Acts, the term "Asia" is ambiguous and refers to either the peninsula as a whole (Ac 19:26–27) or its western section (Ac 2:9, 6:9).

ANCESTOR WORSHIP—An ancient form of superstitious religion in which the living seek to deify the spirits of departed relatives. No evidence exists to indicate that ancestor worship or a cult of the dead was ever part of Israel's religion, although prohibitions against such practices were given (Lev 19:28; Dt 14:1).

ANCIENT OF DAYS, ANCIENT ONE—The name for God in one of Daniel's visions (Da 7:7–22). The imagery depicts God as the divine judge on a fiery throne who presides over the great world empires.

ANDREW (*"manly"*)— Brother of Simon Peter, Andrew was raised a fisherman. The two brothers formed a fishing partnership with James and John. Andrew became a follower of John the Baptist and then was called as one of the first disciples of Jesus (Jn 1:35–40). Tradition says that Andrew was crucified on an X-shaped cross. He is the patron saint of Scotland and also of Russia, because it is believed that he ministered in Scythia, a region north of the Black Sea.

ANDREW, ACTS OF—One of the five apocryphal books of the apostles, written during the third century A.D. (although some have dated it as early as A.D. 190). It survives only in fragments of various versions, but was widely accepted by ascetic sects, who substituted it for the Book of Acts. It describes Andrew's travels and recounts the miracles he performed.

ANDRONICUS (*an DRON ih kuhs; "conqueror"*)—**1.** A deputy under Antiochus Epiphanes (2Mac 4:31). **2.** A relative of Paul who had been imprisoned with him. He was highly regarded by Paul, who called Andronicus and his partner Junia "prominent among the apostles" (Ro 16:7).

ANGEL OF THE LORD—A mysterious messenger of God, sometimes described as God (Gen 16:10–13; Ex 3:2–6) or as a being sent by God in human form.

ANGELS

The popular artistic portrayal of angels as winged beings is generally not supported by biblical accounts. The Bible does describe angels as spiritual beings (Heb 1:14) with super-human power and knowledge (2Sa 14:17, 20; 2Pe 2:1), but they are not all-powerful or all-knowing (Ps 103:20; 2Th 1:7). Angels act as God's messengers to humanity or as agents to carry out divine will. The word "angel" is also applied to people who are messengers of God (1Ki 19:2; Lk 7:24).

Angels are mentioned numerous times in more than half of the biblical books. They have appeared in human form and do care for humanity (Ps 91:11), but the modern conception of everyone having a special guardian angel does not appear in the Bible. When applied to a divine messenger in the New Testament, the word is usually accompanied by a phrase that makes the meaning clear, such as "angels of heaven" (Mt 24:36).

Sometimes angels are depicted as destructive, such as the two angels that razed Sodom (Gen 19:13). The Bible also speaks of fallen angels—those who rebelled against God—whose leader is Satan (Rev 12:9). The Book of Revelation names Abaddon (or Apollyon) as an angel who rules a bottomless pit and is the king of demonic locusts (Rev 9:11).

The Angel of the Lord revealed information or delivered people from harm. This figure usually appeared before a dramatic event—either good or evil—took place involving God's people.

ANGELS OF THE SEVEN CHURCHES—In the Book of Revelation, Christ appears to John in a vision, telling him to send a message to each of the angels of seven churches in Asia (Rev 1–14). The angels may refer to those who presided over these churches, or they may be a personification of each church.

ANGER—Feelings of hostility, ranging from mild displeasure to raging fury. Paul says to be angry but not to sin (Eph 4:26). Jesus displayed anger against those who desecrated the temple (Jn 2:13–17). The Bible makes a distinction between the anger of people and the anger of God, which is considered righteous.

ANIMALS OF THE BIBLE—The Bible mentions an abundant variety of animals, largely because of great geographical variation and climatic conditions. The identification of

Noah gathered two of every kind of animal on the Earth to be carried on the ark so that they could reproduce after the Flood.

many species remains difficult because of ancient methods of classification. For instance, we commonly use the word "animals" to refer to all living creatures that are not plants; the Old Testament uses it in the sense of "mammals" as distinguished from birds, reptiles, and fish. Thus, the bat is a bird and the whale a fish.

ANNA *(AN uh; "grace")*—1. Wife of Tobit. She supported the family during Tobit's blindness (Tob 2:11). 2. Daughter of Phanuel. As an aged widow and a prophetess, Anna proclaimed that the infant Jesus was the long-awaited Messiah (Lk 2:36). 3. Mother of Mary; grandmother of Jesus. She is not mentioned in the New Testament, but is named in the apocryphal Protoevangelium of James.

ANNAS *(AN uhs; "grace")*—A Jewish high priest (A.D. 6–15). His five sons also became high priests, as did his son-in-law Caiaphas (who condemned Jesus to death). Annas was an influential political and religious figure in Jerusalem during the life and trial of Jesus and the early days of the Church (Jn 18:13, 24).

ANNO DOMINI *(AN oh DOM ih nee)*—A Latin term for "in the year of the Lord," this system of dating, which was intended to begin at the birth of Jesus, was based on an Easter cycle developed in the sixth century by Dionysius Exiguus. The birth of Jesus is now believed to have occurred earlier, anywhere from 4 to 7 B.C.

ANNUNCIATION—The announcement by the angel Gabriel to Mary of the conception and birth of Jesus (Lk 1:28–35). In the development of the Christian calendar, March 25 was set aside to commemorate the annunciation.

ANOINT—To pour or cover with oil or ointment. Symbolically, it invested the anointed with power, such as a new prophet (1Ki 19:16) or a king ascending to the throne (1Ki 1:39). Anointing also symbolized God's healing power (Mk 6:13; James 5:14). Jesus' title—Christ—comes from a Greek word meaning "anointing." In the New Testament, he is called the Messiah, a Hebrew term for "anointed" (Ac 5:42).

ANTHROPOMORPHISM—Attributing human characteristics to a nonhuman form (from the Greek words *anthropos*—"human," and *morphe*—"form"). Throughout the Bible, God is depicted with human features, such as feet or arms (Ex 6:6, 24:10) or as having human emotions, such as anger and love (Ex 4:14, 20:6).

ANTIGONUS *(an TIG uh nus)*—The last of the Hasmonean kings and son of Aristobulus II, with whom he was imprisoned at Rome (63–57 B.C.). After Julius Caesar's death in 44 B.C., Antigonus invaded Galilee, but a young Herod the Great—then governor of Galilee—defeated him. Four years later, Antigonus became the Jewish king and high priest. He was deposed in 37 B.C., when Herod claimed the throne.

ANTIOCH *(AN tee ok)*—1. A city in Phrygia (also called Pisidian Antioch) that Paul visited on his first missionary journey (Ac 13:13–14). 2. A city in Syria that became the third most important city of the Roman Empire (after Rome and Alexandria). It was the home base of missionary activities (Ac 13:1–3).

ANTIOCHUS *(An TIE uh kuhs)*—1. The name of 13 kings of the Seleucid dynasty, which ruled Syria. 2. Antiochus IV (Epiphanes), the eighth king of the Seleucid dynasty. He ruled Israel 175–164 B.C. (1Mac 1:10). The Maccabees revolted over his efforts to hellenize them and to suppress Judaism.

ANTIPAS *(AN tih puhs; "against all")*—**1.** Herod Antipas, son of Herod the Great. He ruled as the tetrarch of Galilee. Antipas imprisoned and killed John the Baptist (Mt 14:1–11) and mocked Jesus at his trial (Lk 23:7–11). **2.** A Christian at Pergamum who was martyred because of his faith (Rev 2:12).

ANTIPATER *(AN tih PAY tuhr; "against father")*—Father of Herod the Great. The unofficial ruler of Palestine (63–55 B.C.), Antipater was appointed procurator of Judea in 47 B.C. He received governorships over Jerusalem and Galilee for his sons Phasael and Herod. Antipater was poisoned by his cupbearer in 43 B.C.

ANTONY *(AN toh ee)*—Marcus Antonius. A Roman statesman (c. 82–30 B.C.) who appointed Herod the Great as vassal king of Palestine when Herod named the refortified tower at Jerusalem Antonia in his honor. Antony is not mentioned in the Bible.

APHEK, APHEKAH *(AY fek, uh FEE kuh)*—**1.** A Canaanite city (Jos 12:18) where Joshua defeated the king of Aphek. Herod the Great rebuilt it (c. 35 B.C.) and called it Antipatris (Ac 23:31). **2.** A city not conquered by the end of Joshua's life (Jos 13:14). **3.** A city in the tribal territory of Asher (Jos 19:30). **4.** A city where King Ahab defeated the Syrians (1Ki 20:26–30). **5.** A village in the hill country of Judah (Jos 15:53).

APOCALYPSE *(uh PAHK uh lips)*—John's prophetic vision of the future as described in Revelation, the last book of the New Testament. Bible scholars have interpreted it many ways, and it remains the most controversial book of the Bible. *See* **REVELATION, BOOK OF.**

APOCALYPTIC LITERATURE — Highly cryptic and symbolic literature found especially in the Book of Daniel and Revelation. Apocalyptic books report mysterious revelations (from the Greek *apakalypsis*: "revelation"), mediated by angels, that disclose a supernatural world and focus on events of the end time.

APOCRYPHA, OLD TESTAMENT (*uh POK rih fuh; "hidden"*)—A small group of books written between 200 B.C.–100 A.D. Found in some early Christian versions of the New Testament, they were never accepted as part of the Bible. The apocryphal books are sometimes included in modern Bibles, but they are intended to be used for edification and not for doctrines.

APOCRYPHA, NEW TESTAMENT—Noncanonical religious writings from the first centuries of the Christian era. Much of this writing imitates the style of the New Testament and claims to preserve memories of Jesus and the apostles. Scholars do not call them historically reliable, but they are significant to understanding early Christianity.

APOLLOS (*uh PAH lohs*)—A learned, influential Alexandrian Jew in the early Church. Well versed in the Old Testament (Ac 18:24), Apollos had embraced the teachings of John the Baptist but knew little of the Christian movement. In Ephesus, Aquila and Priscilla instructed him "more accurately" about the Christian faith (Ac 18:26), and he became a persuasive preacher.

APOSTASY—Falling away from the faith (from the Greek words *apo*, "away

APOSTLE

From the Greek word *apostolos* ("to send"), the term refers primarily to the 12 men Jesus chose among his followers: Simon Peter, Andrew, James and John Zebedee, Philip, Bartholomew, Thomas, Matthew, James the son of Alphaeus, Thaddaeus, Simon the Zealot, and Judas Iscariot (Mt 10:2–4). Later, Matthias

replaced Judas (Ac 1:23–26). Generally, an apostle was one who had seen the risen Christ and was commissioned by him to preach the gospel.

Although not associated with Jesus' ministry, Paul considered himself an apostle and so did the early Church. Traditionally, scholars have limited the term to refer to the aforementioned 12 and Paul. The word received wider use in Acts and in Paul's letters: Barnabas and James (the brother of Jesus) are called apostles (Ac 14:14; Gal 1:19). Paul also listed apostles with other ministries (1Co 12:28; Eph 4:11), although some scholars believe Paul used the word as a synonym for "messenger" (2Co 8:23; Php 2:25).

from," and *stasis,* "rebellion"). In the Bible, the term refers to Israel's unfaithfulness to God (Jer 2:19) and the abandonment of Christian faith (Heb 6:6). In the New Testament, Paul predicts a general apostasy from the gospel of Christ (2Th 2:3).

APPEAL TO CAESAR—As a Roman citizen, Paul exercised his right of appeal from the jurisdiction of the local court at Jerusalem to the emperor (Ac 23:11). This transfer of a trial was customarily granted in cases involving capital punishment.

APPHIA (AF ee uh)—A woman who was greeted in Paul's letter to Philemon as "sister" (Phm 1:2). Tradition says that she was the wife of Philemon, who suffered martyrdom.

APPIAN WAY (AP ee un)—The second-oldest Roman highway, named after its builder Appius Claudius (312 B.C.). The 333-mile road unified Italy, bound its two coasts, and eased trade with Greece and the East. When Paul traveled down the road to be imprisoned in Rome, Christians met him along his journey (Ac 28:15).

APPLE—Not the fruit we know today, but the citron, orange, quince, or—more likely—the apricot. The "apple of the eye" (Dt 32:10) became an old English expression used for something extremely precious.

AQUEDUCT—An elevated structure, often supported by a series of arches, on which an open channel brought water to dry areas. King Hezekiah built a tunnel under Jerusalem to bring in water (2Ki 20:20). The three pools of Solomon, located south of Jerusalem, were connected with the capital by two aqueducts built by Herod the Great.

AQUILA AND PRISCILLA (ah KWIL luh; "eagle," prih SIL uh)—A husband and wife (also called Prisca) who lived in Rome until Emperor Claudius ordered all Jews to leave the city. They moved to Corinth, where Aquila made tents.

The couple had a church in their home (1Co 16:19).

AR *(ar)*—A major city of Moab (Nu 21:18). It may also have referred to the region or the entire country of Moab (Dt 2:9). In an oracle against Moab (Isa 15:1), Ar was one of the two principal towns to be destroyed.

ARABAH *(AIR uh bah)*—A major region in Israel, located between Mount Hermon and the Red Sea (Nu 22:1). About 240 miles long, it included the Sea of Galilee and the Jordan River Valley. Before entering the promised land, the Israelites camped in the Arabah.

ARABIA *(uh RAY bee uh)*—A large peninsula between the Persian Gulf and the Red Sea. It was the home of Esau (Gen 36), and its people oppressed the Israelites (Jdg 6:11). Solomon sent ships to Ophir in Arabia to bring back gold (1Ki 9:28).

¹ARAD *(AIR ad)*—A city in the Negeb desert region. When the Israelites approached the Promised Land, the king of Arad defeated them, but Israel won a second battle (Nu 21:1–3).

²ARAD *(AIR ad)*—A man of the tribe of Benjamin (1Ch 8:15).

ARAM *(AIR uhm; "high" or "exalted")*—**1.** Son of Shem and grandson of Noah. He was the ancestor of the Arameans (Gen 10:22–23). **2.** Grandson of Nahor, the brother of Abraham (Gen 22:20–21). **3.** A descendant from the tribe of Asher (1Ch 7:34). **4.** An ancestor of Jesus (Mt 1:3).

ARAM *(AIR uhm)*—A powerful state (or confederation of states) during the first millennium B.C. that fought Israel for control over the region. Saul, David, and Solomon fought their people (1Sa 14:47; 2Sa 8:5–12; 2Ch 8:3–4). Aram came to an end in 732 B.C. when it was conquered by Assyria.

Aramaic ossuary inscription

ARAMAIC *(ar uh MA ik)*—A group of Semitic languages that takes its name from the Arameans. Portions of the Old Testament were written in Aramaic, including large parts of Ezra (Ezr 4:8–6:18, 7:12–26) and Daniel (Da 2:4–7:28). The common language of Palestine in the first century A.D., a few Aramaic expressions appear in the New Testament (Mk 5:41; Jn 20:16).

ARAMEANS *(AIR uh mee unz)*—Semitic people descended from Aram. The Israelites were forced to serve the Arameans for eight years as punishment for their idolatry (Jdg 3:8–10). Many Aramean tribes later became subject to Israelite rule and paid an annual tribute. Saul and David both fought and defeated Arameans (1Sa 14:47; 2Sa 8:3–4).

ARARAT *(AIR uh rat)*—A mountainous region between the Black and Caspian seas where Noah's ark rested after the flood (Gen 8:4). Rather than a single mountain, the word may refer to the mountainous region as a whole, which the Hebrews would have considered to be the high0000

ARAUNAH *(uh RAH nuh; "the Lord is firm")*—A man from whom David purchased a threshing floor to build an altar and protect the Israelites from plague (2Sa 24:16–25). Traditionally, the site has been identified as Mt. Moriah, where

ARCHAEOLOGY

Through archaeological digs, scientists can examine cultures and civilizations from the biblical period. These excavations help to reveal what life was like in biblical times, throw light on obscure passages of the Bible, and increase the historical context of the book. Uncovered artifacts have included inscriptions, buildings, art, fortifications, weapons, tools, and personal implements. Tombs and caves frequently yield well-preserved materials that were buried with the dead.

There have been many significant findings during the 20th century. Thousands of clay tablets written in Babylonian cuneiform were discovered at Nuzi between 1925–41. These tablets have helped to explain several customs mentioned in the early narratives, such as Abraham's adopting his servant Eliezer as heir (Gen 15:2). Excavations at the city of Ras Shamra (1928) have provided a fuller picture of Canaanite religion. The Dead Sea Scrolls (found in caves in 1947) have given new insight on the origins of Christianity and the New Testament. These Qumran biblical manuscripts have provided scholars with copies of all the Old Testament books (except Esther), dating about a thousand years earlier than copies previously possessed.

Solomon later built the temple (2Ch 3:1).

ARCHANGEL—A chief of angels (1Th 4:16). This title is used to describe Michael (Jude 1:9). There are seven archangels named by Jewish tradition: Uriel, Raphael, Raguel,

Michael, Sariel, Gabriel, and Remiel. These may be the angels mentioned in the Book of Revelation (Rev 8:1).

ARCHELAUS *(ahr keh LAY us)*—Also known as Herod Archelaus, he was the eldest son of Herod the Great (Mt 2:22) and his successor as tetrarch of Judea (4 B.C.). His appointment of Eleazer as high priest—and his own extra-marital affairs—enraged Jewish subjects. Because Archelaus oppressed both Jews and Samaritans, Caesar banished him in A.D. 6.

ARCHERS—Soldiers who specialized in shooting arrows from a bow. Ancient armies had archers trained from childhood to be deadly accurate. To draw, war bows required a pull of 100 pounds. The arrows could pierce almost all armor (1Sa 31:2; 2Sa 11:24).

ARCHITECTURE—Early Israelites lived in tents. After they entered Canaan, they began to build houses of stone. These were typically small, one-room homes. In the Jordan River Valley, where mud was plentiful, they developed brick-making. When the Israelites moved back into Palestine after Joshua's victories, they began building four-roomed houses, which became the standard pattern of homes for centuries. By the time of Jesus, there were skilled carpenters, stone builders, and brick layers that could construct elaborate buildings. The wealthy could even afford marble floors and fancy ornamentation, such as gold, silver, or ivory.

AREOPAGUS *(AIR ee OP uh guhs)*—A limestone hill in Athens where the Athenian council met to pronounce justice. Paul may have stood before the council when he made his famous address there (Ac 17:19, 22).

ARETAS (AHR eh tuhs; "goodness" or "excellence")— 1. The name of several Arabian kings. 2. Aretas IV, a king of Arab Nabatea from 9 B.C. to A.D. 40 (2Co 11:32–33). When Herod Antipas divorced Aretas's daughter and married his own sister-in-law (Herodias), Aretas was outraged. He sent his army to kill Antipas, who managed to escape with his life. (Mt 14:3).

¹ARIEL (AIR ee el; "lion of God")—A symbolic name for Jerusalem (Isa 29:1–2, 7). Isaiah may have applied it to the city because the lion was the emblem of the tribe of Judah.

²ARIEL— 1. Two Moabites killed by Benaiah, one of David's mighty men (2Sa 23:20). 2. A man sent by Ezra to get servants for the temple (Ezr 8:16).

ARIMATHEA (ar i muh THEE uh; "heights")—This ancient city was the home of Joseph, who offered his tomb as Jesus' burial place. Arimathea was also Samuel's birthplace (Mt 27:57; Mk 15:43; 1Sa 1:19).

ARIOCH (AR ee ahk; "venerable")—1. One of three kings defeated by Abraham at Sodom and Gomorrah (Gen 14:1, 9). 2. King Nebuchadnezzar's bodyguard. Arioch avoided killing the royal magicians by having Daniel interpret the king's dream (Da 2:14–15).

ARISTARCHUS (ar is TAHR kuhs; "best ruler")—Paul's missionary companion who was captured during a riot in Ephesus. He represented Thessalonians in Jerusalem, accompanied Paul to Rome, and was imprisoned with him. Some believe Aristarchus was a Jew, others a Macedonian (Ac 19:29, 20:4, 27:2; Col 4:10).

ARISTEAS, LETTER OF (uh RIS tay us)—A small Greek book explaining how

45

THE ARK OF NOAH

Noah's three-deck ark (450 feet long, 75 feet wide, and 45 feet high) was not the great sailing ship often described in modern paintings and stories.

Built of gopher wood that was bound by reeds and covered with bitumen, the ark was little more than a water-tight floating container for Noah, his family, and the world's animals (Gen 7:11–8:3). A single side door served as both entrance and exit, and 18-inch-high windows were placed around the boat. A canopylike roof protected the occupants from sun and rain.

After the ark landed on one of the mountains in Ararat and was abandoned by Noah, little is known about what happened to it. There have been expeditions to find the ark, and traditions persist, but nothing conclusive has ever been discovered.

Hebrew Law was translated into Greek. Its contradictions and history make the letter interesting legend.

ARK (*"coffin" or "chest"*)— 1. The ark of the covenant. 2. The ark of Noah. 3. A reed basket that carried the baby Moses when he was set afloat on the Nile (Ex 2:2–5).

ARK OF THE COVENANT (*"built by direction"*)—An ornate acacia wood chest containing the Ten Commandments, a pot of manna, and Aaron's rod. Its lid was called the "mercy seat." God instructed Moses to make the ark, which was carried before Israel in the wilderness as a sign of God's presence and guidance. It was placed in the Holy of Holies until the Jerusalem Temple was destroyed by the Babyloni-

The ark of the covenant

ans in 587 B.C. (Ex 25:10–22; Nu 10:33).

ARM—An ancient symbol of strength. Biblically, it symbolizes God's power over creation and ability to deliver and preserve the people (Isa 40:11, 51:9; Dt 4:34, 33:27; Ps 77:15, 89:13).

ARMAGEDDON *(ahr muh GED uhn; "hill of Megiddo")*—The battlefield where the final great battle between good and evil will take place. John's vision of the "great day of God" (Rev 16:16) will be fulfilled there. Scholars place Armageddon near the mountain of Megiddo, where important battles—from 1400 B.C. to the twentieth century—have been fought.

ARMOR AND WEAPONS—*Armor:* This refers to any type of battle protection that was carried or worn, including shields, metal or leather helmets, archers coats of mail, and greaves for shins. *Weapons:* These were hand implements, including swords, bows and arrows, spears, slings, and metal-tipped rods. Both terms are used in the Bible to describe literal and spiritual battle (Eph 6:11, 13).

ARMY *("strength")*—A group of armed men prepared for battle. The term was first used to describe the Israelite militia (1Sa 13:2). Fighting under God's direction, they were victorious, but they suffered defeat otherwise (Jos 1:3, 5:14; 2Ch 5:14;

1Sa 15). Other spiritual armies under God's command (Jos 5:13; 2Ki 6:17) include Jesus as commander of heaven's army in the final battle between good and evil (Rev 19:11).

ARNON (AHR nahn; "rushing stream")—A river of great strategic importance during biblical times. The Israelites crossed the river, which runs into the Dead Sea, and gained their first territory (Dt 2:24). Many forts were built along its banks (Isa 16:2).

ARPACHSHAD, ARPHAXAD (ahr PAK shad)—The first child born after the Flood. He was Abraham's ancestor and lived to be 438 (Gen 11:10–13). Some scholars believe Arpachshad was not a person but a tribe inhabited by the descendants of Shem.

ARROW—A reed or wood shaft with a flint, bone, or bronze point. Arrows were shot from a bow for hunting or battle. They were

also used for divination (Eze 21:21) and to symbolize evil people (Ps 11:2) and God's judgment (Ps 7:13).

ARTAXERXES (ahr tuh ZURK seez; "brave warrior")—A Babylon king who allowed Ezra and Nehemiah to return to Jerusalem and establish uniform observance of Jewish law during the temple's reconstruction (Ezr 7).

ARTEMIS OF THE EPHESIANS (AR tih muhs)—An Asian mother-goddess who represented human, animal, and plant fertility. The immense temple built in her honor at Ephesus was one of the seven wonders of the ancient world (Ac 19:23).

ASA (AY suh)—The third king of Judah, Asa demanded loyalty to Yahweh. He abolished pagan worship and removed his grandmother as queen because she worshiped fertility gods (1Ki 15:12).

ASAHEL *(AS uh hel; "creature of God")* —**1.** David's half-sister, Zeruiah (1Ch 2:16). **2.** A Levite teacher of the Law (2Ch 17:8). **3.** A temple official responsible for the collection of tithes (2Ch 31:13). **4.** The father of Jonathan (Ezr 10:15).

ASAPH *(AS uhf; "gatherer")* — A Levite who led singing and sounded the cymbals before the ark in worship (1Ch 16:5; 2Ch 5:12). Twelve Psalms (Psa 50, 73–83) are attributed to him. Asaph's sons remained temple musicians until the second temple (1Ch 25:1–9).

ASCENTS, SONGS OF *(uh SENTS)* —Psalms 120–134. These were recited by pilgrims "ascending to Jerusalem" for the New Year's festival celebrated in the temple.

ASENATH *(AS eh nath)* — The daughter of Potipherah (an Egyptian priest of On), Asenath was given to Joseph by the Pharaoh as his wife. She bore Joseph's sons, Manasseh and Ephraim (Gen 41:45–50).

ASH WEDNESDAY—The first day of Lent. Traditionally, on this day a priest smudges ashes on a believer's forehead as a sign of repentance. Protestants dropped the custom, which contradicts Jesus' mandate not to "look dismal or disfigured" when fasting (Mt 6:15–21).

ASHDOD *(ASH dahd; "stronghold")*—A Philistine city that was the center of Dagon (a fish god) worship. The ark of the covenant, when captured by Ebenezer, was taken there and placed in Dagon's temple (Jos 15:45; 1Sa 5:1–8).

ASHER *(ASH ur; "happiness")*—Jacob's eighth son. His descendants were the Asherites (Gen 30:12).

ASHERAH *(uh SHEE ruh; "straight")*—A fertility god-

ASCENSION

Ascension—the belief that a person's spirit was transported from earth up to heaven—was a traditional and common story in religious circles, especially Judaism. Described in great detail, the tales of a special person ascending to heaven are found throughout the Old Testament (Enoch, Gen 5:24; Elijah, 2Ki 2:1–12; Isaiah, Isa 6:11). These stories expand the belief that the soul rose to be with God after death (2Co 12:2–4).

Following his crucifixion and resurrection, Jesus taught his disciples for 40 days. Then he took them to the top of Mt. Olive, and he ascended into heaven. Jesus' ascension to heaven is a cornerstone belief for the Christian Church. It was predicted in the Old Testament (Ps 68:18) and marks the beginning of Christ's rule over both heaven and earth. It is the dividing point between Jesus' earthly ministry (which restores us with God) and his heavenly ministry—where he intercedes in prayer on our behalf (Ro 8:34; Heb 7:25) and prepares a place for us (Jn 14:2).

Before he left, Jesus promised his disciples the presence of the Holy Spirit (Ac 2:32) and assured them of his return to establish God's kingdom (Ac 1:11). Jesus "ascended to the right hand of God" (Mk 16:19; Ac 2:33), a position of power that means Jesus shares in God's rule over all things.

dess worshiped in Canaan. She was represented by a small tree trunk without branches (Dt 16:21). The Israelites were commanded to destroy all objects that represented Asherah so that the objects couldn't contaminate their worship (Dt 12:3).

ASHES—A symbol of mourning or doing penance (Jer 6:26; Mt 11:21; Heb 9:13). Ashes are also used to signify frailty, insignificance, and worthlessness (Gen 18:27).

ASHKELON (*ASH keh lahn; "migration"*)—One of five major Philistine cities on the Mediterranean between Jaffa and Gaza. It was briefly occupied by Judah (Jdg 1:18) and was the birthplace of Herod the Great.

ASHTAROTH, ASHTORETH (*ASH tuh roth*)—**1.** A Canaanite goddess of fertility. The Israelites worshiped her (Jdg 2:13), and Solomon sanctioned the royal cult of Ashtaroth (1Ki 11:5; 2Ki 23:13). **2.** The ancient capital of Bashan, center of Ashtaroth worship.

ASHURBANIPAL (*ah shur BAH ni pahl*)—A king of Assyria (688–633 B.C.) who collected more than 22,000 cuneiform tablets. His library is the basis for what is known of Assyrian literature.

ASHURITES (*ASH ur ites*)—The inhabitants of the kingdom of Ishbosheth. The Ashurites descended from the fourth son of King Saul (2Sa 2:8–9).

ASIA—A large continent east of Europe and Africa. Because ancient borders were not accurately defined, the exact area changed at different times throughout history.

ASIA MINOR—The western part of Asia bordered by the Black, Aegean, and Mediterranean seas. It was the site of much of Paul's missionary work (Ac 19:26).

ASIARCH *(Ay zhee ahrk)*— An honorary title given to wealthy Asian officials who sponsored yearly games and drama to honor the Roman emperor. The Asiarchs in Ephesus were friendly to Paul (Ac 19:31).

ASP *("viper")*—A poisonous snake. It most often refers to the Egyptian cobra and sometimes the European viper or adder.

ASS—A member of the horse family used for carrying goods (Gen 42:26; 1Sa 16:20, 25:18), transportation (Nu 22:21; 2Sa 17:23), and farm work because it was stable-footed and strong. Jesus rode into Jerusalem on one (Mt 21:7).

ASSASSINS—Militant Jewish nationalists who used the element of surprise to murder those considered loyal to the Roman emperor (Ac 21:38).

ASSHUR *(AHS shoor)*—**1.** The second son of Shem (Gen 10:22) and ancestor of the Assyrians. **2.** The ancient capital of Assyria. It was named in honor of Assur.

ASSUR *(AS ur)*—The main deity of the Assyrian pantheon, he was the god of military skill and expertise.

ASSURANCE—The sense of certainty about the truth of a belief. In the New Testament, it often refers to having confidence in God's gift of salvation.

ASSURBANIPAL *(ah soor BAH ni pahl)*—See **ASHURBANIPAL**.

ASSYRIA *(uh SEAR ee uh)*— A great civilization that thrived in Mesopotamia from mid-3000 B.C. to just before the Christian era. Its name comes from its capital city, Asshur. Assyria was a strong military power. Israel feared its attacks and had to pay tribute if taken captive (2Ki 18).

ASTROLOGY

The natural desire to predict the future for individuals and nations gave rise to astrology.

The ancient science of getting information from the stars and heavens originated and was developed by the Babylonians and Egyptians. They believed that changes in the location and alignment of heavenly bodies could foretell events that would take place on Earth. Kings hired astrologers to help them make decisions in planning battles and maintaining their power. Astrologers were also called "magicians" and were sometimes expected to interpret dreams.

Throughout the Bible, astrologers were accused of being charlatans and practitioners of the occult (Isa 47:13; Jer 10:2; Ac 8:9–13). Daniel was said to be Nebuchadnezzar's chief astrologer (Da 4:9, 5:11); however, he claimed it was God, and not the stars, that enabled him to know the meaning of dreams (Da 2:27–28). The three wise men—the "magi"—are perhaps the most well-known astrologers in the New Testament.

ASTARTE (*as TAHR tay*)—The Greek form of Ashtaroth, Astarte refers to any of the fertility goddesses of the Near East.

ATHALIAH (*ath uh LIGH uh; "afflicted by God"*)—The daughter of Ahab and Jezebel. The only woman to reign over Judah, her six-year reign ended when she was killed trying to stop a priestly insurrection (2Ki 8:18, 25–28, 11:1–20).

ATHENIANS (*uh THEE nee uhns*)—People of Athens. They were described as notorious gossips (Ac 17:21) and were denounced for their love of immorality and pagan worship (Ac 17:16–21).

ATHENS (*ATH enz*)—The capital of Attica, a Greek state. It was a center of knowledge in science, literature, and the arts. Paul visited there on his second missionary journey (Ac 17).

ATONE, ATONEMENT (*uh TOHN ment; "reconciliation"*)—The act of making amends for one's wrongdoings. In the Old Testament, atonement referred to a purification that was reached through sacrificial offerings by the high priest in the Holy of Holies. In the New Testament, it is achieved through Jesus, who gave himself as the sacrifice (Jn 3:16; Ro 5:11).

ATTALIA (*at uh LIGH uh*)—The chief harbor on the coast of Asia Minor, Attalia was named after Attalus II of Pergamum. Paul and Barnabas passed through Attalia on their way to Antioch (Ac 14:25–26).

AUGUSTUS (*aw GUHS tuhs; "venerable"*)—A title added to Julius Caesar's name by the Roman Senate. The term meant "reverend" and implied he was divine.

AUTHORITY—Biblically, ultimate authority belonged to God, and all other is subordinate (Ro 13:1). To Jesus, serving others was the greatest power (Mt 20:25–26).

AUTHORIZED VERSION—Any Bible translation that is endorsed by the authority of the Church. The term is generally used to refer to the King James English translation, which was first published in 1611.

AVENGER OF BLOOD—A belief that justice for murder was gained when the next of kin killed the accused. Such counter-vengeance often wiped out entire families (Gen 9:6; Nu 35:21).

THE DAY OF ATONEMENT

To the Hebrews, forgiveness was considered a privilege, a gift of God's mercy and graciousness. The Day of Atonement was a special day set aside for people who were sorry for their sins and wanted forgiveness. Observed on the tenth day of the seventh month, it was a day of strict fasting and no work.

Through a complicated series of rituals, the temple and people (including the high priest) were purified. Two sacrifices were made: one for the high priest, the other for the people. The high priest, dressed in white linen, carried the blood from the sacrifice into the Holy of Holies (the sacred inner room of the tabernacle), where he would sprinkle it. Then he would lay his hands on the back of a live goat that was set free to roam in the desert, symbolizing that the sins of the people had been taken away. It is from this practice that we get the word "scapegoat" (Lev 16).

Contemporary Jews still celebrate the Day of Atonement with solemn prayer and fasting, but they no longer offer animal sacrifice.

AZARIAH, PRAYER OF (*az uh RIGH uh*)—An apocryphal story. Thrown into a fiery furnace, Azariah prays as the flames increase; he and his companions aren't hurt, while the Chaldeans are destroyed.

AZEKAH (*uh ZEE kuh; "dug over"*)—A Judean town where Goliath and the Philistines camped before their encounter with the Israelites and David (1Sa 17:1).

BAAL-BERITH *(BAY uhl BEE rith)*—A Canaanite god whom the Israelites worshiped at the shrine in Shechem (Jdg 9:4).

BAAL-GAD *(BAY uhl GAD; "Baal of good fortune")*—A town near Mount Hermon that marked the northern boundary of Joshua's conquests (Jos 11:17, 12:7, 13:5).

BAAL-HAZOR *(BAY uhl HAY zor; "village of Baal")*—Absalom's mountain home near Ephraim where, during a celebration, his servants killed Amnon at Absalom's instigation (2Sa 13:23–29).

BAAL-MEON *(BAY uhl MEE ahn; "lord of the house")*—An Amorite city on the frontier of Moab that was rebuilt by the Reubenites. It is also known as Beth-Baal-Meon (Nu 32:38; Eze 25:9).

BAAL-ZEBUB, BEELZEBUB *(BAY uhl ZEE buhb; "god of the fly")*—1. The deity worshiped at Ekron. King Ahaziah asked Baal-Zebub if he would recover from a fall in the palace (2Ki 1:2). 2. Prince of demons in the New Testament (Mt 10:25).

BAAL-ZEPHON *(BAY uhl ZEE fahn; "lord of the north")*—The place the Israelites camped just before crossing the Red Sea in their flight from Egypt (Ex 14:2).

BAASHA *(BAY uh shuh; "bravery")*—A King of Israel who gained power by killing Jeroboam's family. His reign ended when Zimri killed his son, an action that was seen as God's judgment against Baasha's militant ways and his encouragement of pagan religions (1Ki 16).

BAAL

According to Canaanite beliefs, Baal was a fertility god who controlled the forces of nature, and each farming area had its own version of him. Although there were many Baals, El—as father of men and of all the gods—was the chief of all Canaanite gods. Astarte, Baal's wife, exhibited her power through violence and promiscuous sex.

In general, these gods were brutal and arbitrary in their dealings with people. It gave them great delight to interfere in human affairs, without any thought of the consequences.

While Israel was forbidden to worship Baal, strong cultural influences often led them to join in such rites as temple prostitution (1 Ki 22:38). King Athaliah in Judah and Queen Jezebel in Israel supported Baal worship (2 Ch 5:5; 1 Ki 16:31, 32). The prophets—and some kings—denounced Baal worship and called for Israel to be faithful to God (2 Ki 23:4–5; Jer 19:4–5).

BABEL (BAB ul; "The gate of God")—A city on the Plain of Shinar where the reign of Nimrod began (Gen 10:10) and the Tower of Babel was built.

BABYLON (BAB i lahn)— The political and religious capital of the Babylonians and their empire. It was located south of present-day Baghdad, Iraq.

BABYLONIA (bab i LOH nee uh)—A great empire, dating to 4000 B.C., noted for its advancements in

TOWER OF BABEL

Expert builders, the Babylonians wanted to construct a tower that could reach into the heavens. When God saw their tower (which was likely located on the Plain of Shinar), their true motive—a plan to "make a name" for themselves (Gen 11:4)—was exposed, showing their break from dependence on God. As punishment, God confused the builders' languages so that they couldn't understand one another.

In a play on words, the author of the story takes *babel* ("gate of God") from the Hebrew word *balal*, which means to confuse or confound. In English, it sounds like "babble," which means to say meaningless words. The biblical story suggests that human migration was influenced by language differences. More importantly, the story suggests that when humankind is not in unity with God, people—and nations—are also not in fellowship with one another.

astronomy, mathematics, and literature. Babylonians are credited for many discoveries later developed by the Greeks.

BACA, VALLEY OF *(BAY kuh; "weeping")*—A Palestine valley populated with balsam trees that ooze resin and appear to be "weeping." Pilgrims journeying to Jerusalem had to pass through this arid region (Ps 84:6).

BADGERS' SKINS *("striped skins")*—Animal skins used to make clothing, shoes, and containers to carry water. These skins were also used for the outer covering of the Tabernacle (Ex 26:14). Many scholars believe that the term may refer to precious dolphin or porpoise skins.

BALAAM *(BAY luhm; "glutton")*—A Hebrew priest. Balak (the Moabite king) sent for him to curse the Israelites. En route, an angel spoke to Balaam's donkey. The donkey scolded Balaam, who decided to bless rather than curse. Later, Balaam turned to paganism (Nu 22–24). In the New Testament, he is a symbol of a hypocritical teacher (Jude 1:11; 2Pe 2:15).

BALAK *(BAY lak; "destroyer")*—The King of Moab who convinced Balaam to curse Israel and limit the Israelites' power as they advanced toward the Promised Land.

BALANCES *("two scales")*—Two pans on a horizontal bar suspended by a cord from either the hand or a rod. They were accurate tools for weighing items (such as coins), but some

Justice holding balances

people were tempted to use them fraudulently as "wicked balances" (Mic 6:11).

BALM OF GILEAD *(BAHLM of GIL ee uhd)*—An ointment made of unknown spices and herbs. It was produced in Gilead and was noted for its healing ability (Jer 46:11).

BALSAM TREES *(BAWL suhm)*—Shrubs or bushes of the Judean hills that seep a white, foul-smelling sap. Also called mulberry trees, they provide good protection and concealment (2Sa 5:23–24; 1Ch 14:14–15).

BAPTISM

An outward sign of an inward change, the water of baptism cleanses the heart, mind, and soul of sinful old ways and brings rebirth and membership into the Church. To receive this gift of God's forgiveness and acceptance requires a decision to change, to belong to Christ and the Church.

Christian baptism grew from the Jewish cleansing ritual of baptizing Gentile converts into Judaism after circumcision. Baptism was important in the foundation of the early churches because it served as entry into the congregation. The first baptisms were immersions—like the one John the Baptist held for Jesus, who spoke of coming "up from the water" (Mt 3:16). John baptized many people as a sign of their repentance. Although Jesus did not perform baptisms, the disciples baptized thousands in his name (Ac 6:15–30).

Baptism rituals vary by religious denominations. Some, like Baptists, immerse only adults, while others, such as Roman Catholics, accept infant baptism. Some Protestants sprinkle water instead of performing complete immersion.

BAMOTH, BAMOTH-BAAL
(BAH moth)—A place from which the plains of Moab are visible. King Balak took the Hebrew priest Balaam there to watch and curse the advancing Israelites (Nu 21:19, 22:41).

BANQUET—Feasting, singing, and dancing at special occasions (Am 6:4–6). Guests were welcomed with a kiss and had their feet washed (Lk 7:44, 45). The people's happiness at the coming of the Messiah was like a banquet (Isa 25:6); the Last Supper was a banquet (Lk 22:14).

BAR-JESUS *(BAHR JEE suhs; "son of Jesus")*—A Jewish court magician and false prophet. He tried to persuade Sergius Paul not to listen to Paul and Barnabas (Ac 13:6–12). Bar-Jesus was temporarily blinded after Paul denounced him.

BAR-JONA *(bahr JO nuh; "son of Jonah")*—The surname of the Apostle Peter (Mt 16:17).

BARABBAS *(buh RAB uhs)*—A prisoner arrested for a political murder. He was released by Pilate in a Passover custom, at the crowd's urging, instead of Jesus (Mt 27:16).

BARAK *(BAYR ak; "lightning")*—An Israelite, commanded by Deborah, a judge, to fight Sisera (Jdg 4:6). This successful battle is recorded in the Song of Deborah (Jdg 5:1–31).

BARLEY—An important grain because it was cheaper than wheat, barley was a staple food for people and animals (Lev 3:2). It was also a commodity to trade—and was often used for bribes (Eze 13:19, Hos 3:2). Palestine was known as the land of wheat and barley (Dt 8:8).

BARRENNESS—A synonym for infertility. Being barren was a cause for regret and scorn (1Sa 1:10). Children were considered God's blessing, but the lack of them was seen as God's curse (Ex 23:26).

BARTHOLOMEW *(bahr THAWL uh myoo)*—One of the 12 apostles (Mt 10:3), perhaps Nathaniel (Jn 1:45).

BARNABAS

An early Christian convert, Barnabas sold some of his land and donated the money to the apostles to give to the poor (Ac 4:37). He brought Paul, following his conversion, to the apostles and convinced them that Paul was sincere and not a spy as they feared.

Later, Barnabas was sent to establish a new church in Antioch (Ac 11:22). His ministry was so successful that Paul joined him, and together they preached, taught, and collected money for the poor in Jerusalem. During their mission work in Cyprus and Asia Minor, Barnabas proved he was a great spiritual leader. He and Paul both attended the Jerusalem Council and were sent from there to spread the word.

However, Barnabas disagreed with Paul about letting John-Mark travel with them on the second missionary journey. They separated, and Barnabas traveled with Mark, revisiting Cyprus. His split with Paul was apparently not a serious rift, for Paul wrote well of him (1Co 9:6).

BARTIMAEUS *(bahr ti MAY uhs)*—A blind beggar healed by Jesus (Mk 10:46–52). Jesus remarked on his persistence, gratitude, and belief that Jesus was the son of God.

BARUCH *(buh ROOK)*—Jeremiah's scribe (Jer 32:12, 36:4), who recorded and read his prophecies to the people (Ne 3:20). After the scrolls were destroyed, he rewrote them.

BARUCH, BOOK OF *(buh ROOK)*—An apocryphal book, from Jeremiah's scribe Baruch to the exiles in Babylon. Some believe there were three authors.

BARZILLAI *(bahr ZIL eye; "made of iron")*—David's friend who brought him provisions (2Sa 17:27–29). Because of his old age, Barzillai declined David's invitation to join the royal court at Jerusalem and sent his son instead.

BASHAN *(BAY shun)*—A fertile land east of the Sea of Galilee noted for cattle and wheat (Dt 32:14; Isa 2:13). Bashan produced oak trees used for ship oars (Eze 27:6).

BASIN—A biblical term for a bowl. The largest basins

BATHING

A lack of water made bathing hard to do during biblical times. Bathing usually meant partial bathing, such as washing only the hands and face or rinsing the feet in a foot bath after a long trip. Full-body bathing was not often mentioned, though Pharaoh's court bathed in the Nile (Ex 2:5). Excavations have uncovered bathing rooms in the homes of royalty and the wealthy. Bathsheba was bathing the first time David saw her (2Sa 11:2).

Washing or bathing was a key part of purification rites before worshipers could approach God. Priests bathed before entering the temple (Ex 30:19–21). Only people in mourning went unwashed (2Sa 2:20). The Old Testament custom of washing the hands and face before meals was carried over into New Testament daily life (Mk 7:3).

Bathing was also used as a symbol. God is said to be able to wash away sin (Isa 4:4), and Jeremiah connected the outward bathing of the body with the inward cleansing of the spirit to gain salvation (Jer 2:2).

were used in the temple (Ex 12:22); the smallest were for wine and liquids (Ex 24:6; Jn 13:5).

BATHSHEBA (bath SHEE buh)—The wife of Uriah (a soldier in David's army), Bathsheba committed adultery with David (2Sa 11). After arranging Uriah's murder, David married her and had four sons including Solomon (2Sa 5:14; 1Ch 3:5). She later wielded political power as King Solomon's mother.

BATTLE—Biblical battles involved two opposing divisions of soldiers, spearmen, archers, and slingers advancing at a trumpet sound. Priests accompanied the Israelite army to help determine God's will (1Sa 14:8), and the ark of the covenant was taken to guarantee God's help. Later, chariots and horses were used. Duels often preceded battles.

BDELLIUM (DEL ee yuhm)— A fragrant, yellowish,

gummy tree sap (Gen 2:12). Valued as a perfume, it was often listed with gems because of its importance (Gen 2:12; Nu 11:7).

BEARD—Facial hair worn for male dignity. Plucking or covering a beard was a sign of mourning (Isa 15:2). Israelites were forbidden to cut the corners of their beards, a heathen practice.

BEASTS (of the Apocalypse)— Lawless symbols of force (Da 7; Rev 13:11–18). One beast comes from the "bottomless pit"; the other is called the "false prophet." Jesus destroys both.

BEAUTIFUL GATE—A site in Jerusalem where Peter and John healed a paralytic (Ac 3:2, 10).

BED—A thick sleeping mat. The poor slept on the ground, and the wealthy had elaborate bedsteads (Am 6:4; Est 1:6). Beds were also used for private devotion (Gen 47:31).

BEATITUDES

A popular literary form in biblical times, beatitudes are blessings that begin with a phrase such as "blessed is he" or "happy is he." They typically honored righteous individuals that resisted evil (Ps 1:1, 2; Pr 8:34).

Good behavior had a promised blessing from God and assured his continued presence. In the Old Testament, beatitudes are found in the writings of psalmists and sages (not always with a heavy religious tone). In the New Testament, they appear in Matthew, Luke, and Revelation.

Through his beatitudes, Jesus gave his disciples—and later the Church—goals to which they should aspire (Mt 11:6, 13:16; Jn 20:29). He described the qualities that should characterize disciples and the rewards they could expect (Mt 5:3–11; Lk 6:20–22). Even suffering could be a blessing because of the lessons it could teach about God's steadfastness (Ps 94:12).

"Making one's bed in Sheol" signified the death of people and nations (Job 17:13–14; Eze 32:24–25).

BEELIADA *(bee uh LYE ah duh)*—One of David's sons (1Ch 14:7). His name was changed to Eliada—"God knows"—to avoid using a word close to "Baal." (2Sa 5:16).

BEER *(BEE ur; "well or cistern")*—An unknown well site on the Hebrews' journey (Nu 21:16–18). Jotham fled to Beer to escape his murderous brother Abimelech (Jdg 9:21).

BEER-LAHAI-ROI *(BEE ur luh HIGH roy)*—An unknown well site where

Hagar encountered an angel (Gen 16:7, 14). She called it the "well of one who sees and lives." It was also Isaac's home (Gen 24:62, 25:11).

BEER-SHEBA *(beer SHEE buh; "seventh well")*—An important well town in south Judah. Abraham and Abimelech made a covenant there (Gen 21:31); God appeared to Jacob (Gen 46:1); and Elijah fled to Beer-sheba to avoid execution (1Ki 19:3). Amos chastised its people for their sins against God (Am 8:14).

BEHEMOTH *(beh HEE muth)*—A large animal that could swim and climb, possibly an elephant or hippopotamus (Job 40:15).

BEL—The chief Babylonian god, Baal (Isa 46:1). Bel was also known as Marduk or Merodach to the Hebrews (Jer 50:2).

BEL AND THE DRAGON—An addition to the Book of Daniel (found in the collection of apocryphal books) ridiculing idolatry and heathenism.

BELIAL *(BEE li uhl)*—A word meaning "wickedness" or "lawlessness" for which there is no proper noun in the Old Testament (Dt 13:13; Jdg 19:22.). In the New Testament, it became a name for Satan.

BELSHAZZAR *(bel SHAZ uhr)*—A Babylonian ruler and the grandson of Nebuchadnezzar. Daniel told Belshazzar that God was displeased with him. That night, Belshazzar was killed and Babylon was defeated by the Persians (Da 5:1–30).

BELTESHAZZAR *(BEL teh SHAZ uhr; "may God protect his life")*—A Babylonian name given to Daniel by Nebuchadnezzar's steward (Da 1:7, 2:26).

BEN-AMMI *(ben AM ee; "son of my people")*—The child born to Lot from an inces-

BELOVED DISCIPLE

The identity of this unnamed but well-loved and trusted disciple remains a mystery. Some scholars believe it is the Apostle John, the son of Zebedee (Lk 22:8; Ac 3:1, 8:14). The early Church also held this belief, repeatedly naming him as the beloved disciple. John was at the crucifixion (so Jesus could have spoken to him there), and he was at the tomb of Christ. Others believe it is Lazarus, Jesus' close friend—and the only man Jesus said that he loved (Jn 11:3, 5, 11, 36). Jesus raised Lazarus from death, which may explain why Lazarus was the only person—at first—to recognize the resurrected Jesus.

Speaking from the cross, Jesus entrusted his mother Mary to "the disciple whom he loved," who took her to his own home (Jn 19:26–27). It would have been easy for either John or Lazarus, who lived nearby at Bethany, to do this. Yet another theory is that this is not a particular man, but an ideal follower of Christ whom we should imitate.

tuous relationship with one of his daughters (Gen 19:38).

BEN-HADAD (*ben HAY dad*)—A title given to Syrian rulers who were thought to be descendants of the Syrian deity Hadad, the god of storm and thunder (1Ki 5:18).

BEN-HINNOM, VALLEY OF (*ben HIN ahm*)—The site of a refuse dump southwest of Jerusalem where corpses of criminals and animals, along with rubbish, were burned. It was popularly called "gehenna," an ancient term for hell.

BENJAMIN

The only full brother of Joseph, Benjamin was the youngest and favorite son of Jacob. Benjamin was well loved and did not possess the jealousy and hatred that led the other brothers to sell Joseph into slavery.

During a famine, Jacob reluctantly allowed Benjamin to join his brothers on a trip to Egypt to purchase grain. While there, Joseph—whom his brothers did not recognize—concealed a silver chalice in Benjamin's knapsack and had him arrested. His brothers, worried that Benjamin's loss would cause their father to grieve to death, tried to persuade Joseph to keep one of them in Benjamin's place. In time, Joseph disclosed his identity to his brothers, and they promised to bring Jacob to Egypt, reuniting the family so they could survive the famine.

Benjamin had 10 sons who became a large tribe called the Benjaminites. Their portion of the Promised Land included Jerusalem, and Benjamin's descendants included King Saul and the Apostle Paul.

BENEDICTION—A prayer for God's blessing or an acknowledgment that God's blessing is already present (Nu 6:24–26; Ro15:13).

BENEDICTUS *(ben eh DIK tus)*—The song or prophecy of Zacharias (Zechariah), John the Baptist's father (Lk 1:68–79). He describes Jesus as a spiritual—not military—leader.

BENEFACTOR—A first-century title that Egyptian and Syrian kings stamped on their coins to show services rendered. Jesus forbade this practice (Lk 22:25).

BENJAMIN GATE—A gate in the city of Jerusalem, perhaps Nehemiah's Sheep Gate (Jer 37:13, 38:7).

BEREA/BEROEA *(BEE ri uh; "watered")*—A prosperous Macedonian city that Paul visited on his second missionary journey (Ac 17:10–14). After Paul fled opposition, Timothy and Silas stayed there.

BERNICE *(buhr NIH see; "bringing vitality")*—The eldest daughter of Herod Agrippa I (Ac 12:1). She lived incestuously with her brother Agrippa (Ac 25:13), in whose company she heard Paul. Bernice tried to prevent a massacre of the Jews by Florus.

BETH—The second letter of the Hebrew alphabet and the Hebrew number two. It was also a common word for "house" that was often used with a proper noun (such as "Beth-Anath").

BETHABARA *(BETH AB ura)*—John baptized people at this ford or stream, located somewhere beyond the Jordan River (Jn 11:18). Older manuscripts call it Bethany.

BETH-ANATH *(BETH ay nath; "house of Anath")*—An unknown city near Naphtali (Jos 19:38). The Israelites forced its inhabitants into slave labor.

BETHANY *(BETH uh nee; "house of misery/unripe figs")*—A small town near Jericho (southeast of Jerusalem) that was frequented by Jesus. It was the hometown of Jesus' friends Mary and Martha and their brother Lazarus, whom Jesus raised from the dead (Jn 11:1, 12:1). Jesus' ascension (Lk 24:50–51) happened nearby.

BETH-AVEN *(BETH ay vuhn; "house of vanity or iniquity")*—A wilderness border town of Benjamin (Jos 18:12). Amos and Hosea criticized its inhabitants for their idolatry of golden calves.

BETHEL *(BETH EL; "house of God")*—A sanctuary city north of Jerusalem. It is mentioned more than any other city in the Old Testament except Jerusalem. God met Jacob in a vision there (Gen 28:10–22), and later Josiah restored worship of Jehovah (2Ki 23:15).

BETHESDA *(beh THEZ duh; "house of mercy or outpouring")*—A spring-fed pool near the Sheep Gate in Jerusalem. The lame and ill stepped into its allegedly

BETHLEHEM

One of the oldest towns in Palestine, Bethlehem was only a small village during the time of David. Located south of Jerusalem, it was home to Ruth and Boaz. Its real prominence came as the birthplace of Jesus, probably in a cave rather than a manger.

Caves were used as shelter for cattle. Mary and Joseph, who were in Bethlehem to enroll in the census for taxation, would have known where to find them. The shepherds who came to honor Jesus were likely working on hillsides outside of town (Lk 2:1–20). The Magi, from countries in the East, followed a star to the birthplace in Bethlehem. Fearful of this newborn king, Herod murdered all the infant boys within the city in an attempt to kill the baby Jesus (Mt 2:16–18).

Many holy sites have been built around the area, but we cannot be certain about the exact location of Christ's birthplace. Queen Helena, Constantine's mother, built a chapel over the caves where the birth may have taken place.

healing waters (Jn 5:1–16). It was there that Jesus healed a man who had been ill for 38 years.

BETH-HARAN *(BETH HAY ruhn)*—A fortified city that offered protection for herds of sheep. Located east of the Jordan River (Nu 32:36), it belonged to the tribe of Gad. Later, the city was renamed Julius in honor of Augustus' wife.

BETH-HORON *(BETH HO rahn)*—These twin towns (Upper and Lower Beth-Horon) in the hills of Ephraim were strategically located on the road to Jerusalem (Jos 16:3, 5). Their slopes helped Joshua defeat the Amorites.

BETHLEHEM, STAR OF *(BETH leh hem)*—The star announcing Jesus' birth (Mt 2:2), as predicted in Numbers 24:17 and Isaiah 60:3. Its unusual brightness attracted curious astrologers, probably from Persia, Babylon, or Arabia. Scientists believe it may have been Halley's Comet, Jupiter, Venus, Saturn, or a supernova.

BETH-MARCABOTH *(BETH MAHR kuh bahht; "house of chariots")*—A town given to Simeon on the Judean-Philistine border (Jos 19:5; 1Ch 4:31). Chariots were made and stored there as part of Solomon's weapon trade (1Ki 9:19).

BETH-PEOR *(BETH PEE awr; "house of Peor")*—A site in the hill country east of the Jordan where Israelites camped before entering the Promised Land. After reminding the people of the law, Moses died and was buried there (Dt 3:29).

BETHPHAGE *(BETH fajh; "place of young figs")*—A village somewhere northwest of Bethany (Mk 11:1) where a young colt was taken for Jesus to ride into Jerusalem (Mt 21:1–11). Jesus condemned the fruitless fig tree nearby (Mt 21:18–20).

BETH-SHAN

Marked by a 70-foot tell (mound), Beth-Shan has been occupied continuously since prehistoric times. This ancient city was of strategic importance because it was located near an important travel route that linked Egypt and Damascus. It was abundant with cultivatable soil, good water, and wonderful weather for growing. While scholars disagree, many presume it was also the place of worship of an Egyptian serpent god.

When the Philistines defeated Saul, they displayed his severed head in a Beth-Shan temple and fastened his body (and the bodies of his sons) to the city's walls (1Sa 31:10). It is believed the city was finally taken under control by the Israelites during the reign of King David as a way of avenging Saul's brutal death. During the Christian era it became known as Scythopolis, a major Greek city.

BETH-SAIDA, BETHSAIDA *(BETH SA duh; "house of fishing")*—A village on the Sea of Galilee near Capernum (Jn 1:44) that was the home of Peter, Andrew, and Philip. It was there that Jesus fed 5,000 people with "loaves and fishes" (Lk 9:10–17).

BETH-SHEMESH *(BETH SHE mish; "house of the sun")*—An important town, northwest of Judah near the Philistine border, where Israel conquered Judah (2Ki 14:11). Solomon's granaries were here (1Ki 4:9).

BETH-SHITTAH *(BETH SHI tuh; "house of the acacia")*—A town in the Jordan Valley (location unknown) where the Midianites fled after they were overthrown by Gideon (Jdg 7:22).

BETH-ZUR *(BETH ZUR; "house of rock")*—A fortress town in the mountains of Judah north of Hebron (Josh 15:58). It was crucial in the Maccabean wars (1Mac 6:26).

BETROTHAL—The first stage of the biblical marriage transaction (Ex 22:16). Betrothal was often considered as binding as marriage (Jdg 14:15; Mt 1:18). A man committing adultery with a betrothed woman was stoned to death.

BEULAH *(BYOO luh; "married")*—The symbolic and poetic name for the restored land of Israel. The term expresses a close relationship to God as husband and provider (Isa 62:4).

BEYOND THE JORDAN—Territory east or west of the Jordan, depending upon the writer's perspective. Five of the times it appears in the Bible, it means west, as in the burial of Jacob (Gen 50:10–11).

BIBLE—A collection of the books of the Old and New Testaments used as the inspired words of God. Its primary theme is redemption. God's promises made in the Old Testament are fulfilled in the New Testament through Jesus. There are numerous translations of the Bible available in many different languages and dialects.

BIBLICAL CRITICISM—Techniques applied to biblical writings to help find their original wording, authorship, and sources. Experts compare different texts in search of accuracy, which is the basis for interpretation.

BILHAH *(BIL hah)*—
1. Rachel's maidservant and Jacob's concubine. She was the mother of Dan and Naphtali (Gen 29:29, 30:1–8). **2.** A town of Simeon. (1Ch 4:29).

BILL OF DIVORCE—A written document that a man gave to his wife before sending her away (Dt 24:1–3). Under the law, only men were allowed to initiate a bill of divorce. In the New Testament, Jesus limited the rules governing divorce (Mt 5:31–32, 19:7–9).

BINDING AND LOOSING—A rabbinical term for the Church's authority to decide what is forbidden. ("...whatever you bind on Earth will be bound in heaven, and whatever you loose on Earth will be loosed in heaven.") Jesus gave this authority to Peter and then to the apostles (Mt 16:19, 18:18).

BIRTH, NEW—A personal rebirth, or change, from an old sinful life to a new one through faith in Christ as a result of the Holy Spirit's work (Jn 3).

BIRTHRIGHT—The privileges of the firstborn son. He received a double portion of the inheritance (Dt 21:15–17), the rights to the family name, and a chance for priesthood. Esau lost his birthright by selling it to Jacob for a meal (Gen 25:29–34), and Reuben lost his through sin (Gen 49:3–10).

Engraving of a birth scene

BIRTHSTOOL—A special chair designed for a woman to sit upon during labor and delivery. The Hebrews described it as "double stones" (Ex 1:15–21).

BISHOP (*"overseer"*)— Originally a general term for a Church leader, it evolved into a title for the chief authority of God over a given region. The Bible states that a bishop must be a kind, honorable person (1Ti 3:1–7) who

74

THE VIRGIN BIRTH

A young woman, Mary was a virgin when she gave birth to her son, Jesus. This miracle was a sign from God that her child was the chosen Messiah that had been prophesied in the Old Testament (Isa 7:14–24; Mic 5:2). God's power was revealed in this mysterious event.

Born of a virgin and the Holy Spirit, Jesus is both man and God—a spiritual miracle that was the result of a physical miracle (Mt 1:18, 20). The event did not go unnoticed: Magi followed a wandering star, angels sang, and King Herod became frightened (Lk 2:8–14; Mt 2). No other similar story has been found in earlier Jewish literature.

looks after his local congregations as a shepherd does his flock (Ac 20:28).

BITHYNIA *(bi THIN ee uh)*— A wooded, fertile country that Paul and Silas tried to visit (Ac 16:7). Peter preached there (1Pe 1:1), and councils were held in Nicea and Chalcedon.

BITTER HERBS—Unknown plants eaten at Passover as a reminder of the difficult Exodus (Ex 12:8; Dt 29:18). Horseradish is used today.

BITTER LAKES—The Great and Little Bitter Lakes connected to the Red Sea and the Gulf of Suez before filling with silt. Some scholars think the fleeing Israelites crossed the Red Sea there.

BITUMEN *(bi TYOO min)*— Mineral pitch used to waterproof boats and cement bricks in the Tower of Babel (Gen 11:3). Sodom and Gomorrah's defeated kings were tossed into bitumen pits (Gen 14:10).

BLASPHEMY (*BLAS feh mee*)—Contempt for God, an unforgivable offense punishable by death (Lev 24:10–23). According to the temple leadership in Jerusalem, Jesus' claim to divinity was considered blasphemy, resulting in crucifixion (Mt 26:65).

BLESSED—Highly favored (Gen 12:3; Lk 14:14). Jesus taught that even the poor were blessed, because they belonged to God (Mt 5:3).

BLESSING—God's grace to his people. In the Old Testament, it was believed that an individual's wealth and good fortune was a sign of God's blessing (Pr 10:22; Lev 26:3–13). In the New Testament, Jesus spoke of the meek and poor as blessed with spiritual wealth. Blessings were used to protect the community (Gen 48:14–15), family, and children.

BLINDNESS—A common affliction from infectious disease or dust (Lev 21:18). Blindness also symbolized a lack of vision (Ps 82:5; Mt 15:14).

BLOOD—Mentioned 400 times in the Bible, blood was considered the river of life. In the Old Testament, animal blood was used in sacrificial offerings to atone for sin. According to the law, blood was unclean (Dt 12:23). In the New Testament, the blood of Christ symbolized the redemption of mankind through Jesus. Christians reenact the "drinking" of Christ's blood at communion (Mt 26:28).

BLOOD, FIELD OF—*See* **AKELDAMA.**

BLOOD, FLOW OF—A hemorrhage, perhaps from menstruation (Lev 15:19–24) or dysentery (Lk 8:43). Paul and Jesus cured sufferers (Ac 28:7–8; Mk 5:25).

BOANERGES (*boh uh NURH jeez*; "*sons of thunder*")—A nickname Jesus gave James and John—because of their

BODY OF CHRIST

In the New Testament, Christ's body has several symbolic meanings. It is the human body of Jesus, whose resurrection guarantees the believer's resurrection (1Jn 4:2; 1Co 15:35). It is also the bread used at the Last Supper, which Jesus said was "my body broken for you" (Mt 26:26). Paul used the term to describe the Church (Ro 12:5), with each part or member given a special task to benefit all.

Today, the entire community of Christians is considered the "body," with Christ as the "head" of the Church (Ro 12:4; 1Co 12:12). Through the sacrament of baptism, people are welcomed into membership of this Body of Christ. Each person is to use his or her unique gifts to fulfill a useful function so that the whole body can be nurtured and live. There is no gift, or person, better than the other, for they all work together.

Romans and Corinthians focus on unity among local Church members (1Co 12:12), while Colossians and Ephesians talk about the universal Church. They all stress that Christian unity centers upon Christ and that each person can choose to support (or undermine) this unity.

tempers—when he called them as disciples (Mk 3:17).

BOAZ *(BOH az; "quickness" or "strength")*—A Bethlehem farmer whose field was gleaned by Ruth. They married and their son, Obed, was David's grandfather (Ru 1–4).

BODY—1. Our natural physical body, created by

THE FEAST OF BOOTHS

Also called Feast of the Tabernacles, this harvest festival and religious celebration was the most sacred and important of Israel's three great annual pilgrimage feasts. Held in Jerusalem on the 15th day of the Tishri (the seventh Jewish month), the festival had two purposes: to recall Israel's long tent life in the wilderness and to celebrate the grape and grain harvests (Dt 16:13–15). It lasted seven days (with two days of special observance).

The people lived in booths (small shelters of branches) to remind them of their wanderings during the Exodus (Lev 23:39–43). Those too far away celebrated at their hometown synagogue. Priests conducted religious ceremonies, leading a morning procession to the spring of Gihon to fill a pitcher with water. The worshipers waved myrtle, willow, and palm branches in one hand and lemons or citrons in the other. Jesus and his disciples attended the Jewish feast, where he preached and taught. When he was challenged, Jesus answered, "My teaching is not mine, but his who sent me" (Jn 7:16).

God to live on Earth (Ro 12:1). **2.** A spiritual body (1Co 15:35–38), dwelling place of the Holy Spirit.

BONES—The strongest part of the body, bones signified strength (Gen 2:23) and kinship (Gen 29:14).

They also represented hopeless death, as in "dry bones" (Eze 37:1–12).

BOOK OF LIFE—A symbolic roster of God's believers (Ex 32:33; Rev 3:5). To be "blotted out" is to be cut off from God's favor. In the

New Testament, the Book of Life lists the righteous, whom Christ redeemed for eternal life (Php 4:3).

Assyrian boundary stone

BOUNDARY STONES—Stones used to mark property boundaries (Jos 13:21). It was forbidden to remove these landmarks (Dt 27:17).

BOWELS—Numerous Hebrew words meaning the heart of the emotions or digestive organs (Gen 15:4; La 1:20).

BOZRAH *(BAHZ ruh)*—A fortress city in Edom (Gen 36:33) noted for sheep. Prophets predicted its destruction (Am 1:12; Jer 49:13, 22).

BREAD—1. Ground barley or wheat (mixed with water, salt, and leavening) that was shaped and baked. Unleavened bread was used during Passover. It was an essential food and was used for trade (Eze 4:9). 2. A general term for food. 3. A symbol of Christ. Jesus called himself the "bread of life" (Jn 6:33, 35) and used bread to symbolize his body.

BREAD OF THE PRESENCE—Twelve fresh loaves, representing the Twelve Tribes, that were placed on the tabernacle table as an offering of thanksgiving (Ex 24:4). They were changed each Sabbath when priests ate the old loaves (Lev 24:5).

BREAST—A symbol for nourishment (La 4:3; Lk 11:27) and sacrifice (Ex 29:26). Hitting the breast

79

BREASTPIECE OF THE HIGH PRIEST

A sacred article of clothing, the breastpiece consisted of a square pouch made of gold, blue, scarlet, and purple material. It was folded into a nine-inch square and worn by the high priest (Ex 28:15–30).

This pouch was adorned with four rows of precious stones, each inscribed with the name of one of the Twelve Tribes of Israel. It was held together by four gold rings, and the upper rings were fastened to two more engraved gems on the shoulders (Ex 28:9–12, 22–25).

The breastpiece served two purposes. First, it held the Urim and Thummim, the stones that the priest would cast to make decisions. This lot-casting was believed to be how God let the people know his will and judgment, with the priest acting on his behalf.

The second reason for this elaborate garment was to set the high priest apart as someone special—as Israel's ambassador or representative to God. By wearing and showing the breastplate as he approached God, he carried the entire nation into the holy presence. The high priest was considered the conduit of God's will for man (Mal 2:6–7).

meant anguish (Lk 18:13); leaning on it, affection (Jn 13:23).

BRETHREN OF THE LORD—
1. Brothers, half-brothers, or cousins of Jesus, listed

BREASTPLATE

Because the breast was a vulnerable target in battle, warriors often wore a breastplate for protection. This piece of armor was basically a covering of scales, chain mail, or solid metal. The breastplate was attached to (or worn over) a leather tunic. Other pieces of armor protected the back and areas not covered by the breastplate (1Ki 22:34).

Iron breastplates, as well as fancy and multicolored ones, are described as part of the apocalypse (Rev 9:9, 17). The breastplate was also used as symbolic armor for the soul. The Lord was described as a great warrior who "put on righteousness like a breastplate" (Is 59:17). The New Testament encourages Christians to put on the "whole armor of God," which includes faith and love (Eph 6:14; 1Th 5:8).

as James, Joseph (or Joses), Simon, and Judas (Mt 13:55). Nonbelievers during Jesus' ministry, they united with the disciples after his resurrection (Ac 1:14). 2. Christian family unity (Mt 25:40; Jn 13:34).

BRICK—The most common building material in the biblical world. Clay, reinforced with straw or sand, was sun- or kiln-dried. When Pharaoh refused to give the Israelites enough straw to bind the clay, they rebelled (Ex 5:15–19).

BRICK-KILN—A type of pottery kiln for baking clay bricks (1Sa 12:31). The furnace into which Daniel and his friends were cast was likely a brick-kiln (Da 3:6). Kiln-dried bricks were rare in Palestine until Roman times.

BRIDE, BRIDEGROOM—Marriage was a common

BREATH

Represented in the Old Testament by the Hebrew word *ruah* ("wind" or "spirit"), breath is a symbol of God's gift of life to the world.

In the beginning, God created all living creatures by giving them breath (Gen 1:30). Later, God gave the "breath of life" to humankind through Adam, who was made from the dust of the Earth (Gen 2:7).

God's spirit was present at creation and guided Israel's history. The breath of God could bring punishment (Job 4:9; 2Th 2:8) or it could restore life, as it did Ezekiel's valley of dry bones (Eze 37:9).

In the New Testament, breath represents divine and human spirit (Job 3:28, 27:3) and is the source of wisdom and understanding. The Holy Spirit was promised by Jesus (Ac 1:5, 8) and appeared in a "rushing wind" at Pentecost.

metaphor for the union between God and the Church. God's joy with the people of Israel was compared to that between newlyweds (Ps 128; Isa 54:6). Jesus also described himself as a "bridegroom" (Mk 2:19).

BRIDE OF CHRIST—A term for the Church (Rev 21: 9–10). The relationship between God and his people was often portrayed as a marriage, with Christ as the bridegroom (Isa 62:5; Eph 5:25).

BRIMSTONE (*"burning stone"*)—Sulfur, a yellow crystal used medically and in fumigating. It burned easily and symbolized eternal punishment. Brimstone springs were on the shores of the Dead Sea (Gen 19:24).

BRONZE (BRAZEN) SEA—A large basin in the front of the temple for washing sacrifices and where priests washed their hands (2Ki 25:13).

BRONZE (BRAZEN) SERPENT—A cast-bronze figure Moses put on a pole in the wilderness after God sent serpents to punish the Israelites. All who looked at it were healed (Nu 21:4–9). Hezekiah later broke it as an idol (2Ki 18:4).

BROOK—A small stream, full in winter but dry in summer (Nu 34:5). They were mentioned by name to mark national or tribal boundaries.

BROOK OF EGYPT (*"wadi [river] of torrent"*)—A dividing line between Canaan and Egypt (Gen 15:18; Nu 34:5). It was also the southern boundary of Judah (Jos 15:4, 47).

BROTHERLY LOVE—The friendship and hospitality between neighbors, family members, and the Christian fellowship (Ro 8:29, 12:10; 1Th 4:9). The Old Testament meaning was love for a fellow Israelite. Jesus said it was love for all, especially within the Church (Mt 5:43–48).

BULRUSH—Marsh plants, growing up to 20 feet high, that were used to make ropes, sandals, baskets, and papyrus. Baby Moses was found in the bulrushes of the Nile and adopted by Pharaoh's daughter (Ex 2:1–10).

BURDEN—1. A heavy load that troubles the body or mind (Nu 11:11). Christ offers to help us lighten our burdens (Mt 11:30). 2. An Old Testament warning from God of his judgment. God put the burden on the prophets, who passed it to the people.

BURIAL—The Egyptians embalmed the dead and buried them with their

BURNING BUSH

While tending his flock near Mount Horeb, Moses received the call from God to deliver the people of Israel from slavery. He turned and saw that an unidentified thorny bush was on fire but was not consumed by the flames (Ex 3:2–3). Moses understood that this miracle was an act of a vibrant and all-powerful God who could fulfill the holy covenant that had been made to Moses and his ancestors (Ex 2:24, 3:6, 6:5). Moses, however, was afraid to look at the bush (Gen 3:24; Ex 19:5, 18).

possessions. The Israelites did not follow these practices. Bodies were washed, anointed, and wrapped in linen cloths. Corpses were placed in caves or tombs (Ecc 6:3; Isa 14:20), often on the day of death. Burial was accompanied by a public display of grief from friends and relatives. It was considered a terrible humiliation not to have a burial place. *See* **MOURNING.**

BURNT OFFERING—The ritual sacrifice of a perfect animal (usually a ram or goat) to God for atonement of one's sin. Blood was sprinkled on the altar to dedicate the sacrifice (1Ki 3:4; 2Ch 29:27), and the entire animal (except for the skin) was consumed by fire.

BYBLOS (*BIB lohs*)—The Greek name for an ancient Phoenician seaport city (originally called Gebal) that God gave the children of Israel (Jos 13:5, 6). Byblos was famous for its stonemasons and shipbuilders.

CABUL *(KAY bul)*—An unproductive border city of Asher. Solomon gave the city to King Hiram in return for help building the temple. Displeased, Hiram called the land Cabul ("as good as nothing") as a pun (1Ki 9:13).

CAESAR *(SEE zuhr)*—A title and family name of Roman authority and power. Paul appeared before Caesar (Ac 25:6–12).

CAESAR'S HOUSEHOLD—Servants of the Roman emperor. These included relatives, slaves, and other individuals who performed domestic, medical, educational, literary, and secretarial service. They were well respected (Php 4:22).

CAESAREA *(ses uh REE uh)*—A prosperous seaport city on Israel's Mediterranean coast (Ac 8:40). Built by Herod the Great, Caesarea was known for its magnificent buildings and advanced aqueduct system. Paul passed through there on several of his missionary journeys (Ac 9:30).

CAESAREA PHILIPPI *(ses uh REE uh fi LIP eye)*—A city in the foothills of Mount Hermon. Simon Peter confessed his faith in Jesus as the Son of God near here (Mt 16:13–18). The designation "Philippi" (named after Herod's son Philip) distinguished it from the seaport Caesarea.

CAIN *(KAYN; "to acquire")*—The eldest son of Adam and Eve, Cain was a farmer. He murdered his brother Abel and, unrepentant of his crime, became a fugitive. He married a woman from Nod with whom he had a son, Enoch (Gen 4:1–16).

CAIAPHAS

Joseph Caiaphas was a high priest of Jerusalem during the years A.D. 18–36. His father-in-law, Annas, was high priest before him and still had a strong influence over legal proceedings.

The office of high priest was also a political position, which explains how Caiaphas came to preside at the trial of Jesus. He was among those who feared the people's allegiance to Jesus would destroy the nation and agreed that bold action was needed.

After he was betrayed by Judas, Jesus was sent that night for trial to Annas (Jn 18:12–23), who sent him on to Caiaphas that same night (Jn 18:24–27). Caiaphas, who had prophesied that it was better for Jesus to die as a sacrifice for the entire Jewish nation, sent him on to Pilate (Lk 11:49–50).

Several weeks later, Caiaphas, Annas, and other members of the Sanhedrin investigated Peter and John because of their preaching about Jesus' resurrection. Caiaphas was also involved in persecutions of early Christians described in the Book of Acts.

CALEB (*KAY leb;* "*dog*" or "*rabid*")—A tribal leader whom Moses sent to check the Promised Land. Everyone except Joshua resisted Caleb's desire to attack. For his demonstration of faith, he was allowed to enter the Promised Land (Nu 13:30; Jdg 1:12–15).

CALENDAR—The Hebrew calendar was based on agricultural seasons (Ex 23:16), solar-lunar cycles, and religious festivals (Dt 16:1–17; Ac 20:6, 16; Lev 23:24).

CALF, GOLDEN—An idol that Aaron created from melted

earrings during the Exodus (Ex 32:3–4). It was probably a gold-laminated wooden frame. Angered when he saw the people worshiping the false idol, Moses pulverized it, mixed it with water, and made the people drink it.

CALVARY (*"skull"*)—An unknown, skull-shaped hillside outside Jerusalem where Christ was crucified. Jesus was also buried near Calvary (Jn 19:17, 20, 41).

CAMEL'S HAIR—An expensive material woven of camel's hair. John the Baptist's "camel's hair" clothing (Mt 3:4; Mk 1:6) was probably made from camel skin.

CANA (*KAY nuh*)—An unknown village close to Capernaum. At a wedding in Cana that he attended with his mother, Christ performed his first miracle: turning water into wine (Jn 2:1–11).

CANAAN, CANAANITES (*KAY nuhn, KAY nuh nites*)—The Promised Land of Palestine. The descendants of Noah through Ham (Gen 9:18, 10:15–19), Canaanites were primarily traders and craftsmen. They invented the linear alphabet (Nu 13).

CANANAEAN (*KAY nuh nee uhn; "zealot"*)—A Jewish patriotic party member from Cana. Simon the Apostle was called "the Cananaean" (or "the zealot") to distinguish him from Simon Peter (Mt 10:4).

CANDACE (*KAN duh see; "pure"*)—A title held by a succession of Ethiopian queens. The evangelist Philip converted a minister of Candace's court to Christianity (Ac 8:26–39).

CANON (*KAN uhn*)—**1.** The authorized books of the Bible that the Church accepts as authentic and inspired by God (Zec 1:4, 7:7, 12). **2.** An ancient measuring rod or ruler that was used for building.

CAPERNAUM

The city of Capernaum was built on the northern shore of the Sea of Galilee. Near a political border, it had a customs station and a military base for Roman soldiers. One of the centurions there helped build a local synagogue (Lk 7:1–5).

Although Jesus was brought up in Nazareth, he called Capernaum "home" and used it as the headquarters for his ministry (Mt 4:13, 8:8–9; Mk 2:1). He performed many miracles there, including healing a paralytic (Mark 2:1–12). In Capernaum, he called Matthew—a tax collector—to be a disciple (Mt 9:9). The people, however, were apparently indifferent to his ministry, prompting Jesus to condemn it as one of the cities that had seen his works but didn't repent: "And thou, Capernaum, which are exalted...shalt be brought down" (Mt 11:23, 24).

It remained an entirely Jewish settlement, and even Jewish Christians still held to the Law, attended synagogue, and avoided mixing with Gentile Christians—although they taught, healed, and spoke in the name of Jesus. The city, which was built of local black volcanic basalt, was continuously occupied from the first to seventh centuries.

CANON OF THE OLD TESTAMENT (KAN uhn)— The approved 39 books of the Old Testament. Compiled before the time of Christ, little is known of the selection process.

CANON OF THE NEW TESTAMENT (KAN uhn)— The approved 27 books of the New Testament. These books have more documented evidence to support their authenticity than other writings. (A letter from A.D. 170 lists most of them.) Despite challenges, the current canon has remained unchanged since the fourth century.

CAPHTOR (*KAF tawr*)—A seacoast town that was the original home of the Philistines (Jer 47:4). Some scholars believe it may have been the Mediterranean island of Crete.

CAPPADOCIA (*kap uh DOH shee uh*)—A highland, frontier province in Asia Minor that produced excellent horses and wheat. Worshipers from Cappadocia attended Pentecost (Ac 2:9).

CAPTAIN—A military leader who commanded a unit of 50, 100, or 1,000 troops (Gen 21:22; Ex 18:25). A captain was entrusted with decision-making and judging responsibilities (Isa 3:3; Pr 6:7).

CARCHEMISH (*KAHR kem ish*)—The Hittite capital. It guarded the main route across the Euphrates River and was the site where Nebuchadnezzar gained control of Syria-Palestine (2Ch 35:20).

CARMEL (*KAHR mel;* "*garden-land*" or "*fruitful land*")—A wooded hillside on Palestine's coast. Isaiah declared that Mount Carmel showed the beauty of God's creation (Isa 35:1–2).

Christ as a young carpenter

CARPENTER—A craftsman skilled in woodworking. Jesus learned the trade from Joseph, who made furniture and yokes in his Nazareth shop (Mk 6:3). A carpenter's square is the Christian symbol for Jude

89

and Thomas; a saw stands for James.

CART, WAGON—A wooden, wheeled vehicle pulled by oxen or cattle and typically used to haul farm produce. A special cart carried the ark of the covenant (1Sa 6:7–14).

CASTLE—A fortified building or stronghold (Pr 18:19). David converted the Jebusite castle into his home, the City of David (1Ch 11:5, 7).

CATHOLIC EPISTLES/ LETTERS—The seven letters of the New Testament, written by James, Peter, John, and Jude. They may be written to a general audience or the universal Church rather than to specific congregations.

CATTLE—Counted as wealth, cattle were raised for their milk, meat, hides, and horns. Cattle were also used for animal sacrifices, and their manure was burned as fuel (Gen 13:2).

CAVE—Natural or man-made hollows in hillsides or cliffs. Caves were used as homes, tombs, and hiding places for precious items like the Dead Sea Scrolls (Jn 11:38).

CELIBACY—A voluntary decision to abstain from marriage in order to give full attention to the Lord's work. Jesus respected, but did not require, celibacy (Mt 19:11), and Paul taught that "... it is better to marry than be aflame with passion" (1Co 7:2, 9).

CENCHREAE *(sen KREE uh)*—A harbor town just east of Corinth. Paul shaved his head there to fulfill a vow (Ac 18:18). Phoebe was a church deaconess at Cenchreae (Ro 16:1).

CENSER *(SEN sur)*—A portable holder to carry live coals and incense (Nu 16:6–7). Tabernacle censers were bronze; temple censers were gold (1Ki 7:50).

CENSUS (*SEN sus*)—A count of population, generally for taxation purposes. Hebrews were required to register according to their tribe (Nu 1:26, 46). Plagues were common in crowded census camps. God punished David because he had "numbered the people" (2Sa 24). The New Testament mentions two Roman censuses (Lk 2:1–5; Ac 5:37).

CENTURION (*sen CHEW ree uhn*)—A Roman military officer who had command more than 100 men (a "century"). The Christian centurion, Cornelius, was one of the first Gentiles baptized (Ac 10).

CERINTHUS (*se RIN thus*)—An early Gnostic, called the false apostle in A.D. 100, who said Jesus was not divine and the world was not created by God.

CHAFF—Grain husks left over after winnowing. It was used as a figure of speech to indicate something worthless (Ps 1:4; Mt 3:12).

CHALDEA, CHALDEANS (*kal DEE uh/uhnz*)—Babylon (or its southern territory) and its tribe, which conquered Judah and carried its people into captivity (Gen 11:28). Since the priests practiced astrology and philosophy, Chaldeans were considered educated people (Ac 7:4).

CHALKSTONES (*"stones of lime"*)—Limestone rocks around Palestine. They were compared to idolatrous altars that must be pulverized to gain forgiveness (Isa 27:9).

CHAMBERLAIN (*CHAME bur lin*)—A guardian of the private palace chambers (Ac 12:20), harem, or treasury. In the Old Testament, the word signified eunuch.

CHANGES OF RAIMENT—New clothes, particularly festival attire, that was used as payment or tribute. They

91

CHARIOT

Pulled by one or more swift horses, chariots were used primarily by people of wealth and prestige for ceremonial processions or battle (1Sa 8:11). By the time of Solomon—who had 1,400 chariots and a stable for horses—they were in great use (1Ki 9:15–19).

Chariots were mostly made of light construction, using wood and leather with as little bronze or iron for fastenings as possible. Wheels, with four to eight spokes, stood about waist high (although some were larger). The open-back cart usually held three men: driver, warrior, and shield bearer. The charioteer was always a skilled driver (Ac 8:26–39). Horses were yoked to a pole, and the archer's equipment and spears were mounted on the chariot's sides.

The Israelites, who were often attacked by enemies with chariots, didn't have their own chariots until the time of David. Although fast in battles and on flat ground, chariots were of little use on hilly, rocky areas—the first place the Israelites attacked and conquered.

were exchanged as gifts (Gen 45:22).

CHEBAR *(KE bahr)*—A river or canal in Babylonia. The Jewish exiles set up their camp near its banks. The prophet Ezekiel received his vision there (Eze 1:1, 3, 3:15).

CHEDORIAMER/ CHEDORLAOMER *(KEHD or lay OH muhr)*—A king of Elam. He ruled Babylon and captured Lot from Sodom. Abraham and his men recovered the captives and killed the king (Gen 14:1–16).

CHEMOSH *(KEE mosh)*—The chief god of the Moabites (Nu 21:29). Worship practices included the sacrifice of children. Solomon built a high place for Chemosh that Josiah later destroyed (2Ki 23:13).

CHENOBOSKION *(KEN ah bos kee uhn)*—An ancient Egyptian town east of the Nile. It was the site of one of the earliest Christian monasteries. Gnostic literature was discovered there in 1945.

CHERITH *(KEE rith)*—A brook ("wadi") located east of the Jordan River, probably in Gilead. During a drought, God instructed Elijah to drink water from the Cherith (1Ki 17:3, 5).

CHERUB, CHERUBIM *(CHER uhb, CHER uh bim)*—1. A mythological winged sphinx, bull, or lion with a human head. They guarded the Garden of Eden (Gen 3:24), and appeared in Ezekiel's visions (Eze 10:1–22). Renaissance artists painted cherubs as tiny winged boys. 2. An unidentified place in Babylon (Ezr 2:59).

CHIEF PRIEST—A supervisor of priests or ministers. The chief priest wore special robes, made offerings and sacrifices (Lev 4, 6), and announced God's will (Nu 27:21).

CHILD, CHILDREN—Children were considered blessings from God; barrenness was seen as God's punishment (Gen 33:5; Ps 127:3; Pr 10:1, 17:6). A firstborn Hebrew belonged to God and required a temple payment to be redeemed (Nu 3:40–51). Children were carefully named. They were tended as they helped in the home, field, and workshop. Jesus loved and blessed all children (Mt 18:1–4).

CHILDREN OF GOD—Obedient followers of God (Heb 12:5; Eph 5:1). Jesus and Paul affectionately called their followers children. Christ urged the people to become childlike and humble (Mt 18:2–6). A sinful person was considered a "child of the devil" (1Jn 3:10).

CHINNERETH (*KIN i reth; "harp"*)—A freshwater lake—also called the Sea of Chinnereth—located near the city of the same name (Nu 34:11; Jos 19:35). It was later called the Sea of Galilee.

CHLOE (*KLOH ee; "first shoot of green grass"*)—A Christian woman of Corinth (1Co 1:11). Her people warned Paul of church dissension.

CHORAZIN (*ko RAZ in*)—A town near the Sea of Galilee where Jesus preached. He criticized its people for ignoring his message (Mt 11:21). Ruins, including a synagogue, mark its location.

CHRISTIANS—An early nickname for the followers of Christ. The term, which originated at the church of Antioch in Syria, appears only three times in the Bible (Ac 11:26, 26:28; 1Pe 4:16). It was not widely accepted by Christians until the second century.

CHRISTMAS—The anniversary of Christ's birth. It has been observed on December 25 (or January 6 by Orthodox Christians) since the fourth century. The Roman festival Saturnalia influenced the modern Christmas customs of feasting, candles, and gift-giving.

CHRISTOLOGY (*KRIS tahl o jee*)—The study of Christ's divine and human natures. The Gospel of John is one of the best sources.

CHRIST

Jesus of Nazareth—the son of Mary—was called Christ ("anointed one"), the title of the promised savior (Mk 1:14–15, 2:19–22). His birth in Bethlehem was prophesied as the coming of the Messiah (Gal 4:4). Little is known of his childhood until age 12, when he lingered after Passover to talk with the rabbis.

Jesus was baptized by John the Baptist, and during his brief three-and-a-half year ministry, he called 12 men to join him as disciples. He taught them how to preach, teach, and heal in his name. Jesus healed many people, defying the law by associating with lepers and prostitutes. He performed many miracles (Mk 4:35–41), forgave sins, and taught in parables. His claim to be the Son of God was considered blasphemy by religious leaders. After Judas—one of his disciples—betrayed him, Jesus was sentenced to death. The crowd had the chance to free him (a Passover custom) but released Barabbas instead.

After being crucified on a cross, Jesus was buried in a borrowed tomb. The third day after his death, he appeared—resurrected—to the women who visited to the tomb and later to many of his disciples. Before ascending to heaven to be with God, Jesus promised to return to complete what he had begun and to bring a new age of judgment and a gathering of the faithful.

CHRONICLES, BOOKS OF *(KRAHN i kulz)*—A pair of Old Testament books that trace the history of Israel and kings who obeyed God. Both books are believed to have been written by a single unknown author. 1 Chronicles covers the period from Adam to David; 2 Chronicles covers Solomon to Syrups (king of Persia).

CHRONOLOGY OF THE OLD TESTAMENT—A time line of history, arranged in the order the events happened in the Old Testament. Since little evidence remains from ancient times, dates are based on extrabiblical sources and genealogy in the Scriptures. It begins at creation and ends with the return of the exiled Jews around 450 B.C.

CHRONOLOGY OF THE NEW TESTAMENT—A time line of history, arranged in the order the events happened in the New Testament. Because early Christians didn't keep many records, dates are based on records of rulers or provable events. It begins with the birth of Jesus between 6 and 4 B.C. and ends with

the spread of the early Church somewhere around the first century A.D.

CHURCH—The entire community of God's people (Ac 2:37–41; 1Co 12:12). Members of Christ's spiritual body (Eph 1:22–23) are joined in baptism, communion, and spirit.

CHURCH GOVERNMENT—A set of general procedures for the sharing of leadership and decision-making responsibilities within the Church. Based on New Testament teachings, they stress Christ as authority (Ac 15:28). The New Testament mentions the Church offices of deacon, elder, and bishop.

CHUZA (KOO zuh)—Herod's steward. Chuza's wife, Joanna, supported and followed Jesus, who healed her (Lk 8:3).

CILICIA (si LISH ee uh)—A district in the southeast corner of Asia Minor. Its chief city was Tarsus, the birthplace of Paul (Ac 21:39).

CIRCUMCISION—The religious rite of removing the foreskin of the penis, performed by a rabbi. An ancient custom, circumcision was universal among Jews, Egyptians, and other cultures. To the Hebrews, it symbolized obedience to God's law (Gen 17:9–14; Gal 5:1–12).

An ancient cistern

CISTERN—An earthen or stone reservoir designed to collect rain. Public cisterns could hold up to two million gallons (Dt 6:11). Empty, they were sometimes used as prisons (Gen 37:24; Jer 38:6).

CITADEL (*"height"*)—A fortified or stronghold area of a city. It was usually built in a strategic, commanding location (1Ki 16:18; 2Ki 15:25).

CITIES OF REFUGE—Six Levitical cities that were designated as asylums where a person who had unintentionally killed someone could be safe until his case was tried before the city's elders. If he was found innocent of deliberate murder, he could remain protected there until the high priest died (Nu 35:9–28).

CITIES, LEVITICAL—Forty-eight outlying cities given to the Levites by God (Nu 35:1–8; Jos 21) to carry out their teaching ministry (Dt 33:10). Six of these cities ("cities of refuge") offered legal protection (Dt 4:41–43, 19:1–13).

CITIZENSHIP—A claim of residency through birth or naturalization (Ac 21:39; Lk 15:15). A legal citizen had more benefits and responsibilities than an alien. Paul, proud of his

CITY OF DAVID (JERUSALEM)

The Jebusite stronghold of Zion was located in Israel's central mountains. David captured the area (perhaps by crawling through an underground water shaft) and made it his royal home (2Sa 5:6–9). He enclosed 12–15 acres within walls and made Jerusalem the capital and a religious center. The ark of the covenant was kept there while he gathered materials to build a temple.

Later, Solomon built an elaborate temple, the city walls were enlarged, and walls were built around the temple, giving the place the look of a fortress. David was buried there (as were several other kings). Throughout history, the city and temple were destroyed and rebuilt several times (2Ki 25).

Herod the Great rebuilt the walls and temple, but the construction wasn't completed during Jesus' lifetime. In A.D. 70, the Romans destroyed the temple and city. It was again rebuilt in A.D. 135 by Hadrian, who changed the city's name to honor a pagan god and forbade Jews to enter. It was not until the reign of Constantine in the fourth century that Jews were allowed to return to the City of David.

Roman citizenship, taught that Christians are citizens of a heavenly realm and should live accordingly (Php 1:27, 3:20). Citizenship was probably proven with a document similar to a passport.

CITY—A group of permanent Hebrew dwellings, often surrounded by a wall and built on a hill (Gen 4:17). Early cities were small and offered few amenities other than protection against enemies. As cities grew, they became centers of trade and government and boasted technological advances, such as elaborate sewage systems.

CLAUDIUS *(KLAW dee uhs)*—The unpopular fourth Roman emperor (A.D. 41–54). He banished Jews from Rome (Ac 11:28, 18:2) and tried three times to get rid of Christianity. A predicted famine happened during his reign.

CLAUDIUS LYSIAS *(KLAW dee uhs LIS ee us)*—A Roman military tribune in charge of the Jerusalem garrison. He rescued Paul from Jewish rioters. Later, he protected Paul by sending him to Caesarea (Ac 21:24–23:25).

CLAY TABLETS—Ancient writing materials of smoothed wet clay marked with a stylus in wedge-shaped letters (cuneiform). Kiln- or sun-dried, they were often placed in clay envelopes. Of the thou-

sands excavated, the earliest tablet dates to 3000 B.C. and describes everyday life.

CLEOPAS *(KLEE oh puhs; "renowned father")*—A disciple who met, but didn't immediately recognize, Jesus on the Emmaus Road on resurrection evening (Lk 24:18). Later, he spread the news.

CLOPAS *(KLOH puhs)*—The husband, son, or brother of one of the Marys standing beside Jesus' cross. (Jn 19:25).

CLOTHING—Early biblical people wore animal skins (Gen 2:25). Later, clothing was made from wool, flax, silk, linen, and camel's hair. Typically, a tunic (coat or robe) was worn under a mantle and fastened with a girdle that held a sword or money (Jdg 3:16; Mt 10:9). Women wore veils, and their clothing was more colorful than men's garments (Gen 24:65).

CLOUD—Bearers of rain, clouds symbolized God's

CLEAN AND UNCLEAN

In the Old Testament, the Israelites made a clear distinction between what was holy and unholy to God. These ancient practices from earlier tribal life developed into a system of ritual laws overseen by the high priests. Observed for both spiritual and hygienic reasons, these laws reminded the people of the gap between them and God and the need to prepare before coming into his presence.

God's people were to be free from all contamination—physical, moral, and spiritual. Uncleanness resulted from idolatry, specific bodily functions (especially menstruation and intercourse), certain foods and animals, diseases (such as leprosy), murder, and contact with dead bodies (Hos 6:10; Dt 12:19). People who became unclean were unfit to approach God in worship until certain procedures of cleansing were fulfilled (Lev 5:2–3, 7:19–21, 22:2–8). Purification included waiting periods, rituals with water or fire, and altar sacrifice (Lev 10:10).

The New Testament focused on spiritual cleanness rather than dietary or physical. Christ "cleansed" by word (Jn 15:3). His blood on the cross cleansed the sins of the people, so that purification rituals were no longer required (1 Jn 1:7).

presence. He used clouds to guide the Israelites (Ex 13:21–22) and confuse the Egyptians at the Red Sea (Ex 14:24).

COAT—A long outer garment. Sometimes, it may have been dyed with vegetable extracts, such as Joseph's coat of many colors (Gen 37:3).

COCKCROW—The third of four divisions of time during the Roman night watch (evening, midnight, cockcrow, and morning). Named after the rooster's predawn call, it represented the hours between midnight and 3 A.M. (Mk 13:35).

CODEX *(KO deks)*—The earliest form of books. Papyrus sheets were folded in the middle and sewn together at the spine. Christians may have used codices to distinguish their bibles from the Jewish synagogue scrolls. Originally, all of Paul's letters were bound in one book.

COELE-SYRIA, COELESYRIA *(see lee SEAR ee uh)*—A region between the Lebanon and Anti-Lebanon mountains. It was also used as a general term to describe all of Palestine and Phoenicia.

COHORT—A battalion of 600–750 infantrymen and 240 cavalrymen, or about one-tenth of a legion. Cohorts were posted at forts in frontier towns.

COINS—Introduced after the Exile, coins replaced bartering and weights as the main monetary system. Israelites had to use their captors' coins. A drachma (about 16 cents) was a day's wages.

COLLECTION (PAULINE CHURCHES)—A relief fund collected by Paul from other churches to ease the poverty in the Jerusalem church (Ac 24:17).

COLONY—Retired Roman soldiers and aristocracy that were permitted to live in conquered territories. They served as unofficial garrisons and eased the crowding in Rome (Ac 16:12).

COLOSSIANS, LETTER TO THE—Paul's letter (circa A.D. 61), to the church at Colossae—a small group of Jews, Greeks, and Asians reluctant to change. He

COLOSSAE

An important ancient city, Colossae (kuh LAH see) was located in the Roman province of Asia. The great trade routes from Ephesus and Sardis both met there. It was the site of a good water supply that could be easily defended. When the road was moved farther west toward Laodicea, the city lost some if its importance.

Epaphras, who was converted by Paul at Ephesus, was sent to start the church in Colossae. This took place during Paul's three-year stay in Ephesus on his third missionary journey (Ac 19:10). Although concerned about the church, Paul never preached in Colossae and had apparently not visited there when he wrote his letter to the Colossians.

Philemon and his slave Onesimus were members of the early church in Colossae, which was troubled by heresy and a tendency of its members to listen to false prophets and resist change (Col 4:9). The area was destroyed by a violent earthquake around A.D. 60. There is no mention of this in Paul's letter, perhaps because it happened before news reached him in Rome.

addressed their worship of angels and false teachers (Col 1:15).

COLORS—Hebrews had few terms to describe colors, so many descriptions refer to a color's brightness rather than its particular hue. They made natural dyes to decorate their clothing, skin, and buildings (Eze 27:16; Jer 22:14). White represented purity (Mk 16:5); red, blood; and purple, princes (Lk 16:19).

COMING OF CHRIST, SECOND—Christ's promised return to complete his ministry, defeat sin, and save his followers (Heb 9:28). Godlessness, heresy, and natural changes are signs of his impending return (Mt 24:3–14).

COMMANDMENT, NEW—Jesus' directive to his disciples to "love one another. Just as I have loved you" (Jn 13:34). Jesus also summarized the Old Testament commandments by urging his followers to love God and one another (Mt 22:35–40).

COMMISSION, GREAT—Jesus' instructions that his disciples go into the world to preach, teach, and heal in his name (Mt 18:18–20), an ongoing commission.

COMMUNION *(kuh MYOON yuhn; "a sharing")*—A sacrament of bread and wine, reenacted in Christian fellowship as a reminder of God's covenant and Christ's sacrificial fulfillment. It recalls the last meal "shared" between Christ and his disciples (Lk 22:14–23; 2Co 9:13).

COMPASSION—The divine and human qualities of mercy. Prophets taught that anyone who experiences God's compassion should extend it to others (Dt 10:18). It is the theme for Jesus' parable of the Good Samaritan (Lk 10).

CONCUBINE—A secondary, lawful wife that could be taken to ensure a male heir (Gen 16:2–3). Their rights were protected, and there was no moral stigma (Ex 21:7–11).

CONFESSION—A public statement of faith in God or admission of sin (Lev 5:5; Jas 5:16; 1Jn 1:9). Confession of sin is required for God's forgiveness, but the Bible gives no specific instructions (Mt 5:24).

CONGREGATION—A gathering of God's followers (Ex

103

27:21) either as a group or in a synagogue (Ac 13:43). The Bible often used the word to describe the entire Israelite community rather than a local church (Eph 1:22).

CONGREGATION, SOLEMN ASSEMBLY—A group gathered by appointment for a special reason, such as the Feast of Unleavened Bread (Dt 16:8) or Solomon's temple dedication (2Ch 7:9). The Greek New Testament word is "church."

CONQUEST OF CANAAN—The Israelite invasion and occupation of Canaan (an early name for Palestine). The conquest was generally peaceful, and the Hebrews introduced their culture and religion to the region (Nu, Jos, Jdg).

CONSCIENCE—An inner awareness that one's actions match a personal standard of right and wrong (Ac 23:1). Not mentioned in the Old Testament, the New Testament stresses a good conscience in relation to God (Ro 2:14, 15; 1Co 8:10).

CONTENTMENT—Satisfaction. The acceptance of things as they are—without anxiety or envy—under the security of God's loving wisdom. (Ps 37:7; Php 4:11).

CONVERSION—The turning—or returning—to God, marked by new behavior. In the Old Testament, conversion meant rejecting false gods. In the New Testament, it meant accepting salvation through Christ (Ac 26:18).

COPPER—1. A reddish metal, first used as a simple ornament and later used in tools (Ezr 8:27). 2. A small coin that symbolized generosity (Mt 10:9).

CORBAN (KOR ban)—A sacred offering given to God, often referring to money (Mk 7:11). It was

CORINTH

During the time of Paul's missionary visit, Corinth (*KOR inth*) was a cosmopolitan city brimming with merchants, seamen, slaves, and colonists. Located between Greece and Peloponnesus, it was also a place where all the pagan deities were worshiped.

Morality was low, and many cults, mystery religions, and philosophies were popular. To live "like a Corinthian" was to live the most self-indulgent type of life. Christianity wasn't taken seriously by the Corinthians. They thought it was a religion of the unlearned and unsophisticated.

Against great odds in this culture, Paul founded the church at Corinth during his second missionary journey (Ac 18:1–8). Many of its early members were from the lower, uneducated classes of people. They found it difficult to change or rid themselves of the influences of their surroundings and peers. Paul's two letters to the church contain his teachings on Christian love, the Lord's Supper, Christian ministry, and resurrection.

Filled with many beautiful buildings, Corinth was prosperous until the Middle Ages. After a large earthquake destroyed the city in 1858, it was rebuilt about three miles away from the original site.

not to be used for secular purposes.

CORD, ROPE—Strips of animal skins, vines, or bark, or flax spun into thread, which are then twisted or braided into a single strand. The term was often used figuratively to describe entanglement in sin (Job 36:8; Pr 5:22).

CORIANDER SEED *(ko ree AN dur)*—1. The small, globe-like fruit of an annual plant that was used to season food. Manna was compared to coriander seed in appearance (Ex 16:31; Nu 11:7).

CORINTHIANS, FIRST LETTER OF PAUL TO THE—An epistle from Paul to the morally lax city of Corinth. It addressed problems with early Gentile converts, often from lower socioeconomic classes. The "love" chapter (1Co 13) is one of the most well-known passages of Scripture.

CORINTHIANS, SECOND LETTER OF PAUL TO THE—Paul's second letter offering advice to the church in the prosperous but immoral city of Corinth, where early Christians reverted to their previous lifestyle. Paul urged them to give Christ first place in their lives.

CORNELIUS *(kohr NEEL ee uhs)*—A devout Roman centurion who was instructed in a vision to talk to Peter (Ac 10:2). After his own vision, Peter baptized Cornelius and his family, beginning the practice of allowing Gentiles into Christian fellowship (Ac 10:34–35).

CORNERSTONE—A large stone placed at a building's foundation where two walls meet, helping bind them together (Job 38:6). It was an Old Testament symbol of stability and faith (Isa 28:16). In the New Testament, Christ is called the chief cornerstone (Mt 21:42; 1Pe 2:6).

CORRUPTION—The perishable, temporary nature of the physical body and material world. It is contrasted with the everlasting, incorruptible life saved for believers (1Pe 1:4).

CORRUPTION, MOUNT OF—A hilltop east of Jerusalem at the south end of the Mount of Olives. Solomon built a high place there—

which Josiah later destroyed—to honor the gods of his foreign wives (1Ki 11:7).

Cos/Coos *(KOS, KOOS)*— A large mountainous island (with a city of the same name) about a day's sail from Rhodes (Ac 21:1). Paul visited there on his third missionary journey. Cos was famous for its wines, ointments, and purple dyes.

Cosmetics containers

COSMETICS AND PERFUMERY—Beauty and restorative aids, such as incense (Pr 7:17). Made of pulverized minerals, vegetables extracts, and animal fat, they were disapproved by biblical writers (2Ki 9:30). Perfumed oils were used to anoint Christ's head (Lk 7:37).

COUNCIL OF JERUSALEM—A conference at Jerusalem between Church officials and Paul and Barnabas, who negotiated how to receive Gentile converts into the Church (Ac 15: 2–29).

COUNCIL—A Jewish governing body. In the Old Testament, the council represented the nation after the Persians granted Jews control of their own affairs (Ezr 7:28). In the New Testament, local congregations were given educational, legal, and religious responsibilities. It also described the Sanhedrin, or high court (Mt 10:17).

COUNSELOR—An advisor. Used as a proper name to describe God (Ps 16:7, 32:8) and the Holy Spirit

(Jn 14:16, 26). In the Old Testament, the term referred to the seven counselors who advised kings (Ezr 7:14).

COURT—1. A system of justice. The Sanhedrin was the high court in Jesus' day (Mt 26:57–68). 2. A king and his advisors. 3. An enclosed yard of a home, tabernacle, or temple. The tabernacle court was 100 cubits long and 50 cubits wide (Ex 27:9).

COUSIN—Usually a child of an uncle or aunt, but the word is often translated as "kinsman." Luke refers to Elizabeth as Mary's cousin, but the exact relationship is not known (Lk 1:36).

COVENANT, BOOK OF—The first book of laws for the Hebrew people. It covered a wide range of subjects, including slavery, murder, and thievery (Ex 20).

COVET—To desire something wrongfully or with evil intent. The term first appears in the Ten Commandments (Ex 20), then again in Deuteronomy (Dt 5:21).

COVETOUSNESS, GREEDINESS—A desire for more. Covetousness was considered sinful behavior that angered God (Jos 7). In the New Testament, Mark names greed—or avarice—as one of the evils that defile a man (Mk 7:22).

COW—A farm animal that provided labor, milk, meat, and leather. The Israelites also used young bulls in rites of sacrifice (Ex 29:1).

CREATURES—Four "living creatures" were seen in Ezekiel's dream (Eze 1:5). Each creature had four faces: that of a man, a lion, an ox, and an eagle. These were cherubim who carried God's throne. They also appear in the Book of Revelation (Rev 4:7).

CREED—A statement of Christian belief and doc-

CREATION

The biblical account of God's creation of the universe and humanity—often referred to as the Creation Hymn—covers seven days (Gen 1–3).

The first step, according to this poetic description, occurred when God willed the appearance of light (Gen 1:3). On the second day, he separated the waters and formed the sky (1:6–8). The third day brought the emergence of land and vegetation (1:9–13). On the fourth day, the sun, moon, and stars became visible (1:14–19). On the fifth day God ushered into existence the creatures of the sea and the birds (1:20–25). On the sixth day, he created the land animals and humans—his crowning achievement (1:24–31). On the seventh day, he rested.

Because of its various uses in the Bible, the exact meaning of the word "day" as used in this story is not known. It could represent a 24-hour time period, or it could denote some other span of existence. According to scientists, however, rock formations and fossil remains do verify the order of events as narrated in the Book of Genesis to be correct.

trine. Three ancient creeds, while not found in the Bible, are based on passages from the New Testament (1Co 15:3).

CREEPING THINGS—Animals that crawl on the ground. They were considered by the Israelites to be ceremonially unclean. The Old Testament lists certain animals (including mice and reptiles) that "swarm upon the earth" and were not acceptable for the Israelites to eat or touch (Lev 11:29–30).

CRESCENS *(KRES enz; "increasing")*—One of the 70 disciples, Crescens was an assistant to Paul. He left Paul at Rome and went to Galatia (2Ti 4:10).

CRETE—An island southeast of Greece, between the Aegean and Mediterranean seas. Paul visited Crete—also called Candia—on his journey to Rome.

CRIME AND PUNISHMENT—The first crime reported in the Old Testament was Cain's murder of his brother Abel (Gen 4:8). God put a curse on him as punishment. Moses lists crimes and punishments in Exodus 21–23, including retaliation ("an eye for an eye," Ex 21:24–25) and compensation of money and goods (Ex 21:18–36). Stoning and hanging were common methods of capital punishment.

CRISPUS *(KRIS pus; "curled")*—A ruler of the synagogue in Corinth (Ac 18:7–8) who was baptized by Paul (1Co 1:14). As a ruler, Crispus arranged the service, announced the readers and preachers, and kept order.

CROWN OF THORNS—The soldiers who led Jesus away to be crucified put a purple robe on him and made a crown of briers to place on his head. Then they mockingly saluted him as "King of the Jews." (Mt 27:29; Mk 15:17; Jn 19:2).

CUBIT *(KYOO bit)*—An ancient measure of length from the elbow to the middle finger, about 18 inches. The term was first mentioned in the Book of Genesis, when God instructed Noah in building an ark (Gen 6:14–16).

CULT PROSTITUTE—A man or woman who engaged in ritual prostitution as part of Baal worship. The Israelite Law forbade this pagan practice (Dt. 23:17–18). King Josiah rid the temple of all evidence of Baal worship (2Ki 23).

CRUCIFIXION

Crucifixion, one of the cruelest forms of punishment known to man, was practiced routinely by the early Romans.

This painful and agonizing torture began when the victim was stripped of his clothes and placed on the cross, arms outstretched along the crossbars. An inscription was placed above the head to indicate the prisoner's crime. Four soldiers kept watch so the person could not be taken down by friends or family and revived. The victim was left hanging to suffer hunger, thirst, and pain, and then to waste away and die. Sometimes the legs were broken to hasten death.

Jesus' crucifixion took place on Golgotha ("Skull Hill"), believed to be just outside the north wall of Jerusalem near the Damascus Gate. Condemned to die for the crime of blasphemy, Jesus was forced to carry his own cross to the place of crucifixion, but a man named Simon of Cyrene helped Jesus to carry his heavy load.

A death by crucifixion could take as many as four to six days. In Jesus' case, it took only six hours (Mt 27:32–56; Mk 15:21–41; Lk 23:26–49; Jn 19:17–37). The cross has since become a symbol of the Christian religion.

CUMMIN *(CUM in)*—A plant of Palestine (Isa 28:25; Mt 23:23). The aromatic seeds of this herb were used for seasoning; the leaves and roots were used for medicinal purposes.

CUNEIFORM *(kyoo NEE ih form)*—A type of writing used by the Assyrians and

Cuneiform inscription

Babylonians. Wedge-shaped characters, inscribed on clay tablets, stood for words or combinations of words. Ancient cuneiform inscriptions have helped to identify biblical sites.

CUP—An open container, with or without handles, for dipping or drinking. The cup became a symbol for one's lot in life (Ps 16:5). It also represents the blood that Jesus shed for his people.

CUPBEARER—A high-ranking, trusted officer or attendant who personally filled the king's cup and served his wine (Gen 40:1). Pharaoh's chief cupbearer introduced Joseph to the king, enabling Joseph to rise to a high position in the king's court.

CURSE—To utter profanities or express a wish for harm to come to another person. Noah uttered a curse to his son Ham (Gen 9:25). In the New Testament, Christians are told not to curse their fellow human beings (Jas 3:10).

CUSH (*Kush; "black"*)—1. The son of Ham and the grandson of Noah (Gen 10:6). 2. The Hebrew name for an African country called Ethiopia.

CUSHAN-RISHATHAIM (*KU shan rish a THAY im*)—The wicked king of Aram Naharaim, the northern part of the area later called Mesopotamia. He held the Israelites prisoner for eight years until he was overthrown by Othniel.

CUSHION—A bag—usually stuffed with animal hair—that was used for sitting, kneeling, or lying down. Because of its portability, the cushion was the only furniture used by the biblical tribes of tent-dwellers.

Cylinder seal

CYLINDER SEALS—Personal seals made of soft stone in the shape of a cylinder. In Bible times, people used a seal to mark important papers. When rolled over wax or clay, the seal made an impression that was like a signature. Jezebel wrote letters in her husband's name and placed his seal on them (1Ki 21:8).

CYPRUS *(SY pruhs)*—An island in the Mediterranean located off the coast of Syria. It was the birthplace of Barnabas (Ac 4:36). The first of Paul's three missionary journeys began there in the town of Salamis, where he and Barnabas preached to the Jews (Ac 13:4–5).

CYRENE *(sy REEN)*—A Greek city in Libya, North Africa, with a large Jewish population. Simon, who carried the cross for Jesus on the way to the crucifixion, was from Cyrene (Mk 15:21).

CYRUS THE GREAT *(SY ruhs; "son")*—The Persian king who captured Babylon in 539 B.C. He was sympathetic to the Jews and issued a decree that enabled them to return to their homeland and rebuild Jerusalem (Ezr 1:1–3).

DAGON *(DAY gahn)*—The principal god of the Philistines, whose temples were at Gaza and Ashdod. He was the father of Baal and was worshiped extensively, even by the Israelites (1Sa 5:2–5).

DALMANUTHA *(dal mah NOO thuh)*—A town on the northwest shore of the Sea of Galilee where Jesus and his disciples went after feeding 4,000 people (Mk 8:10).

DALMATIA *(dal MAY shee ah)*—A city on the Adriatic Sea, also known as Illyricum, located in a mountainous district north of Greece. Both Paul and Titus preached there (2Ti 4:10).

DAMASCUS *(duh MAS kuhs)*—The oldest city in the world, known for its fine cloth. It was on the road to Damascus that Saul was converted (Ac 9:1–25), and he did his first preaching in that Syrian city.

DAMASCUS GATE—One of the chief gates of Jerusalem, located on the north wall toward the road leading to northern Palestine and Damascus.

DAMN, DAMNATION—To damn is to pronounce judgment on a person or object. Damnation is the condemnation to eternal punishment because of sin. The Bible states that believers in Christ will be saved; nonbelievers will be subjected to eternal damnation (Mk 16:16).

[1]DAN *("judge")*—The fifth son of Jacob, born to Rachel's maid, Bilhah (Gen 30:6). Dan was the last of the Twelve Tribes of Israel to receive its allotment of land (Jos 19:40).

²DAN—The northernmost city of Palestine. A well-known expression, "from Dan to Beer-sheba" (Jdg 20:1), referred to all of Israel from north to south. The main source of the Jordan River was located in this area.

DAN-JAAN *(dan JAY an)*—An ancient city, also known as Leshem or Laish (2Sa 24:6). It was attacked and burned down by the Danites, then rebuilt and renamed Dan (Jdg 18).

DANCE—Dancing was often part of religious celebrations among the Israelites to thank God for a good harvest or a great victory (Ex 15:20).

DANIEL *("God is my judge")*—A prophet of the Old Testament. He was one of the first captives taken from Jerusalem to Babylon. He became an advisor to King Darius and interpreter of his dreams. His strong religious convictions landed him in the lion's den, where he was rescued by God's angel (Da 6:10–23). Three stories attributed to Daniel, but not included in the original text of the Bible, are contained in the Apocrypha: The Song of the Three Holy Children, The History of Susanna, and The History of the Destruction of Bel and the Dragon.

DANIEL, BOOK OF—An Old Testament book whose principal character is the prophet Daniel. Chapters 1–6 are historical. Chapters 7–12 are comprised of Daniel's dreams.

DARIUS *(DAH ree uhs; "he who upholds the good")*—The name of three Persian rulers: Darius the Mede, associated with Daniel (Da 6); Darius Hystaspes, who favored the Jews (Ezr 6:1–15); and Darius of Persia, who was defeated by Alexander the Great (Ne 12:22).

DARKNESS—Three major episodes of total darkness

DAVID

The second—and best known—king of Israel, David was a mighty warrior, a strong spiritual leader, and the father of King Solomon.

While he was still a shepherd boy, David (the youngest son of Jesse) was interviewed by the prophet Samuel. Samuel's mission was to find a new king to replace Saul, who had disobeyed God. Samuel identified David as God's choice to succeed Saul and secretly anointed him as future king of Israel. David returned to his shepherding duties and developed his reputation as a musician.

Ironically, when Saul learned he was to be replaced, he sent for David to cheer him up with music. Soon David became Saul's armor-bearer. When the Philistine army declared war on the Israelites, David fought the giant Goliath and became the new hero of Israel.

Saul became jealous of David's popularity and repeatedly attempted to kill him, so the young hero fled for his life. At Saul's death, David was crowned king. A just ruler, David watched his kingdom grow. His 40-year reign was flawed by some serious mistakes, but he acknowledged his sins and remained faithful to God. In return, God promised him an everlasting kingdom. That promise fueled Israel's hope for a messiah.

occur in the Bible: at the Creation (Gen 1:2); during the time of the Exodus in Egypt (Ex 10:21–28); and at the crucifixion of Christ (Mt 27:45). Darkness has often been interpreted as a lack of spiritual light or separation from God (Lk 1:79).

DATHAN (*DAY thuhn; "strong"*)—A Reubenite chief who joined in a conspiracy challenging the leadership of Moses (Nu 16:23). The earth swallowed up the leaders of the rebellion; the rest of the group were consumed by fire (Nu 16:1–35).

DAUGHTER—A word used in Scripture to designate any female relative: daughter, granddaughter, cousin, sister, or wife. It can also mean the female inhabitants of a place, such as the "daughters of Zion" (Isa 3:16).

DAVID, CITY OF—*See* **CITY OF DAVID.**

DAY—1. The period of time between two sunrises. 2. The time from sunrise to sunset (Jn 11:9). The day was divided into 12 watches. Early morning was the first watch, and noon was the sixth. 3. An event, an era, or a span of life.

DAY OF ATONEMENT—The most solemn day of the Jewish year, held in the tenth month (Tishri) and marked by fasting, burnt sacrifice, confession of sin, and a plea for forgiveness. Instructions for the ritual are found in the Book of Leviticus (Lev 16).

DAY OF JUDGMENT, DAY OF THE LORD—The time when every person will be judged by God and assigned either to heaven or eternal fire. Paul calls it the day when God will judge the secrets of men (Ro 2:16).

DAY OF THE LORD—The day of Christ's coming, when God will triumph over his enemies and bless his people (Joel 1:15). The phrase occurs five times in the Book of Joel, and many times in the writings of the other prophets.

DAY'S JOURNEY—The distance typically traveled by one person in a day. On the Sabbath, Jews were allowed to travel only

2,000 cubits, the distance between the tents and the ark in the tabernacle.

DAYSPRING—A poetic name for the arrival of dawn (Job 38:12). The word is used to denote the coming of the Messiah (Lk 1:78).

DAY STAR—Venus, the most brilliant star in the sky, seen in the east just before sunrise. In the Book of Revelation (Rev 22:16), Jesus declares Himself to be the Morning Star or Messiah as predicted in the Old Testament (Nu 24:17).

DEACON (DEE kuhn)—A man chosen by the disciples to assist in the work of the growing Church (Ac 6:1–6). Stephen was among the first seven young men of good reputation selected to care for the widows and orphans, assist at communion, receive contributions, read the gospel, and baptize.

DEACONESS (DEE kuh nes)—A woman assistant in the early Christian Church, performing duties similar to those of a deacon. The New Testament names Phoebe and others as "servants" of the Church (Ro 16:1).

Restoration of ancient scrolls

DEAD SEA—The lake known in the Bible as the Salt Sea (Gen 14:3), forming the eastern border of Jerusalem. Due to the high concentration of salt, marine life cannot exist in it.

DEAD SEA SCROLLS—Scrolls of ancient manuscripts discovered in 1947 in caves at Qumran near the Dead Sea. They contain frag-

DEBORAH

Deborah was among the 12 judges sent by God to help his people. At that time, the Twelve Tribes were not unified, and Israel had no strong government. The judges administered justice in their local areas, but primarily they were leaders in the battles against Israel's enemies.

Deborah held court under a palm tree in Ephraim, settling disputes for the Israelites. She was also a prophetess, making predictions and interpreting God's messages to her people. She sent for Barak, a military leader, and informed him of God's command that he take 10,000 men to Mt. Tabor to defeat Sisera, commander of the Canaanite army. Barak refused to go unless Deborah accompanied him. She agreed, but she informed Barak that because of his timidity, the honor for conquering Sisera would go to a woman.

Sisera gathered his troops at the Kishon River. Barak's army came down the mountain and killed them all. Sisera escaped and hid in the tent of a woman, Jael, who drove a stake through his head (fulfilling Deborah's prophecy). God's victory was celebrated in Deborah's Song (Jdg 5), one of the oldest examples of Hebrew literature. Deborah was also the name of Rebekah's nurse (Gen 35:8).

ments of nearly every book of the Old Testament.

DEATH—Natural death is the end of physical life (Gen 25:11). Spiritual death is seen as separation from God (Lk 1:79). Through his resurrection, Jesus conquered death and made it possible for the faithful to attain eternal life (Jn 5:24).

DEBT, DEBTOR—The Law of Moses forbade Jews from collecting interest on debts, and every seven years debts were forgiven. This law was often disregarded, and debtors were victimized, imprisoned, or enslaved (Mt 18:21–26).

DECALOG (*DEK uh lawg*)— The basic laws of the Hebrews, inscribed on tablets (Dt 4:13) and given by God to Moses at Mt. Sinai (Ex 20). They are known more popularly as the Ten Commandments.

DECEIT—The act of concealing the truth or misleading. It was listed as one of the evils of the human heart (Mk 7:22). Israel was frequently accused of deceit (Hos 11:12). By contrast, Christ was sinless and without deceit (1Pe 2:22).

DECISION, VALLEY OF—A valley, mentioned only in the Book of Joel, where God will gather all the nations for judgment because of their shameful treatment of Israel (Joel 3:2, 14). Another name is the Valley of Jehoshaphat (Joel 3:12).

DECREE—An official order or ruling. King Nebuchadnezzar issued a decree that landed Shadrach, Meshach, and Abednego in a blazing furnace because they wouldn't worship gold idols (Da 3:10). It was a decree from Roman emperor Caesar Augustus that sent Mary and Joseph to Bethlehem at the time of Jesus' birth (Lk 2:1).

DEDICATION—A setting apart of persons or things for God's purpose. Dedications in the Old Testament include the altar in the tabernacle (Nu 7:84), the city wall (Ne 12:27), and the firstborn males of each family (Ex 13:12).

DEDICATION, FEAST OF—A festival to celebrate the restoration of the temple after Judas Maccabeus drove out the Syrians. Held on December 25, it lasted eight days. It was mentioned only once in the Bible, when Jesus attended the celebration (Jn 10:22).

DEER—One of the animals the Israelites were allowed to eat. Because it had a split hoof and chewed cud, it was considered "clean" (Dt 14:5).

DEHAVITES, DEHAITES (di HAH vites, di HAY ites)— One of the nomadic tribes of Persia, they were deported to Samaria after the captivity of Israel. They protested the rebuilding of Jerusalem and refused to pay their taxes if the city was restored (Ezr 4:9).

DELILAH (deh LYE luh; "small" or "dainty")—A Philistine woman who used her charms to trick Samson into revealing the secret of his strength, then betrayed him to his enemies (Jdg 16:4–20).

DELUGE—The flood that God sent to wipe out the human race because of its sinfulness. The rain lasted 40 days, and even the mountains were covered. All people—except Noah and his family—were destroyed (Gen 6–8).

DEMAS (DEE muhs; "popular")—A Christian worker and helper to Paul while he was imprisoned in Rome (Col 4:14). Demas later deserted Paul and went to Thessalonica (2Ti 4:10).

DEMETRIUS (deh MEE tree uhs; "belonging to Demeter")—A disciple of John. In a glowing letter to his friend Gaius, John praised Demetrius for his good reputation and truthfulness (3Jn 1:12).

DEMON—An evil spirit or influence associated with the devil and described throughout Scripture as "unclean." They were said to possess superior intelligence as well as strength, yet they shuddered at the name of God (Jas 2:19).

DEMON POSSESSION—In biblical times, it was believed that the possession of a person by unclean spirits caused physical problems and mental derangement. During his ministry, Jesus drove out many demons. He once sent a legion of unclean spirits into a herd of pigs (Mk 5:10–14).

DEPUTY—A person chosen to act as a substitute or assistant to a public official. The word is sometimes translated as proconsul. Proconsuls were appointed by the Roman Senate to govern in the provinces for one year (Ac 13:7).

DERBE *(DUR bee)*—A Lycaonian city on the road from Tarsus to Iconium. It was visited by Paul on two missionary journeys. On one occasion, Paul was stoned by Jews in Lystra, so he and Barnabas fled to Derbe (Ac 14:6).

DESCENT INTO HADES— *Hades* is the Greek name for the place of the dead, or the grave, rather than a place of punishment. (In Hebrew the word is *Sheol*.) The creeds of the Christian Church speak of Jesus' descent into Hades—or hell—just before his resurrection.

DESERT—1. A general term for uninhabited wilderness (Mt 3:1), pasture lands, or a desolate waste (Isa 48:21). 2. A specific area on the plain of Jordan and the Dead Sea, called Arabah (Jos 11:2).

DESIRE—To crave or want; a strong wish for something. Paul urged early Christians to conquer sinful desire and to live a holy life (Gal 5:16). Desire

DENARIUS

The most common Roman coin in New Testament times, the denarius was about the size of a dime. Minted mostly in silver, it was issued in gold on rare occasions. The value of the coin fluctuated according to the generosity of the moneylenders. In silver weight, it was worth 20 cents or less—but it was worth much more in buying power because it represented a day's wage (Mt 20:2).

At the feeding of the 5,000, the disciples balked at buying 200 denarii worth of bread (Mk 6:37). The perfume Mary used to anoint Jesus' feet cost 300 denarii, nearly a year's wages (Jn 12:5). The unforgiving servant in the parable was owed 100 denarii, more than three months' salary (Mt 18:28).

Each new emperor had his own coin, stamped with his image and inscriptions. When the Pharisees asked if they should pay taxes, Jesus pointed to the face on the coin and told them to give Caesar what is Caesar's and give God what is God's (Mt 22:15–22). Some of these coins are still in existence today. The lettering on these coins has supplied scholars with historical information and has helped to verify the accuracy of the Bible.

can indicate a hunger or longing for God.

DESOLATING SACRILEGE—An idolatrous object placed on the altar of the temple. It disrupted worship and caused great distress among the Jews, who considered it a sign of the end of the world (Mt 24:15).

DEUTERONOMY, BOOK OF—The fifth book of the Old Testament. It contains a reiteration of the laws and a review of the history of the Israelites. The Song of Moses and an account of Moses' death are also included.

DEVIL—1. An evil spirit. 2. A name for Satan, God's enemy, who attacks humans through temptation and deception. In the New Testament, Satan tried to tempt Jesus (Mt 4:3).

DEW—Drops of condensed moisture that form on cool surfaces. Dew falls heavily in Palestine in spring and fall. Since rainfall is not abundant, dew is important to agriculture. In the Bible, it is a symbol of blessing and refreshment (Mic 5:7).

DIANA OF EPHESIANS—An Asian fertility goddess, also called Artemis, worshiped at the great temple at Ephesus. Paul's preaching caused a riot in Ephesus because it disrupted the business of the silversmiths who made shrines and idols of Diana (Ac 19:24–35).

DIASPORA (*dye AS por uh*)—Jews living outside of Israel. From a Greek word for "dispersion," the Diaspora describes hundreds of thousands of Jews who lived in Mediterranean countries during the New Testament era.

DIBLATH, DIBLAH (*DIB lath, DIB luh*)—A place in northern Israel, 50 miles south of Hamath, believed to be Riblah. God pronounced judgment on Palestine "from the desert

DISCIPLE

The men and women who became followers of Jesus were sometimes called disciples. Included in this circle were the apostles, 12 men (plus Paul) that Jesus gathered, trained, and sent out to preach the gospel.

The terms *disciple* and *apostle* are often interchangeable. (In Matthew 10:1, the word *disciples* is used; in the next verse (Mt 10:2) the men are called *apostles*.) First to be called by Jesus were the fishermen: Peter, his brother Andrew, James, and his brother John. Next were Philip and Bartholomew (Nathanael), Thomas, and Matthew the tax collector. Later came James, Thaddeus, Simon, and Judas Iscariot.

These men were instructed to minister only to the Jews; they were not to go among the Gentiles. Their mission was to cure the sick, raise the dead, cleanse lepers, cast out demons, and announce the coming of Christ's kingdom. They were to take nothing with them, and they were instructed not to accept payment (Mk 10:5–10). The cost of discipleship was the complete surrender of self, family, and all material possessions (Lk 14:25–33).

to Diblah" because of the people's idolatry (Eze 6:14).

DIDYMUS *(DID i mus)*—A Greek word meaning "twin," and another name for Thomas (Jn 11:16). He was one of the 12 apostles, remembered most for his doubting. He would not believe Jesus had risen until he had seen the nail prints in his hands (Jn 20:24).

DINAH *(DYE nuh; "justice")*—The daughter of Jacob and Leah, Dinah was raped by Shechem. He agreed to marry her, but her brothers Levi and Simeon avenged her by attacking Shechem's city and killing all the males in the town (Gen 34).

DIONYSIUS THE AREOPAGITE *(dye uh NI see uhs; ar ee OP a gyte)*—A member of the Areopagus, the supreme court of Athens, which met on Mars Hill. He was converted through the preaching of Paul (Ac 17:34).

DIOTREPHES *(dye AHT ruh feez; "nourished by Zeus")*—A church leader in Asia Minor who refused to accept the teachers sent by John the apostle. He excluded from the church anyone who welcomed the missionaries (3Jn 1:9).

DISCIPLE WHOM JESUS LOVED—*See* **BELOVED DISCIPLE.**

DISEASE—The Jews believed disease was punishment for their sins (Jn 9:2). As Jesus healed the sick, he encountered leprosy, blindness, deafness, mental disorders, paralysis, and other conditions that were prevalent during biblical times.

DISPERSION—The scattering of the Jews to other lands outside of their own country through the Babylonian captivity. Their religion went with them and influenced the spread of the gospel, because the mission of the apostles was to convert the Jews (Ac 2).

DIVIDED KINGDOM, DIVIDED MONARCHY—At the death of King Solomon in 975 B.C., the Hebrew nation split into two kingdoms: Judah in the south under King Rehoboam; and Israel in the north under Jeroboam.

DIVINATION—The attempt to foretell future events through the use of potions, dreams, omens, cards, dice, and other mystical devices (1Sa 15:23). Divination was considered a gift from God to the prophets, but it was condemned in other instances as a pagan practice.

DIVORCE—The breaking of the marriage contract. In the Old Testament, a man could divorce his wife by giving her a written bill of divorcement (Dt 24:1–4). A woman could not get a divorce. In the New Testament, Jesus said that man and woman are joined together by God and that bond should not be broken by man (Mt 19:6).

DIZAHAB (*DIZ uh hab*)—A place in the Arabian desert near the Gulf of Arabia. It is believed to be the location where Moses gave his farewell address (Dt 1:1).

DOCTRINE—The teachings of a particular religion, government, or other group. Paul was concerned with having a sound doctrine that builds up faith and protects against false teaching (Titus 1:9).

DOCUMENTARY HYPOTHESIS—A proposition set forth by scholars regarding the authorship of the Bible. The hypothesis was that the Five Books of Moses were not written by Moses, but were derived from four separate documents.

A gatepost in Citadel of Mycenae

DOORPOST, GATEPOST, POST—1. The parts to the doorway of a building, including the lintel and side posts (1Ki 6:33). 2. A post was a runner or messenger (Job 9:25).

DORCAS *(DOR kuhs)*—A female disciple who lived in Joppa. She helped the poor by sewing coats, robes, and other clothing for them. When she died, Peter raised her from the dead. This miracle attracted many converts to Christianity (Ac 9:36–43).

DOTHAN *(DOH than)*—A town in Samaria where Joseph was thrown into an empty pit, then later sold to spice merchants (Gen 37:17, 24).

Noah's hands holding a dove

DOVE—A bird first mentioned in Genesis (Gen 8:8). After the Flood, Noah released a dove to find out if the waters had receded. At Jesus' baptism, the Holy Spirit descended on him "like a dove" (Mt 3:16).

DOWRY *(DOW ree)*—The marriage price paid to the bride's family by the prospective bridegroom as a compensation for the loss of her services. Because he had no money, Jacob offered to serve Laban for seven years in exchange for Rachel (Gen 29:18).

DRACHMA *(DRAHK muh)*—A Greek coin that had nearly the same value as the Roman denarius and the Hebrew shekel. It represented a day's wage. The coin mentioned in Jesus' parable of the lost coin was likely a silver drachma (Lk 15:8–9).

DRAGON—The original Hebrew word for dragon has several meanings: a crocodile, a sea monster or whale (Gen 1:21), or a jackal (Job 30:29). The "great dragon" in Revelation is Satan (Rev 12:9).

DRESS—Basic articles of clothing in biblical times included a tunic or shirt; a cloak, which protected

DREAMS

The interpretation of dreams, highly developed and practiced by ancient people, continued to flourish during biblical times.

Soothsayers, diviners, and fortune-tellers were prevalent, not only in the pagan world, but also among the Israelites, who believed that God communicated through dreams. Moses condemned all abhorrent practices, including the divination of dreams (Dt 18:10). Nevertheless, kings routinely employed royal diviners to find meanings for their dreams, but often these were tricksters who failed to furnish satisfactory interpretations. Jeremiah criticized false prophets who only pretended to receive revelations from God (Jer 23:25).

In the Old Testament, God gave both Joseph and Daniel the power to interpret royal dreams. King Nebuchadnezzar had a troubling dream that none of his sorcerers could explain. God revealed the meaning to Daniel. When he relayed the message to the king, Daniel was promoted, showered with gifts, and made a ruler in Babylon (Da 2).

Joseph was in prison when Pharaoh called upon him to interpret two dreams. God told Joseph there would be seven years of plenty and seven years of famine, and Joseph advised the king to reserve food for the lean years. Pharaoh was so pleased he made Joseph ruler over all of Egypt (Gen 41).

against the weather or was used as a blanket at night; a turban; and sandals.

Women of the time also wore a high cap and veil. *See* **CLOTHING**.

DRINK OFFERING—A mixture of olive oil and wine that was offered to God along with the burnt offering. It was presented every morning and evening at the entrance to the tent of meeting in the tabernacle (Ex 29:40, 41).

DRUNKENNESS—Having one's senses impaired by an excess of wine or spirits. It caused problems for Noah and Lot (Gen 9:21, 19:33). In his letters, Paul warned Christians against drunkenness and other sinful acts (Gal 5:21).

DRUSILLA (droo SIL uh)— The daughter of Herod Agrippa I. She was the wife of Felix, the governor of Judea who put Paul in prison (Ac 24). Both she and her husband listened to Paul preach (Ac 24:24).

DUALISM (DOO uh liz uhm)—The belief that recognizes two opposing life principles, good and evil; and two parts to man's nature, a body and a soul.

DUMAH (DOO mah; "silence")—The son of Ishmael and probably the founder of the Ishmaelites tribe of Arabia (Gen 25:14). It was also the name of the place inhabited by the tribe.

DUNG—Animal excrement, also called manure. Dung was dried and used as fuel (Eze 4:12, 15). When animals were sacrificed, the dung had to be burned outside the camp (Ex 29:14).

DUNG GATE—One of the 11 gates of Jerusalem in Nehemiah's time. It was located near the southwest corner of the wall and was probably the gate leading to the rubbish dump in Hinnon Valley (Ne 2:13).

DURA (DOO ruh)—A plain in the province of Babylon where Nebuchadnezzar set up a golden statue. He gathered his officials together and commanded them to fall down and worship it (Da 3:1).

EAGLE—The largest bird of prey in Palestine. It was listed among 20 birds that Israelites were forbidden to eat because they were considered unclean (Lev 11:13).

EAR—As part of an ordination ritual, the blood from a sacrificial lamb was placed on Aaron's earlobe (Ex 29:20).

EARNEST—A sum of money paid to make a contract binding; a first installment guaranteeing that full payment will be made. Paul encouraged people to accept the spirit of God as the earnest, or first installment, of our inheritance (2Co 1:22).

EAR OF GRAIN—The part of the cereal plant that con-tains the flowers and fruit. In Pharaoh's dream, the ears of grain signified seven years of plentiful harvest and seven years of famine (Gen 41:22).

EARRINGS—Ornaments, typically made from silver or gold, that were worn in the ears. The golden earrings of the Israelite women were given to Aaron to make a golden calf (Ex 32:2–4).

EARTH—The Bible uses the word to refer to both the world and the soil or ground. In Genesis, God called the dry land earth (Gen 1:10).

EARTHEN VESSELS—Clay jars or pitchers used extensively in the wilderness to keep drinking water cool. The clay pots were fragile and easily shattered, so potters were kept busy making replacements (Jer 18:1–6).

EARTHQUAKE—A vibration of the earth's surface that

can cause destruction of buildings and loss of life. The most notable earthquake in the Bible occurred at Jesus' death (Mt 27:51–55). Another took place at the site of his resurrection.

EAST—The direction of the sunrise. The gate of the tabernacle was on the east side (Ex 38:13). The east gate of the temple was built so the first rays of sun in spring and fall would shine into the Holy of Holies.

EAST, CHILDREN OF THE—The tribes who lived in the east country on the border of Ammon and Moab (Eze 25:4, 10), north to Haran, and south to Arabia.

EASTER—Originally a pagan festival, Easter became a Christian celebration of Christ's resurrection. In the New Testament, it was the time of the Passover Feast (Ac 12:4).

EBED-MELECH (*EE bed MEE lek; "king's servant"*)—An Ethiopian who rescued the prophet Jeremiah from a muddy cistern where he was left to die (Jer 38:7–13). God promised to protect him when the city of Jerusalem was destroyed (Jer 39:15–18).

EBENEZER (*EB eh NEE zer; "stone of help"*)—1. A place of Philistine-Israelite battles. The ark of the covenant was captured here (1Sa 4:1–11). 2. A stone set up by Samuel at Mispah to commemorate Israel's victory over the Philistines (1Sa 7:12).

EBER (*EE behr; "one who crosses over"*)—1. The name of five Old Testament men; most significantly, Abraham's ancestor (Gen 10:21). 2. A possible symbolic name for Hebrews who crossed into the Promised Land from a region beyond the Euphrates.

EBLA (*EEB lah*)—An ancient city, located in modern Syria. Cuneiform tablets, dating from around

EBAL, MOUNT

A mountain north of Shechem, Ebal (*EE bal*) is more than 3,000 feet high—one of the highest points in Samaria (Dt 27:4). Centuries before Moses led his people out of Egypt, God had promised the land of Canaan to Abraham, who built an altar at the foot of Mount Ebal to commemorate the occasion (Gen 12:6–7).

Hundreds of years later, Moses gave instructions to the Israelites for a ceremony they were to perform as they crossed the Jordan River to claim that land. First, he told them to set up some large stones, coat them with plaster, and write the words of the law clearly upon them. After they crossed the river, they were to set up the stones on Mount Ebal.

Next, they were to build an altar of unhewn stones and burn sacrifices. Then, half of the tribe were to stand on Mount Gerizim (located to the north) and recite blessings; the other half were to stand on Mount Ebal and recite curses of the law. They were to recite in loud voices across the two mountains (with the ark of the covenant placed in the valley between them) and thus renew their covenant with God (Dt 27:1–28:14).

Moses himself never witnessed this ceremony—he died before reaching the Promised Land. It was left to Joshua to carry out the plans on Mount Ebal (Jos 8:30–32).

the third century B.C., were discovered during an excavation of the city's ruins. These tablets appear to verify the events of Genesis 14.

ECBATANA *(ek BAT ah nah)*—The capital city of an ancient empire held by the Medes. It was later conquered by the Persians, Partheans, and Greeks. Ecbatana is significantly mentioned in Old Testament-period apocryphal writings. It was the location of the tombs of Esther and Mordecai.

ECCLESIASTES, BOOK OF *(ek LEE zee AS tees; "assembly speaker" or "preacher")*—An Old Testament book, traditionally ascribed to Solomon. It consists of four major discourses that weigh wisdom against folly.

ECCLESIASTICUS *(ek LEE zee AS ti kuhs; "of the church")*—The longest of the Old Testament apocryphal books, and the only one in which the author gives his name (Sir 50:27). It is also called "The Wisdom of Jesus Son of Sirach."

EDEN *("delight")*—**1.** A garden, created by God, where the tree of life and the tree of good and evil grew. It was the home of Adam and Eve before their sin (Gen 2–3). **2.** A town (Am 1:5). **3.** A term describing a delightful place to live (Isa 51:3; Joel 2:3).

EDER, EDAR *(EE der; "flock")*—**1.** The place of Benjamin's birth and Rachel's death (Gen 35:16–21). **2.** A shepherd's tower (Ps 61:3). **3.** A personal name (1Ch 23:23).

EDOM *(EE duhm; "red")*—A mineral-rich strip of land settled by Esau, between the Dead Sea and the Gulf of Aqabah. It was also called Seir (Gen 36:6–8). It was home to the Edomites, who thwarted Israel's progress (Nu 20:21).

EDOMITES—Descendants of Esau, the Edomites were dreaded enemies of Israel (Eze 35:1–9).

EDUCATION—The Bible requires that minds be prepared for faith (Gen

18:19; Dt 6:4–5; Pr 22:6; Mt 22:37; Eph 6:4). Declarations of faith, such as the Jewish Shemah and the Christian Apostle's Creed, are aids to religious education.

¹EGLON *(EG lahn)*—An Amorite city captured by Joshua, assigned to Judah (Jos 10).

²EGLON—A king of Moab. He dominated Israel for 18 years (Jdg 3:12–14).

EGNATIAN WAY *("Via Egnatia")*—A 500-mile-long Roman road reaching from the Adriatic Sea to the Dardanelles strait. Paul traveled along it in the region of Thessalonica and Philippi.

EGYPT—An ancient nation in northeastern Africa that developed along the Nile River. It was the site of the Israelite captivity and the birthplace of Moses (Ex 1–14). Most of the country was an uninhabitable desert, with the majority of the population living along the Nile. Many Egyptian practices influenced the Israelites.

EGYPT, RIVER OF—An ancient boundary for Israel (Gen 15:18). It was probably not the Nile, but rather the El Arish River south of modern Gaza.

EGYPTIAN, THE—A nationalist fanatic of supposed Egyptian birth, rumored to be the leader of 4,000 dagger-carrying terrorists. Paul was mistaken for this man (Ac 21:38).

EKRON *(EK rahn)*—1. The northernmost of five Philistine maritime cities. Israel's stolen ark was kept here (1Sa 5:10). The city was subdued by Judah (Jdg 1:18); later, it was turned over to Jonathan Maccabeus in 147 B.C. (1Mac 10:89).

ELAH *(EE lah; "oak")*—Israel's fourth king. His brief, two-year rule (c. 900 B.C.) was noted for his

EHUD

Between Joshua's conquest of Canaan and the appointment of Israel's first king, judges ruled the land. After 11 years of peace, a cycle of sin led Israel into 18 years of oppression under Eglon, the Edomite king of Moab. In response to Israel's cries of repentance, the Lord assigned a deliverer from the tribe of Benjamin.

Ehud (*EE hud; "united" or "strong"*) was left-handed, a rare occurrence in biblical times that, in his culture, indicated serious imperfection. He carried an agricultural tribute to the Moabite king, concealing a short dagger beneath his outer cloak. After the usual fanfare of presenting tribute, Ehud promised to tell the king some secret information. Either Ehud was skillfully persuasive or Eglon was carelessly curious, because the king granted the Benjaminite a private meeting.

Ehud approached with his right hand—the expected weapon hand—exposed and unthreatening. He then drew out a short dagger with his left hand and mortally stabbed the king. Ehud escaped to lead Israel to victory over Moab. Eighty years of peace followed (Jdg 3:12–30).

carelessness and carousing. The destruction of his family was predicted in the Old Testament (1Ki 16).

ELAH, VALLEY OF (*EE lah*)— The place of confrontation between David and Goliath (1Sa 17:2). Small stones lined the bottom of the valley waterway.

¹ELAM (*EE lehm; "high-land"*)—A kingdom north

of the Persian Gulf (presently southern Iran).

²ELAM—The name of nine Old Testament men; most notably, the son of Shem, who became the father of the Elamites (Gen 10:22).

ELATH, ELOTH *(EE lath; "lofty trees")*—A port town at the north end of the Gulf of Aqabah near Ezion-Geber. Solomon built ships there (1Ki 9:26). The Edomites captured the city, gaining control of the caravan route from Egypt (2Ki 16:5).

ELDAD *(EL dad; "God has loved")*—One of two men in Israel's camp to prophesy without the official sanction, which was given to 70 elders selected by Moses (Nu 11:26).

ELDER—An Old Testament title for religious-political leaders (Ex 24:1). In the New Testament, the title came to mean an apostolically appointed Church leader (Ac 14:23; 1Ti 5:17).

ELEAZAR *(EE lee AY zahr; "God has helped")*—The third son of Aaron. He became chief priest and assisted both Moses and Joshua (Nu 20:28, 34:16). God chose Eleazar to oversee the red heifer ceremony (Nu 19:1–10).

ELECTION—God's choice to single out things or persons for his holy purpose (Dt 7:7–8; Col 3:12). The community of Israel was called out of Egypt after Passover (Dt 4:20, 14:2). The Christian Church is elected through Jesus Christ (Ro 1:1–6; 1Pe 1:2).

ELECT LADY *("chosen authority")*—A woman who received the second epistle of the Apostle John. The term may be a metaphor for the entire Christian congregation (2 Jn 1:1).

ELEMENTS—Basic elements of the physical world (2Pe 3:10–12). 2. A modern term used for the bread and wine shared at the Last Supper (Mt 26:26–30).

ELEVENTH HOUR—Approximately 5 P.M., it referred to the last working hour of the Palestinian day (Mt 20:1–16). Since Babylonian times, the day was divided into 12 parts between sunrise and sunset (Jn 11:9).

ELHANAN (*el HAH nahn; "God is gracious"*)—**1.** A Bethlehemite who killed Lahmi, brother of Goliath (1Ch 20:5). **2.** One of 30 elite warriors under David's leadership (2Sa 23:24).

ELI (*EE lie; "uplifted"*)—The fourth son of Aaron. A priest-judge of Israel, he trained the young Samuel (1Sa 1:24–28) and befell a tragic personal life (1Sa 2:27, 3:11–14, 4:12–18).

ELIAKIM (*ee LIE ah kim; "may God raise"*)—**1.** The manager of Hezekiah's household (2Ki 19:1–2). **2.** Another name for Jehoiakim (2Ki 23:34). **3.** A priest who celebrated Jerusalem's rebuilt wall (Ne 12:41).

4. An ancestor of Jesus (Mt 1:13; Lk 3:30).

ELIEZER (*ee lee AY zur; "God is help"*)—The name of 11 Old Testament men. Among them, Abraham's servant (Gen 15:2) and an ancestor of Joseph, the husband of Mary (Lk 3:29).

ELIHU (*ee LIE hyoo; "he is my God"*)—**1.** A young man who was angry at Job and his friends for their misunderstanding of redemptive suffering (Job 32:6–37:24). **2.** The name of four Old Testament people, also called Eliab or Elie (1Ch 2:13, 6:27, 12:20, 26:1–8).

ELIM (*EE lim*)—A site where the Israelites camped during their journey to Sinai. It was their second stop after crossing the Red Sea (Nu 33:9). Twelve springs and 70 palm trees marked this oasis.

ELISHA (*ee LIE shuh; "God is salvation"*)—A bald-headed prophet who inherited a "double share" of Elijah's

ELIJAH

A ninth-century prophet, Elijah (*ee LIE jah; "the Lord is my God"*) the Tishbite was described as "a hairy man" who wore a leather belt around his waist. Perhaps, rather than being hairy himself, he wore a cloak made of hair (Zec 13:4).

While nothing is known of his family, his probable home was Gilead (2Ki 1:8), and he may have lived on a hilltop (2Ki 1:9, 4:25). Elijah was not a religious volunteer; he was inducted into God's service at a time when the once glorious kingdom of David suffered a series of inept or evil kings. God's commandments and covenant were ignored (2Ch 21). Even priests and Levites had abandoned Israel for the southern kingdom of Judah.

Elijah made prophetic predictions (2Ki 1:9–17), performed miracles (2Ki 4), and gave declarations of coming justice (1Ki 21:20–26). He condemned the worship of Baal and the idolatrous ways of Ahab and Jezebel. Elijah's victory in a contest against 450 prophets of Baal is one of the Bible's best-loved stories (1Ki 18–19). Elijah ascended to heaven in a whirlwind (2Ki 2:11), and many await his return (Mal 4:5).

spirit. He prophesied—often concerning the Syrians—during the reign of King Jehoram in the ninth century B.C. (2Ki 2).

¹ELISHAH (*EL ee shah; "God saves"*)—The great-grandson of Noah and father of the Japathic nation (Gen 10:4).

²ELISHAH—A coastal town that supplied blue and purple dyes to Tyre (Eze 27:7).

ELIZABETH

The story of Elizabeth is recorded in the Gospel of Luke (Lk 1). She is descended from the family of Aaron, the high priest of Israel—whose wife was also named Elizabeth (Ex 6:23).

Elizabeth lived with her husband, the priest Zechariah, in a town near Jerusalem. A barren woman (considered a disgrace in her culture), she was well beyond her childbearing years when God said to Zechariah, "Your wife Elizabeth will bear you a son, and you will name him John" (Lk 1:13). When the child was conceived, the angel Gabriel declared that their son, John the Baptist, would be great in God's sight; he would prepare the people for the Lord.

Elizabeth's relative, Mary, the mother of Jesus, came to see her to announce her own pregnancy, but before she spoke a word, the baby Elizabeth carried suddenly moved inside of her. Filled with the Holy Spirit, Elizabeth cried out to Mary, "Blessed are you among women, and blessed is the fruit of your womb!" (Lk 1:42).

ELKANAH (el KAH na; "God has taken possession")—**1.** A grandson of Korah (1Ch 6:25). **2.** Samuel's father. God allowed him to sire the son with his infertile wife Hannah if they would dedicate the child to God's service (1Sa 1:1). **3.** An ancestor of Samuel (1Ch 6:25, 35). **4.** A mighty man of David (12:6). **5.** An assistant to King Ahaz (2Ch 28:7).

ELLAZAR (el EH zahr)—The home of Arioch, one of five tribal chiefs from eastern Palestine—south of the Dead Sea—united against Abram (Gen 14).

ELOHIM *(EL o him; "the mighty")*—An ancient name for a deity. It was used in the Old Testament 2,500 times to indicate the one true God (Isa 45: 18–25).

ELOI, ELOI, LAMA SABACHTHANI *(EE lo y, EE lo y, lam mah sah BAK tha nee; "My God, my God, why have you forsaken me?")*—An Aramaic phrase that appears in Psalm 22 (Ps 22:1). It was quoted by Jesus from the cross (Mt 27:46).

¹ELON *(EE lon)*—**1.** A judge of Israel for 10 years (Jdg 12:11). **2.** Son of Zebulum (Gen 46:14). **3.** Father-in-law to Esau (Gen 26:34).

²ELON—A border city of Dan (Jos 19:43).

EL SHADDAI *(el shah DIE; "God Almighty" or "God of the mountain")*—A name for God in the Old Testament. Mentioned 48 times, the term implies that God alone creates and sustains (Gen 17:1–8).

ELYMAS *(EL ee mas)*—A sorcerer who influenced Sergius Paulus, proconsul of Cyprus. Also called Barjesus, he was temporarily blinded in an encounter with the Apostle Paul (Ac 13:4–13).

ELZAPHAN *(ELZA fahn)*—An ancestor of Moses (Ex 6:22). A Kohathite Levite, he was chosen with his brother to assist Moses after God judged Aaron's sons (Lev 10:1–7).

Embalming process in Egypt

EMBALMING—Never practiced in Israel, the Egyptians developed this method for preserving dead bodies. A cleansed body was filled with palm

141

wines, oil of cedar, spices, and aromatic substances. It was then steeped in a niter solution, carefully bound in cloth, and heat-treated. The embalming of both Jacob and Joseph was performed by Egyptian physician-servants (Gen 50:2–3, 24–26).

Tapestry depicting the Magi

EMBROIDERY—Needlework of colored and precious metal threads. Monuments suggest that the Israelites learned this art while in Egypt. It was often mentioned in tabernacle preparations (Ex 26–39). Embroidered cloth was desirable war booty (Jdg 5:30; Eze 27:7; Sir 45:10).

EMIM *(EE mim; "terrors")*— Also called the Rephaim, this race of giantlike people inhabited a region east of the Dead Sea (Gen 14:5). They were former inhabitants of Ar (Dt 2:10–11).

EMMANUEL *(ee MAN yoo el; "God is with us")*—A name given Jesus at his birth (Mt 1:23). The prophet Isaiah said the name would be given to a young savior as a sign of hope to Israel (Isa 7:14, 8:8).

Christ at Emmaus

EMMAUS *(e MA uss)*—A village seven miles from Jerusalem. Two followers of Jesus were met by the resurrected Lord there (Lk 24:13–32; 1Mac 3–4).

EMPEROR—A supreme Roman ruler, the emperor was considered divine and worthy of worship. In the

EN-GEDI

A sparsely populated area on the edge of Judah's desert, En-gedi (*en GED ee; "the spring of the wild goat"*) was a well-shaded oasis, rich with underground streams and warm springs. Located about three hours from Bethlehem (Jos 15:62), it was a fertile place, home to flower blossoms (SS 1:14).

The nearby wilderness was barren and subject to hot, dangerous winds. Ravines and deep caves in high limestone cliffs provided hiding places for fugitives, malcontents, and wild animals. The most famous of En-gedi's fugitives was David. Enormously popular in Israel, David had King Saul's daughter, Michal, as his wife and the king's son, Jonathan, as his most loyal friend. Growing insanely jealous, Saul led 3,000 men into the wilderness to destroy David.

Saul stopped to relieve himself inside the cave where David and his men hid in darkness. Though his men urged him to kill the king, David refused. Instead, he crept up and stealthily cut away a portion of Saul's garment, then proclaimed his loyalty to the king (1Sa 24).

New Testament, emperors affected life through taxes (Mt 22:17–22), their power (Lk 2:1; Ac 25:11), and authority (Ac 17:7; 1Pe 2:17). *See* **CAESAR.**

ENCAMPMENT BY THE SEA— A God-appointed camp located north of the Red Sea. It was there that the Israelites escaped Egyptian charioteers by the miracle of parting water (Ex 14).

ENDOR *(en DOR)*—A town in the Plain of Kishon that was never fully wrested from the Canaanites. It was associated with the victory of Barak over the Canaanite commander Sisera (Jdg 4–5). Before his final battle, King Saul sought occult help from a medium in Endor (1Sa 28:3–25).

En-Eglaim (en EG la him)—A place near the west shore of the Dead Sea. It played a prominent role in Ezekiel's God-given vision of Israel's restored glory (Eze 47:10).

Enoch (EE nok; "dedicated" or "initiated")—1. Son of Cain. A city was named for him (Gen 4:17). 2. Son of Jared in the line of Seth. Known for his godly life, Enoch was taken to heaven without having to die (Gen 5:18–24). 3. Grandson of Abraham (Gen 25:4). 4. Reuben's first son (Gen 46:8).

Enoch, Books of—Influential intertestamental writings of apocalyptic nature. The 108 chapters, which are arranged into 5 books, display great awareness of civilization and nature. Jude 13–14 may be a quote from 1Enoch.

Enos, Enosh (EE nosh; "mortal")—An ancestor of Christ and son of Seth (Lk 3:38). At his birth "people began to invoke the name of the Lord" (Gen 4:26). Enos lived for 905 years.

En-Rogel (en RO gehl; "fountain of feet")—A spring south of Jerusalem in the Kidron Valley where fullers cleaned garments by stomping their feet. David stationed spies here during the rebellion of Absalom (2Sa 17:17).

En-Shemesh (en SHEM ish; "spring of the sun")—A spring near Jerusalem, toward Jericho. It separated the territories of Benjamin and Judah (Jos 15:7).

Envy—In Hebrew, the word literally means "to become intensely red," referring to jealousy. In the Old Testament, Rachel

EPAPHRODITUS

The Philippian church of Macedonia was the first European church founded by Paul. In a gesture of great kindness, the church sent aid to the apostle while he was imprisoned. Epaphroditus (*eh PAF roh DIE tuhs; "handsome" or "charming"*), a deputy of the church, was the courier of the church's love for Paul.

Whether it was caused by his perilous journey to Rome, the crowded and diseased conditions of the city, or overwork, a terrible illness brought Epaphroditus close to death. When he was well enough recovered, Paul recognized the worries of Philippian Christians and the homesick longings of Epaphroditus himself, so he sent his much-loved friend home.

Epaphroditus carried with him the apostle's letter filled with tender gratitude and strong encouragement for the church to receive Epaphroditus with honor (Phm 4:10–20).

(Gen 30:1) and Joseph's brothers (Gen 37:11) exhibited envy. A similar Greek word is found in the New Testament (Gal 5:26; 1Pe 2:1).

EPAPHRAS *(EP uh fras; "charming")*—A Christian leader credited with founding the church at Colossae. The Apostle Paul praised his loyalty to churches in the Lycus Valley (Col 1:3–8; Phm 23).

EPHESIANS, LETTER TO THE— The least personal of Paul's four prison epistles. Only Tychicus, the bearer of the letter, is named. Its main theme is the mystery of church unity (Eph 1:9–10).

EPHESUS *(EF eh suss; "the landing place")*—The capi-

Paul preaching in Ephesus

tal city of Asia Minor. By the first century, it was the world center for worship of Artemis, a fertility goddess (Ac 19:23).

EPHOD *(EEF od)*—An ornately woven garment for the High Priest of Israel. Each shoulder held a precious stone engraved with six tribal names. A gold breastplate of 12 precious stones hung from gold chains (Ex 28:4). *See* **BREASTPIECE OF THE HIGH PRIEST.**

EPHPHATHA *(EF fuh thuh; "be opened")*—An Aramaic command spoken as Jesus healed a deaf man. Mark translates the term into Greek for his readers (Mk 7:34).

EPHRAIM *(EE fra im; "fruitful")*—Joseph's son. He was given the patriarchal blessing of Jacob (his grandfather) that was intended for his older brother Manasseh. Ephraim's descendants inherited land in the conquest of Canaan (Gen 48).

EPHRATH, EPHRATHAH *(EF rath)*—A Judean town close

High priest wearing an ephod

146

ESAU

Isaac and Rebekah's eldest son, Esau (*EE soh; "hairy" or "shaggy"*) was a ruddy-skinned hunter, favored by his father over his younger twin, Jacob. Against God's Covenant—and to the grief of his parents—Esau married Canaanite women (Gen 26:34). His gentler brother, Jacob, held his mother's favor and married according to tradition.

As the firstborn son, Esau had birthright privileges of spiritual blessings, clan leadership, and a double portion of his father's possessions. In a shortsighted moment of hunger, he bargained away his birthright to Jacob in exchange for some food (Gen 25; Dt 2:4, 21:17). Later, when their father Isaac arranged to bless his eldest, Rebekah and Jacob deceived the dying man and robbed Esau of his gift (Gen 27). Fear of Esau's rage drove Jacob away to the family's ancestral home in northern Mesopotamia.

Though robbed of his expected future, Esau attempted to please his father by taking an approved wife (Gen 28:6–9). Twenty years later, living prosperously in Seir as the father of the Edomites, Esau again met Jacob. Rather than seek revenge, Esau "ran to meet and embraced" his brother. He graciously forgave past grievances (Gen 32). In the New Testament, "Esau" is used for the Edomites, a people judged by God (Ro 9:13).

to Bethlehem. It was the possible site of Rachel's grave (Gen 35:19). It was home to the Ephrathites, part of David's clan. Micah spoke to the Ephrathites of a future Messianic work (Mic 5:1–2).

Ephron *(EE fron)*—A Hittite man who sold to Abraham land containing the Cave of Machpelah for Sarah's burial. Following Mesopotamian custom, Abraham weighed out his payment to him in silver (Gen 23).

Epicureans—Adherents to a fourth-century ethical philosophy. They were self-disciplined, frugal, and did not believe that a divine power interacted in human affairs. The Epicureans opposed Paul at Athens when he spoke of resurrection (Ac 17:16–34).

Epistle—A formal letter, often written with the aim to teach. The New Testament contains 21 epistles, addressed to individuals or churches, that deal with specific needs or problems. These letters were written by Paul, Peter, John, and Jude.

Erastus *(ee RAS tuhs; "beloved")*—**1.** Paul's companion from Ephesus and fellow worker with Timothy (Ac 19:22). **2.** A city treasurer of Corinth (Ro 16:23).

Erech *(EE rek)*—One of several great cities of lower Babylon settled by Nimrod (Gen 10:10). It is named Uruk in Babylonian literature. It was located 160 miles from modern Baghdad.

Esarhaddon *(EE sahr HAD ehn)*—A king of Assyria during the seventh century B.C. A proud conqueror of Egypt, he was responsible for deporting exiled Jews to Palestine (Ezr 4:2).

Eschatology *(es kuh TAHL uh jee)*—A division of Christian theology devoted to studying the events surrounding the last days of history and the destiny of humankind. It also examines the use and duration of time in relation to things of God (1Co 15:32–58; 1Jn 3:1–2).

¹Eshcol *(ESH col)*—An Amorite who was an ally of

ESSENES

A strict Jewish sect, the Essenes are believed to have developed alongside the Pharisees and Sadducees during the Maccabean Revolt (167–160 B.C.). Along with the excavated Dead Sea Scrolls, the writings of ancient historians Philo and Josephus have shed some light on this mysterious group. The Essenes practiced strict adherence to the Law of Moses and Levitical ritual purity. Their separatist community lifestyle emphasized communal meals, daily study of Scripture, and an apocalyptic view of history.

Pictured above are ruins at Qumran, the occasional dwelling place of the Essenes.

Virtually no information exists about the Essenes prior to the period of Herod the Great. Around 76 B.C., they removed themselves from a politically compromised Jerusalem to Qumran, an area of dry hill country less than a mile northwest of the Dead Sea. Depending on political conditions, they moved back and forth until A.D. 68, when Roman soldiers burned the Qumran headquarters.

In 1947, scholars began to discover the community's library (including the Dead Sea Scrolls), which had been hidden in desert caves for 1,900 years.

Abram at the time of Lot's capture. He lived shortly before the rise of the first Babylonian dynasty (Gen 14:13).

²ESHCOL—A *wadi* (brook) in Canaan where Moses' spies cut down grapes to bring back to the Israelites (Nu 13:23). 2. A valley north of Hebron (Dt 1:24).

ESDRAELON (*EZ dra EE lahn*)—1. The plain that divides the hilly region of Palestine between Galilee and Samaria. 2. A place of conflict with Nebuchadnezzar, mentioned in the apocryphal Book of Judith (Jdt 1:8, 3:9).

ESHTAOL, ESHTAOLITES (*ESH tie ohl*)—An Amorite region of Judean lowlands, 15 miles west of Jerusalem (Jos 15:33). It was later given to the tribe of Dan (Jos 40:41). Here, near the home of Delilah, Samson heard God's call (Jdg 13).

ESTHER (*ES ter; "myrtle"*)— A Benjaminite Jew who,

with the help of her cousin Mordecai, became Queen of Persia. She outwitted Haman, an enemy of the Jews (Est 7).

ESTHER, ADDITIONS TO—An apocryphal book with more than 100 verses originally interspersed throughout the Greek translation of the Book of Esther. The verses add religious aspects to the text.

ESTHER, BOOK OF—An Old Testament story that establishes the celebration of Purim. Esther foiled a planned mass murder of Jews (Est 7). God is not mentioned in the book, but the story implies that God can influence human affairs unannounced and that providence prevails.

ETAM (*EE tum*)—1. A fortification near Jerusalem built by Rehoboam (2Ch 11:6). 2. A rock of refuge for Samson after revenging the Philistine murders of his wife and father-in-law (Jdg 15:1–8).

ETERNAL LIFE—Life that is uninterrupted by death. The first biblical reference occurs after the Exile (Da 12:1–2). The New Testament uses the term "age-lasting," which contrasts brief or fleeting life. Eternal life is the reward for repentance of sins and faith in God. It is described—but not formally defined—in the Bible (Jn 3:16, 17:3).

ETHAN (*EE thun;* "*enduring*")—**1.** An Ezrahite writer of psalms. Three of four Old Testament references link this person to the family of Hermen (Ps 89). **2.** A descendant of Levi (1Ch 6:39).

ETHICS, BIBLICAL—The God-given principles of right and wrong. They are established primarily through covenants for the sake of a holy community (Dt 4:36–40; 2Co 3:4–6).

ETHIOPIA—A region of south Egypt rich in natural resources. Also called Nubia or Cush, it was located near modern Aswan. Ebedmelech, an Ethiopian, arranged for Jeremiah's release from the cistern where he had been left to die (Jer 38:7, 39:15).

ETHIOPIAN EUNUCH—A royal treasurer of Ethiopia. A castrated man, he was converted to Christian faith by understanding a Bible passage (Isa 53) through the help of the evangelist Philip (Ac 8:27–40).

ETHNARCH (*ETH nark*)—A Greek title for an overlord who represented a foreign ruler, such as the high priest Simon, who served for Syria (1Mac 14:47). Paul mentions an ethnarch who represented an Arabian sovereign (2Co 11:32).

EUNICE (*"good victory"*)—The mother of Timothy. Her godly life prepared Timothy for faith and service (2Ti 1:5). She may have witnessed the stoning of Paul in her hometown of Lystra (Ac 14:8–20).

EUCHARIST

A pivotal shift from Old Testament Judaism to New Testament Christianity occurred shortly before the death of Jesus, when he shared a Passover meal with his disciples. Like the Paschal Lamb in Israel's Exodus (Ex 29:38–41), Jesus presented his body and blood as a sacrifice. Since his death, resurrection, and ascension, the Church has honored his command to reenact the meal in his memory (Lk 22:19). That practice is variously called The Lord's Supper, Communion, or Eucharist. Though the Lord's Supper is mentioned several times in the Bible (1Co 11:23–26), nowhere is it called Eucharist (a Greek word meaning "thanksgiving"). The term stems from Jesus' prayer of "thanksgiving" before the meal.

EUNUCH—A castrated man. Throughout the ancient world, eunuchs were men of trust and influence—often advisors or guardians to royalty (Gen 39:1; Est 2:3, 14; Ac 8:27). Under the law, eunuchs were excluded from Israel's covenant community (Dt 23:1).

EUPHRATES *(yoo FRAY teez)*—The largest river in Western Asia and one of four that flowed from Eden (Gen 2:14). It was the northern boundary of Israel during the reign of David (2Sa 8:3).

EUTYCHUS *(YOO ti kuss; "fortunate")*—A young man at Troas whom Paul revived after he had fallen from his window seat during Paul's long speech (Ac 20:9–12).

EVANGELIST—One who proclaims good news about God. The word appears three times in the

New Testament and refers specifically to Philip (Ac 6:5, 21:8). As Church government developed, the evangelist became an official position, along with apostles, prophets, pastors, and teachers (Eph 4:11).

EVE *("life giver")*—The wife of Adam. The first woman, she was created from one of Adam's ribs (Gen 2:18–22). Called the "mother of all living" (Gen 3:20), Eve succumbed to temptation and ate the forbidden fruit (Gen 3:6). For this sin, she was punished with increased childbearing pain and banishment from the Garden of Eden.

EVERLASTING LIFE—*See* **ETERNAL LIFE.**

EVIL—Any force that opposes God. It occurs whenever human sin hinders God's will. The New Testament emphasizes the sinful nature of humanity (Ro 3).

EVIL–MERODACH *(EE vil MAIR oh dahk; "man of [the deity] Marduk")*—A king of Babylon who released King Jehoiachin from prison and treated him favorably at Babylon (2Ki 25:27–30).

EVIL SPEAKING—In the New Testament, Paul condemned all foul-mouthed speaking (Eph 4:31). The word may also mean blasphemy—attributing the work of the Holy Spirit to Satan (Mt 12:31–32). In the Old Testament, blasphemy that curses, slanders, or reviles God was punishable by death (Lev 24:15–26).

EVIL SPIRITS—Spirits that oppose God are mentioned throughout the Bible (Gen 6:1–4; Isa 34:14). Some of them are identified as fallen angels (1Pe 3:19–20); others are described as spirits of the wicked dead. *See* **DEMON.**

EWE—A female sheep, especially when full-grown. The Hebrews began as wandering shepherds. Sheep are the most frequently mentioned animals in the Bible (about 750 times).

EXCOMMUNICATION (*"outside the realm of communication"*)—The exclusion of a person from a community or from membership in a group. Israelites who committed serious offenses could be expelled from their society for a period of time. If the offense was serious enough, they were threatened with permanent banishment. This action, similar to a curse or ban, called for divine judgment (Nu 5:21; Jer 19:15).

EXILE (*or Captivity*)—A period of time during which the Judeans were deported to Babylon. The royal family and leaders were deported in 597 B.C., but the major deportation took place in 587 B.C.(2Ki 25:11). The Exile, which was punishment for stray-

ing from God's words, lasted 70 years (Jer 25:12).

EXODUS (*"departure"*)—The Israelites' escape from Egyptian captivity under the leadership of Moses. This became the supreme occasion of divine deliverance and the beginning of the Covenant.

EXODUS, BOOK OF—The second book of the Old Testament. It has two major sections: events related to the Israelites' deliverance from Egypt, and the establishment of God's Covenant at Mt. Sinai.

EXORCISM—Ancient societies believed that evil powers could take over a person. A variety of methods were used to cast out evil spirits, including chants, spells, and potions. In the New Testament, Jesus exorcized spirits by commanding them to leave (Mt 12:24–28).

EXPIATION (*"to make satisfaction"*)—The removal, cleansing, and forgiveness

EZRA

A Jewish priest-scribe who was skilled in the law of Moses, Ezra (*"help" or "helper"*) played a major role in reestablishing Israel after the exile in Babylon and spiritually uniting the nation.

He held a high position in the service of the Persian king Artaxerxes. The king commissioned him to return to Jerusalem in 457 B.C. and help establish order among the people of the new community (Ezr 7:11–16). He led 5,000 Jews from Babylon to Jerusalem.

After his arrival, Ezra discovered that many Jews had married foreign wives (Ezr 9:1–2). After a period of fasting and prayer, he declared that they should abandon all mixed marriages and restore the exclusiveness of the Israelites. Although painful, Ezra's purge of foreigners was successful, because it preserved Israel's national identity and religious adherence to the laws of Moses.

For the next 13 years, he taught the law and helped the people make it the basis for their daily lives. Because of his teachings, the Israelites repented their national sins and renewed their commitment to God. He also instituted a strict observance of the Sabbath and the giving of temple offerings and sacrifices.

Ezra was also the name of a priest (also called Azariah) who returned from the Exile with Zerubbabel (Ne 12:1).

of sins. In the Old Testament, sins could be expiated through sacrifice (Isa 27:9). In the New Testament, Jesus takes away sin (Jn 1:29; 1Jn 2:2).

EYE—Throughout the Bible, the eye was used as a symbol for the heart or mind (Ecc 17:8; Eph 1:18), or as a way to grasp insight. Those without understanding were said to have their eyes blinded (Isa 6:10).

EYE OF A NEEDLE—A figure of speech that was used by Jesus to show the extreme difficulty of the wealthy entering into God's kingdom (Mk 10:25). He said it was easier for a camel to pass through the eye of a needle.

EZEKIEL (*ee ZEE kee uhl; "God strengthens"*)—A prophet-priest who was taken into exile in Babylon in 597 B.C. The intensity of his prophecy was marked by numerous visions, mute trances, and symbolic actions (Eze 3:1–3, 24–27).

EZEKIEL, BOOK OF—The collected writings of Ezekiel to the Jews who were exiled in Babylon. The book is grouped thematically into four major sections: oracles of doom (Chapters 1–24); oracles against foreign nations (25–32); oracles of restoration and hope (33–39); and visions of a purified community (40–48).

EZEL (*EE zel*)—The site of a stone where David hid until Jonathan, the son of King Saul, informed him of his father's anger toward him (1Sa 20:19–35). Fearing for his life, David bade a final farewell to his good friend and fled to the hills.

EZRA, BOOK OF—The 15th book of the Old Testament. Written by the Jewish priest Ezra, this historical narrative begins with the decree that permitted the Jews (who were exiled in Babylon) to return to Jerusalem and rebuild the temple. The book ends with Ezra's moral reforms, which included ridding the land of mixed marriages (Ezr 9–10).

FACE—The most individually identifiable part of the human body, the face was often used figuratively for the entire person. The faithful are urged to seek God's face, meaning divine favor (Ps 27:8). God's face is also connected with blessing, as well as disfavor (Nu 6:25–26; Ps 34:16). Believers are promised that one day they will see God face to face (1Co 13:12).

FAITH—The "assurance of things hoped for, the conviction of things not seen" (Heb 11:1). Faith requires trust in, and reliance on, God. In the Old Testament, faith means "to be true or trustworthy" to God. In the New Testament, the term usually refers to a personal commitment to Jesus Christ.

FALL, THE—The disobedience of Adam and Eve that caused them to lose their state of innocence in the garden (Gen 3). The fall was the introduction of sin into the world and, along with it, the subjection of all humanity to death (Ro 5:12).

FALSE CHRISTS—Impostors who claim to be messiahs (Mt 24:24). Similar to Antichrists, they attempt to lead the faithful astray (1Jn 2:18). Many false Christs, proclaiming themselves saviors, appeared prior to the destruction of Jerusalem in A.D. 70.

FAMILY, HOUSEHOLD—The basic social unit of those related by kinship and sharing a common residence. Israelites typically formed large households. Headed by the oldest living male, they consisted of immediate and extended

157

FAMINE

The prolonged scarcity of food, accompanied by extreme hunger, was one of the many curses God promised for disobedience (Dt 28:48).

Famine was listed as one of God's four great acts of judgment—along with war, evil beasts, and pestilence (Eze 4:21). In a land dependent on rainfall, the most frequent cause of famine was drought. Famine also resulted from blight, ravaging insects, and human agents (particularly warfare).

The Israelites saw famine as a form of chastening or divine punishment (Isa 51:20). The Bible's most widely known famine was the seven-year famine predicted by Joseph when he interpreted Pharaoh's dream (Gen 41). Other famines occurred in the times of Abraham and Isaac; as punishment because Saul mistreated the Gibeonites (2Sa 21:1); throughout the period of the judges; and during the times of Elijah and Elisha.

A worldwide famine, which occurred when Claudius was the Roman emperor, prompted Christians to help believers in Jerusalem (Ac 11:27–30). Figuratively, Amos referred to a famine of hearing the word of the Lord (Am 8:1), when divine judgment would fall.

families, such as multiple spouses and their offspring, grandparents, servants, concubines, and even sojourners (Gen 46:5–7, 26).

FASTING—The deliberate abstinence from eating (and sometimes drinking) to humble oneself before God. It was often observed as a sign of penitence or mourning (1Sa 31:13), or a means of preparation to receive divine revelation. In the early Church, believers fasted before making important decisions (Ac 13:2–3).

FATHER—1. A male parent, grandfather, or remote ancestor. 2. The founder of an occupation or social group (Gen 4:2). 3. A male who acts toward another with paternal kindness (Gen 45:8). It was used as a title of respect for a teacher or elderly man (1Sa 10:12). 4. God, either as creator of the human race (Mal 2:10) or as the loving parent and guardian of his spiritual children (Ro 8:15).

FEAR—Fear or awe of God is considered the beginning of knowledge and wisdom (Pr 1:7, 16:16) and can lead to faith (Ps 34:11). Love for God creates anguish—or fear—at the thought of moral evil or rebellion (Ps 51:6–12).

FEASTS—Annual celebrations that commemorate important religious or community events. Significant feasts include Passover/the Feast of Unleavened Bread (God's sparing the firstborn males during the Exodus); the Feast of Weeks/Firstfruits (the first wheat harvest); the Feast of Booths (Israel's life in the wilderness); and Purim (the foiling of Haman's plot to exterminate Hebrew ancestors).

FELIX *(FEE liks; "happy")*—A governor of Judea appointed by Claudius. When Paul appeared for trial before him, he listened but refused to allow Paul to go free—hoping to receive a bribe. When Nero recalled Felix two years later, Paul was still in prison (Ac 24).

FERTILE CRESCENT—A nonbiblical term for the crescent-shaped strip of land from the Tigris and Euphrates rivers over Syria to the Mediterranean and southward to Egypt's Nile Valley. It served as a land bridge for commerce and military activity between Egypt and the Tigris and Euphrates valleys.

FESTUS *(FES tuhs; "joyful")* — The Roman governor of Judea appointed by Nero to succeed Felix. He heard Paul's defense and wanted him to stand trial at Jerusalem. When Paul appealed to Caesar, Festus sent the apostle to Rome (Ac 25–26).

Fig tree

FIG TREE—A member of the mulberry family that was cultivated for its fruit. Figs were eaten fresh (2Ki 18:31), pressed into cakes (1Sa 25:18), and used as medicine (2Ki 20:7). The Bible used figs as a symbol for peace and prosperity (1Ki 4:25), desolation (Jer 5:17), or impending national distress (Hos 2:12).

FIRE—Aside from home uses, fire was used in war, in various crafts, and to refine metal. Fire had special functions in worship, and a perpetual fire burned in the temple. Fire symbolized holiness or protection (Zec 2:5). God's action was called a "consuming fire" (Heb 12:29), often associated with wrath (Ex 24:17). In the New Testament, fire represents everlasting punishment (Rev 21:8).

FIRSTBORN—According to the law, the firstborn male offspring belonged to God (Ex 13:12–15). Firstborn animals were sacrificed to the Lord. A temple payment was required to "redeem" a firstborn male child from God. Firstborn sons inherited a double

FIRE, TONGUES OF

This phrase, which appears only once in the Bible (Ac 2:3), designated the dramatic event of Pentecost.

After his resurrection, Jesus promised that holy signs would follow those who believed. When the disciples gathered together to pray at Pentecost, they heard a sound like wind. Tongues of fire appeared and rested on each apostle, who began to speak in unknown languages (Ac 2:4, 8).

The people who had come to Jerusalem from a variety of Roman provinces for the feast represented a variety of languages. They were astonished to hear the disciples speaking of God's work in their own tongues. Peter declared that the miracle fulfilled Old Testament prophecy (Joel 2:28–30). From that event, speaking with tongues became a sign that the Holy Spirit had been poured out on Gentiles (Ac 10:46) and on John the Baptist's disciples at Ephesus (Ac 19).

Tongues played a prominent role in the early Church as a means of worship, thanksgiving, and prayer. Paul called it a spiritual gift (1 Co 12), but regulated speaking and interpreting tongues in public (1 Co 14). *See* **Glossolalia**.

portion of their father's estate (Dt 21:15–17) as well as the paternal blessing (Gen 27).

FISH, FISHING—Fish was important food during biblical times. The best sources for freshwater fish were the Sea of Galilee and the Jordan River. No specific fish are mentioned in the Bible, but the law distinguished between clean fish (those with scales and fins) and unclean (Lev 11:9–12; Dt 14:9–10). The early Church used the fish as a symbol for Christ because the letters of the Greek word for fish, *ichthys*, formed an acronym for "Jesus Christ, God's Son, Savior."

FLAX—An annual herb that was used to make linen. Israelites soaked harvested flax in water to separate the fibers, then dried them. They crushed the seeds for linseed oil and gave the dregs to the animals for fodder. Jesus' body was likely wrapped in linen cloth made from flax (Mt 27:59).

FLESH—In the Old Testament, Law of Moses specified that the Israelites could sacrifice and eat only the flesh of clean animals (Lev 6). In the New Testament, the word refers to human nature when it is deprived of the Spirit of God or dominated by physical desires (Ro 7:5). *See* **FLESH AND SPIRIT**.

FLESH AND SPIRIT—Flesh represents the sinful nature, urges, and lusts (Eph 2:3) that cannot please God (Ro 8:8). Paul contrasts the works of the flesh with the fruit of the Spirit (Gal 5:19–23).

FLESH-HOOKS—Three-pronged forks used by priests to handle meat provided for sacrifices (1Sa 2:13). Those used at the Jerusalem Temple were made of gold (1Ch 28:17) or bronze (2Ch 4:16).

FOOD—The chief staple in ancient times was bread made from barley, wheat, and emmer. There was also a variety of fruits (figs, dates, pomegranates), vegetables (beans, cucumbers, lentils, onions, leeks, garlic), and dairy products (cheese, curds, butter). Meat was usually eaten only on special occasions.

FOOL, FOOLISHNESS—The opposite of wisdom, foolishness was used as an ethical lesson. Although

THE FLOOD

In an act of divine judgment, God created a catastrophic overflowing of water to destroy a corrupt race of wickedness (Gen 6–8). God commanded Noah, the only righteous person alive, to build a large ark (boat) that would provide shelter for himself, his family, and pairs of each animal species of the earth.

The flood continued for 40 days and nights, destroying the existing world. Only those inside the ark were saved from God's wrath. After the waters subsided and the ark rested on Mount Ararat (Gen 8:4), Noah sent out a raven and then a dove, which brought back an olive branch. He waited seven days and sent out a second dove that did not return (Gen 8:6–12).

Noah left the ark and offered sacrifices to the Lord. God renewed his covenant, promising never to bring such a flood again—a commitment signaled by the appearance of the rainbow (8:13–22).

fools may act naively or impudently, they lack the wisdom that comes with the knowledge of God. Their lack of understanding is revealed through their deeds (Ps 14:1; Mt 7:24–27).

FOOT—Feet were a popular metaphor in the Bible. To "sit at the Lord's feet" symbolized discipleship (Lk 10:38); to "fall at the feet" of someone showed respect and humility (1Sa 25:24); to be put under the feet meant submission and conquest (Jos 10:24).

FOOTSTOOL—A royal piece of furniture (2Ch 9:18) that symbolized a realm over which one had dominion. Heaven was called God's throne, and the Earth his footstool (Isa 66:1). Both the ark of the covenant (1Ch 28:2) and the temple were also called God's footstools. The phrase "make your enemies your footstool" (Ps 110:1) was a promise to vanquish Israel's enemies.

FOOT WASHING—An ancient form of hospitality performed on a guest when he or she entered a house. In prominent homes, slaves loosened guests' sandal straps and washed their feet. At the Last Supper, Jesus washed his disciples' feet, symbolizing both his humility and the cleansing of sin (Jn 13).

FOREHEAD—Because it was such a prominent part of the face, the Israelites wore frontlets and phylacteries on their foreheads to represent their devotion to God (Ex 13:9). God instructed Aaron—and each subsequent high priest—to bear the phrase "Holy to the Lord" over his forehead (Ex 28:36–38). David killed Goliath with a stone to the forehead (1Sa 17:49). God's 144,000 servants (Rev 14:9) are marked there, and the followers of evil will also have a mark on their foreheads (Rev 13:16).

FOREIGNER—A non-Israelite. Foreigners were forbidden to enter the temple (Eze 44:9). The term usually meant someone foreign to the Hebrews—a special, separated nation. In the early Church, distinctions (and hostilities) between Jews

FRANKINCENSE

Frankincense was a fragrant, milky-white substance that was harvested from Boswella trees. It was obtained by cutting into the bark and collecting the gum resin. When hardened, it was used as incense. When heated or burned, it produced a pleasant, penetrating odor similar to balsam.

Valued in ancient times for alleged medicinal qualities, frankincense was used by the Egyptians as a fumigant and as ritual incense, and it was part of the anointing oil for Israelites (Ex 30:34). At the temple, people made offerings of frankincense (Isa 43:23), and priests stored it for later use (Ne 13:5, 9).

Frankincense was set beside the Bread of the Presence (Lev 24:7) and accompanied cereal offerings (Lev 2:1–2). It was a gift from the wise men to the infant Jesus (Mt 2:1), and it was also listed among the cargo of the merchants who wept for the fallen city of Babylon (Rev 18:13).

and non-Jews slowly abated (Eph 2:11–19).

FORERUNNER—An ancient military term for a soldier who ran ahead of the army (or an important person) to announce or prepare for their arrival. John the Baptist acted as Jesus' forerunner (Mt 3:1–12). Jesus entered the Holy of Holies as a forerunner to prepare for the access of his followers (Heb 6:20).

FOREST—Much of the biblical landscape has changed since ancient times, but there were once extensive wooded areas of oak, terebinth, and pine. Trees such as tamarisk, acacia, and honey locust grew in the wilderness area. Prophets spoke symbolically of these forests to represent pride (2Ki 19:23), judgment (Isa 9:18–19), or fruitfulness (Isa 32:15).

FORGIVENESS—The prophets (Isa 1:18–19), Jesus (Mk 2:5–6), and early Christians preached turning from sin and being forgiven (Ac 13:38). In the Old Testament, "forgiveness" is a translation of several different Hebrew words that mean to cover or atone. In the New Testament, the term is a translation of Greek words that mean to loose (Lk 6:37) or pass over (Ro 3:25).

FORNICATION—A general term for sexual intercourse outside of marriage (such as seduction, rape, sodomy, bestiality, incest, prostitution, or homosexuality). The Old Testament uses the word figuratively to represent Israel's abandonment of God (Eze 16:26). Fornication appears in five of Paul's seven lists of sins (1Co 5:11). *See* **ADULTERY.**

FORUM OF APPIUS—A station along the Appian Way, 43 miles southeast of Rome. The site was probably founded during the time of Appius Claudius Caecus, who constructed the highway in 312 B.C. Many Roman Christians traveled there to greet Paul (Ac 28:15).

FOUNDATION—The strong, stable base of a city or building, such as Solomon's Temple (1Ki 5:17). Jesus used the word as a symbol to represent his teachings (Mt 7:24–27). Paul called Christ the foundation of God's "temple" (1Co 3:10–17).

FOUNTAIN—Ancient society distinguished the fountain (or spring)—a source of flowing water—from a cistern or well. Settlements were usually located near natural springs. Figuratively, fountains referred to God's favor and blessings (Ps 36:9).

FOUNTAIN GATE—A city gate in the southeastern part of Jerusalem, near the steps that led to the Gihon Spring (Ne 2:14). Originally built when the city was a Jebusite stronghold, the gate was repaired by Nehemiah. Some identify it with the "gate between the walls" (2Ki 25:4).

FREEDMEN, SYNAGOGUE OF THE—A synagogue in Jerusalem that was attended by former slaves, probably Jews (and their descendants) who were taken to Rome as captives by Pompey in A.D. 63. Members of the Greek-speaking congregation charged Stephen with blasphemy (Ac 6:9–12).

FREEMAN, FREEWOMAN—A person who was born free, as opposed to slaves (or former slaves who received their freedom). Paul used the term to describe those who had been freed by Jesus Christ from bondage to sin (1Co 7:22).

FRIEND OF THE BRIDEGROOM—Similar to the "best man" in a modern wedding ceremony, this person planned, arranged, and presided over the marriage (Jdg 14:20). John the Baptist described his relationship with Jesus as that of a "friend of the bridegroom" who prepared the way for Christ (Jn 3:29).

FRIEND OF THE KING—An important official of the royal court, the "friend of the king" was a trusted advisor and intimate companion (1Ki 4:5). During the Maccabean period, these advisors constituted a distinct privileged class of which there were various ranks (1Mac 2:18).

FRINGES—God instructed the Israelites to wear tassels at the four corners of their garments (Dt 22:12) as a reminder to obey God's commands (Nu 15:38–40). Jesus condemned the scribes and Pharisees who broadened their fringes as a sign of superior piety (Mt 23:5).

FROG—Egyptians revered frogs because their goddess of childbirth, Heket, was portrayed as a frog (or as a human with the head of a frog). Israelites considered frogs unclean. The second plague in Egypt brought frogs into Egyptian homes (Ex 8:2–14).

FRUIT, FRUITS—Biblical fruits included olives, grapes, figs, dates, melons, pomegranates, sycamore figs, mulberries, and nuts (including almonds, pistachios, and walnuts). Fruits were eaten fresh, dried, or were processed into oil, wine, or cakes. Many references to fruit are symbolic: They are rewards given by God (Jer 17:10) or the results of pious actions or attitude (Mt 3:10).

FUEL—Wood and charcoal were common fuels. Other fuels included thorns and vines, the chaff of grain and hay, dried dung, fat remains, date kernels, bones of fish, birds, and animals (Eze 24:5–10).

FULLER—A person who cleaned, whitened, bleached, dyed, thickened, or shrunk cloth. The process involved beating and treading upon the material, as well as scouring it with soap or lye (Mal 3:2). The material was stretched in the sun for bleaching. Because the process generated foul odors, the fuller usually worked on the outskirts of a city, near a source of water.

FUNERAL—The burial of the dead (Gen 23:48). The Israelite funeral ceremony included a procession to

FRONTLET

A visible sign of piety and service to God, a frontlet was a headband or a small, square, leather box that was worn on the forehead between the eyes. It contained four strips of parchment, on which were written quotations commemorating the Exodus (Dt 6:8; Ex 13:9, 16). Every male above 13 years of age was required to wear one during morning prayer, except during the Sabbath and holidays.

Intended for memorial purposes, frontlets also offered protection against certain kinds of evil. In later times, the Israelites wore phylacteries—small cubical cases that held parchments on which were inscribed the words of the law (Ex 13:1–10). In the New Testament, Jesus rebuked Pharisees and scribes who wore extremely large frontlets to impress others (Mt 23:5). *See* **Phylacteries**.

the grave or tomb site. The body was carried on a wooden bier by friends or relatives. Loud public displays of mourning were expected—and sometimes professional mourners were hired (Ecc 12:5). Family and friends wept, wore sackcloth (Isa 50:3), cut their hair (Jer 7:29), or fasted to display their grief (27:30). *See* **BURIAL; MOURNING.**

FURLONG —A measure of distance, approximately 200–220 yards (Lk 24:13; Rev 14:20). Some translations use the term *stadion* (plural, *stadia*), which was 215.5 yards.

FURNACE—A brick or stone structure for heating objects. Furnaces were used to smelt metal ore (Eze 22:20) and refine gold or other metals (Pr 17:3).

GAAL (*GAY uhl; "scarab" or "loathing"*)—The leader of an unsuccessful rebellion of the people of Shechem against Abimelech, who had demolished the city and made it uninhabitable (Jdg 9:26–41).

GABBATHA (*GAB uh thuh; "pavement"*)—A paved courtyard outside the Praetorium (governor's palace) in Jerusalem. Pilate judged Jesus there and released him to be crucified (Jn 19:13).

GABRIEL (*GAY bree el; "God is a warrior"*)—An archangel. In the Old Testament, Gabriel appears only once—in answer to Daniel's prayer (Da 8–9). In the New Testament, the angel announced the coming births of John the Baptist and Jesus (Lk 1:11–20, 26–38). One of two celestial beings named in the Bible.

GAD (*"good fortune"*)—**1.** A son of Jacob. His mother was Zilpah, the maid of Jacob's wife, Leah. **2.** A prophet during the time of David (1Ch 21:9). He guided the king (2Ch 29:25) and wrote an account of David's reign (1Ch 29:29). **3.** A Canaanite god of fortune (Isa 65:11).

GAD, VALLEY OF—The tribal inheritance of Gad. It was located east of the Jordan, between the territories of Reuben to the south and the half-tribe of Manasseh to the north.

GADARENES, GADARA (*GAD uh reenz, GAD uh ruh*)—A major city six miles southeast of the Sea of Galilee. It had a large Greek population and few Jews. Jesus healed a demoniac there (Mk 5:1–10).

GAIUS (*GUY yuss; "commended"*)—**1.** A Macedonian Christian who traveled with Paul. He was dragged into the theater during a riot in Ephesus (Ac 19:29). **2.** A man from Derbe who accompanied Paul on his journey to Asia Minor (Ac 20:4). **3.** A man who housed Paul at Corinth (Ro 16:23). **4.** A Christian from Corinth whom Paul baptized (1Co 1:14), possibly the same man as Gaius 3. **5.** The addressee of John's third letter (3Jn 1).

GALATIA (*guh LAY shee uh*)—A province and a region in Asia Minor, named after the Gaulic (Celtic) population that settled there in the third century B.C. Paul, who evangelized several cities there (Ac 13–14), also wrote a letter to those churches.

GALATIANS, LETTER TO THE—The ninth book in the New Testament. After establishing churches in the region (c. A.D. 50), Paul wrote his letter because its teachers were attacking his authority and insisting on circumcision—and not grace alone—for salvation.

GALEED (*guh LEED; "witness pile"*)—The name that Jacob gave to the pile of memorial stones. He and Laban set up the stones to commemorate their covenant and to delineate the boundary between their territories (Gen 31:47).

GALILEE, SEA OF—A freshwater lake, fed by the Jordan River, that was closely connected with Jesus' ministry. It has three names: Sea of Chinnereth (Nu 34:11), Sea of Tiberias (Jn 6:1), and Sea of Galilee (Mt 4:18).

GALL (*GAWL*)—A bitter herb. It was used as a symbol for bitter punishment (Jer 8:14) or experience (Ac 8:23). At the cross, soldiers offered Jesus gall and vinegar, but he refused to drink (Mt 27:34). Some

GALILEE

The province of Galilee (GAL i lee) in northern Israel was about 45 miles long. The tribes of Naphtali, Asher, Issachar, Zebulon, and (later) Dan settled there when they came from Egypt.

Conquered by Rome in 63 B.C., Galilee was ruled by client-kings for many decades. Herod Antipas ruled Galilee (and Perea) from 4 B.C. to A.D. 39 and built his capital city at Tiberias. After Agrippa's death in A.D. 44, (Ac 12:23), Galilee became a stronghold of those who opposed Roman rule. The Romans crushed Jewish resistance in A.D. 66.

The major part of Jesus' ministry took place in Galilee. His youth and early ministry were spent in Nazareth, although his own people rejected him (Lk 4:16–30), and it was at Cana in Galilee that he changed water into wine (Jn 2:11).

believe that the mixture was given to ease the pain, but others think it was an act of cruelty.

GALLIO *(GAL ee oh)*— Lucius Junius Gallio Annaeus, the proconsul of Achaia (Greece). When the Jews brought Paul before him at Corinth, he dismissed the case. He also refused to take action when the mob beat the synagogue ruler Sosthenes (Ac 18:12–17).

GALLOWS—A device for hanging people. It is mentioned only in the Book of Esther, when Bighthan and Teresh (who had plotted to assassinate the king) were hanged on the gallows (Est 2:23). Haman had a gallows built for Mordecai (Est 5:14) but was himself executed instead.

GAMALIEL *(guh MAY lee el; "God is my reward")*—**1.** A Manassite leader during the Exodus (Nu 1:10). **2.** Rabban Gamaliel I, one of the most respected religious scholars of his day. He intervened with the Sanhedrin on Peter and the apostles' behalf (Ac 5: 33–39). Paul was one of his students.

Game of the 24 squares of Ur

GAMES—The few games mentioned in the Bible are primarily of a combative nature, such as wrestling (2Sa 2:14), foot racing (Ps 19:5), and archery (1Sa 10:18–23). Archeologists have discovered dolls, rattles, and marbles—as well as board games—dating to biblical times.

GARDEN—An enclosed plot of land, generally used for agriculture or recreation. Gardens may have also been used as burial plots or for pagan sacrifices. A garden symbolized prosperity or desolation (Isa 58:11; Jer 31:12).

GATH *("winepress")*—One of five major Philistine cities. When the Israelites conquered Canaan, they were unable to expel the Anakim (a race of giants) from the city (Jos 11:22). Goliath was from Gath (1Sa 13–16).

GATH–HEPHER *(gath HEE fur; "winepress of digging")*— A border town of Zebulun (Jos 19:13), the home of Jonah (2Ki. 14:25).

GAULANITIS *(gaw luh NITE iss)*—A region or district east of the Sea of Galilee. It received its name from its largest city, Golan (Dt 4:43).

173

GAZA—One of five principal Philistine cities. After the Israelites conquered Gaza, it became part of Judah (Jos 15:47). Samson was held prisoner there (Jdg 16:21). Amos and Zechariah pronounced judgment on the city for its transgressions (Am 1:6; Zec 2:4).

Addax (desert gazelle)

GAZELLE—A swift, shy, deerlike animal, slightly smaller than the roe. The gazelle is sandy brown, with stripes marking the face and flank, and ringed horns that curve toward the back. They were symbols of love and beauty (SS 2:9) and a major game-animal for food (1Ki 4:23). *See* **ANTELOPE**.

GEBAL *(GEE bahl; "mountain")*—1. An ancient Phoenician port, renamed Byblos ("Bible") because it was a center for the trading of papyrus. 2. A territory southeast of the Dead Sea mentioned in connection with Moab and Edom (Ps 83:7).

GEDALIAH *(ged uh LIE uh; "the Lord is great")*—1. The appointed governor over those who remained in Judah after most people had been taken into exile. He protected Jeremiah (Jer 39:14). 2. A leader of singers during the time of David (1Ch 25:3, 9). 3. A priest who had to send away his foreign wife (Ezr 10:18). 4. A prince who threw Jeremiah into a cistern for predicting the fall of Jerusalem (Jer 38:1–6). 5. Grandson of King Hezekiah; grandfather of Zephaniah (Zep 1:1).

GEDOR (*GEE dor*; *"wall"*)—
1. A town in the hill country of Judah situated between Bethlehem and Hebron (Jos 15:58). 2. A town in Judah (1Ch 4:18). 3. A town in the territory of Simeon (1Ch 4:39–40). 4. A town in the tribal territory of Benjamin (1Ch 12:7), possibly the same as Gedor 2.

GEHAZI (*geh HAH zee*; *"valley of vision"*)—A servant of Elisha (2Ki 4:8–37). When Elisha healed Naaman (the Syrian army commander), the prophet refused to accept payment for his healing. Gehazi, however, tricked Naaman into giving silver and clothing, which he tried to keep for himself. Because of his deceit, Gehazi and his descendants were smitten with leprosy (2Ki 5).

GEHENNA (*geh HEN uh*)—A narrow valley south of Jerusalem (Jos 15:8). The name came to symbolize final punishment by fire,

and thus the New Testament referred to it as the place of eternal torment. Some Bibles translate the word as "hell" (Mt 5:22, 29–30). *See* **HINNOM, VALLEY OF.**

GELILOTH (*geh LIE lahth*)—A landmark or small area along the road from Jericho to Jerusalem that separated the territories of Benjamin and Judah (Jos 18:17). Tradition has identified it as the inn of the Good Samaritan.

GENEALOGY—A history of a person's (or a group's) ancestry. There are two major types of genealogy represented in the Bible: linear—a single line of descent from a living person to a single ancestor, or from an ancestor to a single living person (Lk 3:23–38; Ru 4:18–22); and segmented—a horizontal or branch form of genealogy relating many members by a common ancestor (Ex 6:14–25).

GENEALOGY OF JESUS CHRIST—Jesus' genealogy—the history of his ancestry—occurs in two gospels. Matthew uses three sets of 14 generations, starting with Abraham and ending with David (Mt 1:1–16). Luke traces the ancestry of Jesus back through Joseph, David, and Abraham to Adam (Lk 3:28–38). Both records reflect the common Old Testament practice of selection and omission of names in such lists.

GENERATION—**1.** Each succession of persons from a common ancestor (Gen 50:23). **2.** An age or period of a body of contemporaries, determined by the normal span of life. The generation lasts as long as any of the members survive (Ex 1:6; Nu 32:13).

GENNESARET (*geh NES uh ret*)—A plain that bordered the northwest shore of the Sea of Galilee (Mt 14:34). During a visit there, Jesus healed the sick. Because of its proximity, the Sea of Galilee was sometimes called the "lake of Gennesaret" (Lk 5:1).

GENTILE (*"nation"*)—A term used by Jews to describe foreigners or non-Jews. The word has its roots in the Old Testament, where it referred to the nations (*goyim*) not driven from the land (Jos 24:11). God strictly separated Jews and called them a chosen nation (Dt 7:1–5). Only in post-biblical Hebrew did it become possible to speak of an individual Gentile (*goy*).

GENTLENESS—Kindness, consideration. Paul names gentleness as part of the "fruit of the Spirit" (Gal 5:22–23), meaning Christians should be gentle toward everyone (Php 4:5; 2Co 10:1).

GERAR (*GEE rar*)—A city near Gaza where Abraham and Isaac stayed during famines and entered into

GENESIS, BOOK OF

The first book of the Old Testament, the name Genesis comes from a Greek word meaning "to be born." Its Hebrew title is "In the beginning," which is taken from its opening words.

The book sets the stage for the ongoing course of history. Genesis divides itself into three sections: a history of the universe, showing God's relation to it and introducing human history (Gen 1–2); the human history before Abraham, showing God's relationship to the human race and introducing the Chosen People (Gen 2:4–11:26); and a history of God's covenant with his people up through their descent into Egypt (Gen 11:27–50:26).

The Book of Genesis is also the story of God and humanity, sin and grace.

agreements with Abimelech (Gen 20:1–2, 15, 26:1–8).

GERASA (*ger RAH suh*)—A major city settled by the Ammonites. It became an important Christian center in the fourth century A.D.

GERIZIM, MT. (*GAIR uh zim*)—A mountain in the district of Samaria. Before entering the Promised Land, six tribes of Israel stood on the slopes of Mt. Gerizim while Moses pronounced the blessings for keeping the law (Dt 27:4–26). Samaritans built their temple on Mt. Gerizim (Jn 4:20).

GERSHOM (*GUHR shum*)— 1. The oldest son of Moses and Zipporah. 2. An alternate name for Gershon, a son of Levi. During the wilderness wanderings, the Gershonites covered and transported the tabernacle furnishings. **3.** A Jew who returned from the Exile with Ezra (Ezr 8:2).

GESHUR *(GESH uhr; "bridge")*—A small Aramean kingdom on the slopes of Mount Hermon. Home to the Geshurites, it served as a buffer between Aram and Israel.

Gesture of prayer

GESTURES—The most common prayer gesture in the Old Testament is "spreading the palms" (Ex 9:29), with God filling the hands of the petitioner with the requested benefit.

Other religious gestures included lifting the hands, kneeling, bowing the head.

GHOST, HOLY—Another name for the Holy Spirit. The word "ghost" comes from an Old English word meaning spirit or soul. *See* **HOLY SPIRIT.**

GIANT—Races of giants are first mentioned in Genesis (Gen 6:4). Israelite spies who ventured into Canaan returned with reports about the huge size of the inhabitants (Nu 13:32–33). The most famous giant was Goliath (from Gath), who was about nine feet tall (1Sa 17:4–7).

GIBBETHON *(GIB uh thon; "height" or "mound")*—A village in the territory of Dan (Jos 19:44). Nadab, a king of Israel, was assassinated there (1Ki 15:27).

GIBEAH *(GIB ee uh; "hill")*—**1.** A city of Judah in the hill country southwest of Jerusalem. **2.** A town in the hill country of

GETHSEMANE

Gethsemane (*geth SEM uh nee*) was an ancient olive oil press that could be found in or near olive groves. After the Last Supper, Jesus took his disciples and went to a place called "Gethsemane," where he pleaded with God to deliver him from the coming events (Mk 14:32–43).

The site is mentioned twice (Mk 14:32; Mt 26:3) before Judas' betrayal of Jesus (Lk 21:37; Jn 18:1–2). Mark and Matthew refer to a place called Gethsemane near the Mount of Olives. John's gospel records neither the name nor Jesus' anguished prayer, but it locates the betrayal in a garden across the Kidron Valley from Jerusalem, on the western slopes of the Mount of Olives. From that citation comes the traditional name, Garden of Gethsemane (Jn 18:1).

Although its precise location is not known, the Roman emperor Constantine's mother designated a possible site in A.D. 325.

Ephraim. **3.** A city in the tribal territory of Benjamin. It was the setting of the rape and murder of a Levite's concubine that led to a civil war against Benjamin (Jdg 19–20).

GIBEON (*GIB ee uhn;* "*hill*")—A city spared from destruction during the Israelite conquest. Masquerading as foreigners, Gibeonites formed a covenant with Israel (Jos 9:1–15). When the ruse was discovered, Joshua honored the covenant but made them servants.

GIFT—Hebrew has 15 different expressions

GIDEON

The youngest son of Joash, Gideon (GID ee uhn; "cutter" or "hewer") was a descendant from the tribe of Manasseh and is counted among the major judges.

When the Midianites (a nomadic tribe of plunderers) overpowered the people, Gideon—a meek farmer—received a call by an angel to deliver Israel (Jdg 6:11–23). First, he was asked to destroy the temples dedicated to the pagan god Baal-Asherath. Fearing reprisal, he carried out his destruction at night (Jdg 6:32).

He then gathered 23,000 Israelites to fight, but he hesitated and asked God for a sign—that a fleece left overnight on the floor would gather dew while the floor remained dry. After receiving the sign, he was still doubtful and asked for another sign—that the fleece would remain dry while the floor gathered dew. This done, God tested Gideon's faith by ordering him into battle with only 300 men. His small army killed 15,000 Midianites and captured two of their kings (Jdg 8:10).

The Israelites offered him kingship, but he refused and said, "I will not rule over you and my son will not rule over you: the Lord will rule over you" (Jdg 8:23). After he retired to his home, Israel had peace for 40 years (Jdg 8:28).

relating to gifts. Sometimes gifts really meant tributes (Jdg 3:15) or bribes (Pr 18:16). The presentation of a gift was usually done with as much ceremony as possible. Refusal to give or receive a gift was a great insult. In the New Testament, Paul declared that Jesus Christ was God's gift to the world (Ro 6:23).

GIFTS OF THE SPIRIT— Abilities or empowerments given by the Holy Spirit. In the Bible, the term was used only by Paul (1Co 12:8–10; Eph 4:7–13; Ro 12:3–8), although spiritual empowerment for particular tasks was mentioned in the Old Testament (Jdg 3:10; Nu 11:29).

GIHON *(GEE hon)*—1. One of four rivers that flowed out of Eden (Gen 2:10,13). 2. A spring in the Kidron Valley. Connected to Jerusalem via an underground tunnel, Gihon was a vital source of water for the city.

GILBOA *(gil BOH uh)*—A mountain (about 1,700 feet high) that guards the eastern pass from the Plain of Esdraelon into the Valley of Jezreel. It was the site of Saul's last battle with the Philistines. His three sons were killed, and the wounded Saul took his own life (1Sa 31).

¹GILEAD *(GIL ee ud; "rocky")*—A densely forested region in Transjordan (Jer 22:6). It was a source of plants from which incense and medicines were made, such as the balm of Gilead (Jer 8:22).

²GILEAD—1. Grandson of Manasseh and ancestor of the Gileadite clan. 2. The father of Jephthah (Jdg 11:1). 3. A descendant of Gad (1Ch 5:14).

GILGAL *(GIL gal; "circle" or "rolling")*—1. The site of the Israelites' first encampment after crossing the Jordan (Jos 4:19–20). Located near Jericho, it became the base of military operations during the conquest of Canaan. 2. A village from which Elijah ascended into heaven (2Ki 2:1). 3. A town located between Dor and Tirzah (Jos 12:23).

GILGAMESH (*GIL guh mesh*)—A Babylonian (Akkadian) poem recounting the exploits of the legendary King Gilgamesh. The tablets containing the poem were discovered among archives at Nineveh.

GIRDLE—A garment that was worn around the waist. They were commonly made of leather, but finer girdles were made of linen, embroidered with silk (or sometimes gold and silver thread), and studded with gold, precious stones, or pearls. A sword or dagger could be suspended from the military girdle. "Girding the loins" denoted preparation for battle.

GLASS—Although ancient cultures made glass and glass beads, it is rarely mentioned in the Bible (Job 28:17; Rev 4:6). In the first century A.D., the Romans made vessels on the end of a hollow metal tube by blowing a bulb of molten glass into a mold.

GLEANING—The practice of gathering or picking up what was left in the fields after reaping (Jdg 8:2; Ru 2). The Law of Moses told farmers to leave gleanings for the poor, the sojourners, the fatherless, and the widows (Lev 19:9–10).

GLORIA IN EXCELSIS (*"Glory in the highest"*)—A Latin expression of praise, originating from the announcement of the angels to the shepherds, "Glory to God in the highest heaven" (Lk 2:14).

GLORY (*"weight" or "importance"*)—A significant theological term; to have glory is to be important to oneself or others. In the Old Testament, the word is used to describe both God and people (Job 19:9). Divine glory refers to God's visible manifestations to humans (Nu 16:19; Ps 102:16). In the New Testament, it primarily refers to the glory of God (Lk 2:9; Ac 7:55), extending the term to include the risen Christ (1Co 2:8).

GLOSSOLALIA (*GLOS uh LAY lee uh; "tongue speech"*)— The act of speaking in languages unknown to the speaker or incomprehensible. In the Bible, the word "tongue" sometimes refers to language, frequently an alien one. Glossolalia was prominent in the early Church from the day of Pentecost (Ac 2). Paul regulated the use of this holy gift (1Co 14). *See* **SPEAKING WITH TONGUES.**

GNAT—A general term— referring to gnats, lice, mosquitoes, midges, or sand flies—associated with the third plague upon Egypt (Ex 8:16–18). Jesus accused the scribes and Pharisees of "straining out a gnat and swallowing a camel," meaning they were scrutinizing the details of ritual impurity while neglecting ethics (Mt 23:24).

GOAD—A long stick with a pin or pointed spike at-

tached. Farmers used the goad to make cattle move, especially oxen (1Sa 13:21). Figuratively, the teachings of the wise were goads that stimulated thought in others (Ecc 12:11). Refusing to acknowledge the obvious was to "kick against the goads" (Ac 26:14).

GOAT—Belonging to the same family as sheep, goats are the hardiest, most versatile of domestic livestock. Raised primarily for meat, ancient societies also used the animal's milk, hair, and skin (Lev 7:23; Dt 14:5; Jos 9:4). Goats were also required as animal sacrifices (Lev 1:10).

GOATSKIN—The roof of the tabernacle was made of goatskins (Ex 26:7), and the Levites used them to cover the tabernacle furniture when they moved. The New Testament describes the wearing of goatskins when destitute as part of the suffering and persecu-

GNOSTICISM

A general term for several diverse religious movements of the first three centuries A.D. Gnosticism (NOS ti siz um) offered salvation from material existence through knowledge (*gnosis*).

Most forms of this religion made a distinction between God (spirit) and the world (matter) and believed that the world was evil, inferior, and opposed the good. God may have created the first order, but each succeeding one was the work of anti-gods and subordinate deities.

Paul condemned such ideas (1 Ti 1–2; 2 Ti 2:16–19). John also argued against such teachings, although he did not specifically name them as Gnostic. Most of what we know about Gnosticism comes from the reports of Church fathers (such as Irenaeus, Hippoclytus, Tertullian, Origen, and Epiphanius), who opposed all forms of the movement.

In 1946, a library of 13 Coptic manuscripts was discovered near Nag Hammadi, Egypt. The manuscripts revealed a complex—and less specifically Christian—movement.

tion endured by Israelite heroes (Heb 11:37).

GOD—A general term for deity. The term was used to refer to the one deity worshiped in the Judeo-Christian tradition (God) as well as for deities worshiped by others (god/gods). In the Old Testament, God was represented by the Hebrew word *El* (or the plural, *Elohim*), which meant power or strength. In the New Testament, the Greek word *theos* was more commonly used.

GOD-FEARERS—A term for Gentiles (non-Jews) who attended synagogue services and observed some of the Jewish law but were not full converts to Judaism.

GODLINESS—A term that was commonly used to show respect for Greek and Roman gods. Probably because of this association, the word seldom appears in the Bible. New Testament writers preferred "righteousness," "faith," or "holiness" to describe the qualities most pleasing to God. In the Old Testament, true godliness—or piety—usually found expression as "loyalty to God," "goodness," or "holiness" (Ps 4:3).

GOG ("Mountain")—**1.** A descendant of Reuben (1Ch 5:4). **2.** A ruler of the land of Magog. Ezekiel prophesied that Gog would ravage Israel before being destroyed by God (Eze 38–39). He may have been Gyges, king of Lydia (c. 660 B.C.). See **MAGOG**.

GOLAN—A city in the territory of Manassah (Dt 4:43). The name became associated with the region surrounding the city. It was part of the plateau of Bashan, east of Galilee.

GOLDEN GATE—A gate in the eastern wall of the old city of Jerusalem. Tradition says the columns separating the passageways were given to King Solomon by the Queen of Sheba. Ottoman Turks walled it up, presumably because both Christian and Jewish traditions believed that the Messiah would use it to enter the city (Eze 44:1–3).

GOLIATH ("exile" or "soothsayer")—**1.** A Philistine giant slain by David with a single stone from his sling (1Sa 17). Physically imposing and heavily armed, Goliath had challenged Saul's army to bring out a champion to fight him. Their combat decided the

GOLGOTHA

Three of the four gospels name Golgotha (GOL guh thuh) as the site of Jesus' crucifixion (Mt 27:33; Mk 15:22; Jn 19:17). The name, defined as "the place of a skull," comes from the Greek word *gulgalta* ("skull"). It was probably named this because of its habitual use for executions (although a less likely explanation is rooted in the physical appearance of the place).

John's account, as well as Jewish and Roman execution customs, indicated that Golgotha was located outside Jerusalem's city walls (Jn 19:20). Roman crucifixion customs and a biblical mention of passersby suggest it was near a thoroughfare (Mt 27:39). Its location remains in dispute.

Since the fourth century, the site now marked by the Church of the Holy Sepulchre has been revered as the location of Golgotha. A rival site—Gordon's Calvary—is located north of Jerusalem and is a favorite site of Protestant pilgrims.

war's outcome. Goliath was likely one of the Anakim, legendary descendants of Anak (Nu 13:28). 2. Possibly a son of Goliath 1 (2Sa 21:19).

GOMER *(GOH muhr; "ember" or "completion")*— 1. The oldest son of Japheth (Gen 10:2) 2. The harlot wife of Hosea. Possibly associated with a fertility cult, she bore him three children. Gomer became a symbol of Israel's unfaithfulness and God's grace (Hos 1:2–3).

GOMORRAH *(guh MOR uh; "submersion")*—One of five cities defeated by Abraham

(Gen 14:2–3, 8). God destroyed Gomorrah and Sodom because of the wickedness of their inhabitants. Only Lot and his family survived (19:24–29). Sodom and Gomorrah became symbols for corruption and the power of divine punishment.

GOOD FRIDAY—A religious holiday that commemorates Jesus' crucifixion, Good Friday is observed on the Friday preceding Easter (Mk 15:42). Traditionally, it was a day of fasting and penance. Post-Reformation practices (observed by both Roman Catholics and Protestants) include a service from noon to 3 P.M., marking Jesus' agony on the cross.

GOOD NEWS—An English translation of the Greek word *evangelion*. In the New Testament, it refers to the message preached by Jesus (Mk 1:14–15) and what God has done for humanity through Jesus

Christ (Ro 1:1–14). *See* **GOSPEL.**

GOOD SAMARITAN—The subject of one of Jesus' parables. The man proved himself a good neighbor by aiding a Jew who was robbed by thieves and wounded (Lk 10:29–37). In New Testament times, a good Samaritan would have been a contradiction because of a centuries-long hatred between Jews and Samaritans.

GOPHER WOOD—Material from which Noah was instructed to build the ark (Gen 6:14). Its identification is uncertain, although it may have been a variety of conifer, possibly a cypress.

GOSHEN (*GO shen; "mound of earth"*)—**1.** A region in the eastern Nile delta where Jacob's family settled (Gen 45:10, 46:28–47:6). It was given as grazing land to the descendants of Jacob. **2.** A part of Canaan conquered by Joshua (Jos 10:41). **3.** A city in the hill country of Judah (Jos 15:51).

GOSPEL—The modern form of the Anglo-Saxon term "god-spell"—a story from or about a god. The Gospel is a message of glad tidings, especially the good news concerning Jesus Christ and salvation (2Co 4:4). *See* **GOOD NEWS.**

GOSPELS, THE—The Good News. The first four books of the New Testament: Matthew, Mark, Luke, and John. They are each a distinctive account of the beginnings of salvation through Jesus Christ. The gospels are not biographies—apart from the infancy narratives, they record only the last part of Jesus' life. Instead, they represent four different perspectives that present Jesus as the world's savior.

GOVERNMENT—The administration of society by those in power. Although the Bible presents a variety of political institutions, details are fragmentary. The Bible warns against the dangers of corrupt government—particularly that of a king. God is seen as the ultimate source of justice (Ps 72:1–4; Ro 13:1, 4).

GOVERNOR—A local ruler who was appointed by a king to oversee a specific district or province of the kingdom. In the Old Testament, the term was used most often to designate the imperial administrators of Babylon and Persia. During Roman times, a governor usually served three years. His primary responsibility was to maintain peace. Pilate was governor over Judea when Jesus was crucified (Mt 27:2).

GOZAN *(GO zan)*—A city and district in northwest Mesopotamia on the Habor River. Assyrian King Tiglath–pileser III deported Israelites to Gozan after the destruction of Samaria (Isa 37:12).

GRACE—In the Old Testament, grace literally means "favor" (Gen 6:8). In the New Testament, grace refers to the unmerited—and freely given—redeeming action of God through Jesus Christ. By God's grace, sin is forgiven and its power broken (Ro 6:14–15; 2Co 8:9).

GRAIN—In the Bible, "grain" was a general term for a variety of cultivated cereal grasses, such as wheat, barley, millet, and spelt. (Some translations use the word "corn" instead of grain.) Because it was such an essential food, grain was a symbol of sustenance. Jesus compared grain to the word of God in his parable about the sowers (Mt 13:3–23).

GRAPES—An important agricultural product during biblical times, grapes were eaten fresh, dried into raisin clusters, or made into wine or vinegar. People gathered grapes in

Israeli children pressing grapes

baskets with much festivity (Jdg 9:27). Grapes often represented God's judgment: Grapes of wickedness were harvested and thrown into the wine press of God's wrath (Joel 3:13; Rev 14:18–19).

GRASSHOPPER—The Bible contains numerous references to grasshoppers and locusts (the words were used interchangeably). These insects migrated in swarms, damaging vegetation in their path (Am 7:1). When Moses' spies returned from Canaan, they

189

GRAVEN IMAGES

Images or statues of deities that were used as objects of worship, graven images were typically sculpted or cast from a mold. God forbade Israelites to make any kind of images—a prohibition that set them apart from their neighbors (Ex 20:3–6).

Worship of idols was an ongoing issue. In a satire on idolatry, Isaiah provided details about making idols (Isa 44:9–20). Joshua's farewell speech urged the people to put away the gods their fathers had served in Egypt (Jos 24:14). Prophets continually spoke against such worship (Hos 11:2; Mic 1:7).

After the Exile, the Jews distanced themselves from idols, and the concern about graven images lessened. In the New Testament, it became more of an intellectual concept, such as equating covetousness with idolatry (Col 3:5; Eph 5:5). *See* **Idols**.

---

described a race of giants that made the Israelites seem "like grasshoppers" (Nu 13:33).

GRAVE—The burial place of the dead. Graves were generally located outside cities (Lk 7:12). Natural caves often became family burial sites (Gen 23). The wealthy sometimes hewed a family tomb out of solid rock and sealed the entrance with a large circular stone in a groove (Jn 19:38–42).

GREECE—A major ancient civilization rooted in a confederation of city-states in the southern Balkan peninsula. Most of its artistic, scientific, and political accomplishments constitute the foundations of Western civilization. Greece, mentioned in only two later books of the Old Testament (Daniel and Zechariah), figures prominently in the New Testament. Three of the cities to which Paul wrote letters (Corinth, Philippi, and Thessalonica) were in Greece—and he visited many others (Ac 16:9–18:18). *See* **ACHAIA.**

GREEK LANGUAGE—Alexander the Great extended Greek culture and language throughout the Mediterranean world. When biblical writers used the term "Greek," they did not mean merely natives of Greece, but all those who had been influenced by Greek culture and were not Jews (Mk 7:26). The New Testament was written in *koine*—a common-language, simplified dialect of classical Greek.

GREETING—Biblical greetings typically included an offering of hospitality, such as a wish for happiness or a blessing. Gestures formed an important part of greetings and included clasping the beard, embracing, and kissing. Kneeling was the usual greeting given to one's superior or to God's representative (Gen 18:2). A holy kiss extended peace and unity, echoing God's reconciliation. In the New Testament, the epistles usually begin with a formal greeting.

GRINDER—1. One whose task was to process grain into flour by rubbing or pulverizing it between two stones that were turned by hand or by animals. Grinding was usually the work of women or slaves. 2. A symbolic word for the molars—worn and decayed teeth—in an allegory about aging (Ecc 12:3–7).

GRUDGE—Harboring a feeling of anger against one's neighbor. Prohibited under Israelite law (Lev 19:18), "ungrudging" behavior was encouraged (Dt 15:10; 1Pe 4:9).

GUARANTEE—A commercial term for the deposit—or down payment—that secured a legal claim or made a contract binding. It is used figuratively in the New Testament for God's gift of the Spirit, which is a guarantee of everlasting life with Christ (2Co 5:5).

GUARD—1. A person assigned to protect an important person or group (Gen 37:36; Ac 28:16). 2. To watch over or protect; to have charge of; or to keep. In the New Testament, God's peace guards believers' hearts and minds (Php 4:7).

GUILT—For biblical writers, guilt was not primarily an inward feeling of remorse or a bad conscience. It involved a situation that had arisen because of sin committed against God or a neighbor.

GUILT OFFERING—A temple offering required when a person had desecrated some holy thing or committed perjury (Lev 5:14; 6:2–5). Its purpose was reparation of damages. The guilt offering consisted of the sacrifice of a ram, the person's confession, and the repayment of damages—plus a 20 percent fine.

GULF—A deep gap or cleft separating two places. Jesus told a parable about a rich man in a place of torment and a beggar in a place of bliss. They were separated by a great gulf or chasm (Lk 16:26).

GYMNASIUM—An important institution in ancient Greek culture, it provided physical education as well as moral and literary training. The gymnasium was much like a preparatory school for aristocratic males who had attained puberty. It helped establish national solidarity and maintain values, particularly in outlying cities of the empire.

HABAKKUK *(huh BAK uhk; "embracer" or "wrestler")*—A pre-exilic prophet of Judah, probably a contemporary of Jeremiah, Zephaniah, and Nahum. Habakkuk lamented the violence and lawlessness that pervaded Judean society and implored God to intervene.

HABAKKUK, BOOK OF—An Old Testament book that contains the revelations of Habakkuk, one of the 12 minor prophets. The author wrestles with this question: Why would God punish his Chosen People by allowing them to be defeated by an evil nation? God's answer was that a person's arrogance has within it the seeds of its own destruction (Hab 2:4). God brings judgment and punishment to all evildoers. The book contains no reference to the prophet's lineage or place of residence, but speaks of Israel's impending defeat by the Chaldeans (Babylonians) (Hab 1).

HABIRU *(hah BY roo)*—A broad social movement of displaced people from about 2000 to 1000 B.C. The Akkadian word, which may have meant "immigrant," does not appear in the Bible. Some believe that the reference to Abraham (Gen 14:13) as "the Hebrew" may indicate that he was considered part of the Habiru.

HABOR *(HAY bohr; "fertile")*—A tributary of the Euphrates River. Along the shores of Habor, the king of Assyria settled some of the Israelites who had been conquered and deported from Samaria (2Ki 17:6).

HACHILAH *(huh KEE luh)*— An unidentified hill in the wilderness of Ziph where David hid from Saul (1Sa 23:19). Saul camped on the same hill in his search for David (1Sa 26:3).

HADAD *(HAY dad; "thunderer")*—1. The eighth son of Ishmael and grandson of Abraham (Gen 25:15). 2. An Edomite king who ruled from Avith (Gen 36:35–36; 1Ch 1:46–47). 3. An Edomite king (1Ch 1:50–51). Because of a textual error, his name appears as Hadar in Genesis 36:39. 4. An Edomite ruler who fled Joab's massacre but later returned as an adversary of Solomon (1Ki 11:14–25).

HADAD–RIMMON *(HAY dad RIM muhn)*—A site on the plain of Megiddo (not far from Jezreel) where King Josiah of Judah was killed and his army defeated by Pharaoh Necho of Egypt (2Ch 35:24). Many scholars believe the name refers to a Canaanite god of vegetation and stormy weather.

HADADEZER *(HAY dad EE zur; "Hadad is help")*—The king of Zobah. A powerful Aramean ruler, he was enlisted to help the Ammonites against David, but was defeated (2Sa 10:6–19). Later, he gathered troops and was defeated a second time. As a result, David exacted heavy tribute from the Arameans and extended his control in Transjordan.

HADRIAN *(HAY dree un)*— Publius Aelius Hadrianus, a Roman emperor (A.D. 117–138). He rebuilt Jerusalem in A.D. 135 as the Roman city Aelia Capitolina. It was populated by Gentiles, with a temple to Jupiter on the site of the Jewish temple. His actions provoked a Jewish rebellion.

HAGAR *(HAY gahr; "flight" or "one who flees")*—An Egyptian maid of Sarai/

HADES

Named after a Greek god of the underworld, Hades was the home of the dead. In the Old Testament, Hades was a translation for several different Hebrew words (pit, stillness, death, deep darkness), the most common of which was *sheol*—the realm of the dead from which people sought oracles.

The act of seeking the dead was forbidden by the law (Dt 18:11), but was practiced (1Sa 28:3–25). Like other Semites, Hebrews believed *sheol* was beneath the Earth (Nu 6:30–33). The souls of the dead—without distinction—went there (Gen 37:35; Ps 31). They also saw *sheol* as open to God (Job 26:6). Because God watched over the spirits of the Chosen People, he was present there (Ps 139:8).

During the intertestamental period, Hades came to be regarded as a place where the deceased awaited judgment. In the New Testament, Hades was the abode of the dead (Ac 2:27, 31).

The notion that the realm of the dead had one or more gates controlling the movement in or out of it was ancient (Isa 38:10; Mt 16:18). The risen Jesus said he had the "keys of Death and of Hades" (Rev 1:18), which implied he had power over life and death. *See* **Sheol**.

Sarah (Gen 16:1). She was made a wife-concubine of Abraham. Hagar bore Ishmael for Abraham when Sarah was childless. When Sarah's own son was born, Abraham cast out Hagar (with Ishmael) to wander in the desert.

HAGGAI (*HAG eye; "festive"*)—A prophet who

encouraged the Israelites to rebuild the temple. He urged them to focus on God and spiritual responsibilities (Ezr 5:1).

HAGGAI, BOOK OF—An Old Testament book containing four sermons of the prophet Haggai. Because the temple they were rebuilding lacked the splendor of Solomon's Temple, the returning exiles stopped work and built themselves lavish homes (Hag 1:4). Haggai urged continued reconstruction, promising God would help them prosper for their diligence (Hag 2:7).

HAGRITES (*HAG rites*)—A nomadic Aramean tribe, wealthy in donkeys, sheep, and camels. During Saul's reign, they were banished from the land east of Gilead (1Ch 5:10, 18–22).

HAIL, HAILSTONES—Frozen snow or rain, hailstones could cause severe crop and property damage. In the Old Testament, hail

was a symbol of God's punishment of the wicked (Isa 28:2).

HALAK (*HAY lak; "smooth"*)—A "bald" (without vegetation) mountain south of Palestine. It marked the southern boundary of Joshua's conquests (Jos 11:17).

HALF-TRIBE—Half of the tribe of Manasseh settled in Gilead (north of Gad's territory) while the other half lived west of Jordan along the Mediterranean Sea. Each was called a "half-tribe" of Manasseh (Nu 31:33–42).

HALLEL (*HAL el*)—A song of praise. At annual feasts, the Israelites sang a group of psalms thanking God for deliverance from Egypt (Ps 113–118). Psalms of praise (Ps 120–136) were also sung at morning prayers.

HALLELUJAH (*"Praise Yah [Yahweh]"*)—A Hebrew exclamation used at the

HAIR

In ancient times, hair growth was a sign of human vitality, giving it religious significance to the Israelites. Allowing hair to grow was an outward sign of one's commitment and vow to God. Samson's mother was instructed not to cut his hair because he would be dedicated to God's  work of rescuing his people from the Philistines (Jdg 13:5).

Long hair on both Israelite men and women signified beauty and pride (Eze 8:3), as long as it was styled in ways avoiding pagan practices. During periods of mourning, pagans would leave their hair mussed and in disarray. The Israelites were required to keep their hair well groomed and trimmed (2Sa 14:26).

On the other hand, excessive attention to the styling and grooming of hair was criticized both by the Old Testament prophets and by the Apostle Paul. In the New Testament, men usually wore short hair, while long hair was proper for women (1Co 11: 14–15). Anointing one's hair with oil or perfumed water was often performed by a host as a sign of hospitality.

beginning of psalms to call people to praise God. The word was adapted to Christian faith as a "call to worship" (Rev 19:1–8).

HAM (*"hot"*)—The youngest son of Noah. He survived the Flood aboard the ark. Ham's descendants included Egyptians, Ethiopians, Libyans, and Canaanites (Gen 10:6–20).

HAMAN (*HAY muhn; "famed"*)—A prime minister of Persia whose plot to kill the Jews was thwarted by Mordecai and Esther. Haman lost his position to Mordecai and was executed (Est 7:10).

HAMATH (*HAY muth; "fortress, citadel"*)—An important city on a major trade route from southern Asia Minor. Hamath marked the northern boundary of Israel (Nu 13:21, 34:8; 1Ki 8:65).

HAMITES (*HAM ites*)—Descendants of Ham, Noah's youngest son. The Hamites were divided into four branches: Cush, Egypt, Put, and Canaan (Gen 10:6–20).

HAMMURABI (*ham uh RAH bee*)—The sixth and perhaps most important of the Babylonian kings. Noted for his famous code of law, Hammurabi was a great diplomat, military strategist, and humanitarian.

HANANIAH (*han uh NIGH uh; "the Lord is gracious"*)— **1.** A common Hebrew name. **2.** The trumpeter at the Jerusalem wall dedication (Ne 12:41). **3.** A Jewish leader who sealed the covenant renewal (Ne 10:23). **4.** A false prophet who opposed Jeremiah (Jer 28:1). **5.** A royal commander under Uzziah (2Ch 26:11). **6.** A God-fearing officer placed in charge of Jerusalem by Nehemiah (Ne 7:2).

HAND—Mentioned more than 1,600 times in the Bible, "hand" is one of the

HANUKKAH

King Antiochus IV, known for his religious intolerance, defiled the Jewish temple by robbing it and erecting a statue of the Roman god Jupiter in the Holy of Holies in 167 B.C.

After a period of pagan worship, a Jewish revolt regained control of the temple. As a means to purify the temple and rededicate its new altar, Judas Maccabeus started the annual festival of Hanukkah ("dedication") in 164 B.C.

Tradition says that Judas found a lamp in the desecrated temple with only enough oil in it to last one day. Miraculously, the lamp stayed lit for eight days of celebration. Following the Roman destruction of the temple in A.D. 70, the tradition was celebrated by individuals in their homes by lighting a lamp on each of eight nights.

Hanukkah is an occasion for the Jewish people to remember and to offer thanksgiving. While attending a Feast of Dedication, Jesus characterized himself as the Son of God, the Messiah (Jn 10:22–38).

most-used words in Scripture. The touch of a hand was thought to communicate authority, power, blessing, and respect (Gen 9:2, 48:13; Mk 6:5; Ac 8:17). The "hand of God" was a common expression that symbolized God's divine action and authority.

HANES (*HAY neez*)—An Egyptian city where representatives from Israel and Egypt met to consider forming an alliance (Isa 30:4).

HANNAH (*HAN uh; "grace"*)—A wife of Elkanah. Ridiculed for being childless, Hannah prayed to God for a child, promising she would give him to God's service. When she bore Samuel, she turned him over to Eli after he was weaned (1Sa 2:1–10).

HANUN (*HAY nuhn; "gracious"*)—1. Son of the Ammonite king Nahash. After he insulted David's messengers, Hanun was defeated by David's army, and his people were forced into slavery (2Sa 10:1–11). 2. A man (or possibly two men) who helped restore Jerusalem's wall (Neh 3:13, 30).

HARA (*HAY ruh; "hill"*)—A city where Israelites of the half-tribe of Manasseh were held captive by the Assyrians (1Ch 5:26).

¹HARAN (*HAY ruhn; "mountainous"*)—Abraham's brother and the father of Lot (Gen 11:27–29).

²HARAN—An important commercial center on the caravan route between Nineveh, northern Syria, and Egypt. Sarah and Abraham lived there (Gen 11:31).

HARLOT—A prostitute. Common on the streets, harlots were also found in the temples of Baal to excite the fertility gods to sexual activity (which ensured productivity of the land). Israel was depicted as a harlot because of its unfaithfulness to God (Eze 16:15–43).

HARMON (*HAHR muhn; "palace"*)—A place of banishment where the "greedy women of Samaria" were taken to be punished, held captive, or killed (Am 4:3).

HAROSHETH (*ha RO sheth; "forest of the Gentiles"*)—A Canaanite town. It was the home of Sisera, commander of the army defeated by Israel (Jdg 4:2, 13, 16).

HARP—A general term for a variety of multiple-stringed musical instruments that were either

HAROD SPRING

Selected as a judge, Gideon was called by God to defeat the nomadic tribe of Midianites, who continually raided and robbed the Israelites throughout Canaan.

Over time, he amassed a large army. In order to test Gideon's faith, God commanded him to reduce its size so that when the Israelites defeated the Midianites they would know it was God's might, not their own, that defeated them.

Gideon sent all but 10,000 of his troops home, but God was still not satisfied. He instructed Gideon to take his men to Harod (HAY rod; "trembling") Spring for a drink. All those who scooped water into their hand and lapped it like a dog were to stay and fight. Those who knelt and drank directly from the spring were to be sent home.

Only 300 men lapped water from their hand (Jdg 7:1–7). The small group of warriors miraculously defeated a larger and far superior army by blowing their trumpets and breaking clay pots, confusing the Midianites and causing them to begin attacking one another (Jdg 7:19–23).

plucked or strummed. Used primarily for worship (Ps 33:2), the harp was rarely used in secular functions (Isa 5:12).

HARROW—To level a field by dragging branches over it to smooth out clods (Hos 10:11).

HART—An adult male deer, possibly of the European red deer prevalent in biblical times. Noted for its strength and agility, it became a symbol for the faithful (SS 2:9).

Ruth surveying the corn harvest

HARVEST—The season of reaping. The Israelites, who depended primarily upon agriculture for their living, celebrated three harvest seasons: barley in April/May (Ruth 1:22); wheat in June/July (Gen 30:14); and vine and tree fruit in September/October. The religious feasts of Passover, Pentecost, and Tabernacles coincided with harvest seasons. In the New Testament, the harvest referred figuratively to the gathering of the redeemed souls (Mt 13:39).

HASIDIM (*HA suh dum*; *"pious or devout"*)—A strict Jewish religious movement. As pagan influence grew and contaminated Jewish worship, the Hasidim were committed to rigid observance of the law and revival of Jewish rituals. The Pharisees and Essenes are believed to have originated from the Hasidim.

HASMONEANS (*haz mo NEE uhns*)—Mattathias, an aged priest, and his five sons who led a successful revolt against the Greeks, forcing pagan religious rituals on the Jews and persecuting those who refused (1Mac; 2Mac).

HATRED, HATE—Aversion or hostility between individuals or groups—or between people and God. To hate God meant to break the covenant (Ex 20:5; Dt 5:9). Conversely,

God hated behavior contrary to the covenant (Dt 16:22). The New Testament challenged believers to love all people, including enemies (Lk 6:27).

HAURAN *(HOW rahn; "caves")*—A city east of the Jordan River. At one point, it formed the northern boundary of Israel (Eze 47:16). Its volcanic soil grew excellent wheat.

¹HAVILAH *(HAV uh lah; "circle")*—1. Son of Cush and grandson of Ham. His descendants became an Arab nation (Gen 10:7). 2. One of the descendants of Joktan (who was a descendant of Shem) (Gen 10:29).

²HAVILAH—A land, abundant with gold and natural resources, through which the Pishon River flowed (Gen 2:11, 12).

HAWK—Several species of these birds of prey are found in Palestine. The most common is the sparrow hawk. The Israelites considered them to be unclean (Lev 11:16).

HAZAEL *(HAY zay el)*—An official of King Benhadad who became king by smothering Benhadad and then committed atrocities against the Israelites (2Ki 8:12).

HAZEROTH *(huh ZEE rahth; "villages")*—A place where the Israelites camped during their wilderness journey. At Hazeroth, Miriam and Aaron questioned Moses' right to be the sole communicator between the people and God (Nu 12:1-2, 33:17-18).

HAZOR *(HAY zor; "court")*—The name of several Middle Eastern cities. The most noted of these was located in upper Galilee on the "Way of the Sea" (a major trade route connecting Egypt with Syria). It was the largest Canaanite city during the second millennium B.C.

HEAD—Biblically, the head was seen as the source of life rather than place of intellect. It indicated a leader of a family (Ex 6:14); a point of origin (Ex 12:2); or a beginning, such as Christ as the beginning of the Church (Eph 5:23).

HEADDRESS—1. A turban (Eze 24:17) or garland worn by a bridegroom (Isa 61:3). 2. A linen cap worn by a priest (Ex 39:28). 3. A general term for any covering for the head (Isa 3:20).

HEALTH, DISEASE, AND HEALING—In the Old Testament, Hebrews considered disease an indication of God's displeasure or punishment (Ex 4:11). In the New Testament, Jesus did not share this belief. He healed the ill, restoring God's intention for life (Lk 4:18).

HEART—The Hebrews regarded the heart as the seat of intelligence, feelings, and will. It was often used to describe the moral nature of humankind (Jer 17:9).

HEAVE OFFERING—Also called a wave offering, this was a portion of sacrifices and offerings that was set apart from the mass and given to Yahweh (Lev 7:30).

HEAVEN—The dwelling place of God and his angels (Dt 26:15; Mk 13:32), and the ultimate destination of believers (1Pe 1:4).

HEAVEN, KINGDOM OF—The sphere of God's reign and power, first announced by John the Baptist (Mt 3:1). Jesus declared that the kingdom was present in his life and ministry and was made known in his casting out of Satan's power (Lk 11:17). Others believed the kingdom was present only in a conditional way and will be completed with the coming of the new heaven and new earth (Mt 5:1–20).

HEBREWS, LETTER TO THE—Written to Jewish Chris-

HEBREW

An ethnic and political designation, the term "Hebrew" refers to the Israelites and their ancestors (Gen 43:32).

Generally believed to be the descendants of Abraham and his family, the Hebrews—God's Chosen People—settled in the land of Canaan after escaping Egypt. Originally, they did not use the word Hebrew to refer to themselves. Instead, the term was used by the Egyptians, Philistines, and other groups to describe the Israelites, who were seen as foreigners (Gen 39:14; 1Sa 4:6, 9).

The Canaanites used the word *'eber* ("opposite side") to identify those people who came from the other side of the Euphrates. Some believe the Hebrew word *'br* ("crossed a boundary") best explains who the Hebrews were. It was used to describe a group of people from the late Bronze Age (1550–1220 B.C.) who became ethnically dissident and disenfranchised. Abraham was believed to be a part of this group (Gen 14:13).

By the time of the kings, the word was replaced by the phrase "people of Israel." In the New Testament, the term refers to Jewish people in Palestine (and of the Diaspora) who were not influenced by Greek culture (Ac 6:1; 2Co 11:22).

tians, this letter by an unknown author claims that Jesus is the fulfillment of the Old Testament and warns them not return to their old Jewish rituals (Heb 6:11–14).

HEBRON *(HEE bruhn; "friendship")*—One of the

oldest and most continuously settled cities south of Jerusalem. Abraham lived there and was buried nearby; David was twice anointed king there (2Sa 2:4, 5:3).

HEGAI *(HEG eye)*—King Ahasuerus' eunuch in charge of the royal harem. He won Esther's trust when she prepared to meet the king (Est 2:3).

HEIR—According to the Law of Moses, the firstborn son inherited the birthright (a double portion of the father's estate), with the remainder divided among other sons. If a man had no sons, his possessions were divided among his daughters (Nu 27:8).

HELAM *(HEE luhm; "fort")*—A place in the Syrian desert east of the Jordan where David defeated King Hadadezer's army (2Sa 10:16).

HELDAI *(HEL dye; "worldly")*—**1.** David's captain who commanded 24,000 men (1Ch 27:15). **2.** A Jewish exile who brought gold and silver for the crown of Joshua when he returned from Babylon (Zec 6:10).

A Flemish painting of Hell

HELL—Not mentioned in the Old Testament, Hell is the home of the damned. A place of continual torment, it is reserved for Satan, his angels, and those who reject God (Rev 20:10–15).

HELLENISTS—Jews who spoke Greek and often adopted Greek ideas and practices (Ac 6:1).

HELMET—A protective battle covering for the head. Ancient helmets were usually made of leather (and sometimes bronze).

HELPER—One who provided aid or relief. The term often referred to God (Ps 30:10, 54:4) or to individuals called to assist others.

HEMAN (HEE mun; "faithful")—1. A Levite and one of King David's musicians. Heman is believed to be the author of Psalm 88 (1Ch 15:17). 2. One of Solomon's sages (1Ki 4:31).

HEMATH (HEE muth; "hot spring")—A fortified town in the territory of the Naphtali tribe. It was known for hot medicinal springs (Jos 19:35).

HEMORRHAGE—In the Old Testament, any contact with blood (which was considered sacred) was prohibited. Those who hemorrhaged were un-

clean; their religious and social life was restricted.

HENADAD (HEN uh dad; "favor of Hadad")—A Levite whose descendants helped rebuild Jerusalem's walls under Zerubbabel and Nehemiah (Ne 3:18).

HEPTATEUCH (HEP ta toohk)—The first seven books of the Bible. Some consider the books of Joshua and Judges so similar that they should be included in the Pentateuch (making it the Heptateuch).

HERALD ("army ruler")—An official who shares a royal proclamation or carries messages between rulers. In the New Testament, the word means "one who proclaims" and often refers to a preacher (1Ti 2:7).

HERBS AND SPICES—Plants used to flavor and prepare food, make incense for medicinal purposes or cosmetics, or prepare bodies for burial.

HERESY (*"take or choose"*)—The different branches of Judaism, such as Pharisees and Sadducees (Ac 5:17). Christianity was considered a sect of Judaism (Ac 24:5). Later, heresy described differing factions within the early Church (1Co 11:19).

HERMENEUTICS (*her meh NEW tiks*)—The science of interpreting the Bible. Scholars use varying criteria to study biblical passages and gain a better understanding of their meaning..

HERMES (*HER meez; "mercury"*)—A messenger for the Greek gods who was widely worshiped as the protector of sheep and cattle (and was believed to control their fertility). Impressed when Paul healed a lame man, people called him Hermes (Ac 14:12–17).

HERMETIC LITERATURE—A collection of religious writings associated with the Greek god Hermes. They discuss creation, human nature, and God. Through repentance, we can escape punishment and enter into God's being. The soul's regeneration purified it from the effects of physical life.

HERMOGENES (*hur MAHJ uh neez; "born of Mercury"*)—An Asian Christian who abandoned Paul and the gospel (2Ti 1:15). The reasons for his desertion are unknown.

HERMON, MT. (*HER muhn; "sacred mountain"*)—The highest mountain in Palestine, believed to be sacred by the Canaanites. Its melting snow is a major source of water for the Jordan River.

HERODIANS—A group of Jews who favored Herod's rule and continually opposed Jesus (Mt 22:16; Mk 3:6).

HERODIAS (*huh RO dee uhs*)—The granddaughter

HEROD THE GREAT

A dynasty of rulers, the Herods governed Palestine from 37 B.C. to A.D. 70. Herod the Great, the most noted of the Herods, ruled over Jews in great splendor. His greatest achievement was his ability to maintain good relations with the Romans while keeping the support of his Jewish subjects.

Herod's political deftness allowed his reign to be, for the most part, peaceful. During his rule, he implemented a massive building program that was beyond any other in Jewish history. He rebuilt the cities of Samaria, Jerusalem, and Jericho. Following the lead of the Hellenistic culture, he constructed many theaters and stadiums and sponsored numerous plays and athletic contests. In 20 B.C., he began his greatest building accomplishment: the reconstruction of the temple in Jerusalem.

But Herod's personal life was quite different from his public accomplishment. He was known to be cruel and fearful of losing his power. This led him to execute three of his sons. He also attempted to slaughter all the Jewish males under the age of two in order to kill Jesus, who, as "king of the Jews," was a threat to his rule.

of Herod the Great. She had John the Baptist killed when he publicly spoke out against her marriage to Herod Antipas, who was her brother-in-law (Mt 14:3–12).

HERODOTUS (*hear RO duh tuhs*)—A Greek historian. His nine-volume history of the Greek relationships with Near Eastern peoples earned him the title of "father of history."

HESHBON *(HESH bahn; "device")*—An important city east of the Dead Sea, continually fought over by the Israelites, Amorites, and Moabites.

HEZEKIAH *(HEZ uh KYE uh; "the Lord is my strength")*—A king of Judah. Known for his piety, he ruled 29 years (2Ki 18:5). Hezekiah brought reform to Judah by destroying all pagan symbols and reopening the temple (2Ch 29:3). He fortified Jerusalem's walls, built towers, and constructed a tunnel assuring good water (2Ki 20:20). His reign weakened when he made political alliances with Babylon, which led to Judah's destruction. At his death, Hezekiah was still honored as a king of great faith.

HIDDEKEL *(HID e kel; "rapid")*—A Hebrew name for the Tigris River (Gen 2:11–14).

HIEL *(HIGH el; "God lives")*—A man who brought God's curse upon himself by rebuilding Jericho (1Ki 16:34). His two sons were killed during the forbidden construction.

HIERAPOLIS *(high ur AHP o lis; "holy city")*—A Roman city. A center for pagan cults, Hierapolis was located near a hot spring believed to have medicinal powers. A Christian church was founded there while Paul was in Ephesus (Col 4:13).

HIGH PLACE—A name for any site where a shrine or temple was built for religious sacrifice, worship, and festivals. These high places gave the inhabitants a feeling of control over the land (Nu 33:52).

HILKIAH *(hil KYE uh; "the Lord is my portion")*—The chief priest under King Josiah. During temple restoration, Hilkiah found an ancient Book of the Law that showed him how corrupt the people had

HIGH PRIEST

The high priest was considered the mediator between God and the Israelites. He performed sacrifices and rituals and acted on behalf of the nation. Also called the chief priest, this lifelong office was passed on to a family member.

High priests were obligated to a higher degree of purity than ordinary priests. The high priest was the only person who had the privilege of entering the Holy of Holies, the sacred inner room of the temple. On the Day of Atonement, he was allowed to enter to sprinkle sacrificial blood on the mercy seat and in front of the ark of the covenant. Then he would place his hand on a goat's head and confess the people's sins. The goat—a "scapegoat"—was led through the people and driven into the wilderness. The people could then stand blameless before God.

After the Exile, the office of high priest gained dignity equal to that of a king. Unfortunately, along with the prestige came ambitious and unscrupulous practices. The office was restored to its former glory following the Maccabean revolt. For Christians, Jesus was the perfect high priest who took on the sins of all people and made a new covenant with God.

become. He cleared the temple of all pagan symbols so purity of worship could be established (2Ki 22:4).

HILL-COUNTRY—Hilly areas not high enough to be called mountains. Biblically, the term refers to the hills in Judea (Lk 1:39).

HILLEL *(HIL el; "he has praised")*—A Rabbinical scholar whose school offered a liberal understanding of Hebrew law. Many of his maxims, which resemble Jesus' teachings, have been preserved.

HIRAM *(HIGH ruhm; "noble")*—A king of Tyre who helped David build his palace and Solomon complete the temple (1Ki 5:2). When Solomon's building program proved too expensive, Solomon sold 20 villages to Hiram (1Ki 5:18).

HIRELING *(HYR ling)*—A person hired for a specific period of time whose wages were paid daily. Unlike slaves, a hireling wasn't part of a master's household.

HITTITES *(HIT ites)*—**1.** A great empire that flourished in Asia Minor from 1800 to 1200 B.C. **2.** The descendants of Heth, son of Canaan. They lived in the hills of Judea near Hebron (Gen 15:20).

HOBAH *(HO buh; "hiding")*—A place north of Damascus where Abraham pursued the four kings who captured Lot (Gen 14:15).

HOLINESS CODE—A series of Old Testament moral instructions regarding sexual conduct, priestly practices, and civil concerns (Lev 17–26). They reflected Israelite concern for ethical and religious purity.

HOLINESS *("separate")*—God's nature as characterized by moral perfection

VALLEY OF HINNOM

A boundary between the territories of Judah and Benjamin, the Valley of Hinnom (HIN ahm; "wailing") was located just outside Jerusalem's Gate of Potsherds (modern Jaffa Gate). It was commonly used to burn rubbish, bodies of criminals, and animals.

The Old Testament identified it as a place where children were cremated as a sacrifice to pagan gods Baal and Molech (2Ki 23:10; 2Ch 28:3; Jer 32:35). King Ahaz participated in these rituals by sacrificing his son, and the prophet Jeremiah implied that child sacrifice was common among the Israelites (Jer 2:23). Because of these rituals, the valley became know as "Slaughter Valley" (Jer 7:32–33, 19:6).

As a consequence for the people's disloyalty and their participation in these horrible sacrifices, God promised a "day of vengeance" when he would allow the enemies of Israel to defeat them (Jer 19:7–9). When Josiah became king, he stopped the pagan practices. Because of its fires and wicked history, the valley was sometimes associated with hell.

(1Sa 2:2). God commanded the Israelites, "You shall be holy; for I the Lord your God am holy" (Lev 19:2). In the New Testament, it was embodied in Jesus, who was called "the holy one of God" (Mk 1:24).

HOLOFERNES *(hahl o FUR neez)*—An Assyrian army general commissioned by King Nebuchadnezzar to conquer the people who failed to worship him. He ultimately failed in his effort and was killed by Judith (Jdt 13:1–10).

213

HOLY OF HOLIES

The ark of the covenant, Israel's most holy object, needed a "most holy place" to be stored in the tabernacle (Ex 25:16). This special room became known as the Holy of Holies.

Only the high priest was allowed to enter the Holy of Holies—on the Day of Atonement. Because God's presence was so awesome, only the most holy of individuals could be in proximity of God's presence. Anyone of lesser spiritual stature would desecrate the Holy of Holies.

The concern to keep the site pure led to interesting practices, such as the high priest wearing golden bells. As long as the bells could be heard ringing, the people knew the priest was performing his ritualistic duties. If the bells stopped ringing, it could mean the priest had become ill or died—and his dead body would defile the Holy of Holies. To guard against such possible corruption, the priest wore a rope around his waist so he could be pulled out in case of tragedy.

HOLY ONE OF ISRAEL—A title given to God in the Book of Isaiah (Isa 1:4, 5:19). In the New Testament, the same title was applied to the Messiah (Mk 1:24; Ac 3:14).

HOLY PLACES—Outer areas of the temple where priests performed routine duties, such as tending lampstands, the table of the Bread of Presence, and the altar of incense.

HOLY SEPULCHRE—A rock-hewn cave belonging to Joseph of Arimathea that became the tomb where Jesus was buried (Mt 27:57–60). Today, the

Church of the Holy Sepulchre stands on the traditional site of Jesus' burial.

HOLY SPIRIT—The third part of the Trinity; a mysterious presence of God. The Holy Spirit calls, empowers, and sustains people to help the Church. It also grants individual gifts (such as speaking with tongues) when necessary to extend the Christian ministry (1Co 12:7; Eph 4:4–7).

HOMOSEXUALITY—Homosexual practices were widespread in the ancient Near East, especially in foreign cults (2Ki 23:7). In the Israelite code of law, homosexual relations were forbidden (Lev 18:22). In the New Testament, Paul condemned the practice as contrary to God's plan for human sexuality (1Co 6:9).

HONEY, HONEYCOMB—A popular biblical food for cooking (Ex 16:31). Honey was believed to have medicinal powers (Pr 16:24).

HOOK—1. A lead ring that was placed in an animal's nose (2Ki 19:28). 2. A small, sickle-shaped knife used by vinedressers (Joel 3:10). 3. An implement used to catch fish (Mt 17:27).

HOPE—Belief that there is a living God who intervenes on behalf of people and can be trusted to fulfill promises. Paul describes hope as one of the three lasting qualities of life (1Co 13:13).

HOPHNI (*HAHF nee; "fighter"*)—A son of the temple priest Eli. Along with his brother Phineas, Hophni violated the law regarding ritual sacrifices at Shiloh. The two priests kept the best parts of the meat sacrifices for themselves (1Sa 2:2). For this, their family was cursed and killed at the battle of Aphek (1Sa 4:11).

HOPHRA (*HAHF ruh; "endures"*)—An Egyptian king who invaded Pales-

tine during King Neb-
uchadnezzar's siege of
Jerusalem but failed to free
the Israelites (Jer 37:5–11).
He was killed fighting
Amasis.

HOR *(HAWR; "hill")*—A
mountain near Edom
where Aaron was buried
(Nu 20:22).

HOREB *(HAWR eb;
"desert")*—The place where
Moses met God in the
burning bush. In that
encounter, God presented
Moses with the terms of
the covenant (Dt 4:10; Ex
19–20).

HORESH *(HO resh;
"wood")*—A place in the
wilderness of Ziph where
David hid from Saul and
formed a covenant with
Jonathan (1Sa 23:15–19).

HORITES, HORIM *(HO rites,
HO rim)*—The ancient
inhabitants of Seir before
Edomite occupation (Gen
14:6). Some believe they
also settled in central
Palestine (Jos 9:6).

HORN—Animal horns—
used as containers or musical instruments—were
symbols of power, victory,
and glory (Dt 33:17). To
"exalt one's horn" meant to
grant victory (1Sa 2:1); to
"cut off one's horn" re-
ferred to defeat (Jer 48:25).

HORNET—God used the
hornet to drive people
from Palestine so the
Israelites could claim it
(Jos 24:12).

HORNS OF THE ALTAR—
Horn-shaped projections
on the corners of ancient
altars. These symbolized
strength and holiness. On
the Day of Atonement,
when priests were conse-
crated, the blood of a
sacrificed animal would be
spread over the horns as a
sin offering (Lev 16:18).

HORSE—In biblical times,
horses were used for transportation, hunting, and
military purposes. They
were associated with pagan
luxury and royal power (Dt
17:16; 1Sa 8:11). The

Israelites were forbidden to have horses, because this showed dependence upon power rather than God. However, they became so common in Jerusalem a special gate was added to the wall (2Ch 23:15; Jer 31:40).

HOSEA (ho ZAY uh; "the Lord has saved")—An Israelite prophet whom God told to marry Gomer, a prostitute. In spite of Gomer's unfaithfulness, Hosea remained loyal to her even after she left him. Hosea's faithfulness symbolized God's faithfulness for the wayward Israelites.

HOSEA, BOOK OF—An Old Testament book containing the message of the prophet Hosea. He spoke against Israel's religious unfaithfulness and personal corruption. The book is a call to return to God and enjoy God's blessings.

HOSHEA (ho SHE uh; "may the Lord save")—1. The original name of Joshua,

later changed by Moses (Nu 13:8). 2. The "puppet king" who served as the Assyrian's leader over Israel (2Ki 17:1–6). 3. Azaziah's son, prince of Ephraim (1Ch 27:20). 4. One of Nehemiah's chief rulers (Ne 10:23).

HOST OF HEAVEN—An Old Testament name for celestial bodies. The term was used to describe the vastness of creation over which God has power (Isa 34:4, 45:12; Jer 33:22).

HOUR—1. A division of time. The Israelite day was measured from sunset to sunset. Roman days were divided from midnight to midnight. 2. A term that indicated an important or opportune moment (Mt 25:13).

HOUSE—Old Testament housing included private dwellings (Dt 6:7), palaces (Jer 39:8), temples (1Ki 8:13), and animal shelters (Ps 104:17). In the New Testament, homes served as the first churches (Ac 1:13, 2:2).

HULDAH (*HULH duh; "weasel"*)—A female prophet. She predicted disaster for the Jews because they abandoned God. However, they would not be punished until after Josiah's reign—because he obeyed God (2Ch 34:8–33).

HUMILITY—The ability to be free from pride and, therefore, in favor with God (2Ch 7:14). Jesus said that humility is the cornerstone of Christian character (Mt 5:3).

HUNTING—Popular among the Egyptians and Mesopotamians as sport and for food. The Israelites seldom hunted, except for food or protection from wild animals. New Testament references to hunting are mostly metaphorical (Lk 11:54, 21:34).

HUR—The name of numerous Old Testament people.

Most noted is a man who helped keep Moses' arms raised, insuring victory over the Amalekites (Ex 17:8–13).

HURAM (*HYOO ruhm; "my brother is exalted"*)—**1.** Another name for Hiram. **2.** A metal worker from Tyre. Solomon hired him to do ornamental work on the temple (1Ki 7:13–14).

HURRIANS (*HYOO ree enz*)—A term either identical to or confused with Horites (Gen 34:2; Jos 9:7). They lived as far north as Gibeon and Shechem until the conquest of Joshua.

HUSBANDMAN (*"tiller of the ground"*)—An ancient term for a farmer, including those who owned their own land and tenants.

HUSHIM (*HYOO shim; "those who hasten"*)—**1.** A male and female name. **2.** Son of Dan, or his descendants (Gen 46:23). **3.** The wife of Shaharaim, a

Benjaminite, and mother of Abitub and Elpaal (1Ch 8:8, 11).

HUZZAB *(HUHZ ab; "fixed")*—An obscure Hebrew word. Some believe it is a personal name; others translate it as "mistress" and believe it refers to the palace of Nineveh (Na 2:7).

HYKSOS *(HIK sos; "rulers of foreign lands")*—A Semitic aristocracy who gained control of Egypt. They ruled during the Fifteenth and Sixteenth Dynasties (c. 1700–1500 B.C.).

HYMENAEUS *(HY muh NEE uhs)*—A Christian teacher whom Paul excommunicated for false teaching on the resurrection. Hymenaeus believed it was only spiritual, rather than a literal bodily resurrection. (1Ti 1:19).

HYMN—A religious song expressing praise, joy, and thanksgiving to God. Hymns were sometimes called psalms or spiritual songs (Eph 5:19). Scripture passages lead to the belief that hymn singing was customary in the early Church (Ac 16:25; Eph 5:19).

HYPOCRITE—One who performs religious ritual and belief only for show. Jesus described the scribes and Pharisees—who followed the law to the letter but were blind to living its intention—as hypocrites (Mt 6:2, 5, 16, 7:5, 15:7; Lk 10:15).

HYSSOP *(HISS up)*—Biblical hyssop was probably the plant we know as marjoram, because common hyssop did not grow in Palestine. It was used as a brush and its oil as a purifying agent in religious rituals (Ex 12:22; Ps 51:7; Heb 9:19).

IBLEAM (*IB lee uhm;
"destroying"*)—A town of
Manasseh's tribe where
Ahaziah (king of Judah)
and Zechariah (king of
Israel) were killed (Jos
17:11; 2Ki 9:29, 15:10).

IBZAN (*IB zan; "famous"*)—
A minor judge whose
home was Bethlehem. He
governed Israel for seven
years following the rule of
Jephthah (Jdg 12:8–9).

ICHABOD (*IK uh bahd;
"where is glory"*)—A name
given to the son of Phinehas, grandson of Eli, when
he heard the Philistines
had captured the ark of the
covenant (1Sa 4:22).

ICONIUM (*eye KO nee uhm;
"image"*)—The capital of
Lycaonia, rebuilt after the
Flood. According to leg-
end, Prometheus made
new people from the mud,
giving new life to those
drowned. Paul and Bar-
nabas visited Iconium
during the first and second
missionary journeys (Ac
13:51–14:6).

Worship of the golden calf

IDOL—Any material figure
that is believed to be an
image of a god and has
become an object of wor-
ship. *See **IDOLATRY; GRAVEN
IMAGES.***

IDOLATRY—Worship of any
god other than Yahweh
through rituals, including

I AM

According to tradition, God becomes known by sharing his name. God's presence was revealed to Moses in the burning bush, where he commanded Moses to speak to the pharaoh and demand that he let the people out of slavery.

Moses asked what he should say so that the pharaoh would know that he spoke on behalf of God. God told him to say to the pharaoh, "The one who is called I AM has sent me to you" (Ex 3:14). This assured Moses that he was speaking to the one true God, whose continuing power and presence would fulfill his promise. "I AM" is related to the Hebrew verb "to be" (*YHWH*, pronounced *YAH way*).

Yahweh—the name of God—was considered by the Jews to be too sacred to pronounce, so they substituted the name Adonai in public readings. In the New Testament, Jesus used the term "I AM" to describe himself. In passages such as John 8:58, Jesus explicitly compared himself with the Old Testament name of God. In John's gospel, the phrase "I AM" appears 24 times.

human and animal sacrifice and prostitution. Idolatry was called "spiritual adultery" (Hos 1:2). In the New Testament, the term refers to anything that leads one away from absolute loyalty to God, such as covetousness, sexual sin, and greed (Eph 5:5; Php 3:19; Col 3:5).

IDUMAEA (*id yu MEE uh; "red"*)—A land south of Judea where the Edomites sought refuge after an Arab tribe took over their homeland.

221

IGAL (*EYE gahl; "redeemed"*)— 1. A spy sent by Moses to scout Canaan (Nu 13:7). 2. One of David's strong soldiers (2Sa 23:36). 3. Son of prophet Shemaiah (1Ch 3:22).

IGNORANCE—Moral, rather than intellectual, deficiency concerning religion. It describes individuals who have no sense of God's presence (Ac 17:23, 30). God often excuses sin resulting from ignorance (1Ti 1:13).

ILLYRICUM (*ih LEAR ih kuhm; "joy"*)—A province of Rome along the east coast of the Adriatic Sea. Paul said that he preached there (Ro 15:19).

IMAGE—A physical representation of a god in human or animal form. The use of such images was strictly forbidden (Ex 20:4).

IMAGE OF GOD—Humankind is said to be made in God's image (Gen 1:26–27). Since God is spirit, it is unlikely that this means we are physically like God. Rather, our substance, moral nature, and spiritual qualities have the likeness of God.

IMMANUEL (*ih MAN yu el; "God is with us"*)—An Old Testament name for the predicted Messiah (Christ). Isaiah foretold of a child who would be born to a virgin and would bring salvation to the Israelites. He would be a sign of God's presence (Isa 7:14).

¹IMMER (*IM ur; "lamb"*)—A priestly leader during the reign of David (1Ch 24:14). His descendants rebuilt the Jerusalem wall (Ne 3:29).

²IMMER—A Babylonian city where Jewish exiles were held captive (Ezr 2:59).

IMMORALITY—Sexual practices contrary to biblical teachings. Paul characterized immorality as "works of the flesh" (Gal 5:19).

INCARNATION

The doctrine of incarnation ("taking on flesh") is a cornerstone belief of the Christian faith. Believers accept that Jesus Christ, God's eternal son, became human and lived among us (Jn 1:14; Ro 8:3). This selfless act bridged the gap between the human and the divine.

Jesus became a part of the created world and joined the ranks of all mortals, whose lives last for a period of time and then end. Christians believe that Jesus experienced all aspects of humanness, including joy, laughter, pain, suffering, temptation, and death. By becoming human, however, Jesus did not diminish his divinity; he took on complete personhood.

While his life was one of sinless perfection, he experienced and understood the intense temptations that come to us. Through his agonizing death, he became the sacrifice necessary for our sins to be forgiven and our relationship with God renewed.

INCENSE—A mixture of aromatic gums and spices burned during religious ceremonies. The fragrant smoke symbolized ascending prayers (Ps 141:2).

INCEST—Sexual intimacy between blood relatives. Forbidden by Hebrew law, it was punishable by death (Lev 18:6–18, 20:11–12).

Sex between relatives by marriage was also taboo—punishable by sterilization of both parties (Lev 20:19–21).

INCREASE—The multiplication of animals and plants by natural reproduction under God's control (Ps 67:6). In the New Testament, the word refers to the numerical and spiritual growth of early Christians (2Co 10:15).

INDIA—A country along the eastern boundary of the territory of Ahasuerus (Est 1:1, 8, 9). Israelites had limited trade and contact with India (Eze 27:15–36).

INHERITANCE—The passing of property from a father to his sons. The firstborn son received double the share of the others (Dt 21:15–17). If there were no sons, the property was divided among the daughters. *See* **BIRTHRIGHT.**

INK—A mixture of lamp-soot, gum, and water that was used with a pen or brush to write. Because it could be blotted, ink became a symbol for that which never lasts (Ex 32:33; Nu 5:23; 2Co 3:3).

INN—A resting place for travelers. The term often referred to a place where hospitality was offered, rather than a building that provided lodging (Ex 2:20; Jdg 19:15–21).

INNER MAN—A term that Paul used to make a distinction between a person's outward appearance and what exists within his or her heart (Eph 3:16). Renewed daily, the inner person seeks loyalty to God (2Co 4:16; Ro 7:22).

INNOCENTS, MASSACRE OF THE—When the wise men did not return and tell Herod where to find the baby Jesus, he ordered the murder of all males in Bethlehem under the age of two (Mt 2:16–18).

INSPIRATION—God's use of the Holy Spirit to motivate people to speak or write about God's message (1Co 2:13).

INTERPRETATION, BIBLICAL—A study of Bible text to determine its meaning—both at the time of writing and at the present time. *See* **HERMENEUTICS.**

IRA (*"watchful"*)—1. David's personal priest (2Sa 20:26). 2. The name of two of David's mighty soldiers (2Sa 23:26, 38).

IRAN—A southwest Asian country where Aramaic is still spoken as it was in Jesus' day.

IRON—A strong, malleable metal used to make tools, farming implements, weapons, armor, and vessels. Israelites used it widely after the decline of the Philistines, who had controlled knowledge of the smelting process.

Ancient iron hoe

IRON AGE—A period of human history (c. 1200–300 B.C., following the Stone Age and Bronze Age) when weapons and tools were made of iron.

IRRIGATION—The watering of crops and plants through artificial means. Elaborate irrigation systems existed as early as 3000 B.C. While there is no word in the Bible for irrigation, its use is implied (Ecc 2:5; Isa 58:11).

ISAAC (*"laughter"*)—The promised son of Abraham and Sarah. When his birth was foretold, both laughed because Sarah was well beyond childbearing age (Gen 18:12). His importance in Hebrew tradition was reflected in the popular phrase, "God of Abraham, God of Isaac, God of Jacob" (Ex 3:6).

ISAIAH, BOOK OF—An Old Testament book of prophetic writings that urge Israel's faithfulness to and dependence upon God alone. Those who turn from God are warned of judgment. The writer offers hope and comfort to the

225

ISAIAH

A great prophet of Judah, Isaiah ("the Lord is salvation") was a poet and statesman. He was also a lifelong resident of Jerusalem (c. 760–690 B.C.).

At 25, he had a vision in which God asked for someone to speak. "Here am I, send me," he answered (Isa 6:8). His 50-year ministry in Israel—spanning the reign of four kings—confronted evil, predicted the future, and interpreted God's will.

Isaiah urged the people to rely on God, not themselves. He cautioned against idolatry (Isa 44:10–11, 57:13) and challenged the rich for gaining wealth at the expense of poor. He warned against believing that security was achieved through military connections instead of God. He also foretold of the birth of a Messiah (Isa 53).

Isaiah's words, recorded in the poetic Old Testament book that bears his name, are similar to Jesus' social justice teachings. Ancient copies of his writings were among the Dead Sea Scrolls found by Bedouin children in 1947.

exiled Jews through the vision of a promised Messiah.

ISCARIOT—Likely a town in Judea, associated with Judas (who betrayed Jesus).

ISHBOSHETH/ISH-BOSHETH *(ish BO sheth/ish BAHSH eth; "man of shame")*—1. The youngest son of King Saul. Also called Ishbaal ("man of Baal"), he was a weak and ineffective ruler and was killed in his sleep. Following his death, David (who was king of Judah at the time) became ruler over all of Israel (2Sa 4:1–12).

ISHI (*ish EYE; "my husband"*)—**1.** An Israelite name for God of the covenant (Hos 2:16). **2.** Descendants of Jerameel (1Ch 2:31), Judah (1Ch 4:20), and the Simeonites (1Ch 4:42).

ISHMAEL (*ISH may uhl; "may God hear"*)—The son of Abraham and Hagar (Gen 25:12; 1Ch 1:28). When Ishmael and Hagar were cast out into the desert by Abraham, God guided them to a well and promised that Ishmael would be the father of a great nation. His descendants are considered to be the ancestors of today's Arab nations.

ISHMAELITES—Ishmael's descendants in Arabia (Gen 25:12–18, 37:28). Joseph's brothers sold him to the Ishmaelites (Gen 37:25–28, 39:1).

ISLAND, ISLE—**1.** Inhabitable land in the midst of water, perhaps the Mediterranean Sea (Isa 20:6, 42:15). **2.** The farthest places on Earth (Isa 41:5).

ISRAEL, KINGDOM OF—Ten northern tribes that separated from Judah at Solomon's death and followed Jeroboam. The kingdom lost half its population and two-thirds of its land because its people failed to follow God's covenant (2Ch 11:13–14).

ISSACHAR (*IHZ uh kahr; "hired worker"*)—The ninth son of Jacob and ancestor to one of the Twelve Tribes of Israel. His tribe settled along major trade routes (Gen 46:13; 1Ch 7:1–5; Dt 33:18–19) and submitted to forced labor to gain wealth (Gen 49:14–15).

ITALIAN COHORT—A Roman military unit at Caesarea when Peter preached. The centurion Cornelius was a captain (Ac 10:1).

ITALY—A country in south-central Europe. Paul visited there and passed on greetings from "those who

ISRAEL

After Jacob (Abraham's grandson) wrestled with an angel of God, his name was changed to Israel, which means "one who strives with God" (Gen 32:28). The name grew to refer to Jacob's descendants (the Twelve Tribes), who became known as the "whole people of God" or Hebrew nation (Ex 32:4; Dt 4:1).

During the wilderness wanderings, the name encompassed all of the tribes, with no distinction between them. The nation was ruled by judges until the desire for a king was answered with Saul.

David ruled all Israel, but rifts gradually developed between the tribes. After Solomon's death, ten northern tribes revolted (1Sa 11:8). Two tribes, Judah and Benjamin, remained loyal to the House of David while the northern ten tribes kept the name Israel and followed Jeroboam as king.

Religiously and morally weak, Israel was abandoned by the prophets, overthrown, and taken captive into Assyria about 722 B.C. (2Ki 17:7–8, 15, 17; Hos 2:13). The southern half of the kingdom was conquered by Babylon in 586 B.C.

come from Italy" (Ac 27:1–6).

ITHAMAR (*ITH uh mahr;* "*place of palms*")—Aaron's youngest son, a priest who calculated the cost of building the Jewish temple (Ex 6:23, 28:1).

IVORY—The Israelites imported ivory tusks (Eze 27:15; Rev 18:12), and ivory was a symbol of wealth (Ps 45:8; 1Ki 22:38). Amos said such luxury ignored people's needs (Am 6:4).

JAAR *(JAY ur; "forest")*—A place where the sacred ark of the covenant is said to have been discovered (Ps 132:6).

JAAZANIAH *(jay AZ uh NYE uh; "Yahweh hears")*—**1.** A common name in early Palestine. **2.** A military captain in Judah who assisted the governor after the fall of Jerusalem (2Ki 25:23).

JABAL *(JAY buhl; "stream")*—The eldest son of Lemach and Adah. He was the ancestral father of the first nomadic herdsmen (Gen 4:20).

JABBOK *(JAHB ahk; "blue river")*—A tributary of the Jordan River. Jacob and his family crossed it the night

God spoke to him (Gen 32:22).

JABESH, JABESH-GILEAD *(jay besh GIL ee uhd)*—A city in Gilead that Saul's army protected from the Ammonites (Jdg 21). When Saul was beheaded and hung on the city wall of Beth-Shan (1Sa 31:8–10), the men of Jabesh-Gilead retrieved and buried him, earning David's praise.

¹JABEZ *(JAY bez)*—The ancestor of a Judahite family (1Ch 4:9).

²JABEZ—A town near Bethlehem, home of several scribes (1Ch 2:55).

JABIN *(JAY bin; "intelligent")*—**1.** A Canaanite king of Hazor killed by Joshua (Jos 11:1–15). **2.** A king of Canaan. He suppressed the Israelites, who—under Deborah and Barak—defeated him (Jdg 4:2–24).

JACHIN AND BOAZ *(JAY kin and BO az; "he will establish" and "in it is strength")*—

229

Twin bronze pillars of Solomon's Temple (1Ki 7:15–22; 2Ch 3:15–17). After the temple's destruction, their metal was taken to Babylon.

JACKAL—A reddish-grey animal similar to the wolf and fox. The jackal ate only carrion and communicated by long howls (Is 13: 21–22; Jer 50:39). It was used as an image of desolation (Job 30:29).

JACKAL'S WELL—A well or spring in the Hinnom Valley between the Valley Gate and the Dung Gate (Ne 2:13).

Jesus at Jacob's Well

JACOB'S WELL—A deep well near Shechem where Jesus met the Samaritan woman (Jn 4:6, 12).

JAEL (*JAY el; "mountain goat"*)—A Kenite woman who killed Sisera, the Canaanite commander, by driving a tent peg through his head while he slept (Jdg 4:17–22).

JAHAZ (*JAY haz; "trodden or open place"*)—An unknown Transjordan city where the Israelites defeated the Amorites (Nu 21:23–24). It belonged to the tribe of Reuben after the Conquest of Canaan (Jos 13:18).

JAHZEIAH (*JAH zee yuh; "may God see"*)—Son of Tikvah. When Ezra ordered the Israelites to divorce their foreign wives, Jahzeiah resisted (Ezr 10:15).

JAIR (*JAIR; "may God shine/enlighten"*)—1. A descendant of Manasseh (Nu 32:41). 2. A Gileadite judge for 22 years (Jdg 10:3–5). His 30 sons controlled Havroth-Jair.

JACOB

The son of Isaac and Rebekah, Jacob ("supplanter" or "grabber") was born holding the heel of his twin brother Esau (Gen 25:22). God blessed him; his mother favored him. These reasons—plus his greedy nature—led Jacob to cheat Esau out of his birthright and Isaac's blessing.

Fleeing to escape his brother's wrath, he dreamed that God stretched a ladder from Earth to heaven. This was a sign reassuring God's promise to Abraham (Jacob's grandfather) that great nations would come from him. Jacob's uncle Leban promised him Rachel, but tricked him into marrying Leah. He finally married both, although he loved only Rachel, with whom he had Joseph.

Escaping from Leban, Jacob had another dream, in which he wrestled with an angel of God. The experience left him with a broken hip and a new name: "Israel" (Gen 32:28).

Isaac welcomed him when he finally returned home. Esau forgave him, living across the Jordan in Seir while Jacob stayed in Canaan before moving many times. The Twelve Tribes of Israel came from his 12 sons, fulfilling the covenant God had made with Abraham.

JAIRUS (*JAYR uhs; "may God establish"*)—A ruler of the Capernaum synagogue. Jesus raised his daughter from the dead (Mt 9:18–26; Lk 8:41–56).

JAMES, LETTER OF—A New Testament epistle written by James, the brother of Jesus, to Jewish Christians approximately 25 years after Jesus' resurrection. He

JAMES

There are two major characters named James in the Bible. The first was called by Jesus to be a disciple. He left his father Zebedee and the family fishing business to do so (Mt 4:21). His brother John and their partner Peter joined him.

James remained among the three men closest to Jesus during his ministry. He witnessed all of the major events, including Jesus' death and resurrection. Jesus nicknamed James and his brother "sons of thunder" because of their tempers and hasty judgments.

James questioned Jesus about who would be first in the kingdom, hoping to earn that honor. In a way he did, for James was the Church's first martyr—killed by Herod Agrippa I, 15 years after Jesus' death (Mt 10:2, 17:1–13; Lk 5:1–10; Ac 1:13, 12:2).

The other James, "James the Just," was the brother of Jesus. He found his faith in Christ after the resurrection. He became the primary leader of the Jerusalem Christians. James was known for wisdom and integrity, which were favorite topics of the Book of James, which he wrote. The Apostle Paul often consulted him.

Under James' leadership, the Church council debated and decided not to require Gentile Christians to adhere to the Jewish laws of circumcision (Acts 15). James was stoned to death, according to the historian Josephus, in A.D. 62.

cautioned against faith without action and urged patience.

232

JANNAEUS, ALEXANDER
(JAHN nay uhs, al ex AN duhr; "Jonathan")—An

unpopular pro-Sadducee king of Judea (103–76 B.C.) whose goal was to expand his borders. His wife, Salome Alexandra, succeeded him and reversed his policies, choosing to side with the Pharisees.

JANNES AND JAMBRES *(JAN ez, JAM breez)*—Two legendary Egyptian sorcerers who challenged Moses' efforts to make Pharaoh free Israel by duplicating his miracles. Paul cited them as examples of troublemakers (Ex 7–8; 2Ti 3:1–9).

JAPHETH *(JAY feth; "may God enlarge")*—The second of Noah's three sons (Gen 9:23–27, 7:13); the ancestor of the people in northern Israel, including the Anatolians.

JAREB *(JAY reb)*—**1.** An Assyrian king from whom Ephraim sought help (Hos 5:13). **2.** An honorary title for king.

JARMUTH *(JAHR muhth; "height")*—A city in Judah that opposed Joshua's invasion (Jos 15:35, 12:11). Returning from Exile, the Israelites repopulated it (Neh 11:29). Pottery and bronzes from the Iron Age (c. 1200–300 B.C.) have been found there.

JASHAR, BOOK OF *(JAY shur; "one who is honest, righteous, upright")*—An ancient Hebrew collection of secular and religious songs and poetry describing heroic acts of Israel's leaders (Jos 10:13).

JASHOBEAM *(juh SHOH bee uhm; "let the people return to God")*—The chief of David's mighty warriors (1Ch 11:11). He was a Hachmonite.

JASON *(JAY suhn; "healing")*—**1.** A common Jewish name sometimes substituted for Jesus and Joshua. **2.** A Cyrene historian who wrote a five-volume book (since lost) about the Maccabean revolt. The Second Book of Maccabees was based on

233

JAWBONE

The rebellious Samson, a Nazirite, killed 30 Philistines after being cheated in a wager. Later, when his Philistine wife and her family were killed, he burned the Philistines' fields.

He was hunted and captured, but the Spirit of the Lord came over him and he was able to break his ropes and grab the jawbone of an ass (Jdg 14:14). With this crude weapon, Samson killed 1,000 men (Jdg 15–16). The battle site was named Ramath-lehi (*"hill of the jawbone"*).

In the Bible, a jawbone was a symbol of the restraining of one's enemy (Isa 30:28). God freed his people by easing the yoke on their jaws (Hos 11:4). Jawbone was sometimes translated as "cheek" (Job 41:2; Eze 29:4, 38:4).

his work. **3.** A man whom Judas sent to make a treaty with Rome (1Mac 8:17). **4.** A Jewish Christian who helped Paul and Silas at Thessalonica (Ac 17:5–9).

JASPER *(JAS pur)*—A precious stone in many colors (Ex 28:20, 39:13) that decorates God's throne and heaven's walls (Rev 4:3, 21:18–19).

JATTIR *(JAT ur; "surpassing")*—A Levitical city in the hillside of Judah southwest of Hebron (Jos 15:48; 1Ch 6:57). David sent a portion of the treasure he seized from the Amalekites to Jattir (1Sa 30:27).

JAVAN *(JAY vuhn)*—**1.** Son of Japheth (Gen 10:2). **2.** A nation of slave and bronze traders, perhaps the Greeks (Eze 27:13), to which Judah and Jerusalem were sold (Joel 3:6).

JAZER *(JAY zur; "God helps")*—An Ammonite city conquered by the Israelites during Moses' time and assigned to the tribe of Gad (Nu 21:32). David recruited its skilled warriors; Judas Maccabeus captured it (1Mac 5:8).

JEALOUSY—In the Bible, jealousy was shown as both a positive and negative emotion. God was described as a jealous (concerned) God who forbade idolatry (Ex 20:5; 1Co 10:22). However, human jealousy was a sin that led to tragedy. Because of their jealousy, Joseph's brothers sold him into slavery (Gen 37:11; 1Co 3:3; Gal 5:20).

JEBUS *(JEE buhs)*—A Canaanite town that David seized for his capital and renamed Jerusalem (Jos 18:28).

JEBUSITES *(JEB yu sites)*—Non-Jewish residents of Jerusalem who resisted Joshua's attack (Jos 15:63). Descendants of Canaan, they chose to remain while David was in power (2Sa 24:16–25). During Solomon's reign, the Jebusites were drafted into royal servitude (1Ki 9:20–21).

JEDAIAH *(jeh DAY yuh; "Yahweh had favored")*—**1.** Son of Shimir. He was a clan leader in the tribe of Simeon (1Ch 4:37). **2.** A Levitical chief who returned to Jerusalem with Zerubbabel (Ne 12:6, 7). **3.** An exile who brought gold and silver for the temple and high priest's crown (Zec 6:10, 14).

JEDUTHUN (*jeh DYOO thuhn*; *"praiseworthy"*)—**1.** The chief musician in David's tabernacle and Solomon's Temple (1Ch 16:41–42, 25:6). He and his sons served as seers or prophets (1Ch 25:1; 2Ch 35:15). **2.** Father of Obed-Edom (1Ch 16:38).

JEHIEL (*jeh HYE uhl*; *"may God give life"*)—**1.** A Levite harpist who was present at the installation of the ark in Jerusalem and throughout David's reign (1Ch 15:18, 20). **2.** A tutor for David's sons (1Ch 27:32).

JEHOAHAZ (*juh HOH uh haz*; *"Yahweh has grasped"*)—**1.** The 11th king of Israel (814–800 B.C.); the son and successor of Jehu (2Ki 10:35). Jehoahaz repeatedly disobeyed covenant law, angering God (13:2, 6). He later repented and was rescued. **2.** An alternate name of Ahaziah, king of Judah (2Ch 21:17).

JEHOHANAN (*jeh hoh HAY nuhn*; *"Yahweh is gracious"*)—**1.** A common Jewish name. **2.** A Levite who served as gatekeeper in the temple (1Ch 26:3). **2.** Ishmael's father, a commander in Jehosaphat's army. **3.** The priest who officiated at the dedication of the walls of Jerusalem.

JEHOIACHIN (*je HOY uh chin*; *"Yahweh establishes"*)—The 19th king of Judah (597 B.C.). At eight years old, he succeeded his father, Jehoiakim (2Ki 24:8). Jehoiachin reigned three months before being sent, with his entire entourage, to Babylon. Treated well, he was freed 37 years later (2Ki 25: 27–30).

JEHOIADA (*jeh HOY ah duh*; *"Yahweh knows"*)—**1.** A chief priest who organized a rebellion against the wicked Queen Athaliah and put Joash on the throne (1Ch 12:27; 2Ch 23). He died at 130 and

JEHOSHAPHAT

The fourth king of Judah (872–848 B.C.), Jehoshaphat saw his father (King Asa) die as a result of following false prophets instead of God. Because of this experience, when Jehoshaphat ascended to the throne he became one of the few God-fearing kings of Israel and Judah. He restored worship of God, destroyed false idols, and set the Law of Moses as the standard (2Ch 19:9).

When three armies joined to attack Judah, he gathered the entire nation to prayer instead of battle (2Ch 20:12). On the day of battle, Jehoshaphat's army discovered the invaders had killed one another. They returned singing praise to God.

His 25-year reign was noted for its consistent efforts to make peace with the northern kingdom (1Ki 22:44), sending priests into Judah to teach the people the "law of the Lord" (2Ch 17:7–9). His son Jehoram, who succeeded him by killing his brothers, reversed his father's faithful ways.

was buried in a royal tomb for his service to Judah and Yahweh (24:15–16). **2.** The father of Benaiah (who served as David's military official) (2Sa 8:18).

JEHOIAKIM (jeh HOY ah kim; "Yahweh will lift up")— A king of Judah (609–598 B.C.); the second son of

Josiah. Jehoiakim murdered the prophet Uriah, who opposed his religious abuses, such as scroll burning (2Ch 36:8; Jer 36:1–32). His 8-year-old son Jehoiachin succeeded him.

JEHORAM (juh HOR uhm; "Yahweh is exalted")—**1.** A

king of Israel (852–841 B.C.); son of Ahab and Jezebel. Although he moved away from pagan worship, he showed faithlessness (2Ki 1:17; 1Ch 3:1). **2.** A king of Judah (849–841 B.C.); son of Jehoshaphat. During his rule, he followed pagan practices, killed his brothers, and rejected his father's faithful ways (2Ch 21:2–4). His widow, Athaliah (daughter of Ahab and Jezebel), killed all of his descendants except a grandson (Joash) who escaped (2Ki 8:16).

JEHOSHABEATH, JEHOSHEBA (*juh HAHSH uh buth; ji HAHSH i buh; "Yahweh is fullness"*)—The daughter of King Jehoram of Judah. She rescued Ahaziah's son Jehoida from the queen mother Athaliah's attempt to murder the royal family (2Ch 22:11; 2Ki 11:2).

JEHOSHAPHAT, VALLEY OF— A place where God will judge pagan nations (Joel 3:2, 12). Also called the "valley of decision" (Joel 3:14), it may be located in the Kidron Valley or it may be merely symbolic.

JEHOVAH (*jeh HO vuh; "to be"*)—God's name, created from consonants of Yahweh (YHWH). Considered too sacred to be spoken, the Hebrews substituted the term Adonai instead (Ex 6:3, 17:15; Isa 12:2). *See* **ADONAI; YAHWEH.**

JEHOVAH-JIREH (*jeh HO vuh JYE re; "the Lord will provide"*)—The site, named by Abraham, where Yahweh provided him with a ram to be sacrificed instead of his son (Gen 22:14). Its location is uncertain.

JEHOZABAD (*jeh HAHZ uh bad; "Yahweh has given"*)— **1.** The servant of King Joash of Judah. He was an accomplice in the king's assassination (2Ki 12:21). Later, he was killed by Joash's son and successor, Amaziah (2Ki 14:5). **2.** A Benjamite commander during Jehoshaphat's reign (2Ch 17:18).

JEHU (*JEE hoo; "he is Yahweh"*)—**1.** A military leader and son of Jehoshaphat. He defeated the wicked Ahab and ruled as king of the northern kingdom (841–752 B.C.), almost ridding the land of pagan worship (2Ki 9, 10). The prophet Hosea condemned his bloody revolution. **2.** A prophet and son of Hanani. He announced the Lord's judgment against King Baasha of Israel (1Ki 16:1, 7, 12). Jehu also warned Jehoshaphat of the Lord's anger at him for joining King Ahab against the Syrians (2Ch 19:2).

JEHUDI (*jeh HOO dye*)—A royal official sent by King Jehoiakim to bring Baruch to read Jeremiah's prophecies (Jer 36:14). Angered by its contents, the king burned the scroll.

JEPHTHAH (*JEF thuh; "Yahweh will set free"*)—A judge in Israel; the illegitimate son of Gilead (Jdg 10:6–12:7). Keeping a rash promise, he sacrificed his daughter. It became an annual custom for Israelite maidens to mourn her death for four days (Jdg 11:40).

JERAHMEEL (*juh RAH mee el; "may God have mercy"*)—**1.** The firstborn son of Hezron. A descendant of Judah through Tamar (1Ch 2:9), he was the head of the Jerahmeelites. Located on Judah's southern frontier, their land was raided by David (1Sa 27:10). **2.** A member of King Jehoiakim's court (Jer 36:26).

JEREMIAH (*JAIR uh MYE uh; "Yahweh lifts up"*)—A major Old Testament prophet. His ministry covered the last five kings of Judah. Jeremiah was often in danger because of his criticisms and warnings (Jer 15:10–21). During the Exile, he fled to Egypt.

JEREMIAH, BOOK OF—An Old Testament book

containing well-documented stories of the prophet Jeremiah's 40-year ministry. Dictated to his secretary Baruch (Jer 36), the book focused on God's covenant relationship to the people of Judah.

JERICHO (*"city of palms"*) — One of the world's oldest cities, Jericho was an oasis in the Jordan Valley (Dt 34:3). It was strategically located along major trade routes. Joshua captured the city; Jesus healed a blind man (Mt 20:29–34), met Zacchaeus (Lk 19:1–10), and set his parable of the Good Samaritan there (Lk 10:30).

JEROBOAM (*JAIR uh BOH uhm; "may the people multiply"*) — **1.** Jeroboam I, king of the northern kingdom (922–901 B.C.). When Solomon attempted to kill him, Jeroboam escaped to Egypt (1Ki 12:1–2, 24). Returning, he was proclaimed king over the ten northern tribes. His refusal to repent after tampering with the calendar brought down his house (1Ki 15:29). **2.** Jeroboam II, 13th king of Israel (786–746 B.C.). He was a vigorous ruler who extended the reaches of the kingdom but tolerated idolatry (2Ki 14:23–29).

JERUBBAAL (*jeh ROO BAY ul; "let Baal contend against him"*) — The name given to Gideon when he destroyed his father's altar to Baal (Jdg 6:32).

JERUEL (*jeh ROO el*) — A wilderness area of the Jordan, where King Jehoshaphat defeated the Ammonites and Moabites (2Ch 20:16).

JESHIMON (*jeh SHIGH mahn; "wilderness" or "desert"*) — **1.** A range of mountains in eastern Judea, reaching to the northwest shore of the Dead Sea. It was home to many fugitives. **2.** A salty desert region below Mt. Pisgah (Nu 21:20).

JERUSALEM

The "city of peace," Jerusalem lies along a mountain range in Palestine—east of the Mediterranean Sea and west of the Dead Sea.

It is considered a holy place to Jews because it is was the "city of David." It is also holy to Christians because it was where Jesus had his ministry. To the Muslims, it is the sacred place where the prophet Mohammed was taken to heaven.

Although it was originally a Jebusite stronghold called Zion (2Ki 19:21), little is known of the city from Joshua's death until the time when David captured it and built a temple there, which was later destroyed (2Ch 12:9).

The city itself was destroyed many times in the following 300 years. Jesus—whose death, resurrection, and ascension took place there—spoke of it with sadness (Mt 23:37; Lk 19:42) and predicted its conquest by the Romans.

¹JESHUA *(JESH oo uh; "Yahweh is salvation")*—A name for Joshua (1Ch 24:11). His descendants may have been returnees from Babylonian captivity (Ezr 2:36).

²JESHUA—A town in southern Judah, northeast of Beer-sheba. It was reoccupied by Jews after their return from captivity (Ne 11:26).

JESHURUN *(JESH uh ruhn; "upright")*—A poetic name for the nation of Israel. The term personified Israel's moral character and history with Yahweh (Isa 44:2; Dt 32:15).

JESSE *(JES ee)*—The father of King David; son of Obed

JESUS CHRIST'S TITLES

In the Bible, Christ is Jesus' most common name (meaning "Messiah," or "anointed one"). Other titles include:

Alpha and Omega
Bread of Life
Everlasting Father
King of Kings
Lamb of God
Lion of Judah
Lord

Mighty God
Morning Star
Prince of Peace
Savior
Son of Man
Wonderful Counselor
The Word

and grandson of Boaz and Ruth (1Ch 2:13–15; Ruth 4:21; Mt 1:5–6).

JESUS BEN SIRA—A philosopher, teacher, and scribe. He wrote the apocryphal Book of Sirach (198–175 B.C.), a collection of wisdom literature.

JESUS CHRIST—*See* **CHRIST.**

JESUS, WISDOM OF—Apocryphal writings from the first three centuries, also known as the Sophia of Jesus Christ. Originally written in Greek, it retells the Epistle of Eugnostos as a dialogue between the resurrected Christ, the 12 disciples, and seven holy women. The manuscript was found in an ancient Christian monastery at Chenoboskion in Egypt.

JETHER *(JEE thur; "abundance")*—Gideon's oldest son (Jdg 8:20). He was afraid to follow his father's orders to kill the Midianites Zebah and Zalmunna.

JETHRO *(JETH roh; "excellence")*—A Midian priest and Moses' father-in-law (Ex 3:1). When Moses fled Egypt, he lived with Jethro, married his daughter Zipporah, and tended his flocks (Ex 2:16–3:1). Later, Jethro came to visit Moses in the wilderness and offered him advice, but chose not to join the Israelites on their journey (Ex 18:1–27).

JEW—A member of the Hebrew race. The word came into common use after the Exile (Ezr 4:12, 6:14). In the New Testament, a Jew was anyone who practiced Judaism, not just someone who lived in Judea (or Israel) (Mk 14:1–2; Ac 22:3; Jn 5:10–18).

JEWELS—1. Precious stones, often believed to have magical powers. Jewels were worn by men and women in rings, bracelets, and necklaces (Eze 27:22; Nu 31:50; 2Ch 3:6; Ex 28:15–21). 2. A symbol for God's New Jerusalem (Rev 4:3; Isa 54:11–12).

JEWISH CHRISTIANS—Early Christians were all Jews, or "believers from the circum-cised" (Ac 10:45). Later, Jewish Christians were distinguished from Gentile believers (Gal 2:12–13). Their insistence on following the Laws of Moses troubled the early Church (Ac 13—15).

Elijah, Ahab, and Jezebel in Naboth's vineyard

JEZEBEL *(JEZ uh bel)*—The wicked wife of King Ahab. A follower of the pagan god Baal, she had hundreds of Yahweh's prophets killed (1Ki 18:13). Jezebel's name has become synonymous with evil and treachery. Elijah prophesied that she would die and be eaten by dogs (1Ki 21:23). During a rebellion, she was thrown out a window to her death, fulfilling the prophecy (2Ki 9:30–35).

¹JEZREEL *(JEZ ree uhl; "God sows, God gathers")*—A fertile city in the Judean hills, south of Hebron (Jos 15:56). It was a strategic military site (Jos 17:16; 1Sa 29:1, 11). Solomon had his winter palace in Jezreel (Am 3:15); Jezebel met her death there when Jehu cast her out a window (2Ki 9:14–37).

²JEZREEL—A descendant of Judah. He was the ancestor of a town by the same name in Judah (Jos 15:56).

JOAB *(JOH ab; "Yahweh is my father")*—David's nephew and a loyal army commander (2Sa 2:16; 1Ch 2:16). He killed David's rebel son, Absalom. Later, he was killed in the tabernacle and buried in his desert home (1Ki 2:34–38).

JOAH *(JOH ah; "Yahweh is brother")*—King Hezekiah's recorder who dealt with the Assyrians at the siege of Jerusalem in 701 B.C. (2Ki 18:18, 26, 37). He was involved in temple reforms and repairs (2Ch 29:12).

JOANNA *(joh AN uh; "Yahweh is gracious")*—The wife of Chuza, Herod's steward (Lk 8:3). One of the women Jesus healed, she tended him and the disciples. Joanna was one of the women who discovered Jesus' empty tomb (Lk 24:10).

JOASH, JEHOASH *(JOH ash; "Yahweh has given")*—**1.** The 9th king of Judah (837–800 B.C.), he assumed the throne at age seven (2Ki 11–12). As an infant, his aunt Jehosheba hid Joash from the queen mother Athaliah's royal massacre. During his reign, he restored the temple using a new form of payment directly to workers (2Ki 12:8, 15). He was murdered by two of his officers and buried in the City of David (2Ki 19–21). **2.** The father of Gideon the judge (Jdg 6:11). He was the caretaker of the Baal

JOB

After being praised in heaven by God for his faithfulness, Job of Uz—a wealthy, pious man—found himself besieged by troubles because God let Satan test his faith.

Satan wagered that if Job lost everything, he would turn away from God. Within a day, Job's livestock were stolen, his ten children died, and his skin developed terrible sores. His friends and neighbors, believing that Job must have done something terrible to warrant such punishment, threw him out of the city. As Job sat in the ashes of his life, his wife urged him to curse God and die.

With his three remaining friends, he sat outside the city gates and mourned for seven days. Why, he lamented, had this happened to him? His friends offered various reasons, including Job's sin and his need to understand God's nature.

Job preferred to meet God face-to-face rather than to believe it was God's intention to harm him. In a whirlwind, God appeared and displayed his might. Job was humbled before God and prayed for his ill-informed friends. His life was restored twofold because of his faithfulness (Book of Job; Eze 14:14).

altar that Gideon destroyed. **3.** The 12th king of Israel (801–786 B.C.), known for his military success. When he visited Elisha, the prophet predicted his victory over the Syrians using bows and arrows (2Ki 13:14–19).

JOB, BOOK OF—An Old Testament book recounting the troubles of Job, an upright man whose good life turned sour because God allowed Satan to test him. He remained faithful even as he grieved and argued, raising the question, "Why does God allow suffering?"

JOCHEBED *(JAHK uh bed; "the lord is glory")*—The wife of Amram; mother of Moses, Aaron, and Miriam (Ex 6:20; Nu 26:59).

JOEL *(JOH uhl; "the Lord is God")*—A prophet who wrote the poetic Book of Joel. He was associated with the Jerusalem Temple but was not a priest (Joel 1:13, 2:17). Little is known of his life.

JOEL, BOOK OF—An Old Testament book containing the prophet's warnings of God's judgment on oppressors (beginning with a locust plague) and a call for repentance. In the New Testament, Peter declared that Joel's promise of God's blessing was fulfilled at Pentecost (Book of Joel; Ac 2:14–21).

JOGBEHAH *(jahg BEE hah; "situated on high")*—A Transjordan city, part of the territory of Gad (Nu 32:35). It was located on the caravan route where Gideon pursued the Midianites (Jdg 8:11).

JOHANAN *(jo HAY nuhn; "Yahweh has been gracious")*—**1.** A Jewish leader who took Jews, including Jeremiah, to Egypt (Jer 40–43). **2.** Son of King Josiah (1Ch 3:15). **3.** A Benjaminite who joined David's army (1Ch 12:2–7). **4.** A Gadite who joined David's army (1Ch 12:8–14).

JOHN, GOSPEL OF—The fourth gospel of the New Testament. Penned by John, the son of Zebedee, it contains numerous stories not recorded in Matthew, Mark, or Luke. John wrote to explore the divinity of Christ and to promote faith (Jn 20:31).

JOHN MARK—Author of the second New Testament

JOHN THE BAPTIST

Elizabeth and Zechariah were an elderly, childless couple when the angel Gabriel announced they would give birth to a son.

At John's birth, Zechariah prophesied that the young boy would prepare the way of the promised Messiah through preaching, teaching, and forgiving sins. He was raised in an orthodox home centered around religious learning and practice.

John may have been a Nazirite (a group of devout Jews) and perhaps lived with the Essenes, a Jewish religious community. He wore camel's hair clothing and lived in the hills until God called him to be a prophet.

During his life, John baptized many people—including Jesus—in the River Jordan. He preached moral integrity, sharing, and sincerity—and prepared the way for Jesus' ministry (Lk 3:4–14). Because he condemned Herod Antipas' immoral marriage, John was arrested by the Jewish ruler and later killed (Mk 6). The disciples praised him long after his death.

gospel. John was his Jewish name, Mark (Marcus) his Roman name (Ac 13:5, 13). He traveled with Paul, then Barnabas, on missionary journeys (Ac 12:25, 13:13). Early tradition says he was Peter's interpreter in Rome and the founder of the church in Alexandria.

JOHN THE APOSTLE (*"son of thunder"*)—A fisherman son of Zebedee and the younger brother of James. A part of the inner circle of Jesus' apostles (Mt 27:56; Mk 1:20), he saw Jesus raise Jairus' daughter from the dead (Mk 5:37). He wrote the gospel bearing his name and three epistles. He may also be the author of Revelations and the man whom Jesus called his "Beloved Disciple." *See* **GOSPEL OF JOHN; EPISTLES OF JOHN.**

JOHN, EPISTLES OF—Three short letters written 60 years after Jesus' resurrection by the Apostle John to encourage Christian matu-rity. 1 John encourages Christians to love one another and warns against false teachers. 2 John, written to a specific church, encourages Christians to seek sound doctrine. 3 John is addressed to Gaius.

JOIADA (*JOY uh duh; "Yahweh knows"*)—A priest and son of Paseah. He helped restore the Old Gate in Jerusalem under Nehemiah (Ne 3:6).

JOIAKIM (*JOY uh kim; "Yahweh raises up"*)—A high priest after the Exile; son of Jeshua and father of Elishabib (Ne 12:10).

JOIARIB (*JOY uh rib; "Yahweh contends"*)—A learned man. Ezra sent him to Casiphia, a village of Jewish exiles, to find Levites to serve at the temple (Ezr 8:16).

JONADAB/JEHONADAB (*JOH nuh dab; "Yahweh is generous"*)—1. The ancestral father of the Rechabites, a nomadic clan who were

JONATHAN

King Saul's son and heir to the throne, Jonathan ("the Lord has given") stood aside to let David—a friend closer than a brother—rule instead. Their friendship was a model of loyalty.

A commander of 1,000 men, Jonathan led his soldiers against a mighty Philistine army while his father attacked from the rear. Hopelessly outnumbered, Jonathan believed that God would ensure victory. He and his armor-bearer killed 20 enemies, sending the rest away frightened (1Sa 14:6).

He befriended David after Saul honored the young shepherd for killing the Philistine Goliath with a slingshot. Later, he defended David against the king's jealousy and protected his friend against Saul's murderous plots. He pledged loyalty and friendship to David "and between my descendants and yours forever" (1Sa 20:42).

Jonathan was killed (along with his father and two brothers) in a battle with the Philistines. His death caused David great grief (1Sa 18–20). Fulfilling a pledge, David cared for Mephibosheth, Jonathan's only surviving relative (2Sa 9:1–13).

forbidden to drink wine, sow seeds, or live in houses. Jonadab lived during King Ahab's rule (Jer 35). 2. A son of Shimea (David's brother). He was a friend of David's son Amnon, for whom he helped plan Tamar's rape (2Sa 13:3, 5, 32, 35).

JONAH (*JOH nuh; "dove"*)— An Old Testament prophet. Under God's guidance, he traveled to Nineveh, urging repentance. His reluctance, the people's changed hearts, and God's mercy are recorded in the Book of Jonah.

JONAH, BOOK OF—An Old Testament prophetic book containing the story of Jonah, whom God sent to urge Nineveh to repent. As a parable, it tells of a person and a nation unable to understand God's mercy. Literally, it's an account of a tempest at sea, a "great fish" that swallows Jonah, and a plant-eating worm that torments him.

JONAS *(JOH nuhs)*—A name given to the prophet Jonah in the New Testament (Jn 21:15–16).

JOPPA *(JAHP uh; "beautiful")*—A coastal city in the territory of Dan (Jos 19:46). King Hiram of Tyre cut and floated Joppa's timbers for Solomon's Temple. Peter restored Dorcas' life in Joppa (Ac 9:36–42), and he had his vision of preaching to the Gentiles there (Ac 10:9–48).

JORDAN, RIVER—The most important river in Palestine, flowing 200 twisting miles from its source near Mt. Hermon to the Dead Sea. The Israelites had to cross it (Dt 3:23–25); John baptized Jesus in its waters (Mt 3:1–17).

JORDAN VALLEY—The Palestinian section of the Great Rift Valley, which runs from Turkey south to Africa, through which the Jordan River flows.

Joseph, Mary, and Jesus

JOSEPH *("may God add")*—1. Son of Jacob and Rachel; the ancestor of an Israelite tribe. His jealous brothers sold him into Egyptian slavery for 20 pieces of silver (Gen 37:3–4; 2Sa 13:18–19). He interpreted

Pharaoh's dream of drought and was released to oversee grain storage against the famine. When his brothers came to buy food, Joseph recognized them and invited them to move to Egypt (Gen 45:16–20). **2.** A carpenter who settled in Nazareth with his wife Mary and son Jesus (Jn 1:45, 6:42). After Jesus' birth in Bethlehem, Joseph was warned in a dream to flee Herod's massacre (Mt 2:13–15). He was a devout Jew who celebrated Passover (Lk 2:41).

JOSEPH OF ARIMATHEA *(ar i muh THAY uh)*—**1.** A wealthy member of the Jewish Sanhedrin (high court). A secret follower of Jesus, he did not take part in the resolution to put Jesus to death. After the crucifixion, Joseph anointed, wrapped, and buried Jesus' body (Mt 27:57, 58; Mk 15:43). **2.** A nominee to replace the Apostle Judas (Ac 1:23); also called Justus 1 and Barsabas 1.

JOSEPHUS FLAVIUS *(jo SEE fuhs FLAY vi uhs)*—A Jewish general, historian, and Pharisee. Interpreter for Titus in Rome after the fall of Jerusalem, he wrote *The Jewish War, Jewish Antiquities,* and his autobiography, *Life*.

JOSES *(JOH seez)*—One of Jesus' younger half-brothers (Mk 6:3). He was also called Joseph.

JOSHAPHAT *(JAHSH uh fat; "Yahweh judges")*—**1.** David's priest. He was responsible for blowing the trumpet before the ark of the covenant when it was brought to Jerusalem (1Ch 15:24). **2.** Joshaphat the Mithnite; one of David's mighty men (1Ch 11:43).

JOSHUA, BOOK OF—An Old Testament book. Named for its main character by an unknown author, the book traces the Israelites entry

JOSHUA

Hoshea was one of Moses' leaders during the Exodus. He was a clever warrior, which earned him a new name—Joshua ("the Lord is salvation"). He accompanied Moses to Mt. Sinai to receive the Ten Commandments and later supported Moses when he condemned the Israelites for making a golden calf idol.

Joshua was the only scout who believed the new land (Canaan) could be conquered. As a reward for his faith, Moses chose him as the new leader who would take the people the final distance into the Promised Land (Ex 17:9). The Book of Joshua is a record of his military victories over numerous kings, all resulting from his faith in God. One of his most dramatic battles was at Jericho when the walls fell (Jos 6:20).

After settling the people in Canaan, Joshua judged land disputes and planned further expansion, keeping to his promise of peace. In a final word to the people, he reminded them of God's covenant (Jos 21:43, 45) and urged them to turn away from idolatry.

into Canaan and the conquest of the Promised Land (Jos 1–12), the events after Moses' death (Dt 34), and the division of the Twelve Tribes of Israel.

JOSIAH *(joh SIGH uh; "the Lord supports")*—A king of Judah (640–609 B.C.) who assumed the throne when he was only eight years old (2Ki 22:1). During his 31-year reign, he fought Baal worship (2Ki 23:1–25; 2Ch 34:1–7). While renovating the temple, he discovered an old Book of the Law that inspired him to enact religious reforms (2Ki 23:8–20). Killed in battle, Josiah was carried by a chariot to Jerusalem, where he was mourned (2Ki 23:30–34).

JOT AND TITTLE *(JAHT; TIT el)*—Jot, or *iota*, is the smallest letter in Hebrew and Aramaic script. *Tittle* is a small stroke distinguishing between similar Hebrew letters. (Mt 5:18; Lk 16:17). Metaphorically, the term indicated something of little importance.

JOTHAM/JOATHAM *(JAY thuhm; "Yahweh is perfect")*—A king of Judah (750–732 B.C.). During his reign, his people prospered despite their idolatry (2Ch 15:32–38). He built the northern temple gate and established many forts and towers throughout Judah. Matthew lists him in Jesus' genealogy (Mt 1:9).

JOURNEY, SABBATH DAY'S— *See* **SABBATH DAY'S JOURNEY.**

JOY—A part of the "fruit of the Spirit" (Gal 5:22–24), biblical joy is a sense of delight and confidence in God, not merely happiness. Joy was considered to be possible even in troubled times (2Co 13:9; 1Pe 1:8). It will be the mood of the final gathering of God and the people (Rev 19:7) but can be achieved now (Lk 15:10).

JOZACAR *(JAHZ uh cahr; "the lord is remembered")*— One of King Josiah's servants who conspired to kill the king (2Ki 12:21). *See* **JEHOZABAD.**

JUBAL *(JOO bahl; "horn player")*—Son of Lamech and Adah; younger brother of Jabal. He was the musical ancestor of "all those who play the lyre and pipe" (Gen 4:21).

JUBILEE, YEAR OF—The fiftieth year in a cycle of Sabbatical years in ancient Israel (Lev 25; Ex 23:10–11). It was begun by the sounding of the ram's horn.

253

Blowing the ram's horn

Leased land was returned to its original owners, Israelite slaves were freed, and debts were forgiven. Scholars debate whether it was actually held.

JUBILEES, BOOK OF (*"Little Genesis"*)—An apocryphal text calling for obedience to the Torah. Written by a Palestinian Jew (c. 168–167 B.C.), it is essentially a rewrite of Genesis 1 through Exodus 12, presented as Moses' vision on Mount Sinai. It is noted for its 364-day calendar.

JUDAH, KINGDOM OF—The territory of a southern tribe of Israel, which began when ten northern tribes of Israel revolted (1Ki 12–22). Its boundaries changed frequently, and Jerusalem was the capital.

JUDAISM—A Jewish religion based on Old Testament. The six-pointed star of David is its symbol. The aristocratic Sadducees and legalistic Pharisees were its major political parties in Jesus' time.

JUDAIZERS—Early Jewish Christians who insisted that Gentile Christians become and "live like Jews" (Gal 2:14).

JUDAS (*"praised"* or *"hammer"*)—A common Greek name for Jude, the brother of Jesus (Mt 13:55) and author of the Letter of Jude.

JUDAS ISCARIOT—The treasurer of the disciples. He betrayed Jesus for 30 pieces of silver, an amount typically charged to some-

JUDAH

A son of Jacob and Leah, Judah ("praised") grew up in a divided household. Jealous of his half-brother, Joseph, he devised a plan to sell him into slavery in Egypt (instead of letting his brothers kill him). Later, Joseph saved Judah and his family from starvation during a great famine.

Judah married a Canaanite woman and had three sons: Er, Onam, and Shelah. When tricked into having children with Tamar (his widowed daughter-in-law), Judah also became the ancestor of Jesus (the "Lion of Judah"). Judah's descendants included David, from whose line Jesus descended (Mt 1:3; Lk 3:30).

Before Jacob died, he blessed Judah, calling him a lion (a symbol of strength in battle). Jacob promised that Judah would become a great leader, a prophecy that became reality through his descendants—the tribe of Judah.

After the Israelites escaped from slavery in Egypt and reached Canaan, the tribe gained extensive land, including the mountainous area around Jerusalem. After Solomon's reign, the Hebrew nation split into two kingdoms: Israel (to the north) and Judah, which included Jerusalem.

one whose ox gored a slave (Lk 22:3; Mt 26:47–56). Jesus foretold the betrayal (Jn 6:70–71). Judas later returned the money to the high priests before hanging himself (Ac 1:18–20). They used it to buy a paupers' cemetery.

JUDE—*See* **JUDAS.**

JUDE, LETTER OF—A New Testament epistle written by Jesus' brother to confront false teachers in unidentified early churches (Jude 4, 12–13).

JUDEA—The Jewish state after the Exile. In the New Testament, it was one of three Roman divisions of Jewish territory (Judea, Galilee, and Samaria).

JUDGES—Charismatic leaders of Israel after the conquest of Canaan. Their history is recorded in the Book of Judges.

JUDGES, BOOK OF—An Old Testament historical book outlining Israel's religious history from Joshua to Samuel. A continuation of the Book of Joshua, its author is unknown.

JUDGMENT—A formal opinion or decision by a judge or by God, whose will is the standard (Isa 10:1–4; Ps 7:8–16). God delivered his judgment as punishment for enemies or as purification for his people (Isa 2:12; Am 5:18). Jesus and Paul

cautioned against unfair judgments (Mt 7:1; Ro 14).

JUDGMENT, THE LAST—God or Christ's final assessment at the end of a person's life and history (1Ti 4:1; Ac 10:42; Rev 22:12). Believers are urged to prepare and nonbelievers to repent (Mt 24:42; Ac 17:30–31).

JUDGMENT DAY—The day when God will judge all people (1Co 4:5; 1Pe 1:17) and sentence the wicked (Mt 5:21; 2Pe 2:9).

JUDGMENT SEAT—A seat on a raised platform where ancient officials heard legal cases and addressed the people. Pilate stood on one when he turned Jesus over to the crowd (Mt 27:19; Jn 19:13)

JUDITH—A widow of Bethulia, a besieged city. To save her people, she tricked the enemy king and cut off his head with his sword. Rather than a real woman, some believe she was a symbol for complete faithfulness. Her account is written in the apocryphal Book of Judith.

JUDITH, BOOK OF—An apocryphal book of the heroic deeds of Judith of Bethulia. It was written to encourage the oppressed Jewish people.

JULIUS—A Roman centurion (Ac 27:1) who treated Paul kindly while taking him to Rome as a prisoner. He prevented Paul's death (Ac 27:42, 44).

JUNIA—A relative of Paul who was imprisoned with him in Rome. Paul called Junia "prominent among the apostles" (Ro 16:7). Junia is a woman's name, but the status of women in the first century make it unlikely that a woman would have held such a position. Some texts use the masculine form, Junias.

JUNIPER—A branched desert shrub that provided shade and supplied charcoal (1Ki 19:4–5; Job 30:4).

JUPITER—Chief of the Roman gods, also identified as the Greek god Zeus (Ac 14:12–13).

JUSTICE—1. Justice is a standard of God and humanity (Php 4:8; Job 19:7; Mt 27:19). Joseph of Arimathea was called a "just" man (Lk 23:50). 2. A legal system in which disputes are judged. The Israelites had a strict set of laws to deliver justice (Lev 19:15; Pr 16:10).

JUSTUS—1. The surname of Joseph Barsabbas, a candidate to succeed Judas Iscariot as disciple (Ac 1:23). 2. Jesus Justus, one of the few Jewish Christians to help Paul (Col 4:11).

JUTTAH (*JUHT uh; "stretched out"*)—A town in the hill country of Judah (Jos 15:55). It became one of the Levitical cities. Tradition says that Mary visited Elizabeth at Juttah, and John the Baptist was born there (Lk 1:39).

gered by the Israelites' constant complaining during their journey, Moses struck a rock at Kadesh, causing sweet water to flow out of it. A sign from God, Moses renamed the site "waters of contention" (Eze 47:19, 48:28).

KABZEEL (*KAB zee el; "may God gather"*)—A city in southern Judah (Jos 15:21). It was the home of Benaiah, one of David's mighty men (2Sa 23:20). After the Exile, it was resettled as Jakabzeel (Ne 11:25).

KADESH (*KAY desh*)—**1.** A general name for sanctuary cities, usually located in mountains, before the time of Israelites. Kadesh usually indicated cities in the south; Kedesh was used for the north. **2.** Kadesh-Barnea.

KADESH-BARNEA (*KAY desh BAHR nee uh*)—An oasis at the southern edge of Palestine. Ishmael was born nearby; Aaron died there (Jos 15:3; Dt 1:38). An-

KADMIEL (*KAD mee uhl; "God is ancient"*)—The head of a Levitical family who returned to Judah (Ezr 2:40).

KADMONITES (*KAD moh nites; "easterners"*)—A race of people who were among the inhabitants of Canaan before the Israelites (Gen 15:19). Called "people of the East," their land was promised to Abraham.

KAIN (*KAYN; "smith"*)—A hill city in southern Judah, southeast of Hebron (Jos 15:57).

KANAH (*KAY nuh; "reed"*)—**1.** A brook that formed the border between the territory of Ephraim and Manasseh (Jos 16:8, 17:9). Today, the Kanah is a tributary of the Yarkon, the largest river in Palestine (although it probably flowed differently in biblical times). **2.** A border city of Asher, southeast of Tyre (Jos 19:28).

KATTATH (*KAT ath; "small"*)—An unknown city on the border of Zebulun (Jos 19:15). It may be the same as Kitron, a city from which the Canaanites couldn't be driven (Jdg 1:30).

KEDAR (*KEE duhr; "dark" or "mighty"*)—The second son of Ishmael (Gen 25:13). He was the ancestor of the Kedarites (Is 21:17; Eze 27:21), or Arabs. A nomadic clan, they lived in tents made of black goatskins, which may have earned them their designation as "sons of the dark." A powerful but brief economic and military force, the Kedarites lived off the land until they were destroyed by Nebuchadnezzar (Isa 21:16–17; Jer 49:28).

KEDEMOTH (*KED eh mahth*)—A Levitical city in the tribal territory of Reuben on the Arnon River (Jos 13:18). Moses sent messengers to Kedemoth from the nearby desert, asking permission of King Sihon to pass through (Dt 2:26).

KEDESH—*See* **KADESH.**

KEDESH IN NAPHTALI (*KEE desh in NAF tuh lie; "holy place"*)—A city of two hills in the tribal territory of Naphtali (Jos 19:37). Later, it was designated a city of refuge (Jos 20:7; Jdg 4:6).

KEILAH (*kee EYE luh; "fortress"*)—A town on the plains of Judah that was rescued by David from the Philistines. King Saul, jealous of David's successes, sent an army to Keilah to kill David (1Sa 23:1–14).

KENATH (*KEE nath; "possession"*)—A city on the east side of the Jordan River settled by the tribe of

Manasseh. The city was captured by Nobah, who then renamed it after himself (Nu 32:42).

KENAZ (*KEE naz; "hunting"*)—The grandson of Esau and son of Eliphaz. He was one of the clan leaders of the Edomites (Gen 36:15, 42).

KENITES (*KEE nites*)—A race of people who lived in the desert area between Palestine and Mt. Sinai. God made a covenant with Abram, giving him and his descendants the land that belonged to the Kenites (Nu 24:21, 22).

KENIZZITES (*KEN iz zites*)—One of ten tribes of Canaan whose land was given to Abram (Gen 15:19). Caleb (Moses' spy) and Othniel (a judge of Israel) were the sons of a Kenizzite (Jos 14:6, 14).

KENOSIS (*kee NO sis; "emptiness"*)—A Greek word that refers to Christ's selfless act of taking on human form. Though he was in the form of God, Christ "emptied himself," took the form of a servant, and was prepared to obey God to the death (Php 2:68).

KEREN-HAPPUCH (*KER en HAP uhk; "horn of eye paint"*)—Job's youngest daughter, born late in his life. She and her two sisters were considered the most beautiful women in the land. Both received an inheritance right along with their brothers (Job 42:14, 15).

KERIOTH (*KEHR ee ahth*)—One of the cities of Moab that received God's judgment because of the people's idolatry and pride. Jeremiah predicted its ruin (Jer 48:24).

KESITAH (*KEH si tuh*)—An ancient unit of money of unknown value. At Shechem, Jacob used one hundred kesitah to purchase land on which to pitch his tent (Gen 33:19).

KETURAH *(kee TOO ruh; "incense")*—The second wife of Abraham. She bore him six sons. As firstborn, Isaac inherited all his father's possessions, but Abraham gave "gifts" to Keturah's sons while he was still living (Gen 25:1).

KEY—In the Bible, a key was a symbol of authority. Jesus gave Peter the keys of the kingdom of heaven so he could open the kingdom for all men to enter and be saved (Mt 16:19; Ac 10:44).

KIBROTH-HATTAAVAH *(KIB roth hah TAY uh vuh; "graves of craving")*—The place of burial for a group of Israelites who craved meat rather than the food God provided. God sent them quails, then struck them with a deadly plague while they were eating (Nu 11:18, 31–34).

KID—A young goat, sometimes used as a sacrifice or burnt offering (Nu 15:11). A kid was often prepared as a meal for friends or visitors (1Sa 16:20).

Two kids in a pasture

KHIRBET-QUMRAN

After the Dead Sea Scrolls were discovered in 1947, archaeologists came upon the ruins of a colony that the Arabs called Khirbet-Qumran (*KEER bet KOOM rahn*), meaning "stone ruin."

At first it was thought to be the remains of an old Roman fort, but when the site was excavated it was found to be a religious community center. Scholars identified rooms once used for worship, study, eating, and washing. They also found a scriptorium with writing tables, benches, and inkwells—enough evidence to conclude that this was the place the scrolls were made.

The community was believed to be that of the Essenes, a strict Jewish sect that broke away from Jerusalem during the second century and called itself "sons of light." Their library contained several hundred scrolls of Old Testament and nonbiblical texts that provided new information about the Bible.

The scroll of Isaiah—made of 17 sheets of leather that were sewn together—was 23 feet long. It was 1,000 years older than any previously discovered biblical texts. Before the Romans swept through Khirbet-Qumran in A.D. 68 to destroy the community, the Essenes were able to hide their manuscripts in clay jars in the nearby caves.

KIDNEYS—Because kidneys are surrounded by fat, they were considered the choice parts of an animal to burn during a sacrifice (Ex 29:13, 22). Kidneys were also regarded as the seat of emotions.

KIDRON (*KID ruhn*)—A valley east of Jerusalem. Jesus had to cross the Kidron Valley on his way to the Garden of Gethsemane (on the Mount of Olives), where he went to pray (Jn 18:1).

KILL—To put to death, or to murder. One of the Ten Commandments forbids killing (Ex 20:13). Jesus declared that anyone who is angry with his brother is subject to the same judgment as one who kills (Mt 5:21).

KILN—An oven where bricks were baked, also called a brick-kiln (2Sa 12:31). Potters used a kiln to fire clay pots, which were used in abundance in biblical times.

KINDNESS—The quality of being friendly, loving, and benevolent toward others. Kindness was listed as one of the "fruits of the Spirit," virtues that Christians should exhibit (Gal 5:22–23).

KING—The male ruler of a country or people. His office is called a kingship. The most important kings of Israel were Saul, David, and Solomon. Christ was called "King of kings and Lord of lords" (1Ti 6:15), but his kingship was a spiritual rather than a temporal realm.

KINGDOM OF GOD, KINGDOM OF HEAVEN—The spiritual reign of God over his faithful people. It began with Christ's ministry and extends into eternity. Jesus urged the people to pray for its coming (Mt 6:10), and later declared that the Kingdom of God was near (Mt 10:7).

KINGS, BOOK OF—The 11th and 12th books of the Old

KINGS OF ISRAEL AND JUDAH

King Saul, David, and Solomon each reigned for 40 years over the united kingdom of Israel. After Solomon's death, his son Rehoboam took the throne. But Jeroboam revolted with ten of the Twelve Tribes and formed the Northern Kingdom, called Israel. The two remaining tribes formed

King David

the Southern Kingdom, called Judah (1 Ki 12:1–24).

Jeroboam quickly established calf worship as the religion of the Northern Kingdom, and all 19 kings worshiped either a golden calf or the Canaanite god Baal. Ahab, who reigned from 875 to 854 B.C., was considered the worst of all the kings of Israel. His wife Jezebel killed the prophets of God and built a great temple to Baal in Samaria.

Judah continued to be known as a nation of God-worshipers, but in reality, most of the kings served idols. Only seven of Judah's 20 kings were faithful to God. Hezekiah, who had the throne from 726 to 697 B.C., was considered the best. Early in his 29-year reign, he destroyed idols and cleansed and reopened the temple.

Both kingdoms came to an inglorious end when Israel was captured by Assyria around 722 B.C. and Judah was captured by Babylon in 586 B.C.

Testament. Originally written as one book, it was split into 1 Kings and 2 Kings during one of its translations. The books trace the history of Solomon, the last king of the unified kingdom of Israel, and all of the following kings of the divided kingdom. They cover a span of 400 years, ending with the captivity of Israel by Assyria in 722 B.C., and the captivity of Judah by Babylon in 586 B.C.

KING'S GARDEN—A garden near the palace, between the two walls of Jerusalem (Jer 39:4), and not far from the Pool of Siloam (Ne 3:15).

KING'S HIGHWAY—An ancient road east of the Jordan River, running north and south through Edom and Moab. Though they promised to keep to the King's Highway on their way to Canaan, the Israelites were refused passage through the Edomite territory (Nu 20:17–22).

KINSHIP—A family relationship. In the Old Testament, Israelite society (which consisted of a variety of households, clans, and tribes) used kinship laws to determine inheritance. Christ broadened the term to include a relationship with God and his spiritual family, which was stronger than human ties (Mk 3:31–35).

KIR *(KEER)*—A Moabite city, possibly near Elam. At the request of King Ahab of Judah, the king of Assyria attacked and destroyed Damascus, then deported the people to Kir (2Ki 16:19).

KIR OF MOAB, KIR-HARE-SETH *(KEER HAR uh seth)*—One of two main Moabite fortress cities. It was built on top of a hill, surrounded by a narrow valley with high mountains on all sides. Moab was the enemy of Israel, and Isaiah

265

prophesied its ruin (Isa 15:1).

KIRIATH *(KEER ee ath; "city")*—1. A Hebrew word that designated a city. 2. An alternate name for Kiriath-Jearim.

KIRIATH-ARBA *(KEER ee ath AR buh; "fourth city")*—An early name for the city of Hebron (Gen 23:2). Sarah, Abraham's wife, died there at the age of 127.

KIRIATH-JEARIM *(KEER ee ath JEE uh rim; "city of forests")*—One of the 26 towns and their villages inherited by the tribe of Benjamin (Jos 18:28). Also known as Kiriath-Baal, it was a center of Baal worship. The ark of the covenant remained there for 20 years (1Sa 7:2), until King David brought it to Jerusalem (1Ch 13:5,6).

KIRIATH-SEPHER *(KEER ee ath SEE fur; "city of books")*—A town in the territory of Judah, later known as Debir. It was

allotted to Caleb, one of the 12 spies Moses sent into Canaan. The town was taken by Othniel, Caleb's brother (Jos 15:15, 16).

KIRIATHAIM *(keer ee uh THAY im; "double city")*—A Moabite town on the east side of the Jordan River. The Reubenites captured the town, then rebuilt and renamed it (Nu 32:37, 38).

KISH *(KISH; "power")*—A Benjaminite born in Gibeon. He was the son of Jeiel and the father of Saul, first king of Israel (1Ch 9:36).

KISHON *(KEE shahn; "curving")*—A river of central Palestine. On the bank of the Kishon, Barak and Deborah defeated the Canaanite general Sisera (Jdg 4). Also, Elijah destroyed prophets of Baal there (1Ki 18:40).

KISS—A common greeting among relatives, friends, guests, and royalty, dating back to the time of Jacob

(Gen 27:26). Ironically, Judas betrayed Jesus with a kiss (Mt 26:48–49). Paul urged Christians to greet each other with a holy kiss to show their love and brotherhood (Ro 16:16).

¹KITTIM *(KIT im)*—The great-grandson of Noah (Gen 10:4).

²KITTIM—A unknown place, possibly Cyprus. Balaam predicted that ships would come from Kittim and conquer Assyria (Nu 24:24).

Greek sculpture of a woman using a kneading trough

KNEADING-TROUGH—A bowl or container in which dough was prepared for making bread. When the Israelites fled Egypt, they took their kneading bowls with them (Ex 12:34).

KNEEL—In biblical times, bending the knee or kneeling was seen as a mark of respect and a gesture of obedience. Kneeling is accepted as the proper posture for prayer and worship (Ac 20:36; Ps 95:6).

KNIFE—In Old Testament times, knives were primarily used to slaughter animals, either for food or sacrifice. A special flint knife was used in circumcision (Jos 5:2,3).

KNOWLEDGE—The word appears more than 200 times in the Bible. The first mention is found in Genesis, which describes "the tree of the knowledge of good and evil" (Gen 2:9). Since God's knowledge is unlimited, the first humans wanted to be like him, so they ate from the tree and committed the original sin. Wisdom and knowledge were sought by leaders throughout the Old Testament. In the New Testament, knowing God—rather than knowing what God knows—is the highest attainment of Christian life.

KOA *(KO uh)*—An Aramaic tribe. Ezekiel prophesied that they would be one of the groups to rise up against Samaria and Jerusalem and carry out God's judgment against idolatry and licentious behavior (Eze 23:23).

KOHELETH *(ko HEL eth)*—A Hebrew word for "one who speaks publicly in an assembly," perhaps a preacher or teacher. This name was given to the writer of the Old Testament book Ecclesiastes, who professed to be King Solomon (Ecc 1:1).

KORAH *(KOR uh; "bald")*—1. A son of Esau and Oholibamah. 2. A son of Eliphaz, Esau's firstborn. Korah became a clan chieftain (Gen 36:5, 16).

KORE *(KOR ee; "quail")*—1. A Levite who was the father of Shallum, the chief gatekeeper stationed at the King's Gate in Jerusalem. 2. The son of Imnah. Kore was in charge of distributing the freewill offerings and consecrated gifts at the temple (2Ch 31:14).

LABOR—God cursed humanity with hard work after Adam and Eve sinned in the Garden of Eden (Gen 3:17–19). In the Old Testament, the Israelites were required to labor six days, then rest on the seventh (Ex 20:9). In the New Testament, Christ offered rest to those who were weary from their labor (Mt 11:28).

LACHISH (*LAY kish*)—A fortified Canaanite city located in a valley 25 miles southwest of Jerusalem. After a long history of attacks and sieges, the town was reoccupied by the Israelites (Ne 11:30).

LADAN (*LAY duhn*)—**1.** A descendant of Ephraim and an ancestor of Joshua (1Ch 7:26). **2.** Son of Gershon the Levite. He served in the temple during the reign of Solomon (1Ch 23:7).

LADDER OF TYRE—A landmark consisting of rocky outcroppings projecting into the sea at Tyre. They are said to have looked like a series of steps leading up into the seaport. Simon Maccabeus was appointed military commissioner of the region "from the Ladder of Tyre to the frontiers of Egypt" (1Mac 11:59).

LAHMI (*LAH my; "warrior"*)—The brother of Goliath the Gittite. In King David's battle against the Philistines, Elhanan, son of Jair, killed Lahmi (1Ch 20:5).

LAMB OF GOD—A name for Jesus by John the Baptist (Jn 1:29). He was referring to Christ's role as a sacrificial figure who was to die in place of sinners (Isa 53:4–7).

LABAN

First mentioned in the Bible when he helped arrange the marriage of Isaac and Rebecca (Gen 24), Laban (LAY buhn; "white") was Jacob's rich uncle and father-in-law. After Jacob tricked his brother Esau out of his birthright and family blessing, he fled to his uncle's home in Haran to escape his brother's wrath.

Laban's daughter Rachel caught Jacob's attention, and he offered to work seven years for Rachel's hand in marriage. After the seven years were served, a wedding took place—but Laban substituted his older daughter Leah for Jacob's beloved Rachel. When Jacob awoke next to the wrong woman, he realized too late that Laban had tricked him. It was the first of several deceptions he used on Jacob. In exchange for taking Rachel as his second wife, Jacob agreed to serve another seven years. When that time was up, Laban demanded another six years of service in exchange for a share of the family's sheep flock.

Eventually, Jacob fled with his family. Laban pursued and caught up with Jacob, who complained that Laban had cheated him, changed his wages ten times, and would have sent him away empty-handed if God had not intervened. The two men made an agreement not to harm one another, and finally they parted (Gen 29:15–30).

LAME, CRIPPLED—In the Old Testament, the lame could not become priests because they were not without blemish (Lev 21:18). In the New Testament, Jesus' miracles included healing the lame, the maimed, the blind, and the mute (Mt 15:30).

LAMECH *(LAY mek; "wild man")*—The name of two lines of Adam's descendants. Lamech who descended from Cain, fathered Jabal, Jubal, and Tubal-Cain (Gen 4:18). Lamech, the descendant of Seth, was the father of Noah (Gen 5:25).

LAMENT—An expression of grief or sorrow. The Book of Lamentations consists entirely of laments over the fate of Jerusalem. Some laments are found among the poetry of the Psalms and the books of the prophets.

LAMENTATIONS, BOOK OF—An Old Testament book containing five poems that mourn the destruction of Jerusalem and the suffering of its people, as well as prayers for help and forgiveness.

LAMP—Typically made of pottery or bronze, ancient lamps burned oil. They were used both in households and in the temple.

Oil-burning lamp

The lamp became a symbol for God's word and guidance (Ps 119:105; 2Sa 22:29).

LAMPSTAND—A holder for oil-burning lamps. The Old Testament gives explicit instructions for making a lampstand for the tabernacle. It was to be constructed of one piece of hammered gold, with a base and shaft and six branches. Each branch held a cup, shaped like an almond blossom, in which a lamp rested (Ex 25:31–40).

271

LAMB

Often used as food for important occasions, the meat of lambs was considered a delicacy among the ancient Hebrews (Dt 32:14). Most of the Old Testament references, however, centered around the use of the lamb as a burnt offering or sacrifice for sin. The first mention of the sacrificial lamb occurred when Abraham prepared to sacrifice his son Isaac. At the last moment, God provided Abraham with a lamb to substitute for his son (Gen 22:7).

Lambs were an important part of the daily offering at the tabernacle: one lamb in the morning and another in the evening (Ex 29:38–41). Seven male lambs—each a year old and without blemish—were required for Sabbath, monthly, and festival offerings. The Paschal Lamb was the leading figure in the observance of the Passover Feast. The lamb was to be killed on a specific date, its blood sprinkled on the doorposts and lintels, and the meat roasted—not boiled—and eaten.

In the New Testament, the Crucifixion took place during Passover, with Christ as the unblemished sacrificial lamb (1Co 5:7). John the Baptist called Christ "the Lamb of God who takes away the sins of the world" (Jn 1:29, 36).

LANCE—A weapon with a sharp-pointed metal head on a long shaft, such as a spear or javelin. A Roman soldier pierced Jesus' body with a lance as he hung on the cross (Jn 19:34).

LANDMARK—A stone or pillar used to mark the boundary of property. Moving these markers was considered a serious crime against one's neighbor (Dt 19:14). *See* **BOUNDARY STONES.**

LAODICEA *(lay oh dih SEE uh)*—A wealthy Roman town that became an important Christian city. It was a banking center on an Asian trade route. Paul's letter to the nearby Colossians was also addressed to the Laodiceans (Col 4:16).

LAPPIDOTH *(LAP ih dahth; "torches" or "flames")*—The husband of Deborah (a prophetess and judge of Israel), mentioned only once in the Bible (Jdg 4:4).

LASEA *(la SEE uh)*—A seaport town on the coast of Crete. Luke mentions Lasea in connection with Paul's missionary journey to Rome (Ac 27:8).

LASHA *(LASH uh)*—A town near Sodom and Gomorrah. It was used to describe the extent of the Canaanite territory, "from Sidon . . . as far as Lasha" (Gen 10:19).

LASHARON *(luh SHAH ruhn)*—One of a long list of towns conquered by Joshua, the successor to Moses, and given to the Israelites as their allotment of land (Jos 12:18).

LAST DAYS, LATTER DAYS—A Christian expression for the end of the world. According to the Gospel of Mark, "no one knows the day or the hour," but these days will be marked with persecution, conflict, and the destruction of the entire Earth (Mk 13:32). A final judgment and punishment will take place, and the second coming of Christ will establish the kingdom of God among believers.

LATIN—The language of the Romans, Latin was also used in Palestine during Christ's time. The inscription on Jesus' cross ("Jesus of Nazareth, the King of the Jews") was written in Hebrew, Greek, and Latin (Jn 19:20).

LANGUAGE OF THE OLD AND NEW TESTAMENTS

The stories in the Old Testament were probably passed on orally from one generation to the next before they were written down.

The Jewish scriptures were originally written in Hebrew. Called "the language of Canaan" (Isa 19:18), Hebrew is the earliest known language and is believed by some to be the original human language. It belongs to the Semitic group of languages, which are read from right to left.

The Hebrew alphabet, originally without vowels, has 22 consonants. Vowels, indicated by dots or dashes, were introduced in the fifth or sixth century A.D. Few changes occurred in the language in the 1,000 years before the Babylonian captivity. Ancient tablets show that Israel's neighbors—the Canaanites, Phoenicians, and Moabites—spoke a similar dialect.

After the captivity, Aramaic began to replace Hebrew as the spoken language. Certain portions of the books of Ezra, Daniel, and Jeremiah were written in Aramaic. By the time of Christ, Aramaic was commonly in use, although Hebrew was still used in the schools and temples. A modern form of Hebrew is the official language of Israel today.

The New Testament books were written in Greek. Spread by Alexander the Great, a common dialect of the Greek language was spoken throughout the civilized world. Greek was considered to be the language best suited to expressing human thought. Paul spoke to the Roman soldiers in Greek (Ac 21:37).

LATTER PROPHETS—The books of the prophets in the Old Testament are divided into two categories: the Former Prophets (Joshua, Judges, Samuel, and Kings) and the Latter Prophets (Isaiah, Jeremiah, Ezekiel, and the 12 minor prophets).

LAVER *(LAH vur)*—A basin for water, located near the door of the tabernacle. Jewish priests used it to wash their hands and feet before approaching the altar (Ex 30:17).

LAW—Rules for conduct imposed and enforced by authorities. Torah, the Hebrew word for law, was the name given to the Pentateuch, the first five books of the Old Testament. The Torah contains the civil and religious laws of the Israelites.

LAWGIVER—The title given to Moses for his role in bringing God's Law—the Ten Commandments—to the people of Israel (Ex 20).

LAWLESS ONE—An imposter who will profess to be Christ in his second coming. Paul warned the Thessalonians about a false messiah—an antichrist—who would try to deceive them with miracles, signs, and wonders (2Th 2:3–8).

LAWSUIT—In the Old Testament, Moses urged the people to be fair and not to be swayed by the crowd when testifying in a lawsuit—especially involving the poor (Ex 23:2, 6). In the New Testament, Matthew advised Christians to settle disputes among themselves instead of going to court (Mt 5:25).

LAWYER—A biblical lawyer interpreted the Law of Moses in the synagogues and schools. The scribes usually served this function. Jesus issued a scathing denunciation of the scribes and Pharisees for their pride and self-righteousness (Mt 23).

LAST SUPPER

On the eve of his betrayal and crucifixion, Jesus gathered his disciples to share a special meal and celebrate the Passover together.

Jesus suddenly broke the bread, blessed it, and offered it to them. He told the disciples they were eating his body, given for them in sacrifice. He then offered them wine, saying it was his blood, shed for them for the forgiveness of sins (Mt 26:17–30).

He urged them to repeat this meal often in remembrance of him and so proclaim that they were all one body with him. The disciples were mystified, but after Christ died on the cross and rose again, their last supper together took on greater significance as they finally understood what he had been telling them.

Since that time, the Lord's Supper—or communion—has become for believers a means to commemorate Christ's death and resurrection, acknowledge his sacrifice, accept forgiveness of sins, and declare their oneness with him. Those who participate in this meal look ahead to the time when Christ will come again (Mt 26:26–28).

LAYING ON OF HANDS—Placing hands on the head of individuals to bless them or dedicate them to God. The Israelites laid hands on the Levites to set them apart for the Lord's service (Nu 8:10).

LAZARUS (*LAZ uh ruhs; "God has helped"*)—The brother of Mary and Martha. A beloved friend of Jesus, Lazarus died while Jesus was away. When he returned a few days later, Jesus raised him from the dead (Jn 11:1–12:19). The miracle attracted many new believers.

LAZARUS AND DIVES (*DI eez; "rich"*)—In one of Jesus' parables, Lazarus was a righteous beggar who died and went to heaven. Dives was an unrepentant rich man who died and went to hell (Lk 16:19–31). The name Dives comes from the Vulgate, the Latin version of the Bible.

LEAD—One of the metals taken in the war against the Midianites (Nu 31:22) and exchanged in trade with Tarshish (Eze 27:12).

LEAH (*LEE uh; "wild cow"*)—The elder daughter of Laban. She was married to Jacob through trickery. Jacob worked seven years in exchange for Rachel, but Leah was substituted for her sister on the wedding night (Gen 29:16–30). Leah became the mother of six of the Twelve Tribes of Israel.

LEAVEN—A substance that makes dough rise. Leavened bread was not to be used for sacrifices or during Passover (Lev 2:11; Ex 13:3). The word was used figuratively as a corrupting influence when Christ warned the disciples about the yeast (leaven) of the Pharisees and Sadducees (Mt 16:6).

LEBANON (*"white mountain"*)—A mountain range along the Syrian coast in Palestine. Its name refers to either its limestone cliffs or snow-capped peaks.

Joshua's conquests included the Valley of Lebanon (Jos 11:17).

LEECH—A blood-sucking worm that clings to the skin. The horse leech was common in Palestine, particularly on animals that drank from the pools.

LEEKS—Bulbous plants resembling the onion, leeks were popular in biblical times for cooking. During their wanderings in the desert (where food was scarce), the Israelites longingly recalled eating leeks while they were in captivity in Egypt.

LEES—The dregs or thick part of the wine that goes to the bottom of the vat. The word has many figurative uses, expressing blessings (Isa 25:6), bitterness (Ps 75:8), and indifference (Zep 1:12).

LEG—In the Old Testament, the word often refers to the legs of sacrificial animals. The iron legs of a statue in Nebuchadnezzar's dream were interpreted to represent the Roman empire (Da 2:32–43). The legs of crucifixion victims were often broken to hasten death (Jn 19:33).

LEGION—A division of the Roman army numbering 6,000 men. The word is used in the Bible to represent a large number (Mt 26:53).

LEHABIM (*lee HAY bim*)—A people descended from Egypt; possibly related to Libyans (Gen 10:13).

LEHI (*LEE hye; "jawbone"*)—A location in Judah where the Philistine army pursued Samson. He picked up the jawbone of a donkey and killed 1,000 men with it (Jdg 15:9–19).

LEMUEL (*LEM yoo el; "devoted to God"*)—A pen name for the unknown king who is credited for writing Proverbs 31. These were maxims his mother had taught him. The king i

believed to have been
Solomon. His mother was
Bathsheba, an influential
woman in the king's court.

LENTIL—A member of the
pea family, the lentil plant
was a popular source of
food in biblical times. Its
seeds were dried and
ground to make meal, or
soaked and cooked to
make stew (Gen 25:29, 34).

LEOPARD—A fierce spotted
animal of the cat family.
Leopards were common in
Palestine in ancient times.
They were depicted lurking
(Hos 13:7–8) and watch-
ing cities (Jer 5:6). Isaiah
described the peaceful
kingdom, where the leop-
ard will lie down with the
kid, its prey (Isa 11:6).

LEPROSY—An infectious
disease considered "un-
clean" by the Israelites. The
symptoms include ulcera-
tions, numbness, and
wasting away of flesh
(resulting in deformity). A
milder form of the disease
may be linked to psoriasis.

An entire chapter of Leviticus deals with the description and treatment of
leprosy (Lev 13).

LESBOS (*LEZ bos*)—A Greek
island in the Aegean Sea
where Paul stopped on his
third missionary journey.
He stayed overnight at
Mytilene, a city on the
southeast shore of the
island (Ac 20:14).

LEVI (*"joined"*)—Jacob's
third son through Leah; an
ancestor of Jesus. He took
part in a plot against his
brother Joseph (Gen 37:4,
28), and in the massacre of
the Shechemites (Gen
34:25–31). Jacob cursed
his sons for their violence,
but the tribe was redeemed
when they killed the wor-
shipers of the Golden Calf
(Ex 32:25–29). *See* **LEVITES.**

LEVIATHAN (*leh VYE uh
thuhn*)—A large marine
animal described as fierce,
mighty in strength, covered
with scales, and possessing
fearsome teeth (Job 41).
This "sea monster" is

God slaying the Leviathan

believed to be a crocodile, but the term may have been used figuratively to symbolize unknown terrors of the world.

LEVIRATE LAW *(LEV ih ret)*—An ancient custom (first mentioned in Gen 38:8) in which a brother (or another male relative) of a deceased man must marry his brother's wife—and father a child—to perpetuate his brother's name (Dt 25:5–10).

LEVITES *(LEE vites)*—Descendants of Levi, the son of Jacob. The men of this tribe served at the tabernacle, assisting the priests (who were from Aaron's family). The Levites were in charge of transporting the ark of the covenant and sanctuary furnishings whenever the tent was moved (Nu 3:5–13, 27–32).

LEVITICUS *(leh VIT i kuhs)*—The third book of the Old Testament. It contains the religious and civil laws of Israel, including regulations for conducting worship, rites of ordination, festivals to be observed, clean and unclean foods, and behavioral concerns.

LIBERTY—In the Old Testament, the focus was on physical freedom. In the Jubilee (50th) year, slaves were given their liberty, debts were forgiven, and property was returned (Lev 25:10). The New Testament used the term for spiritual liberty (2Co 3:17), freedom from the slavery of sin (Jn 8:34–36).

LIBNAH *(LIB nuh; "whiteness")*—One of the places

LEVITICAL CITIES

Because they had helped him to do away with the calf-worshipers, Moses had pronounced a blessing on the sons of Levi, ordaining them for the Lord's service (Ex. 32:25–29). They were to be assistants to the priests and help take care of the sanctuary.

Since they were a people set apart, the Levites were not allowed to cultivate land or work at trades. Neither would they receive an allotment of land as the other tribes had. Instead, for their service in the tabernacle, they were to receive tithes (a portion of crops and livestock) from the remaining Israelites. In turn, they were required to give a tithe of their portion to the priests (Nu 18:20–28).

In addition, Moses designated 48 cities (along with outlying pasture lands) to be given to the Levites in which to reside. This number included six cities of refuge (for people awaiting trial) and 13 cities reserved specifically for the priests of Aaron (Jos 21). The cities were scattered throughout the territories of the other 11 tribes.

in the desert where the Israelites camped as they were led out of Egypt by Moses and Aaron (Nu 33:20).

LIBNI (*LIB nye; "white"*)— A son of Gershon; grandson of Levi (1Ch 6:16–17). His descendants, the Lib-nites, were one of the clans responsible for the care of the tabernacle (Nu 3:18–26).

LIBYA—A country of North Africa, west of Egypt, also called Put. Its downfall was predicted by Ezekiel (30:5) and Jeremiah (46:9).

LIE, LYING—1. Making false statements. Lying is an abomination to God (Pr 12:22), and the Ten Commandments forbid it (Ex 20:16). 2. To be in a reclining position; resting. 3. To "lie with" was a biblical expression for sexual intercourse (Gen 38:8). 4. To "lie with one's fathers" meant to die (Gen 47:30). 5. To "lie in wait" indicated covert action (Jos 8:4).

LIFE—Physically, the period of earthly existence (Gen 23:1). It is a gift given by God at the time of creation (Gen 2:7). Taking a life was strictly prohibited by the law (Lev 24:17; Ex 20:13). Humankind also possesses a spiritual life that was the focus of Christ's ministry (Jn 10:10).

LIFE, ETERNAL—*See* **ETERNAL LIFE.**

LIFE, FUTURE—Immortality. Humankind is promised a future life for everyone. There will be a resurrection of the righteous and the unrighteous (Ac 24:15), but all will be judged and receive what is due. The righteous will live in paradise (Lk 23:43). Those who have done evil will be in Hades (Mt 11:21–24).

LIGHT—The first natural light appeared at the command of God (Gen 1:3). Oil lamps provided artificial light in biblical homes, tabernacles, and temples (Ex 37:17; Mt 5:15). As "the light of the world" (Jn 8:12), Jesus supplied spiritual illumination.

LIGHTNING—During the rainy season in Palestine, lightning was a frequent occurrence. It was looked upon as a show of God's power (Ex 9:23–24). In the New Testament, Luke said that the coming of Christ is as sure as the lightning that flashes and lights up the sky (Lk 17:24).

LILITH *(LIL ith)*—An evil female demon of Semitic

folklore. She was characterized as living in the wasteland with wildcats, hyenas, and goat-demons. Lilith felt at home amid destruction (Isa 34:14).

LIME—A material produced by burning limestone, bones, and shells (Isa 33:12). Lime was used to make mortar, plaster (Dt 27:2), and whitewash for the walls of tombs (Ac 23:3).

LIMESTONE—A common type of rock composed of calcium carbonate. When burned it produces lime. Limestone was easily obtained in the country around Palestine.

LINEN—Thread or cloth made from fibers of the flax plant. Linen clothing was ideal for the warm climate and was widely in use in biblical times (Pr 31:22). The garments of the Levitical priests were made of linen (Lev 6:10), as were burial shrouds (Mt 27:59).

LINTEL—The upper horizontal beam of a doorway. At the first Passover, the blood of the Paschal Lamb was placed there as a sign that God would spare the household's firstborn son (Ex 12:7, 22, 23).

LINUS—One of the members of the Christian Church in Rome who, along with Paul, sent his greetings to Timothy (2Ti 4:21). He is believed to have been the first bishop of Rome.

LION—Hebrews were familiar with lions, which are mentioned many times in different sections of the Bible. They were portrayed as symbols of strength (Jdg 14:18).

LION OF JUDAH—The "Lion of the Tribe of Judah" (Rev 5:5) is a title for the Messiah that was prophesied in the Old Testament (Gen 49:8–10). He was to be a descendant of Judah and David. Christ's birth fulfilled the prophecy.

283

LIP—In the Bible, the word lip was used both literally and as a metaphor for speech and language. In Hebrew, the language of Canaan is the "lip" of Canaan (Isa 19:18).

LITHOSTROTOS *(lith OS truh tuhs)*—A stone pavement beneath the modern-day buildings in Jerusalem. It is believed to be the remains of the judgment hall—or praetorium—where Jesus was brought before Pilate (Jn 18:28, Mt 27:27).

LIVER *("to be heavy, weight")*—The largest, heaviest abdominal organ, the liver was often mentioned in reference to animal offerings to Yahweh (Lev 3:4, 10, 15). Some ancient cultures practiced a form of divination—called hepatoscopy—that inspected animal livers for omens. Except for sacred lots, divination was prohibited to Israel (Dt 18:10). The liver was considered the seat of courage and passions (La 2:11). Hebrews sometimes amended the term to "heart" or "glory" (Ps 16:9).

LO-DEBAR *(LO dee bar; "without pasture")*—A town east of Jordan in Gilead. It was the hometown of Mephibosheth, a cripple whom David invited to permanently join him at the king's table (2Sa 9:1–13).

LOAVES—Biblical bread was usually made from leavened wheat flour. In the temple, a weekly offering of 12 loaves symbolized God's presence (1Sa 21:6) and served as sacrifice (Lev 23:17). As a sign of God's sustaining power, Jesus made five loaves and two fish feed more than 5,000 people (Mk 6). *See* **BREAD OF THE PRESENCE.**

LOCUST—Defined variously as crickets, grasshoppers, worms, or caterpillars. Locusts are mentioned at least 47 times in the Bible.

They appeared as plagues; John the Baptist ate "locusts and wild honey" (Ex 10; Joel 1; Mk 1:6).

LOG—1. A measurement of one or one-half pint; the smallest unit mentioned the Old Testament (Lev 14:10–24). 2. An analogy Jesus used to teach humility and responsibility: "Why do you see the speck in your neighbor's eye, but do not notice the log in your own eye?" (Lk 6:41).

LOGOS (*LOH goss; "speech" or "word"*)—In Greek philosophy, the divine law or creative principle. Biblically, it describes the Word of God; the activity of God's speech (Ps 33:6; Heb 4:12). In the New Testament, the Apostle John describes Jesus as the "living word" who is with God, as God (Jn 1:1–3; Rev 19:13).

LOOM—A hand-controlled device for weaving cloth. Delilah attempted to break the power of Samson (while he slept) by weaving

Weaver's loom

his hair into unfinished cloth on an upright loom (Jdg 16:13–14).

LORD—A title of respect for a superior; also called "master." When referring to God as Lord, the Israelites used the Hebrew word *Adonai* (which implied mastery and majesty) to distinguish it from a human master (Ex 20:2). In the New Testament, Jesus is called Lord using the Greek word *kurios*, which varies in meaning from "Sir" to "God" (Jn 4:11, 20:28).

285

LORD OF HOSTS—A name that depicts God as both a warrior and the heavenly creator.

LORD OF SABAOTH—A name for God; also called "Lord of Hosts." In the New Testament, the term was used for God as one who judges (Jas 5:4; Ro 9:29).

LORD'S DAY—Sunday, the first day of the week. Jesus' resurrection occurred on this day; Christians consider Sunday their day of weekly worship (Rev 1:10).

LORD'S PRAYER, THE—A model prayer that Jesus used when he instructed his disciples how to pray (Mt 6:9–13; Lk 11:2–4).

LORD'S SUPPER—The final meal that Jesus shared with his disciples before his crucifixion. During the supper, Jesus presented his body and blood as a sacrifice. The Church has honored his command to reenact the meal in his memory. *See* **EUCHARIST.**

LOT (*"concealed" or "covering"*)—The son of Haran; nephew of Abraham. Against God's will, Lot moved near the wicked city of Sodom and associated with its sinful people. When God destroyed the city, Lot was instructed to flee with his family without looking back. When his wife did look back, God turned her into a "pillar of salt" (Gen 11:27–31).

LOTS, CASTING—An ancient practice of throwing stones (or drawing them from a pouch) to determine a decision. It was believed that God had influence over the outcome. Many things were decided by the casting of lots, including the selection of leaders and the distribution of conquered territory. In the Old Testament, the high priest used two stones—the Urim and Thummim—to determine divine will.

LUCIFER (*"light bearer"*)—A Hebrew word used in the

Old Testament to describe a Babylonian king who had fallen from power (Isa 14:12). The word has become an alternate name for Satan, the angel who rebelled against God.

LUCIUS *("light")*—1. A church leader at Antioch (Ac 13:1). 2. A church leader at Rome, possibly the same as Lucius 1 (Ro 16:21).

LUKE *("light" or "bright")*—The author of the third gospel and the Acts of the Apostles. He was a traveling companion of Paul, who referred to Luke as a "beloved physician" (Col 4:14).

LUKE, GOSPEL OF—The third book of the New Testament. Written to give an "orderly account" of Jesus' life and teachings (Lk 1:3), it is the longest and most detailed of the four gospels.

LYDDA—A city, located southeast of Joppa, where Peter healed a paralytic man (Ac 9:32–38).

LYDIA *(LID ee uh)*—A woman in Philippi who sold purple cloths in the marketplace. After hearing Paul speak, she converted to Christianity. Her home became the first European house church (Ac 16: 11–15, 40).

LYSIAS *(LIS ee uhs)*—1. A Roman military official who helped Paul (Ac 21:31). *See* **CLAUDIUS LYSIAS.** 2. A Seleucid military commander under Antiochus IV Epiphanes. Lysias attempted to crush a Jewish rebellion against Seleucid oppression.

LYSTRA—A town in central Asia Minor. When Paul performed a healing there, he and Barnabas were mistaken as gods by the people there (Ac 14:6–23). Timothy was a resident of Lystra.

¹**Maacah** (*MAY a kah; "oppression"*)—**1.** A Geshurite wife of David. She was the mother of Absalom. **2.** A wife of King Rehoboam of Judah. Called a "great lady" (1Ki 15), she was an influential queen-mother during the reign of her son Abijah (c. 915–912 B.C.) and grandson Asa (c. 912–871 B.C.).

²**Maacah**—A small desert country near Syria. It was drawn into battle against David (2Sa 10).

Maareh-Geba (*MAY uh reh GEE buh; "west of the Geba"*)—A place of hiding for Israelites who attacked the Benjaminites to revenge the rape of a concubine (Jdg 19–20).

Maccabees, Book of—Four Jewish apocryphal books describing the history of the Maccabean revolt against the Greeks.

Macedonia (*mas eh DOH nee uh*)—An important province of northern Greece. It was part of Alexander the Great's vast empire and was later occupied by Rome. Paul's European ministry began with the call, "Cross over to Macedonia" (Ac 16: 9–10).

Machaerus (*ma KAY rus*)—A fortified mountain stronghold, overlooking the Dead Sea, built by Herod the Great. It was the supposed site of the imprisonment and death of John the Baptist.

Machir (*MAY kir; "sold"*)—**1.** The first son of Manasseh. He was the father of the Machirites (Gen 50:23; Nu 26:28). **2.** A man who helped David during escape from Absalom (2Sa 17:27–29).

MACCABEES

After Rome prevented Antiochus IV (Epiphanes) from a victory over Egypt, the cruel and vain Seleucid king turned his attention to the submission of Palestine. He halted Jewish offerings and traditions. In 167 B.C., he ordered Jerusalem's priests to sacrifice a pig in honor of the cult of Zeus. A statue of the Greek god was set up in the temple (Da 11:28–31; 2Mac 6). Palestinian villages were required to set up similar altars for monthly sacrifices and feasts.

Seventeen miles from Jerusalem, a priest of Modein named Mattathias refused to comply. He killed to defend Jewish faith, then rallied his countrymen to revolt (1Mac 2:44–48). With his five sons, Mattathias led a guerilla war against trained Seleucid troops. After his death, leadership fell to his third son, Judas, who was given the honorary title Maccabees (*MAK a bees; "the hammer"*).

In 164 B.C., in God's name and against all odds, Syria's dominance was broken. After hundreds of years of servitude, Israel finally won independence. Jerusalem's defiled temple was cleansed and rededicated to Yahweh (1Mac 4). Hanukkah is the annual celebration of that Maccabean restoration.

MACHPELAH (*mak PEE luh; "a doubling"*)—A burial cave purchased by Abraham from Ephron. Sarah, Abraham, Isaac, Rebekah, Leah, and Jacob were buried there (Gen 49:29–32).

MADMANNAH (*mad MAN na; "dunghill"*)—A town in the extreme south of Judah, toward Edom (Jos 15:31). It may have been where Solomon's chariots were made.

MADMEN (*MAD men; "dung pit"*)—A Moabite town. It was one of the places named in Jeremiah's prophecies against nations (Jer 48:2).

MADMENAH (*mad MEE nuh; "dunghill"*)—A town situated along the northern route from which the Assyrians attacked Jerusalem (Isa 10:24–31). Its exact location is unknown.

MADON (*MAY don; "contention"*)—A Canaanite town (Jos 11:1). King Jobab of Madon was among the allies who gathered to fight against Israel.

MAGBISH (*MAG bish*)—A place settled by Jewish exiles returning from Babylonian captivity (Ezr 2:30).

MAGDALA (*MAG duh luh*)—A fishing town on the western shore of the Sea of Galilee. Also called Magdalan or Magadan, its residents were known as Magdalenes (Mt 15:39).

MAGDALENE, MARY (*MAG duh len*)—A woman of Magdala from whom Jesus cast seven demons. Present at Jesus' crucifixion and burial, she was the first person to encounter the resurrected Christ (Mk 16:1; Jn 20:11).

MAGIC AND SORCERY—Ancient authorities often sought advice from esteemed magicians who read sacred hieroglyphic writings and omens, interpreted dreams, or made prophetic predictions (Gen 41:8; Da 2:10). Sorcery pertained to magical arts and frequently included drugs, spells, or incantations (2Ch 33:6). Hebrew law forbade these pagan practices (Ex 22:18). The New Testament urged sorcerers to convert to the Christian faith.

MAGISTRATE—A Greek term used by Romans to denote a high rank among military or governmental leaders in the provinces

MAGI

The term magi (*MAY jigh; "wise men"*) was first applied to members of an ancient Persian nature religion. Rather than a god, they worshiped the elements of earth, air, water, and (especially) fire. These priests, who possessed seemingly magical powers, practiced dream interpretation, astrology, and fortune-telling. They also foretold prophecies and studied omens.

In the Old Testament, the word *Rabmag* indicated the chief of the magi (Jer 39:13). During the sixth century B.C., Zoroaster (a pagan prophet) and his followers added a theological aspect to an otherwise godless system. By the first century, magi became a general word for anyone who practiced magic, dream interpretation, or divination (Ac 8:9, 13:6).

The New Testament mentions magi who came "from the East." They traveled a great distance to find the one "born king of the Jews" and to offer him gifts from a treasure chest (Mt 2). Astrology was their means of knowledge. After seeing Jesus and being warned by a dream to avoid Herod, they returned home by a new route. Nowhere in Scriptures are they called kings, nor is the number of those who came mentioned.

(Lk 12:58; Ac 16:20; Titus 3:1).

MAGNIFICAT—A song of praise attributed to Mary, the mother of Jesus (Lk 1:46–55). It is one of three songs recorded concerning the birth of Jesus (Lk 1:68, 2:29).

¹MAGOG (*MAY gog*)—A descendant of Japheth, son of Noah (Gen 10:2). His people were fierce warriors and enemies of Israel.

²MAGOG—A territory ruled by Gog, an enemy of Israel (Eze 38–39). It is connected to a final rebellion against God (Rev 20:8). *See* **GOG.**

MAGOR-MISSABIB (*MAY gor MIS uh bib; "terror on every side"*)—A name that Jeremiah gave to the cruel priest Pashhur, who had him put in stocks (Jer 20:3).

MAGUS, SIMON—A Greek magician converted to Christianity through Philip's preaching (Ac 8).

He attempted to purchase God's power but was severely rebuked by Peter and John.

MAHANAIM (*MAY ha NAY im; "two hosts"*)—A place in Gilead where Jacob encountered God's angels (Gen 32:2). It was later appointed as a Levitical city of refuge (Jos 21:38). Mahanaim was a place of rest for David in his battle against Absalom (2Sa 17:24).

MAHANEH-DAN (*MAY ha nuh dan; "camp of Dan"*)—A site near Zorah, west of Jerusalem. It was the birthplace of Samson (Jdg 13:21–25), and served as a campsite for 600 warriors from the tribe of Dan (Jdg 18:12).

MAHER-SHALAL-HASH-BAZ (*MAY heer SHAAL al HAASH baz; "the spoil speeds, the prey hastens"*)—A name that God commanded Isaiah to give one of his sons. God warned that by the time the child was old enough to speak, Israel and Syria would be conquered by the Assyrians (Isa 8:3).

MAHLI (*MAH lee; "sick or shrewd"*)—**1.** Son of Merari; a descendant of Levi (Nu 3:20). **2.** Son of Mushi. He was one of the Levites David placed in charge of tabernacle songs (1Ch 6:31–48).

MAHOL (*MAY hol; "dance"*)—A man whose family wisdom was legendary, yet paled when compared to that which God gave Solomon (1Ki 4:31).

MAKKEDAH (*mak KEE da; "place of shepherds"*)—A cave in the northwestern part of Judah. Fleeing a slaughter in the battle of Gibeon, a confederation of five Amorite kings hid from Joshua there (Jos 10).

MAKTESH (*MAK tesh; "like a mortar"*)—A place mentioned only by the prophet Zephaniah in a prophecy against Judah (Zep 1:11). Many believe it was located near Jerusalem.

MALACHI (*MAL uh kye; "my messenger"*)—An Old Testament minor prophet and writer of the Book of Malachi. He probably preached during Nehemiah's second mission to Jerusalem while the Jews were under Persia's dominion (c. 450 B.C.).

MALACHI, BOOK OF—The last of 12 Old Testament prophetic books. It was written after the Jews were released from their captivity in Babylon. When they returned to Jerusalem, the people quickly strayed from their worship practices. Malachi was sent as God's prophet to confront the spiritual and social sins of the people.

MALCAM (*MAL kam; "their king"*)—A Benjaminite, son of Shaharaim (1Ch 8:9).

MALCHIAH (*mal KYE uh; "Yahu is king"*)—**1.** A prince

who owned the muddy cistern that held Jeremiah prisoner (Jer 38:6). 2. The name of 14 Old Testament people, including priests, musicians, a wall-builder, and a goldsmith.

MALCHUS (*MAL kus*)—A slave of the high priest. Simon Peter severed his right ear at Gethsemane (Jn 18:10).

MALTA (*MAWL tuh; Canaanite for "refuge"*)—A Mediterranean island, also called Melita. To the amazement of the hospitable islanders, Paul survived a venomous snakebite there (Ac 28:1).

MAMMON (*MAM un*)—An Aramaic word for wealth or riches. Jesus used it to warn against the love of money (Mt 6:24; Lk 16:10–11).

¹MAMRE (*MAM reh*)—**1.** Abraham's home. It was located west of the cave of Machpelah, near Hebron.

²MAMRE—An Amorite ally of Abraham against Meso-potamian kings (Gen 14).

MAN—Words that are translated as "man" occur more than 3,000 times in the Scriptures. The first, which refers to Adam, means "of the Earth" or "human" (Gen 2:7). The last refers to Jesus as the Son of Man (Rev 14:14).

MAN OF GOD—In the Old Testament, the term "man of God" originally referred to prophets. Manoah's wife used the phrase to describe the angel of the Lord who foretold the conditions of Samson's birth (Jdg 13:6; 1Sa 2:27; 1Ki 13:1). In the New Testament, the term identified someone who exhibited outstanding piety.

MAN OF LAWLESSNESS—A title that Paul gave to the antichrist, a deceiver who will lead worldwide rebellion before Christ's second coming (2Th 2:3). He is also called the master of deception (2Th 2:8; 1Jn 2:18).

MANNA

When the Israelites wandered in the wilderness for 40 years, God fed his people with bread that mysteriously appeared every morning (Ex 16:4; Dt 8:3). Called manna (a Hebrew word meaning "what is it?"), it resembled coriander seed but tasted like a honey wafer (Ex 16:31).

Manna—the "grain of heaven"—miraculously rained down on them, but was not always appreciated by the grumbling Hebrews (Ps 78:24; Nu 11:6–7). When the Jews entered the Promised Land, they circumcised all males (as the mark of God's covenant) and celebrated Passover (Jos 5:12). The next day, food was prepared from locally grown crops, and God's provision of manna ceased. A small portion was preserved in the Holy of Holies (Heb 9:4).

In the New Testament, Jesus used the image of manna to teach about himself as the "bread of life" (Jn 6:31–35).

MANAEN (*MAN ay en*)—A prophet-teacher of the church at Antioch (Ac 13:1). He was raised as a foster brother of Herod Antipas.

MANASSEH (*muh NAS eh; "he causes to forget"*)—**1.** The eldest son of Joseph; the ancestral father of the Manassites (Gen 48).

Gideon was a Manassite (Jdg 6:15). **2.** A wicked king of Judah (c. 687–642 B.C.); son of Hezekiah. During his reign (begun at age 12) he practiced idolatry and "did much evil in the sight of the Lord" (2Ki 20–21; 2Ch 33:1).

MANASSEH, PRAYER OF—An apocryphal book attributed to Manasseh. Probably written sometime between the Jewish post-Exile and the Christian era, it contains 15 verses about repentance and hope.

Mandrake

MANDRAKE (*"love apple"*)—An ancient perennial herb. Its leaves were eaten by women to induce pregnancy (Gen 30; SS 7:13).

MANGER—A wooden or stone crib for grain (Isa 1:3). Only one gospel (Luke) records that Jesus was born in a manger (Lk 2:7). Other descriptions of the birth range from a cave to a protective courtyard stall attached to inns for animals of guests.

MANOAH (*muh NO uh; "rest"*)—The father of Samson. Though his wife was barren, an angel of the Lord told the pious couple that they would give birth to a hero who would deliver Israel from the Philistines (Jdg 13).

MANSIONS—A place that God has prepared for his believers. Jesus said, "In my father's house, there are many dwelling places" (Jn 14:2, 23).

MANTLE—An ancient garment, often described as a sleeveless robe or outer wrap (2Ki 2:8, 13). It was used as a symbol for praise (Isa 61:3) and fury (Isa 59:17).

MANUSCRIPTS—The original text of an author's work. The word also refers to any writings prior to the invention of print. Ancient manuscripts appeared on

Torah manuscript

clay, wax, leather, bark, or—most familiar to biblical works—durable papyrus.

MAON *(MAY on; "habitation")*—A hilltop town in Judah. It was also the name of the desert region near the town. David and his men hid there to escape Saul. Maon was the home of Nabal, a wealthy sheepherder who refused to protect David (1Sa 25).

MAONITES—1. Descendants of Caleb; they lived in Maon (1Ch 2:25). The Maonites were listed among the people who returned from exile. 2. A hostile people who oppressed Israel.

MARA *(MAR uh; "bitter")*—A name Ruth chose for herself after enduring terrible suffering, including famine and the loss of her husband and sons (Ruth 1:20).

MARAH *(MAR uh; "bitterness")*—A spring, located somewhere in the wilderness of Shur, where the Israelites found only bitter water after three days of marching with dire thirst. God showed Moses a tree that, when tossed into the spring, made the water sweet (Ex 15:22–25).

MARANATHA *(MAR uh NATH uh; "our Lord has come" or "come, our Lord!")*—An Aramaic expression used by the early Church to affirm belief in Jesus as Lord. It also was used to anticipate the second coming of Christ (1Co 11:25, 16:22; Rev 22:20).

MARDUK *(MAHR dook)*—The chief Babylonian god; also called Merodach or Bel (Jer 50:2, 51:44). In the Babylonian epic of cre-

Marduk

ation, a victorious Marduk turned chaos to cosmos.

¹MARESHAH (*ma REE shuh;* "head place" or "hilltop")—Son of Caleb; father of Hebron (1Ch 2:42).

²MARESHAH—A lowland Judean city, fortified by Rehoboam. It was the birthplace of the prophet Eliezer. During the Jewish revolt, Judas Maccabeus captured the city (2Ch 11, 14; 2Mac 12:35).

MARI (*MAH ree*)—An ancient city of Mesopotamia. It was located at the intersection of two major caravan routes: one connecting Syria to the Mediterranean, the other connecting Assyria to Babylonia. Ancient Mari documents have shed light on the Amorites and on the patriarchal period of Scriptures.

MARIAMNE—The wife of Herod the Great. In a period of conflict for control of the Hasmonean dynasty, Herod—tetrarch of Jerusalem and king of the Jews—married Princess Mariamne I, granddaughter of the Hasmonean ruler Hyrcanus II. Later, Herod had Mariamne assassinated.

MARK (*"large hammer"*)—One of Jesus' disciples and the author of the second gospel. Also called John Mark, he was the son of Mary and a cousin of Barnabas (Ac 12:12). At first unaccepted by Paul, Mark later became Paul's trusted co-worker (Ac 15:38; 2Ti 4:11). Peter called him "my son" (1Pe 5:13).

MARK, GOSPEL OF—The second and shortest of the four New Testament gospels. Attributed to Mark, the gospel was written from Rome sometime between A.D. 50–70. It was set primarily in Palestine, where Jesus ministered. Written for Gentiles, the gospel records the public actions of Jesus.

Mark's frequent use of the word "immediately" reflects his energetic tone.

MARKETPLACE—Ancient marketplaces usually consisted of bazaar stalls that lined city walls or were crowded into a large public square. The marketplace was a gathering place for trade, labor seekers, purchases, bartering, children's play, and the exchange of news (Mt 20:3).

MARRIAGE—The sexual union of a man and a woman, as approved by

Men playing a board game in an Arab marketplace

MARTHA

The sister of Mary and Lazarus of Bethany, Martha was a close friend of Jesus (Jn 11:1). She is mentioned three times in the gospels—twice concerning events in her home.

Because she welcomed Jesus into "her home," it is likely that she was the eldest sister. She appeared to be vigorous and boldly opinionated. On the first of his recorded visits with Martha, Jesus gently chided the woman for her preoccupation with domestic duties (Lk 10:38–42).

When her brother fell ill, she expected Jesus to come quickly and heal him, but the Lord arrived four days after the burial. Martha hurried to meet him as he neared her house. She spoke honestly with him, "...if you had been here, my brother would not have died."

One of Scripture's highest statements of faith occurs when Martha declares to Jesus, "I believe that you are the Messiah, the Son of God, the one coming into the world" (Jn 11:21–27).

God (Gen 2:24). In the Old Testament, marriage was considered necessary to ensure family and national survival. Hebrew law encouraged monogamy, but recognized polygamy—especially in cases of childlessness. Old Testament weddings often required little ceremony (Gen 24:67; Nu 30). In the New Testament, marriage was considered a holy sacrament (1Co 7:1–7).

MARS HILL—Known in Greek as *Areopagus* (AR ee OP uh guhs; "hill of the war god"), it was an imposing 400-foot limestone hill in Athens. The Athenian council (high court) met in a building atop Mars Hill. Paul preached there (Ac 17:15–24).

MARSH—Low, reedy wetland. Few marshes existed in Palestine, but the Nile Delta marshes may have been described (Job 8:11; 1 Mac 9:42). Marshes were sometimes symbols of future blessing (Eze 47).

MARSHAL—A rarely used Hebrew word for an appointed officer who mustered soldiers for duty (Jdg 5:14; Jer 51:27). It was used figuratively to describe the action of God (Sir 17:32).

MARTYR *("witness")*— Originally, a martyr was a general term for a witness, such as someone who oversaw a legal contract (Gen 21:30). After the deaths of Stephen, James, and others, the word evolved to mean those who died as they witnessed for God (Ac 7, 12; Heb 11).

MARY, THE VIRGIN—A young girl, betrothed to Joseph, who conceived a "child from the Holy Spirit" and named him Jesus. Joseph had "no marital relations with her until she had borne a son" (Mt 1:25). Mary was present when Jesus performed his first miracle in Cana, and she saw him die on the cross.

Aerial view of Masada

MASADA *(muh SAH duh; "mountain fortress")*—A 20-acre sheer-cliffed fortress south of Qumran in eastern Judea, west of the Dead

301

MARY

Six women of the New Testament were named Mary. The popularity of the name probably resulted from the fame of Mariamne (a Hasmonean princess, wife of Herod the Great) or, historically, from Miriam (sister of Moses). Each Mary had a different relationship with Jesus:

1) The sister of Martha, a student of Jesus' teachings (Lk 10:39).

2) The mother of John Mark. She was prominent in the Jerusalem church (Ac 12:12).

3) The mother of James and Joseph (Mt 27:56).

4) Mary of Magdala, from whom Jesus cast seven demons (Mk 16:9).

5) A Christian worker honored by Paul (Ro 16:6).

6) The mother of Jesus (Mt 1, 2). (*See* **Mary, the Virgin**.)

Some difficulty exists in placing Mary 3 (the "other Mary"). She was in the company of women who served Jesus; she was at the cross and witnessed his burial (Mk 15:47). Cleopas was her husband, yet Alphaeus is named as the father of her son James (Jn 19:25; Mt 10:3). Either this is one man identified by two names, or the two passages are unrelated.

Sea. Fortified by the Hasmoneans, it was used by the Herod family until Jewish rebels captured it in A.D. 66. Seven years later, the Jewish Zealots resisted Roman occupation for seven months before nearly all chose suicide over surrender.

MASHAL, MISHAL (*MAY shal; "who is as God?"*)—A pasture-land boundary town belonging to the tribe of Asher. It was later given to the Levites (1Ch 6:74).

MASKIL (*MAS kil*)—A word of uncertain meaning that appears in the title of 12 Bible psalms. It may refer to a musical accompaniment for the songs.

MASORAH, MASORETIC TEXT (*mah SOR uh; "tradition"*)—The traditional Hebrew text of the Old Testament. It was established mostly in the eighth and ninth centuries A.D. by the Masoretes, Hebrew scholars who developed a vowel system for the vocalization of the text.

MASSA (*MAS eh; "burden"*)—The descendants of Ishmael, Abraham's son by Hagar (Gen 25:14). Ancient manuscripts locate them in northwest Arabia, near the Persian Gulf.

MASSAH (*MAS uh; "testing"*)—A place near Rephidim that was without water. After a long march, the thirsty Israelites tested God by disputing with Moses, who feared for his life (Ex 17:1–7). God commanded Moses to strike a rock, which sprung forth water.

MASTER—A lord or owner. In the Bible, a number of different Hebrew and Greek words are translated as "master" to describe positions of authority. The meanings vary from an owner of slaves or servants, to a teacher, ruler, or rabbi. (Eph 6:9).

MATTANIAH (*MAT uh nye uh; "gift of the Lord"*)—Eight Old Testament men are named Mattaniah. The most notable was Judah's last king. He was crowned by Nebuchadnezzar, who changed Mattaniah's name to Zedekiah (2Ki 24:10–19).

MATTATHIAS (*MAT uh THIGH us; "the Lord's gift"*)—**1.** A priest who, with his five sons, started a Jewish revolt against Seleucid rule. He was the ancestral father of the Maccabeans. **2.** A captain of Maccabean forces (1Mac 11:70). **3.** The last of the famous Maccabeans, Antigonus, took this name. **4.** The name of two ancestors of Jesus (Lk 3:25).

MATTHEW (*"gift of Yahweh"*)—One of the original 12 apostles called by Jesus (Mt 9:9; Mk 3:18). Also named Levi, he was a tax collector and the son of Alphaeus (Mk 2:14). Matthew is traditionally accepted as the author of the first gospel.

MATTHEW, GOSPEL OF—Honored as the first of the four gospels, Matthew's book was written to Jewish readers. It describes Jesus—the promised Messiah who fulfills all righteousness (Mt 3:15)—and the disci-ples, who were commanded to carry the good news to all nations (Mt 28:19). Matthew's gospel alone uses the word "church" (Mt 16:18).

MATTHIAS (*muh THIGH us; "gift of Yahweh"*)—The man selected to replace the betrayer Judas among the apostles (Ac 1:23). He was chosen by prayer and casting of lots (Ac 1: 15–26).

MATTOCK (*MAT uk*)—A single-headed pickaxe of wood or iron. Also called a hoe, it was used for turning soil in mountainous areas where there was a lot of stone (Isa 7:25).

MAUNDY THURSDAY (*MON dee; "holy week Thursday"*)—A holy day, traditionally observed on the Thursday before Easter, that commemorates the Last Supper. It celebrates the humility of Jesus washing his disciple's feet, and his command to love one another (Jn 13:34).

MEADOW—Originally, the Hebrew word for meadow (*Abel*) meant "marshy, reedy ground" (Gen 41:2). Later, it referred to a delightful expanse of ground (Ps 65:13), such as Abelmeholah, the "meadow of the dance" (Jdg 7:22).

MEAL OFFERING—Also called a grain offering, it was one of five offerings included in the law given to Moses on Mt. Sinai (Lev 2:1–16, 6:14). The offering was to be made from the finest flour without the use of leaven.

MEALS—Biblical treatment of food and etiquette was highly ordered. Mourning called for fasting; guests received honor through food (Gen 18:1–8). Ordinary meals, served on floor mats, occurred twice a day (Ex 16:12). Formal meals used low tables where guests reclined to eat (Jn 21:20).

MEASURE—Various Hebrew and Greek units of weight or capacity are found in the Bible (Gen 18:6; Rev 6:6). In the Old Testament, the Levites determined the standards of quantity and size (1Ch 23:29). The New Testament speaks of God's spirit as given without measure (Jn 3:34).

MEAT OFFERED TO IDOLS—Ancient meat markets obtained some of their meat from sacrificial offerings and sold it primarily to the poor. Early Christians struggled with the appropriateness of eating meat offered to pagan idols (1Co 8:1–13).

MECONAH (*meh KO nuh*)—A region in southern Judah, between Ziklag and Ainrimmon. Meconah "and its villages" were settled by the Judeans and Benjaminites (Ne 11:25–30).

MEDAN (*MEE dan; "strife"*)—The third of six sons of Abraham and Keturah. He was the ancestral father of an Arabian tribe in eastern Palestine (Gen 25:1–6).

MEDEBA (*MED eh buh; prob. "water of quiet"*)—A Moabite village near Heshbon, named in song and prophecy (Nu 21:21–30; Isa 15:2). It was assigned to the tribe of Reuben (Jos 13:9). Mattathias' son, John, was murdered by a Medeba man (1Mac 9:36–42).

MEDES (*MEEDZ*)—A race of Indo-European people who lived in Media, an ancient country in northwest Iran. Cyaxares, a king of Mede, built the magnificent city of Ecbatana (the capital of the Median Empire) and joined forces with Babylon to destroy Nineveh (Tob 14:12–15).

MEDIATOR—One who brings reconciliation between parties. In the Old Testament, the word referred to the office of prophets and priest (Jer 1:1–4). In the New Testament, Jesus mediated the reconciliation between sinful people and a holy God (1Ti 2:3–5).

MEDITERRANEAN SEA (*"Sea in the Middle of the Earth"*)— Also called the Great Sea, the Mediterranean Sea is the world's largest inland sea. It has played an important role in the fortunes of civilizations from ancient times to today. The sea was also significant to Christian mission work (Ac 13).

MEDIUMS, WIZARDS— Ancient diviners. They attempted to break through the unknown with magical arts, incantations, or reading of signs. (Lev 19:31; 1Sa 28). *See* **MAGIC AND SORCERY.**

MEEKNESS—A gentle disposition of mind and heart that abolishes one's superior feelings over others, regardless of circumstance. Meekness was named as a strong quality of mutual love (Col 3:12).

MEGIDDO (*meh GID oh*)—A city along the Great Road

between Gaza and Damascus; Main traffic passed through the Carmel Mountains there (Jos 17:11; 2Ki 23:28–30). Megiddo is the site of remarkable archaeological finds.

MELCHIZEDEK (*mel KIZ e dek; "king of righteousness"*)—A king-priest of Jerusalem who blessed Abraham and offered him bread and wine (Gen 14:18). He became a symbol of priestly greatness, exceeded only by the Messiah (Ps 110:4; Heb 4–5).

MELECH (*MEE lek; "king"*)—Son of Micah. A Benjaminite, Melech was a descendant of Jonathan and Saul (1Ch 8:35).

MELITA (*MEL i tah*)—*See* **MALTA.**

MELZAR (*MEEL zahr; "overseer"*)—An ancient title, usually translated as "steward" or "guard." The word was used to describe the man charged with the care of Daniel and his companions (Da 1:11, 16).

MEMORIALS—Stones, words, designated days, or rituals that served as reminders of an important event. Passover is a memorial of God's sparing of the firstborn of Israelites in Egypt (Ex 12:14). In the New Testament, the Last Supper established the Eucharist (communion), which is repeated as a memorial of Jesus (Lk 22:19; 1Co 11:24).

MEMPHIS—A major city of Egypt, and its capital during much of the Old Kingdom (c. 2700–2200 B.C.). It was later superseded by Thebes and never regained its former political importance. Jeremiah warned Jews not to flee to Memphis, because God was going to send destruction on Egypt (Jer 2:16, 44:1).

MENE, TEKEL, UPHARSIN (*MEE neh, TEK uhl, yoo FAR sin; "numbered, weighed, divided"*)—An Aramaic inscription written on the wall of the Babylonian King Belshazzar's banqueting hall by a mysterious disembodied hand. Daniel translated the words to mean: God has numbered your days. You have been weighed and found wanting. Your kingdom is divided between the Medes and Persians (Da 5:25–28).

MENELAUS (*MEN uh LAY uhs; "comforter"*)—A priest in Jerusalem who bribed Antiochus IV Epiphanes for the office of high priest in 171 B.C. It was the first time the high priest had not descended from Aaron.

MENORAH (*meh NOR uh*)—A seven-branched lampstand. It was specified as one of the furnishings for the wilderness tabernacle (Ex 25:31–40). Solomon's temple used ten menorahs (1Ki 7:49), but when the temple was rebuilt after the Babylonian exile, they again used a single lampstand (Zec 4:1–6). The feast of Hanukkah focuses on the progressive lighting of the branches of the menorah.

MENSTRUATION—Under Levitical law, a woman's monthly flow of blood made her unclean for seven days. Everyone who touched her during that time of impurity was considered unclean until evening.

MEONENIM, OAK OF (*meh AHN eh nim*)—A tree near Shechem; probably the same as the oak of Moreh. Also called "diviner's oak," it may have been named after soothsayers who practiced there (Jdg 9:37).

MEPHIBOSHETH (*meh FIB oh sheth; "utterance of shame"*)—1. A son of Saul. He was one of seven male descendants of Saul that David handed over to the Gibeonites to be killed. This action was considered vengeance for the blood-guilt that Saul had incurred by killing Gibeonites (2Sa 21:8). 2. Son of Jonathan;

MERCY SEAT

A rectangular lid of gold that covered the ark of the covenant, the mercy seat measured approximately 45 by 27 inches. Surrounding the lid—and wrought as one piece with it—were four cherubs. The four cherubs faced each other and were bent downward with their wings outstretched over the mercy seat. It was there that God communed with the people (Ex 25:17–22).

In Solomon's Temple, once a year (on the Day of Atonement) the high priest was allowed to enter the Holy of Holies (the sacred inner room where the ark was kept). There, he burned incense (a symbol of worship) in the presence of God. The smoke rose and enveloped the mercy seat in a cloud.

The high priest then sprinkled the blood of a sacrificed animal on the mercy seat, thus making atonement for himself and the nation. The mercy seat became synonymous with the presence of God (2Ki 19:1).

grandson of Saul. Paralyzed since childhood, he lost his family and all means of support. David, remembering his covenant with Jonathan, returned the family lands to him (2Sa 9).

MERAB (MEER ab; "increase")—A daughter of King Saul, who promised her to David as a wife, but changed his mind and gave her to Adriel (1Sa 14:49, 17:25). David married her younger sister, Michal.

MERARI (mer AHR eye; "bitter")—1. The third son of Levi (Gen 46:11). He was the founder of the

Merarites, one of the three Levitical families. In the wilderness, the Merarites transported much of the tabernacle materials (Nu 3:35–37). In David's time, they served as temple musicians (1Ch 25:3).

MERATHAIM (*mer uh THAY im; "double rebellion"*)—A symbolic name for Babylon (Jer 50:21).

MERCY—Kindness and love. In the Old Testament, mercy was used to describe God's faithfulness within the covenant relationship. God showed mercy even to those who broke the law (Da 9:9). In the New Testament, the word typically referred to the fulfillment of God's promised kindness through Jesus Christ (Lk 1:54; Titus 3:5–6). Many Christian benedictions mention mercy (1Ti 1:2).

MERODACH (*MAIR uh dahk*)—Hebrew for Marduk, the patron deity of Babylon. *See* **MARDUK**.

MEROM (*MEE rahm; "high place"*)—A city in Galilee. It was listed among the cities captured by Tiglath-pileser in 733 B.C.

MEROM, WATERS OF—A major water source near the city of Merom in Galilee. It was the site where the Israelites, under Joshua, defeated an alliance of northern Canaanite rulers (Jos 11:5–7).

MEROZ (*MEE roz*)—A city that was cursed in the Song of Deborah for its failure to aid the Israelites in the battle against Sisera (Jdg 5:23). The battle itself took place in the Jezreel Valley.

¹**MESHA** (*MEE shuh*)—1. Son of Caleb (1Ch 2:42). 2. A king of Moab who paid tribute to Israel's King Arab (2Ki 3:4). After Arab's death, he rebelled against Israel. Mesha's own report of the war is inscribed on the Moabite Stone. 3. A Benjaminite born in Moab (1Ch 8:9).

²**MESHA**—A place named as a boundary of the region inhabited by the descendants of Joktan (Gen 10:30).

MESHACH (*MEE shak*)—A Babylonian name given to Mishael, one of Daniel's three companions who refused to worship Nebuchadnezzar (Da 1:7). Thrown into a furnace, they were preserved by God (3:13–30).

MESHECH (*MEE shek;* "draw" or "drag")—**1.** Son of Japheth (Gen 10:2). **2.** Son of Shem (1Ch 1:17). **3.** Descendants of Japheth who traded in slaves and vessels of bronze (Eze 27:13).

MESHELEMIAH (*muh SHEL uh MY uh;* "the Lord repays")—A Levite gatekeeper of the tabernacle during the time of David (1Ch 9:21).

MESHULLAM (*meh SHOO luhm;* "friendship" or "reconciliation")—**1.** An ancestor of Josiah's secretary Shaphan (2Ki 22:3). **2.** Son of Zerubbabel (1Ch 3:19). **3.** A leader of the tribe of Gad (1Ch 5:13). **4.** A Benjaminite (1Ch 8:17). **5.** The father of Sallu the settler in Jerusalem (Ne 11:7). **6.** A Benjaminite who was among the first to return from the Exile (1Ch 9:8). **7.** A member of an important priestly family (Ne 11:11). **8.** A priest of the house of Immer (1Ch 9:12). **9.** A Levite who helped oversee temple repairs (2Ch 34:12). **10.** A leader who sought Levites to serve in the postexilic temple (Ezr 8:16). **11.** One who opposed Ezra's decree to divorce foreigners (Ezr 10:15). **12.** One who divorced his foreign wife after the Exile (Ezr 10:29). **13.** Son of Berachiah; he repaired Jerusalem's walls (Ne 3:4). **14.** Son of Besodeiah; he repaired Jerusalem's walls (Ne 3:6). **15.** A person who stood on the platform with Ezra during

MESSIAH

In the Old Testament, the word messiah ("anointed one") generally referred to a person who had been anointed with the holy oil, such as the high priest or the king (Lev 4:3–5; 2Sa 1:14–16).

Later, a messiah was promised who would be empowered by God to deliver Israel (Jer 23:5–6). A descendant from the royal line of David, he would be king of the Jews, a political leader that would defeat their enemies and usher in a golden era of peace and prosperity (Ps 2:2, 18:50, 89:38).

In fact, David was such a heroic king that he became one model of the messiah. But the chief model for the deliverer was Moses, who brought both spiritual renewal and political freedom to the people (Dt 18:15). In the New Testament, the word referred to Jesus' role as the predicted spiritual deliverer who set believers free from sin and death (Mt 1:1).

the reading of the law (Ne 8:4). **16.** A priest who helped seal the new covenant (Ne 10:7). **17.** An Israelite chief who helped seal the new covenant (Ne 10:20). **18.** A priest of the family of Ezra (Ne 12:13). **19.** A postexilic priest (Ne 12:16). **20.** A postexilic gatekeeper (Ne 12:25). **21.** A prince of Judah who participated in the dedication of Jerusalem's walls after the Exile (Ne 12:33).

MESOPOTAMIA—An ancient region between the Tigris and Euphrates rivers, also called Shinar, Chaldea, Ashur, and Bavel. Writing and literature was developed there. It was later home to the kingdoms of Assyria (north) and Babylonia (south). Modern Iraq encompasses much of Mesopotamia.

METHEG-AMMAH *(METH eg AM uh)*—A place David took from the Philistines (2Sa 8:1). Its location is unknown.

METHUSELAH *(meh THOO zeh luh)*—Son of Enoch and grandfather of Noah. At age 187, he fathered Lamech—and lived another 782 years. He died at the age of 969, the oldest recorded age in the Bible (Gen 5:21–27). He is named among the ancestors of Jesus (Lk 3:37).

ME-ZAHAB *(MEH zay hab; "waters of gold")*—Grandfather of Mehetabel, the wife of King Hadad (Gen 36:39).

MICAH *(MYE kuh; "who is like the Lord?")*—**1.** A man of the hill country of Ephraim during the period of the judges (Jdg 17–19). **2.** A descendant of Reuben (1Ch 5:5). **3.** Son of Merib-Baal of Saul's line (1Ch 8:34–35). **4.** Son of Zichri (1Ch 9:15). **5.** A man sent to Huldah to ask about the newfound book of the law (2Ki 22:12). **6.** An Old Testament prophet and author of the Book of Micah (Mic 1:1).

MICAH, BOOK OF—An Old Testament prophetic book that declares God's anger against injustice. This collection of messages has two major themes: punishment for Israel and Judah (Mic 1:2–5:15); and the announcement of judgment and salvation from their ruptured relationship with God (Mic 6–7).

MICAIAH *(mih KAY yuh; "who is like the Lord?")*—**1.** A prophet who risked his life and went to prison for prophesying that King Ahab would die in battle (1Ki 22:8). **2.** The mother of King Abijah (Abijam) of Judah (2Ch 13:2). **3.** A prince whom King Jehoshaphat sent to Judah to instruct the people in the law (2Ch 17:7). **4.** Son of Gemariah; he was a friend of Jeremiah (Jer 36:11–13). **5.** A priestly musician who took part in the postexilic dedication of Jerusalem's walls (Ne 12:41). **6.** A postexilic priest (Ne 12:35).

Michael (*"who is like God?"*)—**1.** A spy whom Moses sent into Canaan (Nu 13:13). **2.** A man from the tribe of Gad (1Ch 5:13). **3.** A descendant of Gad (1Ch 5:14). **4.** A Levite; descendant of Asaph (1Ch 6:40). **5.** A descendant of Issachar (1Ch 7:3). **6.** A descendant of Benjamin (1Ch 8:16). **7.** A Manassite who joined David at Ziklag (1Ch 12:20). **8.** A descendant of Issachar (1Ch 27:18). **9.** Son of King Jehoshaphat (2Ch 21:2). **10.** The head of a family that returned after the exile (Ezr 8:8). **11.** One of two archangels named in the Bible. Michael is first mentioned when he supported Daniel (Da 10:13). In Revelation, he is described as a warrior who leads other angels in a struggle with Satan's rebellion (Rev 12:7).

Michal (*MY kuhl; "who is like God?"*)—Daughter of King Saul; one of King David's wives (1Sa 14:49; 18:27–28). Michal demonstrated greater loyalty to her husband than to her father by helping David escape the jealous Saul.

Michmash (*MIC mash*)—A city located in the territory of Benjamin where Saul fled from the Philistines (1Sa 13).

Michtam (*MICK tam*)—A word of unknown meaning that appears in the heading of six psalms (Ps 16, 56–60). It may explain how to sing the psalm.

Midian (*MID ee uhn; "strife"*)—The fourth son of Abraham and Keturah (Gen 37:28). His descendants were the Midianites, a tribe who seduced the Israelites into idolatry (Nu

25:1–9). Gideon destroyed the Midianites (Jdg 6–7).

MIDRASH *(MID rash; "search out")*—A form of biblical interpretation. These Jewish commentaries on the Hebrew Bible paid close attention to individual words and grammatical forms to discover truth not seen on the surface.

MIDWIFE—A woman who assisted in the childbirth process. The most extensive biblical reference occurs when two midwives, Shiprah and Puah, disobeyed Pharaoh's command to kill male Hebrew babies (Ex 1:15–21).

MIGDAL *(MIG duhl)*—A military defensive tower within a city (Jdg 8:17), on its walls (2Ch 32:5), or projecting outward from them (Ne 3:25–27).

MIGDAL-EL *(MIG dal el; "tower of God")*—A fortified city in the tribal territory of Naphtali (Jos 19:38).

MIGDAL-GAD *(MIG dal gad; "tower of Gad")*—A town in the lowland plains of Judah (Jos 15:37).

MIGDOL *(MIG dal)*—1. An encampment made by the Israelites when they left Egypt (Ex 14:2). 2. A site in northeastern Egypt where Jews fled after Nebuchadnezzar destroyed Jerusalem (Jer 44:1).

MIGHTY MEN—Brave warriors who risked their lives for David (2Sa 23:8–29). The term was also used for the courageous warriors who served under Joshua (Jos 1:14, 6:2).

MIGRON *(MIG rahn)*—Town in the territory of Benjamin on the outskirts of Gibeah (1Sa 14:2). It was also named as a stop along the route of an Assyrian attack on Jerusalem (Isa 10:28).

MILCAH *(MIL kuh)*—1. Daughter of Haran; the wife of Nahor (Gen 22:20–22). 2. One of five daughters of Zelophehad who received her father's inheritance (Nu 36:11–22).

MILCOM (*MIL kum*)—The Ammorite name for Baal, a Canaanite fertility god. Solomon introduced the worship of Milcom (1Ki 11:5, 33); Josiah abolished it (2Ki 23:13). *See* **BAAL.**

MILDEW—Fungus that attacked crops in damp weather. Mildew and blight are often mentioned together and seen as God's judgment for disobedience (Dt 28:22; Hag 2:17).

MILETUS (*my LEE tuhs*)—An important port in Asia Minor, founded in 324 B.C. It was a center for of Greek art and philosophy. Because it had four harbors, it was also a popular commercial port. Paul met elders from Ephesus at Miletus for a farewell (Ac 20:15–38).

MILK—There were two Hebrew words for milk. One described fresh milk.

The other—cultured milk—was similar to yogurt and was also called curds (Isa 7:22). Milk was a symbol of plenty (Ex 3:17; Dt 32:14). In the New Testament, it referred to simple teaching (1Co 3:2) or unadulterated truth (1Pe 2:2).

MILL, MILLSTONE—A variety of tools were used to grind grain into meal or flour. The task was usually done by two stones—often made of black basalt—that rubbed or turned against each other (Isa 47:2; Mt 24:41).

MILLENNIUM (*mi LEN ee uhm*)—A period of a thousand years. The word was also a general term for a lengthy period (2Pe 3:8). Millennium appears six times in the Book of Revelation, and some accept that as a literal time for when Christ will reign on Earth (Rev 20).

MILLO (*MILL oh*)—A building or part of a city

constructed on a raised platform. The millo of Jerusalem was part of the city's fortification when David captured it (2Sa 5:9). Later, it was repaired by Solomon (1Ki 9:15).

MINA (*MEEN uh*)—A weight of money that varied throughout the Old Testament period. By New Testament times, it weighed about a pound (Lk 19:13, 16).

MINAEANS (*min AY uhns*)— An ancient Semitic tribe of Arabia; also called Meunim (1Ch 4:41). They are mentioned as temple servants (Ezr 2:50).

MIND—An English translation of various Hebrew and Greek words used to describe the human capacity for thinking, judgment, and intention. In the Bible, "heart" is often used as an equivalent of "mind" (Isa 65:17). The heart was seen as the seat of human emotion, intellect, and will.

MINEANS (*Mih NEE uhns*)—*See* **MINAEANS**.

MINING AND METALS—The Bible mentions iron (Dt 8:9), copper (Eze 24:11), beryl (Ex 28:20), onyx (Job 28:6), and chrysolite (Eze 1:16), all of which were mined. The most detailed description of mining occurs in the Book of Job (Job 28:1–11).

MINISTER—1. A personal attendant (1Sa 2:30; Jos 1:1). 2. To engage in priestly service (Ex 28:35). Christ was the high priest (Heb 8:6); Paul ministered the gospel to Gentiles (Ro 15:16). 3. A representative, usually of God. It comes from the Greek word *diakonos*, from which we get the word "deacon" (Php 1:1).

MINISTRY—Practical helpfulness or service to others (1Co 16:15), especially through preaching, visiting, providing for physical needs, and teaching (2Co 5:18).

MIRIAM

The sister of Moses and Aaron, Miriam played a major role in the delivery of the Israelites from Egypt.

When the baby Moses was found in a basket by Pharaoh's daughter, Miriam arranged for his own mother to become his wet nurse (Ex 2:4–8). After the miracle at the Red Sea, Miriam led the Israelite women in a victory song (Ex 15:20–21). During the 40 years in the desert, Miriam shared leadership with her brothers.

Called a prophet, she considered her prophetic ability equal to that of Moses. Miriam and Aaron spoke against Moses when he married a Cushite (Ethiopian) woman, but their criticism went beyond his choice for a wife. Apparently jealous of his authority over Israel, they openly complained about Moses (Nu 12).

God rebuked Miriam, and afflicted her with leprosy. Aaron begged Moses to forgive them and to intercede with God for her. Moses agreed, and she was healed. Miriam is not mentioned again until her death and burial at Kadesh in the wilderness (Nu 20:1).

MINNITH (*MIN ith*)—One of 20 cities captured from the Ammonites by Jephthah (Jdg 11:33). It was famous for growing high-quality wheat, which it shipped to Tyre (Eze 27:17).

MINT—Any of several strongly scented ancient herbs used for cooking and medicine, and as air fresheners. Jesus used mint—an inexpensive plant—as a symbol to condemn the scribes and Pharisees, saying they paid attention to trivial details (mint, dill, and cummin) of ritual laws but avoided the important matters of justice, mercy, and faith (Mt 23:23; Lk 11:42).

MIRACLES—An act of God's intervention in human events. Miracles appear almost exclusively in five periods: the deliverance of the Hebrews from Egypt and their establishment in Canaan under Joshua; the life-and-death struggle of true religion under Elijah and Elisha; the Exile, when God proved himself more powerful than heathen gods; the ministry of Jesus, when miracles attested to his person and work; and during the time of the Acts of the Apostles and the ministry of Paul, when the Church was being established.

MIRROR—Ancient mirrors were made of polished metal (Job 37:18), often bronze; they were disk-shaped and handheld, with handles of sculpted or decorated metal, bone, or ivory. Glass mirrors were not available until Roman times.

MISHAEL (MISH ee uhl; "who is what God is?")—**1.** A Levite. He and his brother Elzaphan carried the bodies of Nadab and Abihu, who had been struck dead by God, out of the camp (Ex 6:22). **2.** An aide who stood at the left hand of Ezra while he read the Book of the Law (Ne 8:4). **3.** A Hebrew name of one of Daniel's companions, whose name was changed to Meshach (Da 1:6–7).

MISHMA (MISH muh; "hearing")—**1.** The fifth son of Ishmael (Gen 25:14). **2.** A descendant of Simeon (1Ch 4:25–26).

MISHNAH (MISH nah)—A collection of rabbinic laws created around A.D. 200. They are arranged in 63 treatises that deal with all areas of Jewish life—legal, theological, social, and religious. For many, the Mishnah ranks second only to the Hebrew Scriptures, and serves as a link between Jews in Israel and those around the world.

MISREPHOTH-MAIM (*MIZ re fath MA im*)—A place near the Mediterranean Sea where Joshua chased the Canaanites after defeating them at the Waters of Merom (Jos 11:8).

MITE, WIDOW'S—The only Jewish coin mentioned in the New Testament was the widow's mite, a small copper coin and the least-valued in circulation. When Jesus saw a poor widow give two mites to the treasury, he said that it was more valuable than the large sums donated by the rich (Mk 12:41).

MITHREDATH (*MITH ruh dath; "gift of Mithra"*)—**1.** The treasurer of King Cyrus of Persia who restored the temple treasures to Shesh-bazzar (Ezr 1:8). **2.** A Persian official who wrote to King Artaxerxes I opposing the rebuilding of Jerusalem (Ezr 4:7).

MITRE (*MY tur*)—A turban, made of fine linen, that was worn by Israel's high priest. Attached to the turban was a gold pendant (or diadem) inscribed "Holy to the Lord." The pendant was affixed in front by a blue lace (Ex 28:4).

MITYLENE (*mit uh LEE ne*)—A wealthy port and the major city of the island of Lesbos. Paul briefly stopped there on his third missionary journey, en route from Troas to Miletus (Ac 20:14).

MIXED MULTITUDE—A term for the many non-Jewish slaves who left Egypt with the Israelites during the Exodus (Ex 12:38). In the postexilic period, it is used in the restricted sense of those of foreign descent who had to be separated from the Jews (Ne 13:3).

MIZAR (*MY zar*)—A hill or mountain within sight of Mt. Hermon (Ps 42:6).

MIZPAH, MISPEH (*MIZ pah, MIZ peh; "watchtower"*)—**1.** A name given to a mound of stones to symbolize a covenant between Jacob and Laban (Gen 31:49). **2.** A region near the foot of Mt. Hermon, called "land of Mizpah" and "valley of Mizpeh" (Jos 11:3, 8). **3.** A city in Judah (Jos 15:38). **4.** A city where Benjaminites raped and murdered the Levite's concubine (1Ki 15:22). **5.** A town or city in Gilead (Jdg 11:29, 34). **6.** A city in Moab (1Sa 22:3).

MIZPAR (*MIZ pahr*)—An Israelite who returned with Zerubbabel from the Exile (Ezr 2:2).

MIZRAIM (*MIZ ray im*)—The second son of Ham. The term was also used for his descendants. In the Old Testament, Mizraim was occassionally used as the name for Egypt (Gen 10:6,13).

MNASON (*NAY suhn*)—A Christian, originally from Cyprus, with whom Paul stayed on his final visit to Jerusalem (Ac 21:16).

¹MOAB (*MOH ab*)—**1.** A son of Lot by his oldest daughter (Gen 19:37). He was the ancestral father of the Moabites.

²MOAB—A nation east of the Dead Sea. Its history was closely linked to the Hebrews during the time of the judges (Jdg 3:12–30), the monarchy (1Sa 14:47), and the divided monarchy (2Ki 3:13–27). Prophets often spoke against Moab (Isa 15–16; Jer 48).

MOABITE STONE—A black basalt stone that bears an inscription celebrating the victory of King Mesha of Moab over Israel during the ninth century B.C. (2Ki 3:4–27). Mesha honored his god Chemosh for the victory. The stone is one of the only surviving examples of the Moabite language.

MOLADAH *(moh LAY duh; "generation")*—A city in the extreme south of Judah (Jos 15:26). It was specifically allocated to Simeon (Jos 19:1–2). After the Exile, it was resettled (Ne 11:26).

MOLECH *(MOH lek)*—A deity to whom Canaanites offered children as sacrifices (Lev 18:21, 20:2–5; 2Ki 23:10; Jer 32:35). Worship of Molech was abhorrent to the God of Israel.

MOLID *(MOH lid; "begetter")*—Son of Abishur; a descendant of Judah (1Ch 2:29).

MOLTEN SEA—Also called the Bronze or Brazen Sea, this great basin was made by Solomon. It stood in the inner court of the temple between the altar of burnt offerings and the sanctuary where priests washed their hands and feet (1Ki 7:39).

MONEY—Bartering was originally the method of exchange; cattle was the early standard of value. Until the introduction of coins, the most common media of exchange were metals measured by weight (Gen 23:16).

MONEY BOX—A small container for carrying coins. Judas Iscariot took care of the common money box of Jesus and his disciples (Jn 12:6, 13:29).

MONEY-CHANGERS—Bankers who exchanged one nation's currency (or one size of coin) for another. They charged a fee for their services. Every Israelite 20 years old or older had to pay an annual tax, so some money-changers operated in the Court of the Gentiles in the temple area. All money had to be minted by the coinmakers of Tyre (to avoid the pagan images of ancient Rome).

MOON—The lesser light (Gen 1:16), created as a sign at night and a marker

MONOTHEISM

Most of the major religions of the biblical world involved many deities. The worship of one supreme being was an important characteristic of the Hebrews—and a central teaching of the Old Testament.

Hebrew creed stated: "Hear, O Israel, the Lord our God, the Lord is one!" (Dt 6:4). This belief was not the result of philosophical speculation; it came from God's divine self-revelation and was understood by experience (Dt 4:35). Although early accounts speak of other gods (Ex 12:13; Nu 33:4), God commanded Israel not to obey those deities, saying "you shall have no other gods before me" (Ex 20:1–6). By 750 B.C., the concept of monotheism was clear. Amos declared that God would judge various nations of idol worshipers (Am 1–2).

In the New Testament, Jesus affirmed the monotheistic convictions of Judaism (Mk 12:29). Several epistles emphasized the oneness of God (1 Co 8:6) and the Christian belief in "one Lord, one faith, one baptism" (Eph 4:5).

of the night sky (Jer 31:35). God forbade the Jews to worship the moon (Dt 4:19). They relied on the moon to measure time, mark off moons (months), and determine the day of the Passover and other feasts. At the end of time, the moon will darken because God's light (rule) will be everlasting (Isa 60:19, 20; Rev 21:23).

MORDECAI (*MOHR duh kye;* "*consecrated to [the pagan deity] Marduk*")—**1.** A Jew who returned from exile with Zerubbabel (Ezr 2:2). **2.** He raised Esther, his orphaned cousin, and enabled her to become the queen of Persia's King Ahasuerus.

MOREH (*MOH reh; "teacher"*)—**1.** A place at Shechem distinguished by a prominent tree where God first spoke to Abraham (Gen 12:6–7). **2.** A hill in the Jezreel Valley where the Midianites camped in preparation for battle against Gideon's forces (Jdg 7:1).

MORESHETH-GATH (*MOH reh sheth gath; "possession of Gath"*)—The birthplace of the prophet Micah (Mic 1:14).

MORIAH (*mor RYE uh*)—**1.** A mountain where Abraham was commanded by God to sacrifice his son Isaac (Gen 22:2, 4). **2.** The location of the Jerusalem temple, originally a threshing floor (2Ch 3:1). Some believe the altar in the temple was on the exact site where Abraham intended to sacrifice Isaac.

MORTAR AND PESTLE—Used by ancient masons and builders, mortar was the material that held bricks together. It was mixed with asphalt, clay, straw, mud, or other elements (Gen 11:3). The mixture was ground by a pestle, which was made of wood or stone; sometimes the mixture was trodden by workers (Na 3:14).

MOSAIC—Relating or pertaining to Moses. The law that God gave to Moses is often called the Mosaic Law.

MOSERAH, MOSEROTH (*moh ZEE ruh, moh ZEE rawth; "bonds"*)—A place where the Israelites camped on their journey to Canaan (Dt 10:6).

MOST HIGH—A popular Old Testament name for God, especially in Psalms (Ps 7:17, 91:1). The phrase is a common translation of a Hebrew adjective that means "high" or "exalted" when it is applied to God.

MOSES

The first great leader of the Hebrew people, Moses is regarded as the author of the first five books of the Old Testament (the Pentateuch). He is revered for his daring leadership and diplomacy, as well as the giving of the divine law.

Moses was born in Egypt when the Hebrews were enslaved to Pharaoh (Ex 2:2). His parents were Amram and Jochebed of the tribe of Levi. Saved from death by Pharaoh's daughter and raised in the royal household, he later fled from Egypt after killing a slavemaster.

On Mt. Sinai, God appeared to Moses and commissioned him to rescue the Israelites from slavery. Moses returned to Egypt, where he performed miracles and asked Pharaoh to release the people. When the Israelites finally left Egypt, Moses was the intercessor between God and the Israelites. Before Moses' death, God showed him a view of the Promised Land—the land he would never walk upon—from the top of Mt. Nebo.

Most Holy Place—Also called "Holy of Holies," this phrase designated the innermost room of the tabernacle (Ex 26:34). Only the high priest was allowed to enter it—and only on one day a year—to make atonement for the people (Lev 16).

Mother of Pearl—The iridescent inner layer of mollusk shells. It was one of the materials used in the mosaic pavement at Ahasuerus' extravagant banquet at Susa (Est 1:6).

Mount, mountain—Mountains were a dominant feature of the biblical landscape. The Bible frequently refers to mountains as dwelling places (Gen 36:8), places of refuge (Jdg 6:2; Mt 24:3), lookouts (Mt 4:8), landmarks (Nu 34:7), assembly sites (1Sa 7:3), cemeteries (2Ki 23:26), and scenes of battles (1Sa 23:36).

Mountain of God, Mountain of the Lord—A mountain upon which God was to be worshiped. It was important to the Hebrews that their worship did not take place on a mountain dedicated to a pagan deity. At first, all Jews worshiped at Mt. Zion, but King Manasseh built a temple on Mt. Gerizim (Ne 13:28). For 400 years, the separate places of worship divided the Jews and Samaritans. (Jn 4:20).

Mourning—Mourners were expected to express their grief by openly shrieking or weeping (Mk 5:38), tearing their own clothes (1Sa 1:2), wearing sackcloth and ashes (Isa 22:12), and cutting their hair (Jer 16:16) or shaving their heads. To increase the public display, professional mourners were sometimes hired (Jer 9:17–22; Mt 9:23). There were specified mourning periods, lasting from seven days (Gen 50:10) to three weeks (Da 10:2).

MOUSE—An unclean animal (Lev 11:29), the mouse was not eaten by Israelites, except in heathen rites (Isa 66:17). Field mice destroyed crops and could carry plagues (1Sa 6:4–5).

MULBERRY—A tree cultivated in Syria for its leaves, on which the silkworm fed. A drink was made from the berries with honey and spices.

MUMMIFICATION—An elaborate embalming technique practiced in ancient Egypt and spread to other cultures. The expensive process took up to 70 days and included the removal of major organs. Jacob and Joseph were embalmed (Gen 50:1–4, 26), but it was not a customary Jewish practice.

MURMURING—The complaining of the Israelites after they left Egypt. A repeated theme in the Book of Exodus, murmuring emphasized the rebelliousness of the people. In the New Testament, the word refers to any type of resentful complaint (Mt 20:11).

Ancient musical cymbals

MUSIC—Music was an important part of everyday biblical life. It was played at parties (Lk 15:25) and to welcome heroes and celebrate victories (Ex 15:20). Music was a ceremonial part of making war and crowning kings (Jdg 7:18–20). David, a musician himself, organized a Levitical choir and orchestra for temple services. Hebrews used three types of instruments: strings (lyre, harp), percussion (cymbals, tambourine), and wind (ram's horn, flute, trumpet).

327

MUSTARD SEED—Mustard was a common biblical plant, grown for spice and for the oil in the seeds. The mustard seed was a symbol of great growth. Although the seeds were quite tiny, the black mustard plant often grew 10 feet tall (Mt 13:31).

MYRA (*MY ruh*)—The chief city of Lycia in Asia Minor. While being transported to Rome as a prisoner, Paul was transferred to a ship there (Ac 27:5–6).

MYRRH (*MER*)—An aromatic extract from a stiff-branched tree with white flowers and plumlike fruit. Myrrh was used in anointing oil (Ex 30:23), as perfume (Ps 45:8), and for embalming (Jn 19:39). The Magi presented it as one of their gifts when they journeyed to see the infant Jesus (Mt 2:11).

MYRTLE—A large evergreen shrub that grows densely along rivers. The Jews used its green leaves to adorn their booths during the Feast of Tabernacles (Ne 8:15). They also used its fragrant leaves for perfume.

MYSIA (*MIS ee uh*)—A region of northwestern Asia Minor. Paul passed through two towns in that area, Troas (Ac 16:8, 11) and Assos (20:13). Pergamum was also in the region (Rev 1:11).

MYSTERY—That which is unknown or hidden from human understanding. In the Old Testament, the word occurs only in the Book of Daniel (Da 2:18). In the New Testament, it refers to secrets revealed through the Holy Spirit (Ro 16:25).

MYTHOLOGY—Ancient stories about gods or supernatural beings that explain the origins of customs, institutions, phenomena, or a culture's beliefs. In the New Testament, the word myth refers to false and foolish stories (1Ti 1:4).

¹NAAMAH *(NAY uh muh; "pleasant")*—**1.** The sister of Tubal-Cain. She was listed in the lineage of Cain (Gen 4:22). **2.** An Ammonite who married Solomon and bore him Rehoboam (1Ki 14:21).

²NAAMAH—A city in the lowlands of Judah (Jos 15:41).

NAAMAN *(NAY uh muhn; "pleasantness")*—**1.** A Benjaminite who settled in Egypt (Gen 46:21). **2.** The leprous commander of the Syrian army who was healed by immersing himself seven times in the Jordan River (2Ki 5). Jesus recalled the incident as an example of God's care for a Gentile (Lk 4:27).

NABAL *(NAY buhl; "foolish")*—A wealthy sheepmaster who refused to give food to David and his men even though they had protected his people from marauders (1Sa 25:2–39). David swore vengeance, but before he could act, Nabal's wife met David with food and asked him to forgive her husband. When Nabal heard of his wife's action, he suffered a heart attack (or stroke) and died. David married his wife.

NABLUS *(NAB luhs)*—A city just west of Shechem. It was founded by Roman Emperor Vespasian in A.D. 72 as Flavius Neapolis, a settlement for Roman army veterans. Today it is a large Palestinian Arab town.

NACHOR *(NAY kor)*—*See* **NAHOR.**

NADAB *(NAY dab; "generous" or "noble")*—**1.** The eldest of Aaron's four sons. After being ordained a priest, he offered "unholy"

NABOTH

A native of Jezreel, Naboth owned a vineyard located next to the palace of King Ahab (1Ki 21). The king wanted to buy the vineyard, but Naboth refused because the land was part of his family inheritance.

After seeing that Ahab was despondent, Queen Jezebel devised an evil plan. She wrote to the elders of the village and demanded that they charge Naboth with blasphemy. Then the queen bribed two witnesses to give false testimony. Naboth was convicted, his land was forfeited to the crown, and he was stoned to death by the villagers—the punishment for blasphemy (Lev 24:16).

Ahab hurried to Jezreel to confiscate the property. There he was met by the prophet Elijah, who pronounced divine judgment on him: Every male in Ahab's house would perish, his dynasty would end, and Jezebel would be eaten by dogs.

Ahab responded with penitence and was spared (1Ki 21:27–29), but his son Joram was slain by Jehu. Joram's body was cast on the plot that had belonged to Naboth. When Jezebel was thrown out a window to her death, and her body eaten by dogs (2Ki 9:30), Jehu proclaimed that Elijah's oracle was fulfilled (2Ki 9:34–36).

fire to Yahweh and died childless (Ex 6:23). **2.** An evil king of Israel (909–908 B.C.). He was the son and successor of Jeroboam I (1Ki 14:20). **3.** A descendant of Judah (1Ch 2:28). **4.** An uncle of King Saul (1Ch 8:30).

NAG HAMMADI *(nag ham MAH dee)*—A town in

northern Egypt where, in 1946, Coptic translations of 13 papyrus volumes of ancient Gnostic writings were found. The discovery made possible a more distinct picture of the contrast between Christian Gnosticism and orthodox Christianity.

NAHALAL, NAHALOL *(nuh HAL al, NAY huh lal)*—A city of Zebulun (Jos 19:15) that was assigned to the Levites (Jos 21:35). It was shared by the Canaanites because the tribe of Zebulun was unable to expel them (Jdg 1:30).

NAHALIEL *(nuh HAY li el; "valley of God")*—A site near Mt. Pisgah where the Israelites camped (Nu 21:19).

NAHASH *(NAY hash; "serpent")*—1. An Ammonite king defeated by Saul (1Sa 12:12). 2. An Ammonite king who befriended David (2Sa 10:2). 3. The father of David's half-sisters Abigail and Zeruiah (2Sa 17:25).

¹NAHOR *(NAY hor; "snorting")*—1. Abraham's grandfather, who lived to be 148 years old (Gen 11:22). 2. Abraham's brother and the husband of Milcah (Gen 11:26).

²NAHOR—A city in northwest Mesopotamia where Abraham sent his servant to obtain a wife for Isaac (Gen 24:10).

NAHSHON *(NAH shahn; "diviner")*—Son of Amminadab; brother-in-law of Aaron (Ex 6:23). He was a leader of the tribe of Judah during the wilderness wanderings (Nu 2:3). Nahshon was listed among the ancestors of David and Jesus (Ru 4:20–22; Lk 3:32–33).

NAHUM *(NAY hum; "comforter")*—1. A prophet sent to the wicked people of Nineveh to warn them of God's coming judgment. His words are recorded in the book of Nahum. 2. A descendant of Zerubbabel. He is listed among the

NAMES OF GOD IN THE OLD TESTAMENT

Some Old Testament names for God included:

1) *Yahweh* (older translations used *Jehovah*)—The most important name in the Old Testament, it appears 6,828 times—usually translated as "Lord" (Ex 3:14). There is no exact definition, but it roughly means "The One Who Is" or "The One Who Exists." The name was considered too sacred to be spoken by the Israelites.

2) *Yahweh Sabaoth*—This name, which occurs 279 times in the Old Testament, means "Lord of hosts." It describes God as the one who rules heavenly armies.

3) *Adonai*—Meaning "the Lord," *Adonai* is a plural term for majesty. It was used as a title of respect to address a superior. After the Exile, worshipers verbally used *Adonai* to replace the sacred name of *Yahweh*.

4) *El*—The common Semitic name for god, *El* occurs 238 times in the Old Testament. *El* has many appellations, such as *El Shaddai* ("God Almighty"; Gen 17:1), *El Elyon* ("God Most High"; Ps 47:2–3), and *El Roi* ("God who sees"; Gen 16:13–14).

Other names for God include *Elohim* (which appears 2,600 times) and *Eloah* (57 times, mostly in the Book of Job). God is also identified as *Branch of Righteousness* (Jer 23:5–6), *Wisdom* (Pr 8), *Shepherd* (Isa 40:11), *Father* (Dt 12:6), *Brother* (1Sa 14:3), *Kinsman* (Gen 31:41), *Redeemer* (Ps 19:14), and *Ancient One* (Da 7:9).

ancestors of Jesus (Lk 3:25).

NAHUM, BOOK OF—A short, prophetic Old Testament book in which Nahum predicted the destruction of Assyria and its capital, Nineveh. Unlike Jonah, who had delivered a message of mercy and forgiveness to the wicked people of Nineveh 100 years earlier, Nahum issued a harsh warning of inescapable justice. The prophecy was fulfilled by the fall of Nineveh in 612 B.C.

Ancient nails

NAIL—Metal nails, usually made of bronze or iron, were used by biblical carpenters. They were hand-forged and about the same size as our modern nails (1Ch 22:3). The nails used at Jesus' crucifixion, however, were large iron spikes (Jn 20:25), which translate as "pegs."

NAIN—A city in Galilee where Jesus raised a widow's only son from the dead (Lk 7:11–17).

NAIOTH *(NAY oth; "habitation")*—A place in or near the city of Ramah in the territory of Benjamin. Samuel lived there, and David fled to Naioth to escape King Saul (1Sa 19:18).

NAOMI *(nay OH mee; "pleasantness" or "my joy")*—The mother-in-law of Ruth. After her husband and two sons died while living in Moab, Naomi returned to Bethlehem. Devoted to her dead husband's mother, Ruth accompanied Naomi on the journey. Later, Ruth mar-

333

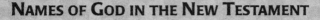

NAMES OF GOD IN THE NEW TESTAMENT

1) *God*—The most common name in the New Testament, God (*Theos*), appears 1,326 times. The Septuagint (Greek translation of the Old Testament) generally translated *Elohim* as *Theos*.

2) *Lord*—In the Old Testament, the major designation of God—*Yahweh*—is translated as "Lord" (*Kyrios*) in the Septuagint. Most of the 719 New Testament occurrences of Lord refer to Jesus as the exalted Christ (Ac 2:36; Jn 20:28).

3) *Father*—For Jesus, "Father" was the principal designation of God. He used the common Jewish phrase "Our Father" (Mt 5:45, 6:9), as well as the informal Aramaic word *Abba* ("daddy" or "poppa") (Mk 14:36), which was appropriated by the Church (Ro 8:15; Gal 4:6).

4) *The Almighty*—This name is found several times in the New Testament (2Co 6:18; Rev 2:8).

5) *Alpha and Omega*—The first and last letters of the Greek alphabet represented God as the beginning and the end of all creation, and thus the only God. It was used only in the Book of Revelation (Rev 1:8, 21:6).

6) *The Holy One*—This Old Testament title for God appeared five times in the New Testament (Rev 16:5; Lk 4:34).

Other common names for God included *King* (Mt 5:35), *Judge* (Jn 8:50), and *Savior* (Lk 1:47).

ried Boaz and became an ancestor of David and Jesus (Ru 4:21–22; Mt 1:5).

NAPHISH (*NAY fish*; *"numerous"* or *"breath"*)—Son of Ishmael (1Ch 1:31). He was the founder of a clan defeated by Israel at the Jordan River (1Ch 5:19).

NAPHTALI (*NAF tuh lye*; *"wrestle"*)—The sixth son of Jacob (and the second of Bilhah, Rachel's handmaid), he was the father of the tribe that bears his name (Gen 30:7–8). Naphtali had four sons, which divided the tribe into four families (Gen 46:24).

NAPHTUHIM (*NAF tuh him*)—A descendant of Mizraim, the second son of Ham (Gen 10:13). Some scholars believe the Naphtuhim to be a tribal family that settled in the Egyptian Delta.

NAPKIN—In the New Testament, a nobleman's slave concealed his pound in a napkin for safekeeping (Lk 19:20). The word is also used for a cloth wrapped around the face of the dead, such as with Lazarus and Jesus (Jn 11:44, 20:7).

NARCISSUS (*nahr SIS uhs*; *"daffodil"*)—The head of a Christian household in Rome whom Paul greeted (Ro 16:11).

NARD—A costly, fragrant ointment that was prepared from a plant native to the Himalayan mountains in India. Nard was used as a perfume (SS 4:13). The woman of Bethany used it to anoint Jesus before his death (Mk 14:3).

NATHAN (*NAY thun*; *"gift"*)—**1.** Son of David and Bathsheba; older brother of Solomon (2Sa 5:14). **2.** An important prophet during the reign of David and Solomon (2Sa 7:2–17; 1Ch 17:1–15). **3.** An Aramean from Zobah (2Sa 23:36). **4.** The father of two of Solomon's officials (1Ki 4:5), perhaps the same as Nathan 1 or 2. **5.** A descendant of Judah (1Ch 2:36). **6.** Brother of Joel (1Ch 11:38), probably the same as Nathan 3. **7.** A leader whom Ezra sent to find Levites for the temple (Ezr 8:15–16). **8.** A man who divorced his foreign wife after the Exile (Ezr 10:39), probably the same as Nathan 7.

NATHANAEL *(nuh THAN ee uhl; "god has given")*—One of Jesus' chosen disciples (Jn 1:45). Because his name does not appear on other apostolic lists, scholars have identified him most commonly as Bartholomew.

NATIONS—Non-Israelites were often grouped under the term "nations" (Ex 15:14). In the Old Testament, God promised to protect the Israelites against foreign nations. God also commanded his people to turn away from the idolatry of other cultures (Dt 7:22–26). The Bible teaches of God's sovereignty over all nations. Jesus was sent as a light to the nations (Gentiles) (Lk 2:32).

NATIONS, TABLE OF—A list of ancient genealogy found in the Book of Genesis (Gen 10). It bridges the gap between humanity's beginnings and Israel's beginnings. The three divisions follow the lineage of Noah's three sons: Shem, Ham, and Japheth.

NAZARENE—A person from Nazareth. Because Jesus grew up there, the term is applied to him in all four gospels and Acts of the Apostles (Ac 10:38). It was also used once to describe the early Christians (Ac 24:5).

NAZARETH—A village in lower Galilee where Jesus spent his boyhood (Mt 2:23; Lk 1:26). It was an insignificant agricultural village close to an important trade route to Egypt.

A view of Nazareth

NAZIRITE *(NAZZ ih rite)*—Israelites who entered into a special vow to God for a period of time (Nu 8:1–2; 1Sa 1:1–11). Nazirites pledged to refrain from wine and other intoxicants, to not cut their hair, and to not touch dead bodies. Samson was dedicated as a Nazirite by his parents before birth.

NEAPOLIS *(nee AP oh lis; "new city")*—A seaport for the city of Philippi. Paul landed there on his second missionary journey (Ac 16:11).

NEBAIOTH *(neh BAY yahth; "heights")*—Ishmael's oldest son. He was the ancestor of the Arab tribe of Nabaiati (Gen 25:13).

NEBAT *(NEE bat; "view")*—The father of Jeroboam I, the first king of the northern kingdom (1Ki 12:16).

NEBI SAMWIL *("high place")*—A 3,000-foot peak north of Jerusalem. It was important because it overlooked the tribal boundary between Benjamin and Judah.

¹NEBO *(NEE bo; "prophet")*—1. A Babylonian god of writing and wisdom; son of Marduk. 2. An Israelite whose 52 sons returned from the Exile (Ezr 2:29).

²NEBO—A Transjordan city conquered by the Israelites. It was given to the tribe of Reuben.

NEBO, MT. *(NEE bo; "prophet")*—The mountain where Moses viewed the Promised Land (Dt 32:49). God told him he would see but not enter the land. Moses died there and was buried nearby (Dt 34:1).

NEBUCHADNEZZAR (*neb yu kud NEZ ur; "may [the deity] Nebo protect"*)—A powerful Babylonian king who conquered Judah and forced many of its people into exile (2Ki 24–25). God delivered messages to the king through Daniel and three Jewish captives. Later, God punished Nebuchadnezzar for his pride by striking him with madness. The king repented, was healed, and ruled in obedience to God.

NECK—It was an ancient custom for victors to place a foot on the neck of the defeated (Jos 10:24). A bowed neck symbolized submission; a stiff neck, stubbornness (Dt 9:13).

NECO (*NEE ko*)—Pharaoh who defeated Josiah at Megiddo (2Ki 23:29). Neco was later defeated at Carchemish by King Nebuchadnezzar (2Ki 24:7).

NECROMANCY—An ancient form of witchcraft in which a medium talked with the dead about the future. Considered black magic by the Israelites, it was forbidden by their law (Dt 18:10–11).

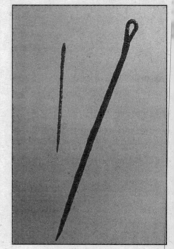

Ancient needles

NEEDLE—Ancient needles were made of bone, ivory, or bronze. Jesus said that it was "easier for a camel to go through the eye of a needle than for someone who is rich to enter the kingdom of God" (Mt

19:24; Mk 10:25; Lk 18:25).

NEGEV *(NEH gev; "southward")*—A section of desert in southern Judah crossed by several important trade routes. Abraham traveled through here en route from Haran to Egypt (Gen 12:9) and settled there after Sodom and Gomorrah were destroyed (Gen 20:1).

NEHELAM *(neh HEL uhm)*—A false prophet who wrote to Zephaniah accusing Jeremiah of being a false prophet (Jer 29:24–31). God promised to punish Nehelam and his descendants for attempting to lead the people astray (Jer 29:32).

NEHEMIAH *(NEE uh MYE uh; "the Lord comforts")*—A governor of Judah who restored Jerusalem's walls in 52 days (Ne 6:15). With Ezra, he made numerous reforms designed to conform with the Law. His deeds are recorded in the book bearing his name.

NEHEMIAH, BOOK OF—An Old Testament book containing a record of Nehemiah's two terms as governor of Judah. In spite of great opposition, he rebuilt Jerusalem after the Exile and initiated many economic and religious reforms.

NEHUSHTA *(neh HUHSH tuh; "brazen")*—Daughter of Elnathan; wife of Jehoiakim; mother of Jehoichin (2Ki 24:8). She was held captive by Nebuchadnezzar in Babylon.

NEHUSHTAN *(neh HUHSH ten; "little brazen thing")*—A bronze serpent created by Moses. When the people in the wilderness complained, God sent poisonous snakes that killed many of the Israelites. After they repented, God told Moses to make the serpent and mount it on a stick. If bitten, an Israelite who looked at the serpent would not die (Nu 21:4–8). The serpent was later destroyed by Hezekiah (2Ki 18:4).

NEIGHBOR—The Bible teaches us to love our neighbor as ourselves (Lev 19:18; Mt 19:19). Half of the Ten Commandments address the treatment of one's neighbors. In the New Testament, Jesus defined neighborly love as the act of extending care to all people, despite their race or social status (Lk 10:25–37).

NEKODA (*neh KO duh; "famous"*)—**1.** The head of the family of Nethinim who, after returning from Babylon, could not prove Israelite ancestry (Ezr 2:60). **2.** The founder of a family of temple servants who returned from Babylon with Zerubbabel (Ezr 2:48).

NEPHILIM (*NEF ih lim; "giant"*)—An ancient race of human giants; descendants of Anak (Gen 6:1–4; Nu 13:33). *See* **ANAKIM, ANAKITES.**

NEPHTOAH (*Nef TOH uh; "opening"*)—A site on the border of Judah and Benjamin, believed to be the spring of present-day Lifta (Jos 15:9).

NEREUS (*NEER ee uhs*)—A Christian in Rome, son of Philolgus and Julia, to whom Paul sent greetings (Ro 16:15).

NERGAL (*NER gahl; "hero"*)—A Babylonian god worshiped by exiles in Samaria. Symbolized by the lion, Nergal was noted for causing destruction and disaster (2Ki 17:30).

NERGAL-SHAREZER (*NER gahl shuh REE zur; "fire prince"*)—Nebuchadnezzar's official who was charged with keeping Jeremiah safe after the capture of Jerusalem (Jer 39:3–14).

NERO (*NEE ro*)—Nero Claudius Caesar, a Roman emperor (54–68 A.D.) who ignored public responsibilities to pursue personal indulgences. He blamed Christian activists for a fire that nearly destroyed Rome and retaliated by persecuting them.

NETHANIAH *(NETH uh NIGH uh; "gift of the Lord")*—**1.** A temple singer (1Ch 25:2). **2.** A Levite law instructor (2Ch 17:8). **3.** The father of Jehudai, an official of Jehoiakim (Jer 36:14). **4.** The father of Ishmael, the murderer of Gedaliah (2Ki 25:23).

NETHINIM *(NETH ih nim; "dedicated")*—Servants who performed common temple tasks (1Ch 9:2; Ezr 8:17–20). They are listed with priests, singers, and Levites as important to temple life (Ezr 2:70).

NETOPHAH *(neh TOH fuh; "dropping")*—A town near Bethlehem where returning exiles settled (Ezr 2:22). It was the home of two of David's mighty men (2Sa 23:28–29).

NETS—Symbolically, nets referred to God's judg-ments (Ps 141:10) and the deviousness of evil people (Ps 9:15).

NEW BIRTH—A spiritual renewal experienced by believers through the work of God's spirit. This new birth changes the heart, allowing response to God through faith (Jn 3:3; 2Co 5:17).

NEW COVENANT—In the Old Testament, God established a covenant—or contract—with his people. The Israelites were required to followed the laws of God, and in return he gave them his favor. The prophet Jeremiah predicted that God would someday create a "new covenant" in which the law would be written "on their hearts" (Jer 31:31–34). Christians recognize the coming of Jesus as the fulfillment of the new covenant. The old covenant required animal sacrifice when it was broken; in the new covenant, Jesus paid for all of humanity's sin by his own death, the perfect sacrifice (Mt 26:28; Mk 14:24).

NEW GATE—A gate of the Jerusalem temple where Jeremiah was tried (Jer 26:10). Its exact location is unknown but is believed to be in the upper court.

NEW MOON—The first day of a lunar month. It was a time of rejoicing, when the Israelites blew trumpets and made sacrifices in thanksgiving to God (Nu 10:10).

NEW TESTAMENT—The second part of the Bible, composed of 27 sacred books. Testament means "covenant." The term "new" not only separates the writings from the Old Testament, but reminds us that a relationship with God is not based upon what we do, but what God has done in the sacrifice of Jesus (1Co 11:25). The New Testament includes the four gospels (Jesus' life and ministry), the Acts of the Apostles (the growth of the Church following Jesus' death), the epistles (letters of instruction to Christians), and apocalyptic writings (which encourage believers that, because of Jesus, good will ultimately prevail over evil).

NEW YEAR—The beginning of a new calendar year. For the Hebrews, the new year was the first day of the seventh month. Trumpets were blown to begin the celebration, but it was then spent as a day of rest (Lev 23:23). The "Feast of Trumpets" was later replaced by Rosh Hashanah.

NICANOR GATE (nigh KAY nor; "conqueror")—A copper gate leading into a courtyard of Herod's Temple. Named for the craftsman who made it, Nicanor Gate was perhaps the gate through which Mary took Jesus to be circumcised (Lk 3:22–35).

NICOLAITANS (nik o LAY tanz)—A Christian group

NEW TESTAMENT APOCRYPHA

The New Testament left numerous questions unanswered. Curious people wanted to know more about many things, such as Jesus' childhood years. This desire to know more led to the writings known as the New Testament Apocrypha (*uh PAHK ri fuh; "hidden"*). This material, which began to be written after the time of the apostles, contained embellishments of the story of Jesus and the disciples.

The writings often claimed to have apostolic authority, but these claims were false. Wary of forgeries, Paul began to verify his signature because it was being faked by other authors seeking to validate their writings (2Th 3:17).

Many of these apocryphal writings were very bizarre and offensive in nature and are believed to have been written to rival pagan literature. However, some of the writings were legitimately intended to shed light on the Christian faith and what it meant to be a Christian.

that practiced pagan rituals and committed fornication (Rev 2:14–15). Both Jesus and the church in Ephesus condemned these practices (Rev 2:6).

NICOLAUS (*nik o LAY uhs; "conqueror of the people"*)— A pagan who converted to Judaism and then to Chris-tianity. He was one of seven "deacons" chosen to meet the daily food needs of Greek widows. It is not likely he was related to the heretical group called the Nicolaitans.

NICOPOLIS (*ni KAHP o lis; "city of victory"*)—An ancient city on the Gulf of Actium

NICODEMUS

A high-ranking Jewish ruler, Nicodemus (*nik o DEE muhs; "victor over the people"*) was a Pharisee and member of the Sanhedrin (high court). After observing Jesus' ministry and miracles, he was curious as to whether or not Jesus indeed had come from God.

He met Jesus at night to avoid criticism by the other Pharisees. In this discussion, Jesus told him that he must be born again, but Nicodemus misunderstood this directive as meaning a second physical birth (Jn 3:1–21).

Later, when Jesus was to be brought before the Sanhedrin, Nicodemus defended his right not to be condemned without a trial. Following Jesus' death on the cross, Nicodemus provided the spices necessary to prepare Jesus' body for burial.

Jesus' encounter with Nicodemus showed that, contrary to common belief, there were Jews of high status interested in Jesus' message. Because Nicodemus did not understand the truth about God's kingdom, John used him as a symbol of how the Jewish nation was "blind to the truth of God" (Jn 1:11, 3:19).

built by Augustus Caesar. Paul spent a winter there (Titus 3:12).

NIGER *(NIGH jur; "black")*—The surname of Symeon, a teacher in the Antioch church. He was called by God to commission Paul and Barnabas on their first missionary journey (Ac 13:1–3).

NIGHTHAWK—A small nocturnal bird of prey, related to the owl and hawk. It was considered unclean by the Hebrews

A sailboat on the Nile River near Elephant Island at Aswan, Egypt

because it ate other animals (Lev 11:16; Dt 14:15).

NILE—The world's longest river, flowing for 4,160 miles. It was the life-stream of Egyptian civilization. The annual flooding of the Nile provided irrigation for crops.

NIMRIM, WATERS OF *(NIM rim; "clear")*—A stream in Moab. Jeremiah and Isaiah predicted that its waters would dry up, causing crops to wither (Isa 15:6; Jer 48:34).

NIMROD *(NIM rahd; "brave")*—Both Babylonian and Assyrian civilizations can be traced to this mighty hunter, warrior, and ruler (Gen 10:8–12). He founded many important cities, including Babel and Nineveh. Many characterized his rule as a "golden age."

NINEVEH *(NIH nuh vuh; "dwelling of Ninus")*—The ancient capital of Assyria, where Jonah was sent to warn the people of its destruction (Jnh 3:4). Jonah's message, while heeded at first, was eventually forgotten by the people. Later, Nahum prophesied the fall of Nineveh, which finally occurred in 612 B.C. Archaeological ruins include many palaces, temples, and Ashurbanipal's library of 26,000 clay tablets.

NISAN *(NIGH san; "standard")*—The first month of the Hebrew calendar. It corresponds to part of March and April.

NISROCH *(NIS rahk; "great eagle")*—A pagan god whom some believe is the same as Ashur. King Sennacherib of Assyria was killed by his two sons in the temple of Nisroch (2Ki 19:37).

NITRE *(NIGH tur)*—A mixture of washing and baking sodas found in deposits around Egyptian lakes. In biblical times, nitre was used to make soap (Pr 25:20).

NOB *(NAHB; "height")*—A town where David fled from Saul, receiving provisions from a priest. When Saul learned this, he killed all the town's priests and destroyed Nob (1Sa 22:19).

NOBAH *(NO buh; "barking")*—A site in Transjordan where Gideon defeated the Midianites (Jdg 8:11).

NOD *(NAHD; "fleeing")*—A land, east of Eden, to which Cain was banished after he murdered Abel. It was noted as a region for nomadic living (Gen 4:16).

NODAB *(NO dab; "noble")*—An ancient tribe of Arabs believed to be descendants of Ishmael.

NOMADS—People with regular migration patterns. Since they moved to find sustenance, they were not considered simply "drifters." Their dependence on each other gave them a strong sense of community. There were three basic types of nomads: hunters and collectors, pastoral, and agricultural.

NORTHEASTER—Strong gale-force east winds. The ship carrying Paul to Rome

NOAH

Noah was a man of deep faith at a time when the rest of the people had lost their obedience to God (Gen 6:1). The world had become so wicked that God decided to destroy not only corrupt humanity but the physical

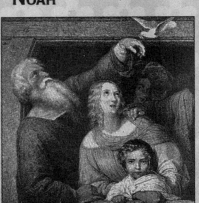

Earth in its entirety with a deluge of water. Because he was righteous and blameless, Noah was chosen by God to survive the Flood (Gen 6:8).

God gave Noah detailed instructions to build an ark that would spare his family and pairs of the world's animals from the waters of judgment. Following the Flood, Noah immediately made a burnt sacrifice in thanksgiving to God for keeping him and his family safe. God then made a new covenant with Noah, promising never again to destroy humankind (Gen 9:1). As a sign of this new agreement, God placed a rainbow in the clouds following the end of the rains.

As the second father of humankind, Noah received the same directive as Adam: "Be fruitful and multiply and fill the Earth." He is said to have lived to be 950 years of age. His three sons—Shem, Ham, and Japheth—and their wives repopulated the Earth.

was hit by one of these winds and driven off-course, eventually landing at Malta (Ac 27:13).

NOSE—Because the nose quivered when upset and made a snorting sound, it was a biblical symbol of anger. A nose ring was a sign of submission (Isa 37:29).

NUMBERS, BOOK OF—The fourth book of the Old Testament, so named because it contains census numbers. The book tells the story of the Israelites' nomadic life after leaving Mt. Sinai until reaching the border of the Promised Land.

NUN (*NUHN; "fish"*)—Joshua's father. He was a member of the Ephraim tribe (Ex 33:11).

NUNC DIMITTIS (*NUHNGK di MIT is; "now let thou depart"*)—A temple blessing pronounced upon Jesus by Simeon one month after Jesus' circumcision. It summarized the belief that Jesus was the Jewish Messiah and a light to the Gentiles (Lk 2:29–32).

NURSE—A woman who cared for—and often nursed—another woman's child (Ex 2:7). Often nurses became a permanent part of the child's family as a trusted servant (Gen 35:8).

NUZI (*NUHZ ee*)—An ancient Mesopotamian city where 5,000 cuneiform tablets were found describing life in the fifteenth and fourteenth centuries B.C. Many of their details of the Patriarchal Age help shed light on things that are not explained in the Bible.

NYMPHA (*NIM fuh; "bridegroom"*)—A wealthy person who housed a Christian church. Paul sent greetings to Nympha (Col 4:15).

OAK—The most common leaf-bearing tree in Palestine, the oak was noted for its strength and girth, but not its height. It was used as a symbol for great power (Am 2:9).

OATHS—A vow showing an intention to keep a promise. In biblical times, oaths were considered sacred and unbreakable. God made an oath to Abraham when he told him that his descendants would be a great nation (Gen 22:16–17; Heb 6:13).

OBADIAH *(o buh DYE uh; "servant of God")*—1. King Ahab's steward who hid 100 priests from Queen Jezebel and arranged the contest between Elijah and Baal's prophets. 2. A prophet who lived after the Exile. An Old Testament book bears his name.

OBADIAH, BOOK OF—The shortest book of the Bible, this Old Testament prophetic work contains the visions of Obadiah. It predicted that God would seek revenge against the Edomites, who rejoiced over Jerusalem's fall and looted the city.

OBED *(O bed; "servant")*—Son of Ruth and Boaz; grandfather of David (Ru 4:16–17). He is the most noteworthy of several Old Testament men bearing this name.

OBED-EDOM *(O bed EE duhm; "servant of Edom")*—A foreign man with whom David entrusted the ark of the covenant. After reclaiming the ark from the Philistines, David saw Uzzah die from accidentally touching it. Afraid, David halted his efforts to transport the ark. Obed-

Edom offered to store the ark in his house. For taking this risk, God blessed Obed-Edom and his household. When David saw this, he resumed moving the ark to the temple in Jerusalem (2Sa 6:1–15).

OBEDIENCE—In the Old Testament, the word referred to the fulfillment of God's will as interpreted by a Hebrew leader such as Moses (Gen 27:8; Ex 19:5). In the New Testament, obedience meant to follow Jesus' example of humility and love (1Pe 1:15; Jn 13:14).

OBELISK (*AHB uh lisk*)—A tall, four-sided Egyptian stone monument that tapered to a pyramid shape on top. It was first associated with the Egyptian sun god Atum-Re.

OBLATION (*ahb LAY shuhn; "spread out"*)—An evening offering of grain or fruits presented to God at the temple (1Ki 18:29).

ODED (*O ded; "restoring"*)—1. Azariah's father (2Ch 15:1). 2. A Samarian prophet who convinced the Israelites to release slaves captured from Judah (2Ch 28:9).

OFFERING—The giving of animals, grains, fruits, and plants as sacrifice to God, either as a form of worship (Gen 4:3–4) or to obtain purification for sin. In Hebrew tradition, offerings were made by the priest on the temple altar on behalf of the entire community.

OFFICERS—Persons with responsibility and authority in civil, religious, or military matters. Moses elected officers to serve as judges (Nu 11:16–17), and Solomon formed 12 districts, each headed by an officer (1Ki 4:5–7).

OG (*AHG; "giant"*)—An Amorite king defeated by the Hebrews. His defeat ended a legend that Og was invincible because of his great size (Dt 3:1–13). He had a huge, specially made iron bed that measured 13 by 6 feet.

OHOLAH *(o HO luh; "tent")*—Sister of Oholibah. The elder of the two harlot "sisters," she was a symbol of Israel, the northern kingdom (Eze 23). God punished her lewd actions by delivering her into the hands of the Assyrians, who killed her.

OHOLIAB *(o HO li ab; "father's tent")*—The craftsman who assisted in the design and construction of the tabernacle (Ex 31:6, 35:34).

OHOLIBAH *(o HAHL ih buh; "my tent is in her")*—Sister of Oholah. The younger of the two harlot "sisters," she was a symbol of Judah, the southern kingdom (Eze 23). God punished her for "playing the whore" with the Babylonians and Egyptians.

OHOLIBAMAH *(oh HOH lih BAH muh "tent of the high place")*— 1. A wife of Esau (Gen 36:14). 2. An Edomite chief; descendant of Esau (Gen 36:41).

OIL, OLIVE—The most common oil in biblical times, it was used in food preparation, as fuel for lamps, and as medicine. Olive oil was also important in religious rituals, such as anointing priests (Ex 22:29, 30:30).

OINTMENT—Beautifully perfumed olive oil, used for religious ceremonies and popular as perfume (Est 2:12; Isa 57:9). When mourning, people would refrain from using them (2Sa 14:2).

OLIVET DISCOURSE—Teachings that Jesus shared with the disciples on the Mount of Olives. This event was recorded in three of the four gospels (Mt 24:3–25:46; Mk 13:3–37; Lk 21:5–36).

OLIVE TREE—A tree that grows about 20 feet tall

Olive tree

with a contorted trunk. Its fruit was harvested for food and oil. The olive tree was a symbol of fruitfulness (Ps 52:8). When shown with the dove, an olive branch represented peace (Gen 8:11).

OLYMPAS *(oh LIM puhs)*— An unknown Christian to whom Paul sent a greeting (Ro 16:15).

OMEGA—*See* **ALPHA AND OMEGA.**

OMER *(O mur)*—An ancient measure equal to one-tenth of an ephah, or little more than two dry quarts by today's standards (Ex 16:18).

OMRI *(AHM ree; "pupil")*— The sixth king of Israel (885–874 B.C.). Said to be the most wicked of Israel's kings, he came to power by assassinating Zimri (1Ki 16:25). Omri cemented ties with Phoenicia through his son's marriage to Jezebel, daughter of the Phoenician king. This political marriage led Omri to condone pagan worship (1Ki 16:26).

ON *("strength")*—A Reubenite leader who rebelled against Moses and joined Korah (Nu 16:1).

ONAN *(OH nan; "vigorous" or "strong")*—The second son of Judah. When his elder brother died, Onan was commanded to marry his widowed sister-in-law. When Onan disobeyed this Hebrew tradition, God put him to death (Gen 38: 7–11).

MOUNT OF OLIVES

The Mount of Olives consists of four summits on a small mountain range overlooking Jerusalem. In the Old Testament, this site was mentioned only a few times, most notably as the place where King David fled during Absalom's revolt (2Sa 15:30).

In the New Testament, however, it was an important place in Jesus' life and ministry. His frequent visits to the home of Mary, Martha, and Lazarus in Bethany would have taken him there. Later, it became his custom to go there alone in the evening (Lk 21:37). The parable of the barren fig tree was told while on the slopes with his disciples (Mt 21:19). It was from this location that Jesus looked over Jerusalem and wept before he entered the city to celebrate the Passover (Lk 19:28–44).

The Garden of Gethsemane, near the Mount of Olives, was where Jesus prayed before his arrest. The top of the mountain is believed to be the place of Jesus' ascension (Lk 24:50).

Because of many traditions and legends around the Mount of Olives, numerous Jewish and Christian shrines have been placed there. Among them are a large Jewish cemetery in anticipation of God's final judgment, which is predicted to occur there (Zec 14); a Christian shrine of the Ascension; and the tomb of Mary.

ONESIPHORUS *(ahn eh SIF o ruhs; "profit bearing")*—A man who received Paul's praise for helping him during his second imprisonment in Rome and for his work in Ephesus (2Ti 1:16–18).

ONESIMUS

A fugitive slave in Rome, Onesimus (*o NES ih muhs*) confessed to Paul that he had run from his master Philemon, and had even stolen from him. Paul and his associates evangelized and discipled Onesimus; soon he had a new identity in Christ. However, Paul urged that he return to Philemon.

Paul wrote a small letter (recorded in the New Testament) urging Philemon to accept Onesimus as a fellow Christian, not a slave (Phm 15). To help persuade Philemon, Paul made a pun based on the meaning of Onesimus' name ("useful"). In essence, Paul says that as a runaway Onesimus was "useless" to Philemon. However, if he accepted Onesimus as a Christian brother—rather than keep him as slave—he became "useful" both to Philemon and Paul (Phm 11). Paul implied in the letter that this was Philemon's obligation as a Christian.

ONO (*OH no; "strong"*)—A Benjaminite town near the southern border of the Plain of Sharon. It became a home for exiles returning from Babylonian captivity (Ezr 2:33).

ONYCHA (*AHN ih kuh; "nail"*)—An ingredient for incense burned on the altar. It was taken from certain shellfish (Ex 30:34).

ONYX (*AHN iks; "nail"*)—A precious biblical stone, onyx was a type of quartz that contained beautiful multicolored bands. It was used to decorate the high priest's breastplate (Ex 28:9) and to adorn the temple (1Ch 29:2).

OPHEL (*O fel; "hill"*)—A 2,000-foot-high ridge between two valleys south of Jerusalem. It was an important part of the fortification of the city.

OPHIR (*O fur; "fruitful"*)— Son of Joktan. A descendant of Shem (Gen 10:29), he dwelled in a territory also called Ophir. The area was noted for its fine gold and other valuable natural resources (1Ki 10:11).

¹OPHRAH (*AHF ruh; "fawn"*)—Son of Meonothai; a descendant of Judah (1Ch 4:14).

²OPHRAH—Gideon's hometown, where he was commissioned by God to deliver Israel from the Midianites (Jdg 6:11).

ORACLE (*OR uh k'l; "speaking"*)—A message from a god, delivered through a dream, the casting of lots, or an inspired prophet (also called a medium). In the Old Testament, the high priest cast the urim and thummim to determine God's will (1Sa 14:41). The Law of Moses was referred to as God's "oracles" (Ac 7:38).

ORAL TRADITION—Material preserved by word of mouth. Scholars believe that most of the Bible was passed down orally for years before it was first written down. As these stories and songs were handed down, they were open to reinterpretation and embellishments. Studying oral traditions has shed much light on the meaning of biblical texts.

ORCHARD—A collection of similar trees planted in the same area (SS 4:13). Orchards were common in biblical lands.

ORDINATION—The "setting aside" of people in the Church for a particular office. Today it is performed through a specific ceremony, including the laying on of hands. Despite many references to ordination in the New Testament, there is no specific set of instructions (Ac 14:23).

OREB (*O reb; "raven"*)—**1.** A Midianite prince executed by Gideon. **2.** A rock marking the site of Oreb's execution. It was named to commemorate Israel's great victory over the Midian army (Jdg 7: 24–25).

ORNAMENTS—The Israelites considered jewelry and other decorative accessories to be signs of wealth and prosperity (2Sa 1:24). Ornaments were not worn by those who were in mourning (Ex 33:4–6).

ORNAN—An alternate form of Araunah. *See* **ARAUNAH.**

ORONTES RIVER (*or ON teez*)—A major river in western Syrian Antioch. It served as an important trade and military route for travelers moving from the Fertile Crescent to the Mediterranean Sea.

ORPAH (*OR pah; "fawn"*)—Naomi's daughter-in-law. After her husband's death, Orpah wished to accompany Naomi to Bethlehem. Instead, her mother-in-law sent Orpah back to her former home in Moab (Ru 1).

ORPHAN (*"be alone"*)—Hebrew law provided for orphans with special tithes and gleanings from the fields (Dt 14:29, 24:19–21). People were urged to show compassion toward children without parents (Ex 22:22; Dt 10:18).

OSSUARIES (*Os soo ear eez*)—Small limestone chests used for secondary burial of bones. Corpses were first placed in traditional burial caves, then—after the body decomposed—the bones were put into an ossuary.

OSTRACA (*OS truh kah*)—Pieces of broken pottery that were used as ancient writing surfaces. Their rough surfaces held inscriptions well. Many important documents have been preserved in this form.

Ostraca found in ruins at Lachish

OSTRICH *(AHS trich; "daughter of greed")*—A common desert bird, the ostrich was considered unclean by Hebrew law because it ate other animals, such as snakes (Lev 11:16). It was a symbol of cruelty and ignorance because the female ostrich abandons its eggs during the day, leaving them exposed to harm (La 4:3; Job 39:14–17).

OTHNIEL *(OTH nee el; "lion")*—Israel's first judge. He was a great warrior who saved his people from the Mesopotamians and established a long period of peace (Jdg 3:7–11).

OVEN—Figuratively, enemies were said to be burned in fiery furnaces (Ps 21:9).

OVERSEER—An ancient supervisor assigned to watch workers or a household (Gen 39:4–5; 2Ch 2:2). In the New Testament, the word referred to a chief Church official (1Ti 3:2; Titus 1:7).

OWL—A nocturnal bird of prey. The Hebrews considered the owl unclean for food because it ate other animals (Lev 11:17).

OX—A common domesticated animal, the term "ox" referred to both the male and the female of the species. They were used for their meat and milk, and for hauling and farming. Several humanitarian rules governing their use are found in the Bible (see Ex 23:4, 12; Dt 25:4).

PADDAN, PADDAN-ARAM *(PAY dan, PAY dan AH ruhm)*—An area in northwest Mesopotamia. Abraham settled there before he reached Canaan. Isaac's wife Rebekah was from Paddan-aram (Gen 11:31, 25:20).

PAGANS—Non-Jews or non-Christians. The word refers to non-Christian Gentiles as opposed to Christian Gentiles (1Co 5:1, 10:20).

PAHATH-MOAB *(PAY hath MO ab; "ruler of Moab")*—The founder of a family that returned from the Exile and, through Ezra's persuasion, divorced their foreign wives (Ezr 10:30). The family signed a covenant to restore observance of the law (Ne 10:14).

PAINT, PAINTING—Few biblical references to paint exist because it was against Jewish law to make images.

PALACE—A heavily fortified residence housing a ruler (2Sa 5:9) and a nation's wealth. David's palace was the first in Israel's history.

PALM TREE—A branchless tree with trunks reaching 75 feet, crowned with dark green leaves. In biblical times, the palm was used for everything from food to shelter. It was a symbol of prosperity (Ps 92:12).

PALM SUNDAY—The day Jesus entered Jerusalem on a donkey to celebrate Passover. He was welcomed by crowds that waved palm branches as they shouted, "Hosanna." Christians traditionally celebrate Palm Sunday on the Sunday before Easter.

PALTITE *(PAL tight)*—An inhabitant of Beth-Pelet.

PALESTINE

From the time Joshua took possession of Canaan to the fall of Jerusalem in the first century, the history of Palestine and Israel are intertwined. The land, which gets its name from Israel's arch-enemy, the Philistines, became the Roman designation for the province of Israel. Prior to that, the Egyptians called it Canaan.

During the Middle Ages, the name "Holy Land" came into use. Its boundaries stretch north and south from Dan to Beersheba, and east and west from the Mediterranean Sea to the Jordan River. Small in size, Palestine is composed of five different geographical regions including coastline, plains, fertile lowlands and valleys, mountain ranges, and deserts.

Because of its location near the Fertile Crescent, there were many important trade routes running through Palestine. The most important were the Way of the Sea (along the coast) and the Kings Highway (from the Gulf of Aqaba to Damascus). Palestine has two seasons: Winter, from November through April, is mild and rainy; summer, from May to October, is hot and dry.

The term was used to describe Helez, one of David's mighty men (2Sa 23:26).

PAMPHYLIA *(pam FIL ee uh; "mixture of nations")*—A coastline region in Asia Minor. Paul visited two of its cities, Pergan and Attalia, during his first missionary journey (Ac 13:13, 14:24–25).

PANNAG *(PAN ag)*—A sweet confection used for

trade between Judah and Israel (Eze 27:17).

PAPHOS *(PAY fohs; "hot")* — A city on the west coast of Cyprus where Paul introduced Christianity to Roman officials (Ac 13:7).

PAPYRI *(puh PIGH ree)* — Multiple sheets of papyrus pasted end-to-end to make a long roll. Because papyrus was hard to obtain, ostraca (pottery fragments) were more common writing surfaces than papyri.

Papyrus plant

PAPYRUS *(puh PIGH ruhs)* — Large ancient

aquatic plants. Their inner stems were cut into thin strips and pressed together to make writing paper. *See* **PAPERMAKING.**

PARACLETE *(PAR uh kleet; "advocate or helper")* — One who champions another's cause. Jesus used the word to describe part of the Holy Spirit's work (Jn 14:16, 26).

PARADISE — A Persian word used three times in the New Testament to describe heaven (Lk 23:43; 2Co 12:4; Rev 2:7). In the Old Testament, paradise refers to gardens of great beauty and splendor (Gen 13:10).

PARALLELISM — A literary style in which similar or opposing thoughts are stated in the same phrase. Hebrew poetry contains many examples of parallelism (Ps 20:8; 29:1; 36:5; Job 11:18).

PARALYSIS — An ailment with a loss of muscular power. Many incidents of Jesus' healings involved

PAPERMAKING

In ancient times, paper was made from the inner pith of the papyrus reed. The outer cover of the stem would be removed, then a series of soaked reed fibers would be laid vertically, each just slightly overlapping the next. On top of these, another series of soaked fibers would be laid horizontally. The two fiber layers would be glued together with a sticky substance, placed in a press, and allowed to dry.

When dry, the pale yellow papyrus sheets were fastened together to become a long roll of paper suitable for writing upon. After the length needed for a particular roll of paper was determined, the side where the fibers ran horizontally was polished by rubbing it with a piece of bone or sea shell. This polishing made the surface smoother for writing.

During later biblical times, sheets were stitched together and glued to form a codex—an ancient form of a book. Larger-size paper was used for official documents and business, while smaller widths were used for literary composition.

people suffering from paralysis (Mk 2:1–12; Mt 8:5; Jn 5:1).

PARAN (*PAY run; "place of caves"*)—A wilderness region of the Sinai Peninsula. Ishmael and his mother Hagar fled there after being expelled from Abraham's camp (Gen 21:21). Moses also dispatched spies from there to scout Canaan (Nu 13:1–3).

PARBAR (*PAHR bahr; "suburb"*)—A structure, located west of the temple, where guards were stationed (1Ch 26:18). Be-

PARCHMENT

PARABLES

Parables are short, memorable, clever stories designed to answer a question or share a truth. Much of Jesus' teachings was given in parables, which usually involved nature (Mt 13:24), everyday life (Mt 13:33), or recent or unusual events (Lk 13:19, 18:2). A popular means of instructing, parables were used frequently in ancient times.

In the Old Testament, there are only two parables: Nathan's story of the poor man with one lamb (2Sa 12:1–14) and Isaiah's parable of the unproductive vineyard (Isa 5:1–7). In the New Testament, Jesus took them to their highest development, enabling common people to understand his message.

Scholars differ on the number of parables Jesus shared, but they agree that this form of teaching was familiar to Jesus. He was said to be a talented storyteller whose insightful stories surprised and delighted his audiences.

cause the word is of non-Hebrew origin, its exact meaning is unknown.

PARCHMENT—Ancient parchment was made from goat or sheep skins that were scraped of hair, soaked in a lime solution, and then stretched on a frame to become smooth for writing.

PAROUSIA (*puh ROO zhi uh; "presence"*)—A Greek word used in the New Testament to describe Jesus' second coming, when he will judge the world and inaugurate the Kingdom of God in all its glory on the Earth.

PARTHIANS (*PAHR thi uhnz*)—Jews living in the

Parthian (or Persian) Empire. Some were present at Pentecost (Ac 2:9).

PARTRIDGE—Wild game birds hunted in the Palestine mountains. The red-legged or rock partridge was a favorite for food.

PARVAIM (*pahr VAY im; "eastern"*)—A place (of unknown location) from which Solomon imported the fine gold used to adorn the temple (2Ch 3:6).

PASACH (*PAY sak; "cut off"*)—The first of Japhlet's three sons; a descendant of Asher (1Ch 7:33).

PASCHAL LAMB (*PAS kuhl LAM*)—The slain lamb

PASSOVER

The Feast of Unleavened Bread—or Passover, as it came to be called—annually celebrates the Israelites' rescue from God's final plague on Egypt (Ex 12:11, 27; Eze 45:21; Lk 2:41; Jn 13:1). On the night when the Lord struck dead all firstborn children in Egypt, he "passed over" the houses of Jews, sparing them from his wrath.

This spring festival traditionally began with a family supper consisting of roast lamb, bitter herbs, and unleavened bread. The head of the household recited the story of that last night in Egypt. Bitter herbs symbolized bondage; unleavened bread represented the haste in which the people left Egypt—their bread had no time to rise (Lev 2:11; 1Co 5:7–8).

Passover was celebrated in every Jewish household; small ones joined together until there were enough people to eat the entire lamb. Jesus and his disciples ate their Passover meal as a family. Christ is called the Paschal, or Passover, lamb (1Co 5:7).

used in the Passover feast. In the New Testament, Jesus is called the Paschal—or Passover—lamb (1Co 5:7).

PASHHUR (*PASH er; "freedom"*)—The name of several Old Testament individuals. They may be the same person because the name occurs in two different contexts: a list of priests after the Exile and a list of people who opposed the prophet Jeremiah.

PASSION—Jesus' redemptive suffering between the last supper and his crucifixion (Ac 1:3; Heb 2:9).

PASTORAL EPISTLES—A general term for three New Testament books: 1 Timothy, 2 Timothy, and Titus. Written by Paul to coworkers organizing new churches, these books are linked together because they contain common themes of Church life.

PATARA (*PAT uh ruh*)—An ancient seaport of Lycia. It was located along trade routes to Egypt. Paul changed ships there en route to Jerusalem (Ac 21:1, 2).

PATHROS (*PATH rohs*)—A southern portion of Egypt. Some Jews fled there after the fall of Jerusalem (Gen 10:13; 1Ch 1:11).

PATIENCE—Steadfastness and long-suffering (Jas 5:10). Patience was called part of the fruit of the spirit (Gal 5:22). It is a virtue prized by God, to whom it was also applied (Ro 2:4, 15:5; 1Pe 3:20).

PATMOS (*PAT mohs*)—A small, wind-swept island in the Aegean Sea where Romans banished exiles, including the Apostle John in A.D. 95 (Rev 1:9). During his 18 months there, John had a vision that was recorded in the Book of Revelation.

PATRIARCHAL AGE—A period of history covering the life spans of the fore-

PAUL

Born as Saul of Tarsus, Paul was a Roman citizen and devout Jew. He was also an active persecutor of the Christians (Ac 7:58–8:3, 26:9). While on his way to Damascus, about A.D. 34, he was blinded and approached by the resurrected Jesus—"Jesus, whom you persecute" (1 Co 9:16–17, 15:10; Gal 1:15–16). After three days of blindness, Paul accepted God's call and became a great apostle to the Gentiles.

Displeased with his change of heart, the Jews harassed him, making him run for his life more than once (Ac 9:23–25; Gal 1:17). He was beaten, imprisoned, harassed, shipwrecked, and bitten by a snake—but he persevered in his newfound calling. Paul was assisted in his work by Barnabas, Silas, and Timothy. A model of great faith, Paul wrote many of the epistles found in the New Testament.

fathers of the Israelites, including Abraham (Heb 7:4), Isaac, and Jacob (Ac 7:8, 9). Scholars place it somewhere in the Middle Bronze Age (c. 1850–1570 B.C.).

PATRISTIC LITERATURE *(Puh TRIS tic)*—Ancient Christian writings not included in the canon, such as Clement, Ignatius, and Polycarp. These men were priests, bishops, and theologians in the generations immediately following the New Testament era.

PAULUS (PAULLUS), SERGIUS *(PAWL uhs SUR jee uhs)*—A Roman deputy in Cyprus who listened to Paul and Barnabas (Ac 13:4–13). When the court magician tried to turn him against Paul, the magician was blinded. Convinced of

God's power, Sergius Paulus became a believer.

PAVEMENT, THE—A stone-paved courtyard, adjacent to Jerusalem's temple, where Pilate tried Jesus (Jn 19:13).

PAVILION—A covered place for hiding. It was used to describe God's protection (Ps 18:11).

PEACE OFFERING—A voluntary animal sacrifice to God. Its meat was shared by the priests of the temple. The offering was made to gain a right relationship with God (Ex 29:40).

PEACE—In the Old Testament, the word was used as a greeting (Gen 29:6) and to describe God's gift of tranquillity. People and nations receive peace from being in a right relationship with God (Ro 5:1; Col 1:20; Php 4:6–7).

PEARL—A precious stone in biblical times, the pearl was called a "crystal" in the Old Testament (Job 28:18).

In the New Testament, it was a symbol of wisdom and something of great value (Mt 7:6, 13:45–46).

PEDAIAH (pe DAY yuh; "Jehovah redeems")—1. The father of Jedudah, who was Josiah's wife and Jehoiakim's mother (2Ki 23:36). 2. A ruler of Manasseh under David (1Ch 27:20).

PEKAH (PEE kah; "to open")—The 18th king of Israel (740–732 B.C.). He murdered his predecessor Pekahiah (2Ki 16; 2Ch 28). Later, he was killed by Hoshea.

PEKAHIAH (pek uh HIGH uh; "Jehovah has opened")—The 17th king of Israel (742–740 B.C.); son of King Menahem. An idolatrous king (2Ki 15:24), he was killed by Pekah.

PEKOD (PEE kahd; "visitation")—An Aramean tribe living near the mouth of the Tigris River (Jer 50:21).

PELATIAH (PEL uh TYE uh; "Jehovah has delivered")—A

PENTATEUCH

The first five books of the Bible—Genesis, Exodus, Leviticus, Numbers, and Deuteronomy—are known as the Pentateuch (*PEN tuh toyk; "five books"*). The authorship is debated, although much is attributed to Moses.

These books, which are central to Jewish heritage and religion, are invaluable in describing how God created the world and dealt with the Israelites. The story of the Hebrews' escape from Egypt and their travels to the Promised Land, en route to receiving the Ten Commandments, are vividly told.

Each story pivots around God's presence, interaction, promise, and will for the people. God's grace and holiness are contained in every encounter through the Israelite's history—a building block for future revelations of God as creator, sustainer, and guide. Each time the people failed to respond as God wished, they were given new chances to become faithful.

leader in Jerusalem who gave "wicked counsel" to the city (Eze 11:1–2). His death was prophesied by Ezekiel (Eze 11:13).

PELEG *(PEE leg; "division")*—A descendant of Shem and an ancestor of Abraham (Gen 10:25; 1Ch 1:25). During Peleg's 239-year life, Noah's descendants were scattered and their language "confused" (Gen 11:1–9).

PELLA *(PEL uh)*—An ancient city in the mountains of Gilead (Mt 4:25). Christians were sheltered there during the siege of Jerusalem in A.D. 70.

PELONITE *(PEL oh night; "separates")*—A designation

(of unknown origin) given to two of David's mighty men, Helez and Ahijah (1Ch 11:27, 36).

PENTATEUCH, SAMARITAN (*PEN tuh toyk, suh MEHR ih ten*)—The Hebrew text of the Pentateuch that was preserved by the Samaritans. It is different in spelling and wording from the Masoretic Text.

PENTECOST—A Jewish harvest festival, also called the "Feast of Weeks" (Ex 34:22). It fell on the 50th day after the beginning of barley harvest. Later, it was a commemoration of the giving of the law at Mt. Sinai. It was transformed into a Christian event when the Holy Spirit was given to worshipers who had gathered in Jerusalem during the Feast of Pentecost (Ac 2). It is traditionally considered to be the beginning of the Christian Church (Ac 2:1–4).

¹PENUEL (*pe NYOO el; "face of God"*)—A town in Trans-jordan where Jacob wrestled with God (Gen 32:30–31). Gideon destroyed the tower in Penuel and killed soldiers who refused to help him fight the Midianites (Jdg 8:8–9).

²PENUEL (*pe NYOO el; "face of God"*)—Grandson of Judah (1Ch 4:4).

PEOPLE (*of the land*)—A phrase used by religious leaders for the poor—or the peasantry. In some cases, it was used to describe people who failed to keep the Hebrew law.

PEOR (*PEE awr; "opening"*)—A mountain peak in Moab where King Balak summoned Balaam to look down and curse Israel (Nu 23:28).

PERAEA (*puh RAY uh*)—See **PEREA**.

PERDITION (*pur DISH uhn; "destruction"*)—The final place of loss for the wicked. Judas Iscariot was called the "son of perdition" (Jn 17:12).

PEREA (*puh RAY uh; "land beyond"*)—A Transjordan territory paralleling the Jordan River and Dead Sea. In the New Testament, it was called "beyond the Jordan" (Mt 4:25). Jesus spent time there.

PEREZ (*PEER ez; "breach"*)—Son of Judah and Tamar. A twin of Zerah, he was an ancestor of David, Jesus (Gen 38:30, 46:12), and the Perezites (Nu 26:20).

PERFECT, PERFECTION—In the Old Testament, perfection often referred to something that was complete, rather than without flaw (Mt 5:48). It often described the quality of a clean sacrificial offering that included all the necessary parts. Only God achieves total perfection. Controversy continues in the Church about humanity's ability to reach perfection.

PERGA (*PER guh*)—A city in Pamphylia where John Mark left Paul and Barnabas on their first missionary journey (Ac 13:13).

PERGAMUM (*PER guh muhm*)—One of the "seven churches of Asia" and a center of Roman rule. It was reportedly an evil city (Rev 1:11).

PERIZZITES (*PER i zights*)—Early inhabitants of Canaan, later driven out or enslaved by the Israelites (Gen 13:7; 1Ki 9:20–21). They lured the Israelites into idolatry and were condemned by Ezra and Nehemiah.

PERSECUTION—The forced prohibition of religious speech and practice. Biblical history is full of persecutors of the Jews (Est 3:6), and later the Christians (Mt 5:10–12; Ac 4:17–18, 5:17–42).

PERSIA, PERSIANS—The largest country in the ancient Near East; modern Iran. Residents were well-educated, skilled craftsmen. The magi who

PETER

The leading disciple among Jesus' original 12, Peter was called the foundation upon which Jesus would build his Church (Mt 16:18). Born as Simon, he was later called Peter (meaning "rock") by Jesus. From Bethsaida (Jn 1:44), Peter, who was married (Mt 8:14), and his brother Andrew had been partners with James

and John in a fishing business at Capernaum (Mk 1:16, 29).

Peter was close to Jesus and witnessed his transfiguration. During the years the disciples traveled with Jesus, he was most often their spokesperson. However, when Jesus was arrested, Peter denied even knowing him.

After the resurrection, Jesus again asked Peter to serve him. Peter preached, healed, and traveled despite the danger. He came to believe Jesus' message was for all people, not just Jews. Preaching to the crowd at Pentecost, he converted 3,000 people.

Despite being jailed, Peter traveled as a missionary to Samaria, Joppa, and other distant places. He was the author of two New Testament letters.

traveled to see infant Jesus may have been from Persia.

PETER, FIRST LETTER OF—A New Testament letter written by Peter to Christians in Asia Minor. He reminded them to act like God's special people and warned of probable persecution.

PETER, SECOND LETTER OF—A New Testament letter written by Peter to reassure that God's promises are dependable.

PETHOR *(PEE thor)*—A place on the western shore of the Euphrates River. It was the home of Balaam (Nu 22:5).

PETRA *(PEH truh; "rock")*—The capital of the Nabatean kingdom, south of the Dead Sea. Ruins from the Roman period include elaborate tombs carved in red sandstone cliffs (Jdg 1:36; 2Ki 14:7).

PHARAOH *(FAY ro; "great house")*—A title for Egyptian kings that was also used as a name. Of the pharaohs mentioned in the Bible, the most frequent was Ramses II, who oppressed the people in Egypt (Ex 9:1–7).

PHARPAR *(FAHR pahr)*—A river in Syria south of Damascus, mentioned with the Abana (2Ki 5:12).

PHASAEL *(fuh SEE uhl)*—The largest of three towers in Herod the Great's Jerusalem palace. Named after Herod's brother, it was also known as David's tower. It underwent many renovations through the centuries.

PHEBE—*See* **PHOEBE**.

PHILADELPHIA *("brotherly love")*—One of the "seven churches of Asia." It was famous for temples and religious festivals (Rev 3:7).

PHILEMON *(fy LEE muhn; "friendship")*—A wealthy Christian and Church leader in Colossae. He owned the runaway slave

Onesimus, who carried Paul's letter to the city's church.

PHILEMON, LETTER TO (*fy LEE muhn*)—The shortest of Paul's New Testament letters, sent with the fugitive slave Onesimus to the church at Colossae. The letter seeks to restore Onesimus to his former master Philemon.

PHILETUS (*fi LEE tuhs;* "beloved")—A man who taught that the resurrection of Christ had occurred (2Ti 2:17–18.)

PHILIP ("lover of horses")— 1. A fisherman from Bethsaida; one of Jesus' 12 disciples (Mk 3:18; Jn 1:44). He brought his friend Nathanael to Jesus. 2. An evangelist who took the gospel to the Samaritans and baptized an Ethiopian (Ac 8:5–8, 26–39).

PHILIPPI (*fi LIP eye*)—An important city and Roman colony in Macedonia where Paul preached, converting Lydia and others. Jailed there, he converted his jailer and family. Its ruins lie in northeastern Greece.

PHILIPPIANS, LETTER TO THE—One of Paul's New Testament letters, addressed to the church at Philippi. The church had sent him a message (and probably money), and Paul wrote back to thank them and urged them to behave as Christians should.

PHILO (*FIGH lo*)—A Jewish writer and philosopher of Egypt who was a contemporary of Jesus. He helped protect Jews against the Roman emperor Caligula in A.D. 39.

PHINEHAS (*FIN ee uhs;* "mouth of brass")—1. Aaron's grandson, therefore a priestly descendant (Ex 6:25). 2. Eli's son. He was killed guarding the ark of the covenant from the Philistines (1Sa 4).

372

PHARISEES

The Pharisees (*FAYR ih seez*) were an important Jewish religious and political party or sect (c. 150 B.C.–A.D. 70). This group of lawyers and scribes worried that disobeying the law would continue the troubles of the Jews. At first, they kept the traditions of the prophets while the Sadducees kept those of the priests. Later, the Pharisees placed higher importance on keeping the exact letter of Jewish law.

They invented many detailed, near-fanatical requirements intended to make it possible to obey all 600 rules they found in the Old Testament. Tithing and ritual purity were of great concern. Their legal-mindedness kept them from understanding the teachings of Jesus, although Nicodemus and Paul are two notable converts. Jesus was concerned that the Pharisees couldn't see beyond the smaller points of the law to the greater idea of love towards all.

Contrary to popular belief, many of the Pharisees defended the early Church and showed interest in Jesus (Mt 22:23–33). Devout, well-intentioned men, they believed that diligent obedience to the law was necessary to be a servant of God (Mt 5:20, Ac 26:4).

PHOEBE (*FEE bee; "bright, radiant"*)—An important woman in the church at Corinth who carried one of Paul's letters (Ro 16:1).

PHOENICIA (*fuh NEESH ee uh*)—A Mediterranean seacoast town near Galilee. Its residents, the Phoenicians, were great shipbuilders and traders in red, blue, and purple dyes made from a sea snail. Jesus visited there (Mk 7:26).

PHILISTINES

This tribe of mighty warriors migrated to the coast of Canaan where they settled in Philistia. They sold their captives into slavery (Am 1:6–8) and ruled several city-states along the Mediterranean seacoast, from Joppa south to Gaza. They worshiped their own gods: Dagon, Ashtoreth, and Baal (Jdg 16:23; 2Ki 1:2). They were a fierce pirate-tribe until they became settled, when they turned their energies to mining iron for making armor and weapons.

The Philistines were also skilled charioteers on the battlefield. At certain times in their history, they were the Israelites' most dangerous enemies. David killed the Philistine Goliath. With his "mighty men," David also defeated the Philistines in several decisive battles (2Sa 5:17–25, 21:18–22). Artifacts reveal that the Philistines wore kilts and feathered headdresses, and used curved-keel boats with high sterns and bows.

PHOENIX *("date palm")*—A harbor of Crete that Paul's ship tried to reach while en route to Rome (Ac 27:12).

PHRYGIA *(FRIJ ee uh)*—A region in Asia Minor that included Colossae and several Galatian cities where the Apostle Paul started churches.

PHYLACTERIES *(fi LAK tur eez; "safeguard")*—Small boxes containing Old Testament verses. Jews wore them on their foreheads and arms while praying. Jesus accused some scribes and Pharisees of wearing larger phylacteries than necessary to call attention to themselves (Mt 23:5). *See* **AMULETS.**

PI-BESETH *(pigh BEE seth; "home of [the cat goddess]*

Bastet")—A city in lower Egypt on the far eastern branch of the Nile. Also called Bubastis, it was mentioned, along with On, in a prophecy against Egypt (Eze 30:17).

PIETY—A religious expression for worshiping God or living a godly life.

PI-HAHIROTH *(pigh huh HIGH ruth; "house of [the deity] Hrt")*—The last campsite of the Israelites before crossing the Red Sea (Ex 14:2, 9; Num 33:7). It was probably located in the far eastern Nile Delta.

PILATE, PONTIUS—A Roman governor of Judea who sent Jesus to be crucified, perhaps against his own conscience (Mk 15).

PILGRIMAGE—A journey to a religious shrine. All male Israelites were required to travel to Jerusalem three times a year: at Passover, the Feast of Weeks, and the Feast of Tabernacles (Ex 23:14–17; Dt 16:1–17).

Women and children often accompanied them on these journeys. Special songs, called Psalms of Accents, were often sung on these occasions (Ps 120–134).

PILLAR OF CLOUD—God's daytime presence shown to the Israelites en route to the Promised Land. It signaled a time to move after stopping (Nu 14:14). It also appeared when Moses interceded for the people, during his argument with Aaron and Miriam (Nu 12:5), and as his death neared (Dt 31:15).

PILLAR OF FIRE—At night, God's fiery presence shown to the Israelites during their journey to the Promised Land (Ex 13:21, 14:9). The pillar served in conjunction with the Pillar of Cloud.

PINNACLE—A pointed roof or peak of the temple from which Satan tempted Jesus to throw himself (Mt 4:5).

PISGAH *(PIZ guh; "cleft")*—A mountain in Moab near the Dead Sea (Dt 3:17; 34:1). There Moses looked upon the Promised Land before dying (Dt 3:27, 34:1–5).

PISIDIA *(pi SID ee uh)*—A mountainous region in Asia Minor that was part of the Roman province Galatia. Paul and Barnabas preached there (Ac 13:14–50).

PIT—1. A deep hole in the ground. Pits were either natural occurrences, like bitumen pits (Gen 14:10), or were man-made, designed to catch rain or hold prisoners (Ps 35:7; Isa 24:22). 2. A biblical term for Hades, the underground home of the dead (Ps 139:8; Nu 16:30).

PITHOM *(PYE thahm; "house of [the deity] Atum")*—An Egyptian store-city built by enslaved Israelites for a pharaoh (Ex 1:11). Its brick walls enclosed 200 yards of food and grain storage.

PLANTS—Biblical plants were important for food, medicine, clothing, and cosmetics. Conflicting descriptions, names, and locations of the same plant complicate identification.

PLOW—An oak-handled farm tool with a sharp blade (or "share"). It was pulled by an ox through soil in preparation for planting. The earliest plows were forked sticks (Am 6:12). Jesus said that "no one who puts a hand to the plough and looks back is fit for the kingdom of God" (Lk 9:62).

PLOWSHARE—The sharp cutting blade of a plow that digs and furrows the soil. Before David, Hebrew farmers had to take their plowshares to their enemies, the Philistines, for sharpening (Isa 2:4; Joel 3:10).

POETRY—Ancient poetry, which was written to express emotions, existed as a literary form before

PLAGUES OF EGYPT

Pharaoh had no intention of letting the enslaved Israelites leave Egypt as Moses requested, but God had other plans. When Pharaoh remained stubborn, God sent ten miraculous judgments against Egypt's people to convince him to set the Israelites free.

Fish in the Nile River died when the water became polluted. Soon there were swarms of frogs, as well as mosquitoes, flies, and locusts. After an outbreak of boils, there came heavy storms and then dust. Cattle died, as did first-born sons (Ex 7–11). This final plague led to the Passover: The angel of death "passed over" Israelite homes, sparing their children. The plagues of Egypt may have inspired the apocalyptic literature of Revelation (Rev 8:7–11, 10, 16:2–4, 21).

prose. Rhythmic and regular, it often accompanied dancing (Ex 15: 20–21). One third of the Old Testament is poetic, including Psalms, Proverbs, Ecclesiastes, and Song of Solomon.

POLYGAMY—Having more than one wife. Although not condemned, the Old Testament stressed that monogamy was the ideal form of marriage (Pr 5:18–19; Mal 2:14–15).

Often kings took several foreign wives for political reasons. By New Testament times, polygamy was rare.

POLYTHEISM (*PAHL ee thee iz'm*)—The belief in and worship of many gods, resulting in idolatry. Hebrew law condemned polytheism and stressed that there was only one God (Ex 20:1–6).

PONTUS (*PAHN tus; "sea"*)—A large area of what is modern Turkey,

377

POTIPHAR

As captain of Pharaoh's guard, Potiphar (*PAHT I fur*) needed slaves to run the complex operation. He was in charge of daily and special activities that catered to very wealthy, demanding Egyptians who needed to be tended and lavishly entertained.

The palace had extensive rooms, grounds, and gardens that required the attention of gardeners, cooks, and servers. It was this need for household help that prompted Potiphar to buy Joseph from the Midianites/Ishmaelites (Gen 37:36, 39:1–6). Recognizing Joseph's potential, he quickly promoted him to household manager. However, Potiphar's wife wrongly accused Joseph of rape. Potiphar felt he had no choice but to put Joseph in prison (Gen 39:6–23).

bordering the Black Sea. Jews from Pontus attended Pentecost in Jerusalem (Ac 2:9).

POOL—A general term for numerous water-related objects, including natural ponds, standing water, cisterns, and reservoirs often used in irrigation (Ps 114:8; 2Sa 2:13; Isa 7:3; Jn 9:7).

PORCH—A flat-roofed area or a covered court supported by columns (Jdg

3:23; Mk 14:68). The word also referred to a shelter for people bathing, such as at the Pool of Bethesda.

PORTICO OF SOLOMON—A covered area on the eastern side of Herod's Temple. Rabbis taught there, as did Jesus (Jn 10:23). Peter healed a lame man there (Ac 3:2–11).

POSTEXILIC PERIOD—The period in Israelite history after the 70-year Babylonian captivity. During this time, the temple was rebuilt in Jerusalem, encouraged by Zechariah and Haggai. Toward the end of the postexilic age, Malachi warned the people about reverting to sinful ways.

POTIPHERA (*po TIF er uh; "the one sent by [the sun god] Re"*)—A priest in the Egyptian city of On. His daughter, Asenath, was Joseph's wife (Gen 41:45, 50).

POTTERY—One of the oldest known crafts. Earthenware was shaped from local clay and then hardened by the sun or by fire. Red clay was common in Palestine. Ancient potters often kneaded the clay with their feet and mixed it with ashes, grit, straw, or dung.

POTTER'S FIELD—A field in the Hinnon Valley, also called Akeldama (Ac 1:19), bought with Judas Iscariot's 30 pieces of silver. He committed suicide there after betraying Jesus. *See* **AKELDAMA.**

Potter's wheel

POTTER'S WHEEL—A foot-turned wheel that ancient potters used to form clay pitchers, bowls, cups, and other pottery. In the Old Testament, the potter and his wheel illustrated God's power to make—and remake—people and nations (Jer 18:1–6).

POVERTY—In the Bible, the poor were considered the responsibility of those who were not impoverished. Poverty became an issue for the Israelites only after they settled in Canaan and were no longer equal, as in

379

the wilderness. In the New Testament, Jesus blessed the poor and emphasized spiritual, rather than material, wealth (Lk 6:20).

POWER—The ability to control or influence others. True power belongs only to God (1Ch 29:11–12; Rev 5:13).

POWER OF THE KEYS—The symbolic authority Jesus held, and gave to the apostles, to "unlock" doors of heaven. He granted Peter the "keys of the kingdom of heaven" (Mt 16:19).

PRAETORIUM (*pri TOR ee uhm*)—Originally, the tent of the commander of a Roman army unit. Later, it became a general term for the residence of a Roman official. Jesus was mocked before Pilate in the praetorium in Jerusalem (Mk 15:16; Mt 27:27; Ac 23:35).

PRAISE—To say good things about and give honor to God (Ps 9:1; Pr 27:2). God's people are expected to praise God and live a worthy life (Php 1:9–11; Eph 1:11–14).

PRAYER—The act of talking with God through petition, confession, and thanksgiving—and believing in God's attentive response (Nu 16:15; Mt 5:44). Prayer can be both personal and communal, private and public. Jesus taught his disciples to pray (Mt 6:9–13).

PREACHING—In the Old Testament, preaching referred to spiritual leaders—such as priests, judges, and prophets—who delivered God's word to the people. In the New Testament, the term described someone who shared the good news of salvation through Christ. Jesus, who was called a preacher and teacher (Mt 4:17; Mk 9:38–40), authorized certain people to preach (Mt 10:1–5). Paul believed preachers were sent by God (Ro 10:15).

PREDESTINATION—The doctrine of God's sovereign design over human destiny (Ro 8:29–30, 9:6–24).

PREPARATION, DAY OF—The day before the Jewish Sabbath. It was a day of ritual cleansing and extra labor—because work on the Sabbath was forbidden (Mk 15:42). The term also was used for the day before Passover, when greater preparations were made (Jn 19:14).

PRESBYTER *(PREZ bih ter)*—A wise, older community leader; also called an elder (1Ti 4:14). The presbytery was a council of elders, such as the Sanhedrin. The designation "elder" became a Church office.

PRESS, WINE—Ancient wine presses were vats or containers with drains to release juice as singing helpers trampled on grapes

(Isa 16:10; Lk 6:38). Palestine soil yielded excellent wines.

PRIDE—Dignified self-respect or, more commonly, arrogant behavior (Pr 16:18). The Bible cautioned against pride.

PRIESTS—Descendants of Aaron. They guarded the ark of the covenant and oversaw the Israelites' relationship with God. Richly garbed, they conducted temple worship (Ex 28:1; Jos 3). Priests were assisted by Levites, who could serve until age 50 (Nu 4:3). Levites tended the temple treasuries and were musicians and gatekeepers.

PRINCES—Men of authority (Gen 23:6; Nu 1:16). The Messiah was called the "Prince of Peace" (Isa 9:6); Beelzebub was the "prince of demons" (Mk 3:22).

PRISCA, PRISCILLA *(PRIS ka, pri SIL uh)*—A wealthy Roman married to her

This is a prison cell typical of those that were used in biblical times.

coworker Aquila (1Co 16:19). She worked with Paul in the church in Corinth (Ac 18:2-3) and went with him to Ephesus (Ac 18:18-26).

PRISON—Biblical prisons were cavelike dungeons or dry wells where prisoners were jailed. Paul converted his prison jailer (Ac 16: 19-34).

PRISON LETTERS—The New Testament epistles written by Paul while imprisoned. These were addressed to the Ephesians, Philippians, Colossians, and Philemon.

PROCONSUL *(PRO kahn suhl)*—A Roman civil and military governor over a major province outside of Rome (Ac 13: 7-8, 18:12). *See* **DEPUTY.**

PROCURATOR *(PRO kyoo ray ter)*—A Roman military and government official. Often they governed over a minor province outside of Rome, holding the same authority as a proconsul (Ac 23:24).

PRODIGAL SON

A central character in one of Jesus' parables, the young son of a caring father asked for his inheritance early. He took it to a distant city, where he squandered it by reveling in a wild and lavish lifestyle.

When disaster hit, in the form of a famine, he had nothing with which to buy food or shelter. He eventually became a farm hand, taking care of pigs (and even envying them their food). He recalled that his father's hired servant lived better than he did now. He decided to go home and work as a servant, realizing how unworthy he was to be his father's son.

However, on his return he was met by a relieved, forgiving father who threw a welcome-home party, despite the older son's objections (Lk 15:11–32). Jesus told this story to point out God's forgiving nature toward those truly repentant.

PROMISE—A pledge, such as God's covenants with the people (Gen 8:21–22; Ex 19:5–6). The New Testament declares that God's promise was fulfilled by Christ (Isa 7:14; Mt 1:22–23).

PROMISED LAND—Canaan, so called because God promised it to Abraham's descendants.

PROPHETS—Divinely inspired forecasters for God. Abraham was the first prophet; Moses is called the greatest of the prophets. Prophets often spoke in story or parable. There were also many women prophets, including Miriam (Ex 15:20), Deborah (Jdg 4, 5), Huldah (2Ki 22:14), Anna (Lk 2:36), and Philip's daughters.

PROVERB

Ancient sayings of wisdom, proverbs were preserved by sages in ancient Israel. Solomon and other wisdom teachers are credited as the authors of the Old Testament proverbs.

Israelites often expressed themselves in proverbs. Themes included wisdom and folly; the righteous and wicked; wealth and poverty; wise talk; hopes and fears; joys and sorrows; anger; and hard work and laziness. Sometimes they were inquisitive (1Sa 10:12). Proverbs often used picturesque phrases to describe common items, "like apples of gold in silver settings" (Pr 25:11).

Associated with the teachings of the wise men (1Ki 4:32; Pr 26:7), proverbs were considered short parables with a hint of insight that reflected a deeper wisdom. Proverbs encouraged people to find and follow godly wisdom and apply it to daily living.

PROPITIATION (*pro pish ee AY shuhn*)—An appeasing act that makes forgiveness and a new relationship with God possible. Jesus did this for all Christians (1Jn 2:2).

PROSELYTE (*PRAHS eh lite; "a stranger"*)—A religious convert. The term primarily referred to a Gentile who became a Jew (Ac 2:10).

PROSTITUTION—Common sexual activity for commercial purposes (Gen 38:17; Lk 15:30). Cult prostitution, which centered around pagan fertility deities, often involved male and female prostitutes (Dt 23:17; 1Ki 22:38). Israel's unfaithfulness was described as "playing the harlot" (Isa 1:21).

PROVERBS, BOOK OF—An Old Testament book of wisdom containing many short, clever sayings designed to be applied to daily living. Possibly written by Solomon and Lemuel, it was probably intended as a textbook for young Jews. Jesus often quoted its proverbs.

PROVIDENCE—The continued activity of God, who preserves the natural order for humanity and the world (Ps 104:29; Heb 1:3). There is a divine plan for everything—even evil falls under God's providential power (Jn 12:31; 1Co 15:24–26).

PROVINCE—A division of a country under Roman rule, created for administrative purposes (Ac 23:34). During Jesus' time, the provinces were orderly, although heavily taxed.

PSALMS, BOOK OF—Called a "bible within a bible," the Book of Psalms is an Old Testament collection of devotional poetry, prayer, and songs. Its author is unknown, but David is credited with many of the psalms. The longest book in the Bible (Psalm 119 is the longest chapter in the Bible; Psalm 117 is the shortest), it was Jesus' prayer book.

PSALMS OF SOLOMON—A collection of 18 poems in the style of the biblical psalms. Part of the Old Testament Pseudepigrapha, it was written by Jerusalem Jews in response to their defeat by the Romans in the first century B.C.

PSEUDEPIGRAPHA (*soo deh PIG rah fuh*)—Jewish writings (c. 250 B.C.–A.D. 200) not included in the Bible, Apocrypha, or Dead Sea Scrolls. They serve as important resources for understanding Judaism at the time of Jesus.

PSEUDONYMITY (*SOO doh nim ih tee*)—The act of writing under a famous assumed name. This prac-

THE FEAST OF PURIM

This annual Jewish festival, observed in February-March, celebrates the victory of Esther over the wicked plot of Haman—a vain nobleman in the court of Ahasuerus (Xerxes)—to kill all Jews in the Persian empire.

The name Purim ("lots") is taken from the superstitious Haman's plan to draw lots, probably with a small stone, to determine the day of the massacre of the Jews (Est 3:7, 9:24). Esther, bolstered by her cousin Mordecai, upset Haman's plans by revealing the plot to her husband, the king. She explained that she was Jewish and would be killed as well. Esther gained permission for the Jews to defend themselves by taking the offensive.

Purim is one of the most popular Jewish feasts. It is celebrated by particularly happy and noisy parties—even to excess. It is also a time for sharing gifts between family and friends, and for giving food and gifts to the poor.

During the festival, the story of Esther is acted out in drama. The congregation boos and shouts each time Haman's name is mentioned. Queen Esther established the order of festival events (Est 9:32).

tice, which was common in the ancient world, makes it difficult to authenticate biblical authorship.

PTOLEMAIS (*tahl uh MAY is*)—The Old Testament name for the ancient city of Acco. *See* **ACCO.**

PUBLICAN (*PUB li kuhn*)—A tax collector in the Roman Empire. Hated by the people, publicans were often local individuals who were hired by the Romans to collect the taxes within their district. Often dishonest, they were considered unclean (Mt 9:10–12).

PUBLIUS (*PUB lee uhs*)—A Roman official on Malta who welcomed Paul and whose father Paul healed (Ac 28:1–8).

PUDENS (*PYOO denz; "modest"*)—A Roman Christian who, with Paul, sent greetings to Timothy (2Ti 4:21).

PUTEOLI (*pyu TEE o lye*)—A city on the Bay of Naples where Paul landed en route to Rome.

PURITY (*PYUR ih tee*)—The quality of being clean and free of contamination. Chastity, ritual cleanness, and freedom from sin are all associated with purity in the Scriptures. Levites were purified for service in the temple (Nu 8:5–22), and many laws of cleanliness are written in Leviticus. Christian believers were advised to set an example of inner purity in their speech and conduct (1Ti 4:12).

PUT—Son of Ham, Noah's son (Gen 10:6). His descendants are associated with Egypt and Libya.

PYTHON—An ancient spirit of divination. According to Greek mythology, Python was the dragon that guarded the oracle at Delphi. It was killed by Apollo. Paul encountered a young slave girl who was said to have this divining spirit (Ac 16:16).

QOHELETH—*See* **KOHELETH.**

QUAIL—A migratory bird that flies close to the ground. Scarce now, they once numbered in the millions. God sent quail to the Israelites in the desert who craved meat instead of manna (Nu 11:31).

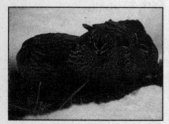

Bobwhite quail sleeping

QUARRY—A pit from which building stone is cut. King Solomon used stone from a quarry to build his temple (1Ki 5:17).

QUARTUS *(KWOR tuhs; "fourth")*—One of the members of the Christian church at Corinth. He sent his greetings to the Roman church through Paul (Ro 16:23).

QUEEN—In the ancient East, queen was usually a title for the mother of a king (2Ki 10:13). The queen-mother often wielded much political power. Exceptions to this custom include Queen Vashti (Est 1:9) and Queen Esther (Est 2:17).

QUEEN OF HEAVEN—A title for the Babylonian goddess of fertility, Ishtar. The Jewish women living in Egypt practiced idolatry. They made offerings to the Queen of Heaven, burned incense to her, and baked cakes in her image (Jer 44: 15–19).

QUICKSANDS—A deep and dangerous bed of shifting sand found along sea-coasts. While bound for Rome, Paul's ship encountered quicksands along the African coast (Ac 27:17).

QUIRINIUS *(kwi RYN ee us)*—Publius Sulpicius Quirinius; the governor of Syria during the time Joseph and Mary traveled to Bethlehem for a census ordered by Caesar Augustus (Lk 2:2). Mary gave birth to Jesus on that journey.

QUIVER—A holder for arrows. Esau took his quiver and bow to the field to hunt game for his father (Gen 27:3). Psalm 127 used arrows in a quiver to represent sons who can protect a father against his enemies.

QUMRAN—*See* **KHIRBET-QUMRAN.**

QUOTATIONS—Phrases or passages repeated from another source. A number of Paul's writings and speeches have been found to contain quotations from the work of the poets Epimenides, Aratus, and Menander. The Old Testament contains quotations from folk literature.

RA, RE *(RAY)*—The sun god of Egypt. Heliopolis (the Greek name for the city of On) was the center of Ra worship. When Joseph became the overseer of Egypt, Pharaoh gave him a daughter of the priest of the cult of Ra as a wife (Gen 41:45).

RA'AMESES, RAMESES *(RAM uh seez)*—1. A common name among the pharaohs of Egypt. 2. A designation for the area of Goshen, founded by Rameses II. Joseph gave his father and brothers land in this area (Gen 47:11).

RAAMAH (*RAY uh muh;
"trembling"*)—A son of
Cush and descendant of
Noah. He was the ancestor
of a tribe that became
known as trade merchants
in spices, precious stones,
and gold (Eze 27:22).

RABBAH (*RAB uh; "great"* or
"citadel")—The chief city of
the Ammonites (known
today as Amman, the
capital city of Jordan). It
was first mentioned as the
site of the "bed" of the
Bashan king, Og—possibly
a sarcophagus (Dt 3:11).

RABBI, RABBONI (*RAB eye,
ra BO nye; "master"* or
"honored teacher")—An
instructor of Jewish law.
Jesus was called Rabbi by
his disciples (Jn 1:38, 49).

RABMAG (*RAB mag*)—The
title of Nergal-Sharezer, a
Babylonian military offi-
cial who was present when
Jerusalem fell to Neb-
uchadnezzar and his army.

RABSARIS (*RAB suh ris*)—
An Assyrian title for a high-

ranking court official and
leader of the army. The
Rabsaris was part of a
delegation sent by King
Sennacherib of Assyria to
invade Judah (2Ki 18:17).

RABSHAKEH (*RAB shuh ke;
"chief cupbearer"*)—An
Assyrian title given to the
spokesperson for the
officers of King Senna-
cherib who were sent to
Jerusalem with an army to
negotiate a surrender.

RACA (*ruh KAH; "worthless"*
or *"empty-headed"*)—An
Aramaic expression of
contempt. Jesus said that
one who insults his brother
by calling him "raca" breaks
God's law (Mt 5:22).

RAHAB (*RAY hab; "broad"*)—
A prostitute who harbored
spies that Joshua sent to
Jericho. She helped them
escape the city. Rahab and
her family were spared
when Jericho was captured
(Jos 2:1–24, 6:22–25).

RAIN—Virtually no rain
falls in Palestine from May

RACHEL

As Jacob approached a well near the city of Haran, he saw Rachel (the daughter of his uncle Laban) preparing to water her flock of sheep. Elated by his cousin's beauty, he rolled the heavy stone from the well and watered the flock for her. Then, according to custom, he kissed her and identified himself as her relative.

Invited to stay at his uncle's home, Jacob set his sights on Rachel. In lieu of wages, he offered to work seven years to gain her as his bride. Jacob was so smitten by Rachel, his seven years of service seemed like "a few days" (Gen 29:20)

On the wedding night, however, Laban substituted Rachel with his elder daughter, Leah (since she was the firstborn daughter). When Jacob complained, Laban suggested he serve another seven years to gain Rachel. Jacob agreed, and finally took Rachel as his wife.

Jacob loved Rachel more than her sister, but it was Leah who conceived children. Rachel remained barren for a long time before she finally became the mother of Joseph. She died during childbirth when her second son, Benjamin, was born (Gen 35:18).

to September. In October and November, the "former rains" occur. Farmers depend upon them to soften the ground for planting. Winter rains take place in December through February. The "latter rains," which fall in March and April, are vital for maturing the grain (Joel 2:23).

RAINBOW—The rainbow was a sign of God's promise to Noah that he would never again send a flood to destroy the human race (Gen 9:12–17).

RAISINS—In biblical times, fresh grapes were eaten in season. But since they had to be harvested quickly, many were dried into raisin clusters and stored for winter use. When David fled Jerusalem, part of his provisions were 100 bunches of raisins (2Sa 16:1).

RAM—A male sheep, used for food and sacrifice (Gen 22:13). Its skin was used for clothing and for covering the tabernacle. The horns carried oil or wine (1Sa 16:1), and trumpets made of rams' horns were used for religious ceremonies (Jos 6:4–6).

RAMAH (RAY muh; "height")—1. The name of a number of biblical cities. 2. An ancient city where the prophet Samuel was born, lived, and was buried (1Sa 1:20, 25:1).

RAMOTH-GILEAD (RAY mahth GIL ee ad; "heights of Gilead")—The location of King Ahab of Israel's final battle. Ahab and King Jehoshaphat of Judah were allies against the army of Aram at Ramoth-Gilead, where Ahab was killed (1Ki 22:1–37).

RANSOM—The price paid to release someone from slavery. In the New Testament, Christ became the ransom to release his people from the slavery of sin (Mk 10:45).

RAPTURE—A theological term that denotes a time when all believers, living and dead, will be "caught up in the clouds together" with Christ to be with him forever (1Th 4:17).

RAVEN—A scavenger bird, the raven was listed in the Law of Moses as unclean and not to be eaten (Lev 11:15). During a drought, ravens brought the prophet Elijah food while he was in the wilderness (1Ki 17:1–7).

REBEKAH

Abraham sent his servant to find a wife for Isaac among Abraham's relatives. After asking for divine guidance, he spotted Rebekah at a well near the city of Nahor. She was not only beautiful, but kind and generous to him. When he asked to sip from her water jar, she gave him a drink and offered to water his camels as well. After the camels finished drinking, the servant learned that Rebekah was indeed one of Abraham's kinsmen. He gave her gold bracelets and a nose ring.

After seeing the gifts given to Rebekah, her brother Laban welcomed the visitor warmly. The servant quickly revealed his mission.

Both the girl's father, Bethuel, and her brother gave permission for her to marry Isaac. More gifts were brought out—and more bargaining took place—before Rebekah herself agreed to accompany the servant and become Isaac's bride.

Rebekah and Isaac met at the family home in the Negev desert, where they were married. A mutual love developed, but she remained barren until Isaac prayed for her. Rebekah soon conceived and became the mother of twins, Esau and Jacob (Gen 24).

REBIRTH—A spiritual second birth, in which a person is renewed and born again by the Holy Spirit through baptism. Jesus told Nicodemus that he could not enter God's kingdom without this rebirth (Jn 3:3–7).

RECHABITES (REK uh bites)—A Kenite tribe living among the Israelites. Founded by Jonadab (son of Rechab), the Rechabites refused material goods, preferring to live simply in tents. They did not drink wine or practice farming. Jeremiah promised this godly tribe that they would never die out (Jer 35:6–7).

RECONCILIATION—The act of restoring a broken relationship. Sin created a break in the loving relationship with God. Christ atoned for the peoples' sins and restored the relationship (2Co 5:18).

RED SEA—A sea that separates Africa and the Arabian Peninsula. The Israelites crossed the Red Sea during their flight from Egypt. Moses parted the waters, and the pursuing Egyptians drowned there (Ex 15:4). Scholars believe a better translation is the "Reed Sea," which may have been a lake or part of the Gulf of Suez.

REDEEMER—One who rescues others from sin by offering a sacrifice. Jesus Christ is called the Redeemer because of his death on the cross.

REFINE—To make pure. An ancient refiner separated pure metal ore from the impurities by passing it through fire. Psalm 12 compared God's promises to refined silver (Ps 12:6). God called Jeremiah a refiner of his people (Jer 6:27).

¹REHOB (REE hahb; "broad" or "open")—1. The father of King Hadadezer of Zobah, whom David defeated in battle. 2. One of the Levites who signed a covenant to obey God's law.

²REHOB—1. A town allotted to the tribe of Asher. 2. One of the northern cities scouted by Moses' spies.

REHOBOTH (ri HO bahth; "open places")—A well dug by Isaac in the valley of Gerar after he was driven from the land of the Philistines by Abimelech (Gen 26:9–22).

REHOBOTH-IR (ri HO bahth EER; "open places of the city")—An area in Assyria on the outskirts of Nineveh. It was one of several cities built by Nimrod, son of Cush (Gen 10:11).

REHUM (REE hum; "merciful")—A deputy of King Artaxerxes' court. He helped write a letter to the king, warning him that the Jews were rebuilding Jerusalem and would no longer pay taxes once they finished (Ezr 4:7–24).

REI (REE eye; "friendly")—A man who remained loyal to David when Adonijah (David's son) attempted to take the throne from his ailing father (1Ki 1:8).

RELIGION—An organized set of beliefs and practices observed by a group or sect, usually involving a moral code. Moses urged the Israelites to pass down their religion to their children and grandchildren (Dt 4:9). Paul called the Pharisees the strictest

sect of the Hebrew religion (Ac 26:5).

REMNANT—The group of Jews who, despite idolatrous influences, remained faithful to God during the Exile. King Hezekiah sent word to the faithful remnant, scattered throughout the land, to return to Jerusalem to worship (2Ch 30:6).

REPENTANCE—A change of mind, involving remorse for wrongdoing and a turning back to God. Both John the Baptist and Jesus called the Jews to repentance (Mt 3:2, 4:17).

REPHAIM (REF ah im)—A race of giants who lived in Palestine before the days of Abraham. Their land was given to the descendants of Abraham (Gen 14:5, 15:20). This fertile valley was the scene of David's victories over the Philistines (2Sa 5:18–25).

REPHAN, REMPHAN (REE fan, REM fan; "Saturn")—A

pagan god, associated with a star, that was worshiped by the Israelites when they were in the wilderness (Ac 7:43).

REPHIDIM *(REF i dim)*—One of the sites where the Hebrews camped in the wilderness. Since no water was available there, Moses struck a rock with his staff, and water sprung forth (Ex 17:1–7).

REPROBATE—One who is beyond hope of salvation because of sinfulness. Paul spoke of hardened sinners whom God rejected (Ro 1:28–32).

RESEN *(REE sen)*—A fortified town between Nineveh and Calah. It was part of the kingdom of Nimrod, a mighty warrior and hunter (Gen 10:8–12).

REST—A period of inactivity; mental or spiritual calm. God rested on the seventh day after creation (Gen 2:2). The Ten Commandments required God's people to rest on the seventh day of the week (Ex 16:23). Christ offered rest for the weary (Mt 11:28).

RESTORATION—The return of Jewish people to their homeland. As the exiles returned from captivity, they resettled in Jerusalem, rebuilt the temple, resumed temple worship, and signed a covenant to follow God's law.

REUBEN *("behold a son")*—Jacob's firstborn son through Leah. He was involved in a plot to get rid of his brother Joseph. Reuben persuaded his brothers not to kill Joseph, but to throw him into a pit (where he planned to rescue him later). Because of an adulterous affair with his father's concubine, Reuben lost his birthright (Gen 49:3–4).

REUEL *(ROO uhl; "friend of God")*—**1.** A priest of Midian who gave his daughter Zipporah to

RESURRECTION

The return to life after death was a vague notion in the Old Testament. Job pondered the question, "If mortals die, will they live again?" (Job 14:14). Daniel also touched on the issue when he said that some who sleep would be awakened to everlasting life (Da 12:2–3).

In the New Testament, the subject of resurrection took on a new significance. During his ministry on Earth, Jesus revived people from death, including Lazarus (Jn 11:1–44), the daughter of Jairus (Mt 9:18–26), and the son of the widow at Nain (Lk 7:15). Then Christ himself was resurrected on the third day after his death on the cross (Lk 24:5). Though changed, his body was clearly recognizable (Lk 24:39).

Paul promised that all people would be judged after death (Ac 24:15). Those who have done evil will be condemned; those who have done good will be resurrected (Jn 5:29). Though believers are to be resurrected with Christ, the physical body will perish and be raised as a spiritual one (1Co 15:42–44). Jesus called himself "the resurrection and the life," and he promised that those who believed in him would live, even though they experienced physical death (Jn 11:25).

RETURN OF CHRIST

On the night before his crucifixion, Christ told his disciples that after his death he would come again to take all believers to a place that he has prepared for them (Jn 14:3). From that time on, his followers have eagerly awaited the fulfillment of that promise. The return—or second coming—of Christ, is known in Greek as the *Parousia* ("coming" or "presence"). The word describes the time when the Lord will return to the Earth in visible form to complete the work begun at his death and resurrection. He will destroy evil and hand over the kingdom to God, who will rule over all (1 Co 15:22–28).

This event is to be preceded by a period of suffering and darkness, after which Christ will come out of the clouds to judge all people and gather his chosen and faithful ones (Mt 24:29–31). The return of Christ is to be sudden and unexpected. No one but God will know the day or the hour (Mt 24:36), but he will arrive in glory as "King of kings and Lord of lords" (Rev 19:16) to take the righteous to a new and sinless existence.

Moses as a bride (Ex 2:16–22). **2.** A son of Esau (Gen 36:4). **3.** A Benjaminite who lived in Jerusalem after the Exile (1Ch 9:8).

REVELATION—The act of making known something that was previously un-known. The entire Bible is a revelation of God, in which he makes his truths, his will, his plans, and his purposes known. The final book of the Bible, which contains a vision of the future, is called the Book of Revelation.

REVELATION, BOOK OF—The last book of the Bible. Also called the "Apocalypse," it is written with a great deal of symbolism and contains a vision of a future heavenly world.

REWARD—Christ spoke often about rewards in heaven. Among those who would receive these heavenly gifts were those who were persecuted for Christ and those who demonstrated love but expected nothing in return (Lk 6:35).

REZEPH (*REE zef*)—One of the towns destroyed by the kings of Assyria. Rezeph was mentioned in a threatening letter that was written to King Hezekiah (2Ki 19:8–12).

REZIN (*REE zin*)—A King of Syria who waged war on Jerusalem. King Ahaz of Judah asked for help from Assyrian King Tiglath-pileser, who then captured Damascus and killed Rezin (2Ki 16:5–9).

REZON (*REE zahn; "prince"*)—An enemy of King Solomon. He led a band of rebels to Damascus, settled there, and became king (1Ki 11:23–25).

RHEGIUM (*REE jee uhm; "break"*)—A town located at the southern tip of Italy. The Apostle Paul spent a day there on his journey from Malta to Rome (Ac 28:13).

RHODA (*"rose"*)—A maid who answered Peter's knock at the gate after he was miraculously released from prison. Eager to tell the others the good news, she forgot to let him in (Ac 12:13).

RHODES—An island in the Mediterranean Sea that Paul passed on his way to Jerusalem (Ac 21:1). The capital city, also called Rhodes, was famous for the Colossus—a gigantic statue of Apollo, called one of the seven wonders of the ancient world.

RIBLAH, RIBLATH (*RIB lah, RIB lath*)—A town on the Orontes River where the king of Babylon passed judgment on King Zedekiah, killing his sons and putting out his eyes (2Ki 25:6–7).

RIGHT HAND—A position of honor. To be placed at the king's right hand was a sign of power (Ps 110:1). After the Ascension, Jesus sat at the right hand of God (Mk 16:19).

RIGHTEOUSNESS—The state of being upright, moral, holy, and just. Righteousness is accorded to God alone throughout most of Scripture (Jn 17:25). Human righteousness can only be achieved through faith in Christ (Ro 3:21–26).

¹RIMMON (*RIM uhn;* "*pomegranate*")—1. A Syrian god with a temple in Damascus. 2. A member of the tribe of Benjamin.

²RIMMON—1. A town in Judah. 2. A town of Zebulun assigned to the Levites. 3. A rock that provided refuge to 600 Benjaminites fleeing from ambush.

RING—Circular ornaments such as earrings, nose rings, and finger rings were worn by both men and women in biblical times. Signet rings, which were engraved with the identity of the wearer, were used to mark sealed documents (Gen 38:18). Rings were a symbol of authority.

RIVER—The important rivers in the Bible included the Tigris, the Euphrates, and the Nile (Gen 15:18). Many rivers were seasonal, flowing primarily during the winter rainy season.

RIVER OF EGYPT—This term likely does not refer to the Nile (Gen 15:18), but to Wadi el-Arish, the southwest border of Canaan (Nu 34:5).

RIZPAH (*RIZ pah;* "*hot stone*")—A concubine of King Saul. After her two sons were killed by the Gibeonites, she watched over the bodies so the birds and wild animals would not disturb them (2Sa 21:8–11).

ROCK—A large outcropping of stone, common in the area around Palestine. Moses struck the Rock of Horeb to get water (Ex 17:6). The Rock of Rimmon was a natural fortress that provided refuge to 600 Benjaminites (Jdg 20:45).

ROD, STAFF—Biblical shepherds used a rod for protection and a staff to rescue stray sheep. Moses' rod summoned hail and lightning (Ex 9:23), caused the sea to part (Ex 14:16), and brought forth water (Ex 17:5–7).

ROMANS, LETTER OF PAUL TO THE—The sixth book of the New Testament; an epistle from the Apostle Paul to the Christian Church at Rome. The letter

The rod of Aaron devouring the other rods before Pharaoh

ROMAN EMPIRE

From the moment Pompey marched in and captured Jerusalem in 63 B.C., the Jews came under the domination of the Roman Republic. During the time of Christ, Rome was a world power, covering the entire Mediterranean area. Its boundaries reached from the Atlantic Ocean on the west to the Euphrates on the east; from the Rhine, the Danube, and the Black Sea on the north to the deserts of Africa and Syria on the south.

Rulers of the empire during New Testament times will forever be linked in history with the beginnings of Christianity. Caesar Augustus began his rule as emperor in 27 B.C. Jesus was born in Bethlehem during his reign (Lk 2:1). Tiberius (Lk 3:1) ruled from A.D. 14 to A.D. 37 and was emperor at the time of Christ's death. Herod became king of Judea under Rome in 37 B.C. and ruled until 4 B.C. During his reign, a series of governors ruled Jerusalem. Among them was Pontius Pilate, who governed A.D. 26–36. He was the man responsible for the trial and execution of Christ. The reign of Nero (A.D. 54–68) was a time of persecution of the Church and included the martyrdom of Peter and Paul.

discusses God's provision of righteousness to humanity through Christ.

ROME—The capital city of the Roman Empire. Located along the Tiber River, it was a governmental and cultural center. Paul was imprisoned there (Ac 28:16).

ROOF—The flat, top portion of a biblical house,

made with tree branches or reeds overlaid with earth and pebbles. A low protective wall was added around the edges for safety (Dt 22:8). The roof was used as a comfortable place to sleep in summer, an area for storing grain and ripening fruit, and for prayer and worship (Ac 10:9).

ROSH (RAHSH; "head")— An offspring of Benjamin. He was one of more than 70 members of the house of Jacob who went to live in Egypt (Gen 46:21).

ROYAL CITIES—Ancient cities in which the royal families and their courts resided (Jos 11:12). They were usually heavily fortified, elaborate, and well-planned for convenience and safety.

RUFUS (ROO fus; "red")— The son of Simon of Cyrene, who carried the cross for Jesus (Mk 15:21). In his letter to the Romans, Paul sent greetings to Rufus and his mother (Ro 16:13).

RUHAMAH (roo HAH muh; "loved one")—The daughter of Hosea and Gomer. She was first called Lo-Ruhamah ("not loved"), symbolic of God's judgment on Israel. The name change signified a restored relationship with God (Hos 1:6–2:1).

RULE, GOLDEN—A rule of moral conduct taken from Matthew 7:12: "In everything do to others as you would have them do to you."

RULER OF THE SYNAGOGUE— A Jewish official in charge of the synagogue services. The ruler appointed people to pray, to read Scripture, or to preach (Ac 13:15).

RUMAH (ROO mah)—The home of Pedaiah, grandfather to Jehoiakim (2Ki 23:36). It is believed to be the same town as Dumah (Jos 15:52).

RUNNER—1. A bodyguard to the king who also carried out his commands (1Sa 22:17). 2. One who

403

RUTH

Ruth was a young widow who became the model for family loyalty and faithfulness. A great famine in Judah sent Elimelech and his wife Naomi to Moab, where their sons took Moabite wives. One of those wives was Ruth.

After Elimelech and his sons died, Naomi decided to return to Judah, urging her widowed daughters-in-law to return to their own homes as well. Orpah went, but Ruth—who was devoted to her mother-in-law—steadfastly refused to leave Naomi.

The two women made their way to Bethlehem. Ruth was determined to put food on Naomi's table—and Naomi was just as determined to find a husband for Ruth. The two goals came together when Ruth went to work in the barley fields of Boaz, a relative of Naomi. Boaz granted her special privileges because of her loyalty to Naomi, and became her protector. A marriage was arranged, and soon Ruth bore a son, Obed, who became the grandfather of King David. Many modern Christian wedding ceremonies include Ruth's touching words to her mother-in-law, vowing to worship Naomi's God and to stay with her until death parted them (Ru 1:16–17).

delivered urgent messages for the king (2Ch 30:6). **3.** A person who ran ahead of the king's chariot to clear the way or make announcements (2Sa 15:1).

RUTH, BOOK OF—The eighth book of the Old Testament. A narrative, its major theme is loyalty and commitment to family and God.

SABAOTH, LORD OF (*SAB a ohth*)—A title expressing God's power, indicating he is Lord over the multitude or over the armies of Israel (1Sa 17:45). *See* **LORD OF HOSTS.**

SABBATH—The day of the week set aside by the Jews for rest and worship, corresponding to the seventh day of creation, on which God rested (Gen 2:3).

SABBATH DAY'S JOURNEY OR WALK—The distance the Jews were allowed to travel on the sabbath day, 2,000 cubits, which is roughly one kilometer (Ac 1:12). It was based on Joshua 3:4 as the distance between the people and the ark.

SABBATICAL YEAR—A year of rest for the land, done every seventh year to acknowledge Yahweh's lordship, even over soil. Also, Jews were to release slaves, forgive debts, and feed the poor during this time (Ex 23:10; Lev 25:1–7).

SABTA, SABTAH (*SAB tuh*)—1. The third of five sons of Cush (1Ch 1:9). 2. A place of Cushite settlement along the East coast of Arabia, near the Persian Gulf (Gen 10:8–12).

SABTECA, SABTECHA (*SAB teh kuh*)—The youngest of five sons of Cush after whom a yet undiscovered Arabian district was named (1Ch 1:9).

SACKCLOTH—Coarse, dark cloth made from goat or camel hair; used for straining or carrying; worn by people in mourning, often ceremoniously slashed (1Ki 21:27; Rev 6:12).

SACRAMENTS—Religious rituals in the Christian

SADDUCEES

This small Jewish political party was mostly comprised of priestly aristocracy and secular nobility. Religious and nationalistic, it was a powerful group.

The Sadducees rejected scribal interpretations and relied directly upon the Torah. They denied developing intertestamental belief in resurrection, calling it unscriptural (Ac 23:8). For them, hope lay not in life after death but in progeny. Neither the law nor the future earned the attention of the Sadducees; their purpose was directed toward the preservation of temple rites.

The influence of the Sadducees fluctuated through a variety of rulers, with their golden era rising between A.D. 6 and A.D. 66. The Jewish revolt of A.D. 66–70, as well as the destruction of the temple and Jewish national identity, pushed the party into ineffectiveness and obscurity.

Church. Efficacy and number differ between Roman Catholics (seven) and Protestants (two). Baptism and the Lord's Supper are commonly celebrated.

SACRIFICE AND OFFERINGS— The law Moses received on Mt. Sinai included five offerings: burnt, grain, sin, guilt, and peace (ordina-tion) (Lev 7:37). The person making the offering gives God something in return for his favor and as an expression of obedience to God's commandments on Mt. Sinai. All or portions of each sacrifice were burnt by an attending priest (Lev 8).

SAFFRON—That part of the crocus flower that collects

pollen; expensive and valued for fragrance, flavoring, and for the orange dye made from it (SS 4:14).

SAINTS—The Old Testament describes them as people dedicated to God. The Greek word *Hagios*, in the New Testament, refers to Christians (Ac 9:13). Specialized meanings evolved in Roman Catholic and Orthodox churches.

SALAMIS (*SAHL ah mihs*)—1. A harbor town tucked under the long eastern arm of Cyprus, a Mediterranean island. Barnabas and Paul preached there in the synagogue (Ac 13:5). 2. A small island 10 miles east of Athens.

SALECAH (*SAL eh kuh*)—A city in the kingdom of Og won by Israelites in the battle of Bashan (Dt 3:8–10). It was built near Damascus on an extinct volcanic cone.

SALEM (*SAY lehm; "complete"*)—For more than two centuries, it was the Canaanite name for Jerusalem or Zion (Gen 14:18). It became King David's capital.

SALIM (*SAH lihm*)—A site near Aenon where both Jesus and John the Baptist were baptizing; a place of abundant water (Jn 3:23).

SALMON (*SAHL mon; "clothing"*)—The father of Boaz, great grandfather of King David; in the Davidic lineage of Jesus (Mt 1:4–5).

SALMONE (*sahl MO nee*)—A high eastern point of Crete past which Paul and his companions sailed with difficulty toward Rome, shortly before being shipwrecked (Ac 27:7–8).

SALOME (*sah LO mee; "peaceful"*)—1. The mother of James and John, who brought spices for the body of Jesus (Mt 27:56; Mk 16:1). 2. The grandniece of Herod Antipas; her dance pleased King Herod and her mother Herodias, and she was rewarded with the head of John the Baptist (Mt 14:3–11).

SALT—A priceless mineral among ancients; a pledge of friendship; a covenant sign between Jews and Yahweh (Nu 18:19); it was sometimes rubbed on newborns to toughen their skin (Eze 16:4).

SALT, CITY OF—A town near the Dead Sea in the wilderness of Judah (Jos 15:62).

SALT SEA—Also called the Dead Sea, it is located at the deepest point of the Great Rift, 60 miles south of the Sea of Galilee. Saline soil of the Jordan Valley causes lifeless water in this, the lowest body of water on Earth (Gen 14:3).

SALT, VALLEY OF—Probably the barren saline area south of the Dead Sea, bordering Edom. It was the site of two victories of Israel over the Edomites, by David and by Amaziah (1Ch 18:12; 2Ch 25:11).

SALVATION—God's deliverance from the power of sin and death; liberty, reconciliation, and eternal life (Ps 27:1; Heb 2; Ro 5:1–11).

SAMARIA—The hilltop capital of Israel's northern kingdom, approximately 40 miles north of Jerusalem. Built by Omri 50 years after Solomon (1Ki 16:24), it was an independent nation under Assyria (2Ki 17:22–41).

SAMARITANS (*suh MEER ih tens*)—The people of Samaria, descendants of Jews married to captives brought to Palestine by Assyria. They established their own temple at Mt. Gerizim. Hostility existed between Samaritans and Jews in New Testament times (Jn 4).

SAMGAR-NEBO (*SAM gahr NEE bo*)—Mentioned in Jeremiah 39:3 (as a name or title); one among Babylonian officials who participated in the subjection of Jerusalem, c. 587 B.C.

THE GOOD SAMARITAN

Whether sincerely or to set a trap, an expert in Jewish law, who considered only his own people as neighbors, asked Jesus, "Who is my neighbor?" Jesus answered with a parable about a man from Samaria.

A Jew traveled along a dangerous wilderness road. He was robbed, beaten, and left for dead. Two Jewish experts on the subject of God and his commandments saw and ignored the wounded man. Help came from a Samaritan, a man closely related to Jews by blood but hated by them.

Centuries before, when most of Israel's northern tribes were exiled, the Samaritan ancestors were left in Palestine. They married captives imported by Assyria and built their own temple on Mt. Gerizim. By the intertestamental period, the spirit of racism was so great between Jews and Samaritans that Jewish travelers circumvented Samaria, which was situated directly between Galilee and Judah.

SAMOS (*SA mos*)—A mountainous island in the Aegean Sea half as wide as its 27-mile length; Paul spent a night there before returning to Jerusalem at the end of his third missionary journey (Ac 20:15).

SAMOTHRACE (*SAM oh thras*)—This was Paul's first stop by sea between Troas in Europe and Macedonia. A mountainous island, it is one of the highest points in the north Aegean Sea (Ac 16:11).

SAMUEL (*SAM yoo el; "name of God"*)—A priest, prophet, and last judge of Israel; from the family of Ephraim, the son of Hannah. 1 Samuel records the

SAMSON

Nearly every event in Samson's life was unusual: his birth, his marriage, his behavior, and his death. Late in the period of judges, most Danites lived in their original tribal land along the Philistine frontier. Dreaded marauders—Amorites and local Canaanites—relentlessly threatened Israelites in the Shephelah. Even before his birth, Samson was called by God as a judge to defend his tribe.

Samson's is the only recorded Nazirite story in the Old Testament (Nu 6). He was called by God and consecrated for life. Neither his mother during her pregnancy, nor he in his lifetime, drank wine or fermented drinks. His hair remained uncut as a sign of his Nazirite consecration.

The blessing of *nazir* carried with it extraordinary strength. Many attempts were made by Samson's enemies to break that power. Delilah especially worked against Samson's success, ultimately giving him over to the Philistines and slavery.

matchless scope of his work for God.

SAMUEL, BOOKS OF—The author of these two Old Testament books is unnamed; originally it was one book. They report 100 years of history, from Samuel's birth through much of King David's reign.

SANBALLAT (*san BAL uht;* "*May Sin [the moon-god] give him life*")—Called "the Horonite." As governor of Samaria, he joined with those opposed to the reconstruction of Jerusalem's walls (Ne 2:10, 4:1).

SANCTIFICATION—A purity belonging to people chosen by and dedicated to God (Ex 19:5–6). The New Testament names Jesus Christ as the author of this holiness (1Co 6:11; Col 1:22).

SANCTUARY—A designated place of worship, whether holy or profane (Am 7:9; Heb 8:2).

SAND—Mentioned at least 35 times and nearly always descriptively, as in Genesis 22:17, which states that Abraham's offspring will be as numerous "as the sand that is on the seashore."

SANDAL—In biblical times, sandals consisted of a wooden or leather sole held to the foot by a thong, panels, straps, or latches; they were hobnailed for warfare. Descriptively used (Ru 4:7; Am 2:6; SS 7:1; Ex 3:5; Mk 1:7).

SANHEDRIN (*san HEE drin*)—The highest Jewish council to administer political and religious concerns. Its origin may date from elders appointed by Moses (Nu 11:16; Mk 14:53; Ac 4:5–22).

SAPPHIRA (*sah FEE ruh; "beautiful"*)—With her husband, Ananias, Sapphira was struck dead for the sin of hypocrisy and falsehood (Ac 5:1–11).

Christian sarcophagus

SARCOPHAGUS (*sar KAHF uh guhs*)—Generally used to describe a stone or terra cotta coffin used for burial by Jews and early Christians.

SARDIS (*SAR dis*)—The mineral-rich capital of ancient Lydia. Conquered by Cyrus of Persia and Alexander the Great, it was later part of the Roman province of Asia. There has been a Jewish community

SARAH

This woman was beautiful enough in her mid-sixties to cause her husband fear of being killed by her powerful admirers. Rather than risking that danger, twice Abraham took advantage of the truth that she was his half-sister by a common father. Both Egypt's Pharaoh, and later the King of Gerar, unknowingly took her as their own without surmising the truth of her married state (Gen 12, 20).

Sarah was unable to bear a child. When an angel announced to Abraham that in her very old age she would become pregnant, Sarah was listening at the entrance of the tent, and she laughed. Then, in fear of God's judgment, she denied her laughter (Gen 18). Later, Sarah and Abraham named their son Isaac, which means "laughter."

When the initial promise of Isaac's birth was made to Abraham, the angel told him to change his wife's name from Sarai to Sarah. The change marked a covenant with God (Gen 17:2). Sarah died at the age of 127 and was buried in the Machpelah Cave (Gen 23).

there since at least the fifth century B.C. (Rev 3:1–6).

SARGON (*SAHR gahn; "the king is legitimate"*)—Found in Isaiah 20:1 (actually Sargon II), a powerful king of Assyria, conqueror of Palestine in the eighth century B.C.

SARID (*SAY rid; "survivor"*)—A town on the north edge of the Plain of Esdraelon near Nazareth; belonging to the tribe of Zebulun (Jos 19:10).

SARSECHIM (*SAR seh kihm*)—One of several Babylonian officials present when Jerusalem was besieged by Nebuchadnez-zar (Jer 39:1–3).

SATRAP (SAY trahp; "protec-tor of the dominion")—A ruler over governors of several small regions that make one province in ancient Persia (Est 3:12; Da 3:2).

SATYR (SAY ter)—Derived from a Hebrew word that

SATAN

Never does the Bible present a universal dualism between God and Satan. He is variously called the devil, Beelzebub, Lucifer, god of this world, or the Deceiver. In a failed rebellion before human history, Satan led legions of fallen angels from heaven. He was judged at the cross of Jesus but continues to exert great influence in the world (Col 2:13; 2Co 4:1–4; Eph 2:1–2), though his final doom is preor-dained (2Thes 2; Rev 12:7–12, 20:10).

The earliest mention of Satan in the Old Testament is in Zechariah 3:1. Rarely is he mentioned in the Old Testament outside the Book of Job, though many see the early history of this angelic creature in the prophecies of Isaiah 14:12–14 and Ezekiel 28:12–15. He is not mentioned by name in Genesis 3, but Satan is credited with prompting the fall of Adam and Eve.

Exile and extreme humiliation of the Jews of the intertestamental period lent to the development of understanding the personal nature of Satan. The New Testament reveals the scope of his power by recording the confrontation between Satan and the Son of God, the one able to forever seal the fate of evil (Mt 4:1–11; Ac 10:38).

describes objects of idolatrous worship, whether demons or wild animals (Rev 18:2; Isa 13:21).

SAUL *(SAWL)*—1. Israel's first king, appointed by the prophet Samuel; brought down by his abuse of power and his jealousy (1Sa; 2Sa; 1Ch). 2. The name by which the Apostle Paul was first known (Ac 7:58–13:9).

SAVIOR—Primarily used in the Old Testament in reference to Yahweh, the one who acts to deliver his people (Ps 17:7). It is also the New Testament title for Jesus (Lk 2:11; Jn 4:42).

SCAPEGOAT—On the Day of Atonement, after a goat sacrifice, a second goat symbolically received the sins of the people, then was turned out into the wilderness to carry the sin away (Lev 16:1–21).

SCARLET, CRIMSON—A dye producing bright reds; made from a scaly insect that primarily attacks evergreen oak and prickly pear trees (Gen 38:27–30; Isa 1:18; Mt 27:28; Heb 9:19).

SCEPTER *(SEP ter; "staff" or "rod")*—An ornate staff, an emblem of authority carried by a sovereign (Est 8:4; Isa 14:5); a rod of correction (Nu 24:17); an object of mockery in the trial of Jesus (Mt 27:29).

SCEVA *(SEE vuh)*—A Jewish high priest whose seven sons in Ephesus attempted to duplicate the powers of the Holy Spirit demonstrated by the Apostle Paul (Ac 19:11–17).

SCHOOLMASTER—A trusted slave responsible for the education, moral training, and supervision of Greek or Roman males between the ages of six and 16. Used analogously for the law (Gal 3:23–25; 1Co 4:15).

SCOURGE—To whip or beat; to punish severely (Jos

23:13). Romans, by law, could aid the investigation of noncitizens by beating them with whips weighted with bone or metal. Jesus was scourged (Lk 23:16, 22).

SCRIBE—A man responsible for copying and interpreting Scriptures (1Ch 2:54, 27:32). Ezra was both a priest and a scribe (Ne 8:13). Jesus confronted scribes (lawyers) who abused Jewish law (Mk 7:5; Lk 11:45–54).

SCRIPTURE—A New Testament term used to describe the Hebrew Bible (Gal 3:8; Mk 12:10). Inspired books added to the Hebrew Bible by the Christian Church form the Christian Scriptures (2Ti 3:16).

SCROLL—A roll of papyrus, leather, or parchment on which books, such as the Bible, were written (Ezr 6:2). Rolled up on a stick, a scroll was usually about 35 feet long. Biblical books such as Luke or Acts would fill one scroll. Longer books required two or more scrolls.

SCROLLS, DEAD SEA—About 500 scrolls and fragments discovered between 1946 and 1956 along the Dead Sea. They have helped to reconstruct Holy Land history from the fourth century B.C. to A.D.135, clarify Jewish religious traditions and early Christianity, and establish the date of a stabilized Hebrew Bible as no later than A.D. 70.

SCYTHIANS (*SITH ee ens*)—A term for barbarous people and nomadic raiders of the Black Sea region (Col 3:11).

SCYTHOPOLIS (*sith OP uh lis*)—The name of Beth-Shan from the Hellenistic through the Byzantine periods; an important city northeast of Jerusalem.

SEA—A major body of water in the ancient world. "The Sea" usually refers to the Mediterranean Sea

(Gen 49:13; Ps 80:11). In Genesis, "the sea" is used as a contrast to dry land (Gen 1:10). It sometimes meant a large river, perhaps the Nile (Isa 19:5). Bodies of water that figured prominently in Biblical times were the Dead Sea, the Red Sea, the Sea of Galilee, and the Mediterranean Sea. Israelites generally regarded the seas as strange and dangerous places. Biblical imagery involving seas indicates God's fierce judgment.

SEA OF GLASS—A term used twice by the Apostle John in Revelation. A sea of clear glass before the throne of God suggests majesty and purity or calmness in contrast to the stormy seas with which the Hebrews were familiar.

SEA MONSTER—In Hebrew usage it refers to large sea creatures, whether real (Gen 1:21) or mythological (Job 3:8). God's taming of the sea and its great crea-

tures became a theme in Israel's faith (Isa 27:1).

Hebrew seals

SEAL—A device of stone or metal engraved with a reverse design for making an impression in clay, lead, or wax. Such impressions were used to identify documents and other objects, and, for security purposes, to place marks on closures. Each personal seal was distinct, to preclude any doubt concerning identity. A seal can represent finality because a sealed container is ready for storage or delivery.

SEBA *(SEE buh)*—A son of Cush; a Hamite or Arabian tribe (Gen 10:7).

SECACAH *(seh KA kuh)*—A town in the Judean wilderness assigned to the tribe

SECOND COMING OF CHRIST

Although the phrase does not actually occur in the New Testament, the "second coming of Christ" was first used by Justin Martyr (c. A.D. 150). Also termed the "return of Christ," both phrases have become popular expressions for Christ's expected return to Earth at the end of the present age. The Greek word for "coming" or "arrival" is *parousia,* and it occurs several times in the New Testament (Mt 24:3, 27, 37, 39; 2Th 2:1, 8). Usually the term expresses the early Christian belief that Jesus would reappear. The idea of his return is expressed more than 300 times.

The night before his crucifixion, Jesus told his disciples that he would return (Jn 14:3). When Jesus ascended into heaven, two angels appeared to his followers and promised that he would return in the same manner as they had seen him go (Ac 1:11). The Second Coming will be his coming in divine majesty and judgment to complete the defeat of evil (1Co 15:24), to judge humanity (Ac 17:31; 2Co 5:10), and to give the blessing of complete salvation to his faithful followers (Heb 9:28). The coming will be visible (Mt 24:30), glorious (Rev 19:16), sudden, and unexpected (Mt 24:27, 42–44). The time of his return is not revealed (Mt 24:36).

of Judah (Jos 15:61). It is probably modern Khirbet es-Samrah, southwest of Khirbet-Qumran near the northwestern shore of the Dead Sea.

SECU, SECHU *(SEE koo)*—A place, perhaps a town, near Ramah. When King Saul arrived at Secu in pursuit of David, whom he intended to kill, the people purposely directed him to Naioth instead (1Sa 19:22).

SECUNDUS *(se KUN duhs)* — One of two Thessalonican Christians who accompanied Paul from Macedonia as he carried the collection for the poor Christians of Jerusalem (Ac 20:4).

SEED — The fertilized and ripened egg cell of a plant, which can sprout to produce a new plant. The Bible also uses the word figuratively: 1. Human descendants (Gen 21:12). 2. Spiritual descendants (believers are Abraham's spiritual seed) (Ro 4:16). 3. The Word of God in Jesus' parables (Mt 13:3–19, 18–33). 4. Jesus' reference to his own death and resurrection (Jn 12:24).

¹SEIR *(SEER)* — An ancestor of the Horites, the original inhabitants of Mt. Seir (Gen 36:20).

²SEIR — 1. A mountain range stretching from the Dead Sea to the Red Sea (Gen 14:6); Aaron died there (Nu 20:27–28). 2. Mountains on the northern border of Judah (Jos 15:10).

SELA *(SEE luh)* — 1. A fortress city, the capital of Edom (2Ki 14:7). 2. A location in the territory of Judah near the Amorites (Jdg 1:36). 3. An unidentified site in Moab mentioned in a prophecy of doom by Isaiah (Isa 16:1).

SELAH *(SEE luh)* — A word of uncertain meaning found 71 times in Psalms (see Psalms 3, 4, 52, 88, and 143) and also in Habbakkuk. It may be a musical notation, a pause in singing for narration, or instructions to the choir or the instrumental accompanists.

SELEUCIA *(seh LOO shuh)* — A seaport near Antioch from which Paul, accompanied by Barnabas and John Mark, began his first missionary journey (Ac 13:4).

SEMITES

The descendants of Shem, the son of Noah (Gen 5:32), were called Semites. In the List of Nations in Genesis 10 (see especially 21–31), Semites refers to those who have a common descent from Shem or who speak a Semitic language.

Geographically, Shem's descendants spread from Lydia eastward through greater Syria, Assyria, and Persia. Curiously, some groups classified as sons of Ham (Gen 10:6–7) also had Semitic languages. The original home of the Semites is unknown because Semitic languages are found all over the Fertile Crescent.

Today, the Semitic family includes most of the inhabitants of Syria, Iraq, Jordan, Israel, Arabia, and parts of Turkey, Lebanon, and North Africa. Through the Jews, Semites have influenced Europe and America; through the Arabs, they have penetrated deep into Africa.

SELEUCID EMPIRE (*seh LOO sihd*)—A dynasty of Hellenistic kings, with its capital at Antioch in Syria. It was one of the largest empires formed from the division of territory conquered by Alexander the Great. Its kings ruled from 333 B.C. until the Roman takeover of the region in the first century B.C.

SELF-CONTROL—Biblical faith depicts human beings as responsible to, and directed by, the will of God. For Paul, self-control was not a human achievement, but was part of the fruit of the Spirit (Gal 5:22–23) and was spiritually cultivated along with other qualities such as love, joy, and peace. Paul also compared self-control to athletes restraining themselves as part of training (1Co 9:25).

SENAAH *(seh NAY uh)*—Head of a family of 3,600 that returned from the Exile (Ezr 2:35). The name is probably identical to Hassenaah, an ancestor of the people who built the Fish Gate in the rebuilt wall of Jerusalem (Ne 3:38).

SENATE, SENATOR—In the Roman Empire, the Senate was a hereditary body of 600 members of the aristocracy who bought their office. The senators met twice a month in or near Rome to approve the emperor's report and to make decrees. In Israel, it was a body called together by the high priest (Ac 5:21). It is likely that Senate and Sanhedrin were used interchangeably.

SENEH AND BOZEZ *(SEE nuh, BO zehz)*—Two sharp rocks in the mountain pass between Michmash and Gibeah where Jonathan and his armor-bearer climbed in an attack on the Philistines (1Sa 14:4–5).

SENIR *(SEE nur)*—The Amorite name for Mt. Hermon, the largest mountain in the Anti-Lebanon range (Dt 3:9). Senir was famous for its fir trees used in shipbuilding (Eze 27:5).

Sennacherib's Prism, an account of his raid into Judah

SENNACHERIB *(sehn NOK uh rib)*—The king of the Assyrian Empire (705–681 B.C.) after the death of his father, Sargon II. Sennacherib was noted for his military campaigns against Judah (2Ki 18). He was assassinated by two of his sons (2Ki 19:36–37).

SEPHAR (SEH far)—A city or mountain (Gen 10:30). Some identify Sephar with Zhafar, between the Red Sea and the Persian Gulf.

SEPHARAD (SEF ar rad)— The home of exiles from Jerusalem (Ob 20), which some identify as Sardis in Turkey.

SEPHARVAIM (seh far VAY im)—A city conquered by Assyria and a place from which King Sargon II sent people to colonize Samaria (2Ki 17:24, 31).

SEPPHORIS (SEF uh ris)—A town in Galilee. During the Hasmonean period (152–37 B.C.), Sepphoris became the administrative center for Galilee. After the destruction of the temple (A.D. 70), the Sanhedrin met there until it moved to Tiberius.

SEPTUAGINT (SEP twuh jint)—A third- to second-century B.C. Greek translation of the Hebrew Bible, produced in Egypt. Both the name and the common Latin abbreviation LXX refer to the 72 Jewish translators. The LXX brought Judaism into the Hellenistic world and became the basis for Judaistic writings in Greek.

SEPULCHRE, CHURCH OF THE HOLY (SEP uhl kur)—A church built on the traditional sight of Jesus' tomb in Jerusalem after the fourth century A.D. Six different Christian groups control the church, which has 22 chapels.

SERAIAH (seh RAY yuh)—**1.** From Judah, father of Joab (1Ch 4:13). **2.** A descendant of Simeon (1Ch 4:35). **3.** David's secretary, also called Shevsha, Sheva, and Shisha (2Sa 8:17). **4.** A high priest when Babylon conquered Jerusalem (2Ki 25:18). **5.** A man who tried

SERMON ON THE MOUNT

The collection of Jesus' teachings found in Matthew 5–7 is the largest portion of uninterrupted teaching in the Gospels. Jesus sat and spoke from a mountain. In setting this model before his listeners, he declared his positive regard for the Law of Moses and said that he had not come to replace the law. The intent of his teaching was to overcome a legalistic attitude.

His sermon begins with a group of blessings (the Beatitudes) and then deals with social duties in a series of contrasts between Jesus' teaching and the ancient legal Jewish traditions. Next, it turns to the private religious duties of almsgiving, prayer, and fasting. Finally, Jesus gave instructions about the inner quality of the spiritual life in many short parables.

The Sermon is the first of five main discourses into which the bulk of Jesus' teaching, as recorded by Matthew, has been collected.

to arrest Baruch and Jeremiah (Jer 36:26). **6.** A man to whom Jeremiah gave a prophetic scroll of oracles against Babylon, instructing him to read it in Babylon and then throw it into the Euphrates River (Jer 51:59). **7.** An army officer allied with Gedaliah at Mizpah (2Ki 25:23). **8.** See

AZARIAH 20 (Ezr 2:2). **9.** The head of a priestly family that returned after the Exile (Ne 21:1). **10.** A priest who sealed covenant renewal, possibly Seraiah 9 (Ne 10:2). **11.** See **AZARIAH 27** (Ne 11:11).

SERAPHIM (*SEAR uh fihm*)—Angelic or heavenly

beings with six wings and human voices, hands, and feet, associated with Isaiah's vision (Isa 6:1–7).

SERGIUS PAULUS *(SIR jee uhs PAWL us)*—The Roman proconsul of the island province of Cyprus. He became a Christian through the preaching of Paul and Barnabas (Ac 13:7).

SERPENT—This term often has symbolic meanings, such as temptation, sin, and evil. Serpents are called cunning (Gen 3:1; Mt 10:16). New Testament passages refer to God's ultimate victory over evil using serpent imagery (Lk 10:19; Rev 20:2–10).

SERPENT, BRONZE—During the Israelites' journeys through the wilderness, they complained constantly, so God sent poisonous snakes among them, which killed many. Moses made a bronze serpent for the afflicted to look upon, and they were healed (Nu 21:4–9).

SERPENT'S STONE—The place where David's son, Adonijah, celebrated his self-established coronation in David's old age (1Ki 1:9). It was probably near En-rogel, south of Jerusalem.

SERVANT OF THE LORD—A title given to the person whose call and mission, sufferings, death, and exaltation are depicted in passages such as Isaiah 53.

SETH—The third son of Adam and Eve. After the death of Abel, Seth comforted them in their grief. God "appointed" Seth as a replacement offspring (Gen 4:25).

SEVEN WORDS, THE—The words of Jesus spoken from the cross. The traditional order is: 1. "Father, forgive them; for they know not what they do" (Lk 23:34). **2.** "Truly I tell you, today you will be with me in Paradise" (Lk 23:43). **3.** "Woman, here is your son," and, "Here is your mother" (Jn 19:26–27). 4. "*Eloi, Eloi, lema sabachthani*," which means, "My God, my God, why have you forsaken me?" (Mk 15:34). 5. "I am thirsty" (Jn 19:28). 6. "It is finished" (Jn 19:30). 7. "Father, into thy hands I commend my spirit" (Lk 23:46).

SEX—Old Testament legislation restricted pre-marital and extramarital sex (Ex 20:14; Lev 20:10). Homosexuality, bestiality, and incest were con-demned (Lev 16:6–18, 22–23).

SHAALBIM, SHAALABBIN (*shay AHL bim, shay AHL uh bin*)—An Amorite city in the territory assigned to the tribe of Dan (Jos 19:24). The Amorites did not give up the city until long after the Israelites settled the land (Jdg 1:35).

SHADOW—This word had several symbolic meanings: brevity of life (Job 8:9; Ecc 6:12), physical weakness and death (Job 14:2), and the shadow of God's hand (Isa 49:2) or wings (Ps 17:8, 91:1), both of which imply divine protection. In New Testament thought, it reflected the Greek idea that a shadow was a lesser likeness of the true being, object, or idea (Col 2:17; Heb 8:5, 10:1).

SHALISHAH (*SHAL ih shuh*)—The region through which Saul passed while looking for his father's lost donkeys (1Sam 9:4).

SHALLUM (*SHAL uhm*)—1. *See* **SHILLEM** (1Ch 7:13). 2. A grandson of Simeon (1Ch 4:25). 3. A descen-dant of Judah (1Ch 2:40). 4. The father of Jehizkiah the Epraimite leader (2Ch 28:12). 5. A man who killed Zechariah; a son of Jabesh, king of Israel (2Ki 15:10). 6. The father of Hilkiah (1Ch 6:12). 7. Keeper of King Josiah's wardrobe, husband of Huldah (2Ki 22:14). 8. An uncle of Jeremiah, possibly Shallum 7 (Jer 32:7). 9.

SHADRACH

While living in Babylon during the Exile, several outstanding young men were taken into the court of King Nebuchadnezzar for training and service. Among them was Hananiah, who was given the Babylonian name of Shadrach.

With Daniel, Meshach, and Abednego, he rose to prominence in the court and won the respect of the king. Although tempted with the indulgences of court life, the four remained true to their God.

Shadrach, Meshach, and Abednego angered Nebuchadnezzar, however, when they refused to bow down to a gold idol. The king ordered them cast into a fiery furnace. To the king's amazement, none of them was hurt, because an angel had protected them from the flames. Recognizing the power of Israel's God, the king released the three, elevated their position in the court, and issued a decree banning any criticism of their religion (Da 1:1–3:30).

The father of Maaseiah, the temple doorkeeper (Jer 35:4). **10.** Also called Johoahaz 3 (1Ch 3:15). **11.** The ancestral head of gatekeepers that returned after the Exile (Ezr 2:42). **12.** A gatekeeper at the temple after the Exile (1Ch 9:17). **13.** A gatekeeper who married and divorced a foreign wife after the Exile, possibly Shallum 12 (Ezr 10; 24). **14.** A man who, with his daughters, helped to repair Jerusalem's walls (Ne 3:12). **15.** A man who helped to repair the walls of Jerusalem (Ne 3:15).

SHALMAN *(SHAL muhn)*—A man who sacked Betharbel (Hos 10:14).

SHALMANESER V (*SHAL muh NEE zuhr*)—When Ululai seized the throne after the death of his father, Tiglath-pileser III assumed the name Shalmaneser V and became the king of Assyria. He conducted a three-year siege against Israel (2Ki 17:1–6).

SHAME—Painful consciousness of guilt for having sinned (Lev 20:17; Jer 2:26). It also refers to disgrace from a sense of failure (Pr 14:34). Conversely, it was considered disgraceful when people had no sense of shame (Jer 6:15; Job 19:3).

SHAMGAR (*SHAM gahr*)—The judge and son of Anath who delivered Israel by killing 600 Philistines with an ox goad as his weapon (Jdg 3:31).

SHAMMAH (*SHAM muh*)—1. A descendant of Esau who was a chief in Edom (Gen 36:13). 2. The third son of Jesse, elder brother of David, and father of Jonadab. He is also known as Shimeah, Shimea, and Shimei (1Sa 16:9). 3. A leading member of David's mighty men (2Sa 23:11). 4. Shammah of Harod, one of David's mighty men (2Sa 23:25).

SHAPHAN (*SHA fuhn*)—1. A man whose reading of the law caused King Josiah to bring reform (2Ki 22:3). 2. The grandfather of Gedaliah, the governor (2Ki 22:12). 3. The father of Elasah, courier to the exiles (Jer 29:3). 4. One named among 70 elders engaging in idolatrous worship in Ezekiel's vision (Eze 8:11).

SHAPHIR (*SHA fir*)—A town mentioned in a prophetic lament over Judah by Micah (Mic 1:11).

SHAREZER (*shah REE zuhr*)—1. The son and murderer of Sennacherib of Assyria (2Ki 19:37). 2. A delegate from Bethel who asked priests about fasting to commemorate the destruction of the temple (Zec 7:2).

SHARON (*SHAR uhn*)—A fertile, thickly forested plain along the Mediterranean coast from Mt. Carmel to Joppa (1Ch 27:29). Rose of Sharon (SS 2:1–2) was a kind of crocus that grew there.

SHARUHEN (*shuh ROO en*)—A city in the tribal territory of Simeon (Jos 19:6), usually identified with Shilhim. It may be identical to Shilim (Jos 15:32) and Shaaraim (1Ch 4:31).

SHAUL (*SHA uhl*)—1. An Edomite king (Gen 36:37). 2. The son of Simeon by a Canaanite woman (Gen 46:10). 3. A descendant of Levi (1Ch 6:24).

SHAVEH, VALLEY OF (*SHA veh*)—The place where Abraham met the king of Sodom and Melchizedek after his defeat of Chedorlaomer (Gen 14:17–18). Abraham built "Abraham's Monument" there (2Sa 18:18).

SHAVSHA (*SHAV shuh*)—A scribe or state secretary of David (1Ch 18:16). Elsewhere called Seraiah, Sheva, and Shisha.

SHEAR-JASHUB (*SHEER JAH shub*)—Isaiah's son, born in the days of King Ahaz and named to symbolize the prophecy that some of the Israelites would return from the Exile (Isa 7:3).

SHEBA (*SHEE buh*)—1. The son of Ramaah, founder of the Hamite/Arabian tribe (Gen 10:7). 2. A descendant of Shem (Gen 10:28). 3. The grandson of Abraham and Keturah (Gen 25:3). 4. A Benjaminite who began a rebellion against David (2Sa 20:1). 5. The head of a Gadite family in the days of Jotham (1Ch 5:13). 6. A city assigned to Simeon (Jos 19:2). 7. Mountainous country in Arabia (1Ki 10:1–13) from which

Israelites obtained gold, gems, and spices.

SHEBA, QUEEN OF—A woman who visited Solomon and, after testing him with hard questions, asserted that his wisdom and prosperity exceeded his fame (1Ki 10:1–13). Jesus called her the "queen of the South" who came from the ends of the Earth to hear Solomon's wisdom (Mt 12:42).

SHEBAT (*SHEE baht*)—The eleventh month in the civil year of the Hebrew calendar (Zec 1:7), corresponding to January-February.

SHEBNA (*SHEB nuh*)—An influential administrator and secretary for King Hezekiah of Judah (2Ki 18:18). Isaiah cursed him for constructing an ostentatious tomb for himself (Isa 22:15–25).

SHEEP—Mentioned more than 500 times in the Bible. Old Testament references are largely literal, while most of the New Testament's are symbolic of Jesus as the shepherd and his followers as sheep (Jn 10; Heb 13:20).

SHEEP GATE—Built after the return from the Exile as part of Nehemiah's reconstruction of the city's walls (Ne 12:39), it was probably located on the north wall of Jerusalem (Ne 3:1).

SHEERAH, SHERAH (*SHEE uh ruh*)—A daughter of Ephraim who built or fortified three villages (1Ch 7:24).

SHEET—Material made from thin sheets of gold, used for making the high priest's ephod (Ex 39:3).

SHEKEL (*SHEK uhl; "weight"*)—A unit of weight that varied, but was approximately half an ounce.

SHELAH (*SHEE luh*)—1. A descendant of Shem and father of Eber; ancestor of Abraham (Gen 10:24). 2. A son of Judah by the daughter of Shua (Gen 38:5).

SHECHEM

1) The son of Hamor, the chief of the city of Shechem. When Dinah, Jacob's daughter, visited among the women of the land, Shechem seized and raped her, then asked his father to secure her for his wife. Lying through their teeth, Jacob's sons agreed—on the condition that all the males of the city be circumcised. The men of the city submitted, with hopes for enrichment through intermarriage with the family of the wealthy Jacob. While the Shechemites were thus incapacitated, Simeon and Levi, two of Jacob's sons, killed all the men, plundered the city, and rescued their sister (Gen 33:18).

2) The son of Gilead and grandson of Manasseh (Nu 26:31).

3) The son of Shemida of the tribe of Manasseh (1 Ch 7:19).

4) A Canaanite and Israelite city in the hill country of Ephraim between Mt. Ebal and Mt. Gerizim, site of the covenant ceremony establishing the Israelite confederation. There, Abraham built an altar to the Lord after his arrival in Canaan. There, also, Jacob pitched his tents, bought a parcel of ground, and like his father Abraham, built an altar.

SHEM—Noah's oldest son, who was one of the eight survivors of the Flood (Gen 5:32–11:1). Shem is considered the ancestor of Israel and of those nations speaking Semitic languages.

SHEMUEL (SHEM yoo el)— 1. A Simeonite (Nu 34:20).

SHEMA

Literally meaning "hear you," Shema is the name and first Hebrew word of the classic Jewish declaration found in Deuteronomy 6:4: "Hear, O Israel, the Lord (Yahweh) is our God, the Lord (Yahweh) alone." According to rabbinical tradition, the Shema originally contained only Deuteronomy 6:4, but it was later expanded to include verses 5–9, a second part (Dt 11:13–21), and a third part (Nu 15:37–41).

The first section includes the twofold injunction to love Yahweh utterly and to manifest this by perpetually calling to mind the commandments. The second part placed the demand for obedience within the framework of a blessing for its fulfillment and a curse for its neglect. The third part concludes with a statement from the introduction to the Ten Commandments.

Rabbinic law established an ancient ritual of reciting the Shema every morning and evening. As a watchword of faith and faithfulness, the Shema constitutes the culmination of the saying recited before death. The declaration was also recited during martyrdom.

The dispute about which of the more than 600 commandments of the law was most important was characteristic of first-century rabbinical discussion. In that context, Jesus quoted from the Shema, and along with Leviticus 19:18, called them the two most important commandments (Mk 12:28–34).

2. Another name for Samuel the prophet-priest-judge (1Ch 6:33). 3. The son of Tola (1Ch 7:2).

SHEOL *(SHEE uhl)*—Biblical term for the netherworld. In poetic and prophetic passages (Dt 32:22; Am 9:2), the reference is to the depths of the earth. More commonly, Sheol is the underworld where departed spirits go—righteous and unrighteous (Pr 9:18).

SHEPHELAH, THE *(shee FEH luh)*—The low hills of western Palestine that provided a buffer between Judah and Philistia, which both countries sought to control because of its strategic location (Jer 17:26).

SHESHACH *(SHEE shak)*—A code name for Babylon. The code followed a Hebrew system known as Atbash where the letters of the alphabet were reversed. Jeremiah used Sheshach when predicting the downfall of the Babylonians (Jer 25:26, 51:41).

SHESHBAZZAR *(shesh BAZ zahr)*—A prince of Judah, appointed by King Cyrus of Persia, who was authorized to return the gold and silver from the temple in Jerusalem (Ezr 1:8, 11).

SHIBAH, SHEBAH *(SHI buh, SHE buh)*—The well from which Beersheba derived its name. During Isaac's time with Abimelech, the well was dug by Isaac's servants (Gen 26:33).

SHIBBOLETH *(SHIB boh leth)*—A password in Jewish civil war used by Gileadites at the fords of the Jordan River to detect the fleeing Ephraimites (Jdg 12:6). Because of a difference in dialect, the Ephraimites could not pronounce the word's initial consonant.

SHIELD—Generally made of metal, although some shields were made of leather or wood; used by a warrior to protect his body from the enemy's weapon. In some versions it is translated as "buckler" (1Ch 5:18; 1Ki 10:16). Figura-

SHEPHERD

Pastoral language was used figuratively throughout the biblical world. It is natural that the Old and New Testaments used shepherd imagery. In many passages, the customs of shepherds were used to illustrate spiritual principles such as: Yahweh being Israel's shepherd (Gen 49:24; Ps 23:1) or Jesus' reference to sheep without a shepherd (Mt 9:36). Shepherds were compared to spiritual overseers (Nu 27:16–17; Jn 21:15–17).

The only literal reference to shepherds in the New Testament was Luke 2:8–20. Elsewhere they appeared in parables and figures of speech, most often in the Gospels. Jesus said his mission was to the "lost sheep of the house of Israel" (Mt 10:6; 15:24). The parable of the lost sheep exemplified God's love for the lost (Lk 15:3–7). The shepherd's separation of sheep from goats was compared to judgment (Mt 25:32–33).

Jesus called himself the good shepherd who knows his sheep by name; they follow him, and he lays down his life for them (Jn 10:1–29). Peter called him the chief shepherd (1 Pe 5:4).

Paul admonished Ephesian elders to oversee and care for the flock, which he equated with the "church of God" (Ac 20:28–30). All who held responsible positions were looked on as shepherds (pastors), and their faithfulness was pointed out (Isa 56:11).

SHILOH

This ancient religious center of Israel was located about 10 miles north of Bethel (Jdg 21:198). Shiloh was the administrative and religious center for the Israelite tribes during the early settlement of Canaan (12th century B.C.). There, they set up the tabernacle (Jos 18:1) and the distribution of land by casting lots (Jos 18:19), and Levites were assigned their cities (Jdg 21). The 10 tribes gathered there to consider renunciation of the two tribes on the east side of the Jordan (Jos 22).

Shiloh became the principal place of worship and center for the priesthood (Eleazar, Jos 21:1–2; Eli and his sons, 1Sa 1:3–10; Samuel, 1Sa 1:24, 3:21) until the capture of the ark by the Philistines. The city never regained its prestige. The loss was complete when Jerusalem became the capital of the kingdom.

Shiloh was in ruins by the time of Jeremiah (Jer 7:12–14), although some people continued to live there (Jer 41:5). In the days of the Greeks and Romans several centuries later, Shiloh was again inhabited.

tively, God is a shield to Israel (Gen 15:1; Ps 3:3).

SHIHOR-LIBNATH (*SHY hor LIB nath*)—A small river that served as the southwestern boundary of the tribal territory of Asher (Jos 19:26).

SHIMEATH (*SHIM ee ath*)—The Ammonite mother of King Josiah's murderer (2Ki 12:21).

SHIMEI (*SHIM ee eye*)—**1.** The ancestral head of the Levites (Ex 6:17). **2.** A descendant of Simeon (1Ch 4:26). **3.** A descendant of Reuben (1Ch 5:4). **4.** A descendant of Merari (1Ch 6:29). **5.** A descendant of David's musician, Heman (1Ch 6:42); possibly Shimei 1. **6.** A descendant of Benjamin (1Ch 8:21). **7.** A descendant of Gershon (1Ch 23:9); possibly Shimei **5**. **8.** A descendant of Kish, ancestor of Mordecai (Est 2:5). **9.** A man who publicly cursed David (2Sa 16:5, 19:16–23). **10.** Possibly another name of Shammah (2Sa 21:21). **11.** An officer of David, loyal during Adonijah's attempted coup (1Ki 1:8). **12.** The head of a division of music ministers (1Ch 25:3). **13.** The overseer of David's vineyards (1Ch 27:27). **14.** Solomon's district governor (1Ki 4:18); possibly Shimei 11. **15.** A Levite who helped purify the temple (2Ch 29:14). **16.** A Levite who helped with temple treasury (2Ch 31:12); possibly Shimei 15. **17.** A grandson of Jehoiachin (1Ch 3:19). **18.** A Levite who married and divorced a foreigner after the Exile (Ezr 10:23). **19.** A man who married and divorced a foreigner after the Exile (Ezr 10:33). **20.** A man who married and divorced a foreigner after the Exile (Ezr 10:38).

SHIMRON (*SHIM rahn*)— The son of Issachar (Gen 46:13), ancestor of the Shimronites (Nu 26:24).

SHIMRON-MERON (*SHIM rahn MIR ahn*)—An ancient royal city of the Canaanites whose king was one of 31 rulers killed by Joshua (Jos 12:20).

SHINAR (*SHY nahr*)—Land of southern Mesopotamia, later known as Babylonia or Chaldea, through which the Tigris and Euphrates rivers flowed (Gen 10:10, 11:2).

SHIPS AND SAILING—By 2000 B.C., Egyptians had built ships to navigate the Nile, but Canaanites held supremacy on the eastern Mediterranean Sea. Jews were not seagoing people;

for them, the sea was a barrier and danger.

SHISHAK *(SHEE shak)*—A Libyan war chieftain who became Pharaoh of Egypt (2Ch 12:1–9).

SHITTAH TREE, SHITTIM WOOD *(SHIH tuh, SHIH tihm)*—Usually translated as acacia, it is a large, thorny tree with rough, gnarled bark; hard-grained and resistant to insects, its wood was used to build the ark of the covenant and the first tabernacle (Ex 36: 20, 37:1).

SHITTIM—A place in Moab, across the border from Jericho (Nu 33:48–49). There Joshua was commissioned to succeed Moses (Nu 27: 23), and from Shittim, 12 men went to spy out the Promised Land (Jos 2:1).

SHOA *(SHOH uh)*—An unknown people mentioned by Ezekiel as one of many who would rise against Judah (Eze 23:23).

SHOBACH *(SHOH bak)*—A Syrian general during the time of David; he was killed in battle against Israel (2Sa 10:16–18). Also called Shophach (1Ch 19:16, 18).

SHOBAL *(SHOH buhl)*—1. A chief of the Horites (Gen 36:20). 2. The son of Hur and founder of Kirjath Jearim (1Ch 2:50–52). 3. A descendant of Judah (1Ch 4:1–2); possibly Shobal 2.

SHOBI *(SHO bye)*—A son of the Ammonite king Nahash who provided food for David when he fled from Absalom (2Sa 17:27).

SHOES—In biblical times, these were generally leather sandals held on by straps (thongs). Shoes were removed indoors (Lk 7:38), and in wealthier homes, a servant stood ready to unloose the thong and remove the guest's shoes (Mk 1:7). In ancient Israel, property was transferred by the symbolic exchange of a sandal (Ru 4:7–8; Am 2:6).

435

SHOVEL—An implement used to clear away ashes from the tabernacle's outer altar. The altar shovels were made of copper, and the ashes were scooped into copper pots (Ex 27:3), which were then carried outside the camp and emptied (Lev 6:10–11). Solomon's Temple had copper shovels for its burnt offerings (2Ch 4:11, 16).

SHOWBREAD—(Shewbread in older translations.) Twelve loaves of unleavened bread placed on a specially constructed table in the holy place of the tabernacle and temple as an offering to God. They were baked of fine flour and arranged in two rows of six each. Priests replaced the bread every Sabbath and ate the old bread (Ex 25:23–30; Lev 24:5–9).

SHROUD—A long cloth used to wrap a corpse. Jesus' body was wrapped in a shroud after the crucifixion (Mt 27:59; Mk 15:46).

SHUA (SHOO uh)—**1.** The mother of one of Judah's wives (Gen 38:2, 12). **2.** The daughter of Heber, and granddaughter of Asher (1Ch 7:32).

SHUAL, LAND OF (SHOO al)—A district near Ophrah toward which the Philistines marched at the time of King Saul (1Sa 13:17).

SHULAMMITE (SHOO lum ite)—A young woman mentioned in Song of Solomon 6:3. The term may indicate the woman's origin from an otherwise unknown town of Shulam.

SHUNEM (SHOO nuhm)—A city north of Jezreel allotted to Issachar (Jos 19:18).

SHUNAMMITE (SHOO nuhm ite)—**1.** Abishag the Shunammite was a lovely young woman who ministered to King David in his old age (1Ki 1:3, 15). **2.** A woman who befriended Elisha (2Ki 4:8–36).

SHUR (SHYOOR)—Desert in the northwest part of the

Sinai Peninsula where the Angel of the Lord found Hagar (Gen 16:7). Shur was a caravan route from Beersheba and Egypt.

SHUR, WILDERNESS OF—A desert region in the Sinai Peninsula, inhabited by Ishmaelites (Gen 25:18). It was the home of Abraham for a time (Gen 20:1). Israelites entered it immediately after leaving the Red Sea (Ex 15:22).

SIBMAH (*SIB mah*)—An area in the rich Moabite plateau allocated to Reuben (Nu 32:36). It was later known for its vineyards.

SICKLE—A farming implement with a simple or compound blade set as a small curve and rigged with a handle to allow short horizontal strokes for cutting grain, grass, or weeds. Workers held the grain in one hand and cut it off near the ground with the sickle. Final judgment is pictured as God reaping with a sickle (Joel 3:13; Rev 4:14–19).

SIDDIM, VALLEY OF (*SID ihm*)—A valley at the southern end of the Dead Sea where the forces of Chedorlaomer defeated the five kings (Gen 14:3–10). The valley was full of asphalt (bitumen) pits that became death traps to the fleeing forces.

SIDON (*SY don*)—Along with Tyre, a leading city in ancient Phoenicia on the Mediterranean coast. A fertile plain inland from the city supported agriculture, but inhabitants depended on sea trade for their livelihood.

SIEGE—A military tactic of surrounding a city, cutting off its supplies and rescue aid, and reducing its resistance to the point of surrender or destruction (e.g., Nebuchadnezzar against Jerusalem, 2Ki 25:1). It can also refer to any prolonged distress or suffering (Job 19:12).

SIGN—A significant act or event that points to or represents God's presence or intentions. They may be miraculous, such as those performed by Moses (Ex 4:1–9), or natural pheomenons such as the rainbow (Gen 9:13) and the infant Jesus (Lk 2:12). In the Gospel of John, each of Jesus' miracles is called a sign.

SIGNET—A device made of stone or metal engraved with the reverse of a design for making an impression in clay, lead, or wax. For security purposes, such impressions placed marks on closures so they could be opened only by breaking the seal. Each personal signet was distinct, to preclude any doubt concerning identity.

SIHON (*SY hahn*)—An Ammorite king. Moses had asked permission to pass peacefully through the kingdom east of the Jordan on the way to the Promised Land. Sihon refused and later attacked the Israelites, but was defeated (Nu 21: 21–32).

SILK—Cloth woven from threads made by the Chinese silkworm. Except for a reference to actual silk in Revelation 18:12, most scholars think the term should be translated as "fine linen" or "costly fabric" (Eze 16:10, 13; Pr 31:22).

Pool of Siloam

SILOAM (*sih LOH um*)—A pool or reservoir in Jerusalem, part of complex waterworks that carried water from the Gihon Spring outside the city

SILAS

This Jerusalem synagogue attendant preserved the scrolls and Scriptures. With his Roman citizenship, writing ability, and ties to the Jerusalem church, he proved useful to the Church at large.

The Jerusalem Council of apostles and elders appointed Silas and Paul to write and deliver their landmark decision to all outlying churches to accept Gentile (non-Jewish) Christians into the Church and to give ethical guidelines for those converts (Ac 15:22–32).

During their travels, Silas and Paul were imprisoned at Philippi; an earthquake destroyed the jail and freed the prisoners (Ac 16:19–29). They were also together during the riot at Thessalonica (Ac 17:4). Later, they went to Berea, where Silas remained with Timothy. Neither Silas nor Timothy followed Paul to Athens (Ac 17:14–15), although they may have caught up with him in Corinth (Ac 18:5).

Silas played an important role in the early Christian work at Corinth. In his letters, Paul called Silas *Silvanus* (1 Th 1:1; 2 Th 1:1).

walls. It was devised by King Hezekiah (2Ki 20:20).

SILOAM INSCRIPTION— Found in 1880, this Hebrew inscription was found on the walls of a tunnel dating from the time of Hezekiah. It describes the building of the tunnel (2Ch 32:30).

SILVANUS *(sil VAN us)*—A form of Silas (2Co 1:19).

SILVER—Mined as early as 3000 B.C. (Job 28:1).

Genesis 13:2 is the first biblical reference: Silver, cattle, and gold marked Abraham as wealthy. Silver was most commonly used for exchange but was also found in decorations, vessels for worship, and trumpets in the tabernacle (Ex 26:19). Most first-century money was minted from silver.

SIMEON *(SIM ee uhn)*—1. The second son of Jacob and Leah (Gen 29:33). 2. A descendant of David, ancestor of Jesus (Lk 3:30). 3. A devout resident of Jerusalem to whom the Holy Spirit revealed he would not die without seeing the Messiah. When Jesus was presented in the temple, Simeon greeted the child as the Savior, blessed Mary and Joseph, and predicted events concerning Jesus and Mary (Lk 2:25–34). 4. A Christian at Antioch of Syria (Ac 13:1). Some believe he was Simon of Cyrene, who bore Jesus' cross (Lk 23:26).

SIMON—1. The father of Judas Iscariot (Jn 6:71). 2. Another name for Peter (Mt 4:18). 3. One of Jesus' 12 disciples, called the Zealot (Mt 10:4). 4. One of Jesus' brothers (Mt 13:55). 5. A leper in Bethany, at whose home Jesus was anointed by a woman (Lk 7:36–50). 6. Leper in Bethany in whose home Jesus' feet were perfumed (Mt 26:6). 7. The man from Cyrene who was forced to carry Jesus' cross (Mk 15:21). 8. A sorcerer (Ac 8:9–25). *See* **SIMON MAGUS.** 9. A tanner from Joppa and friend of Peter (Ac 9:43).

SIMON MAGUS *(MAG us)*— A magician who saw Philip perform miracles in Samaria. Later, he offered money to be able to bestow the Holy Spirit on others. Peter chastised him and he repented (Ac 8: 9–25).

SIN—Anything that violates God's holiness. Biblically, sin is an ever-present reality that corrupts the human race. Although expressed by many Hebrew and Greek words, revolt or transgression is the basic Old Testament concept (Gen 3:1–7). New Testament writers call it lawlessness (1Jn 3:4).

SIN OFFERING—Animal sacrifices, also called guilt offerings, were presented for unintentional or intentional sins for which there was no possible restitution (Lev 4:5–13, 6:24–30), and were supposed to be accompanied by repentance to receive divine forgiveness (Nu 15:30).

SIN, WILDERNESS OF—Wilderness through which the Israelites passed on their journey toward Mt. Sinai (Nu 33:11–12). There they murmured against Moses and Aaron (Ex 16:1–3).

SINEW (sin YOO)—A word that covers a variety of anatomical elements including tendons, ligaments, and possibly muscles. In Genesis 32:32, where Jacob wrestles with the Angel of the Lord, sinew may refer to nerve tissue. Isaiah 48:4 used sinew figuratively for stubbornness.

SION (SI uhn)—1. The peak of Mt. Hermon (Dt 4:48). 2. A Greek form of Mt. Zion (Mt 21:5), referring specifically to Solomon's Temple Mount and generally to the city of Jerusalem (Ro 9:33).

SIRAH, CISTERN OF (SY ruh)—The place where Abner was murdered by Joab and Abishai (2Sa 3:26–27). Its location is unknown, but it was probably near Hebron.

SIRION (SEAR ee UN)—A Sidonian (Phoenician) name for Mt. Hermon, in northern Palestine (Dt 3:9).

SISERA (SIS eh ruh)—1. The commander of the

MT. SINAI

The mountain where God met Moses and gave him the law (Ex 19:3, 20, 31:18) still has an uncertain location. Mt. Sinai is also known by various other names such as "the mountain," "Mountain of God," "Mt. Horeb," "the mountain of Horeb," and "the mountain of God in Horeb." Horeb may refer to a mountain range or ridge, and Sinai to an individual summit on that ridge. The name Sinai was used when the Israelites were actually at the foot of the mountain (Ex 19:11).

The two most likely locations for Mt. Horeb are Jebel Serbal, about 8,000 feet high, in central Sinai, and Jebel Musa, about 7,500 feet high. Jebel Musa has a broad plain at its base, where the Israelites could have camped.

The mountain played an important role in the spiritual development of Moses (Ex 3:1−12). From there the Ten Commandments were given, and at the base, the covenant between God and the Israelites was ratified (Ex 20:1−24:8). God's presence on that peak came to symbolize divine protection (Jdg 5:4−5; Ps 68:8).

The only visit to the mount recorded later in the Old Testament is that of Elijah when he was threatened by Queen Jezebel (1 Ki 19:4−8). In his allegory of the two covenants, Paul used Sinai to symbolize the old system of law (Gal 4:24−25).

army of King Jabin of Hazor, who oppressed the Israelites for 20 years.

Defeated by Deborah, he was killed by Jael while he slept in her tent (Jdg

4:1–22). **2.** A temple servant who returned from the Exile (Ne 7:55).

SISTER—A female sibling, a representative of any female blood relative (Mt 13:56), a member of the same tribe, or a lover (SS 4:9–11). In the New Testament, it is a term for a female person of the community of faith (Ro 16:1).

SITNAH *(SIT nuh)*—One of three wells dug by the servants of Isaac near the Philistine city of Gerar during a dispute over water rights with local herders (Gen 26:21).

SLAVERY

Aside from crown and temple slavery, slave labor played a minor economic role in the biblical period. Privately owned slaves functioned more as domestic servants than as agricultural or industrial workers.

The major source of royal and temple slaves came from war captives (1Ki 9:21; Nu 32:25–47). Private slaves were usually defaulting debtors and their families (Ex 21:2) or those who resorted to voluntary self-sale (Dt 15:16–17).

Slaves were allowed to secure their freedom, and under Jewish law, no Hebrew could be a permanent slave of another Hebrew. After six years of service, a slave was to be released (Ex 21:2). If slaves wanted to continue with their masters, they would have an ear lobe drilled with an awl (Ex 21:5–6).

Spiritually, people apart from Christ are called slaves to sin. This demonstrates that sin has control over their lives (Jn 8:34–36). Paul described Timothy and himself as slaves of Christ Jesus (Ro 1:1; Phm 1:1).

666—The mysterious number of the "beast" in Revelation 13:17–18. In Hebrew and Greek, letters were also used as numbers. Each name had a numerical value of its letters; for example, 666 is the numerical value of "Nero Caesar" in Hebrew. Theories abound to identify a specific individual as 666.

SKIRT—**1.** A loose corner of a garment, like the one David removed from Saul's robe (1Sa 15:27). **2.** The edge of a garment, literally (Ex 28:33–34); figuratively (Jer 13:22–25; La 1:9), a sign of Jerusalem's shame. **3.** The "mouth" of a garment, or collar (Ps 133:2).

SKULL, PLACE OF THE—The site of Christ's crucifixion (Mk 15:22). *See* **GOLGOTHA.**

SLEEP—A common metaphor for death. Several times the Bible says that kings slept or rested with their fathers (1Ki 2:10; 11:43). The Christian dead "sleep in Jesus" (1Th 4:14).

Sleep symbolizes physical laziness (Pr 6:9–11) or moral laxness (1Th 5:6). It can also mean living in safety (Eze 34:25; Ps 4:8).

SLING—Developed by shepherds for protecting their herds against wild animals, it was a simple weapon, made of a small piece of leather using small stones as ammunition (1Sa 17:40). Although simple to construct, it was difficult to fire with accuracy. Benjaminites were famous for the accuracy of their left-handed sling users (Jdg 20:16; 1Ch 12:2).

SMYRNA (*SMER nuh*)—Important trading center during the Roman period, where one of the seven churches in Revelation was situated (Rev 1:11, 2:8–11).

SNAKE—A popular symbol of evil in Scripture (Gen 3; Ps 58:4; Jer 46:22).

SNARE—A device for catching animals and birds (Ps 124:7). The word is

SODOM

This is the most prominent of the five "Cities of the Plain" south of the Dead Sea. It was known for the people's sinfulness, acted out through sexual perversion (Gen 19).

When God decided to destroy Sodom because of its wickedness, Abraham interceded for the city because his nephew Lot lived there. Two angels were sent by God to warn Lot of Sodom's upcoming destruction. They met Lot at the gate, and he invited them to stay at his home.

When the men of the town heard about Lot's two guests, they went to his house demanding that Lot send the two men out so they could have sexual relations with them. Following the custom of Hebrew hospitality, which states a host must provide for the safety of his guests, Lot offered his two virgin daughters to the men in place of his guests. They refused his offer and attacked him. The angels rescued Lot by blinding the townsmen.

The next morning, the angels led Lot and his family out of the town as it was destroyed by fire and brimstone. Lot's wife, ignoring the angels' warning not to look back on the burning city, was turned into a pillar of salt while Lot escaped to safety.

used figuratively in the Bible to mean caught or trapped by evil (Ps 142:3).

SNOW—Snow's whiteness is a symbol of God's purity (Rev 1:14) and the changed nature of the forgiven (Isa 1:18).

SNUFFER *(SNUFF er)*—A small, scissorlike instru-

445

ment, often made of gold, used to extinguish tabernacle lamps (Ex 37:23).

So *(SOH)*—An Egyptian king with whom King Hoshea formed an alliance against Assyria. The Assyrians responded by capturing Samaria and ten tribes of Israel (2Ki 17:4–6).

SOAP—A solution of potash and soda made by filtering water through plant ash; used to cleanse clothes, cooking utensils, and the body (Jer 2:22).

SOCOH, SOCO *(SO ko)*—Several Biblical towns (Jos 15:48; 1Ki 4:10); most notably, a town in Judah near Azekah where David killed Goliath (1Sa 17).

SODOMY—Unnatural sexual acts common in Sodom. Although forbidden by the law (Dt 23:17), many such acts were practiced, even in the temple (2Ki 23:7).

SOJOURNER—Someone who takes permanent residence in and lives by the laws of a country not his or her home (Gen 21:34). The Israelites were sojourners in Egypt (Dt 10:19).

SOLDIER—One who performs military service in return for pay. In ancient Israel, any man above the age of 20 could serve as a soldier (Nu 1:3, 2:2, 10:14). Each tribe formed a regiment in the army.

SOLOMON, PSALMS OF—Short book of 18 psalms written in the first century A.D. and part of the Jewish Pseudepigrapha.

SOLOMON'S PORTICO/PORCH—The covered porch on the east side of Solomon's Temple. Jesus and several of his disciples were believed to have walked there (Jn 10:23; Ac 3:11, 5:12).

SOLOMON'S TEMPLE—Israel's first permanent place of worship after settling in the Promised Land. Planned by David

SOLOMON

Though not the product of their original liaison, Solomon was a son of King David and Bathsheba. Solomon is best known as the third king of Israel—and the wisest of all men (1 Ki 3:9).

Solomon came to power by succeeding his father after having his half-brother Adonijah executed when he conspired to gain the throne. Shortly after becoming king, Solomon had a vision. In it, God asked Solomon what he would like from God. Wisdom, Solomon answered, to know the difference between good and evil as he ruled. God granted his desire (1 Ki 3:4–15).

Solomon is credited as the author of numerous proverbs and songs, the Song of Solomon, the books of Proverbs and Ecclesiastes, and two Psalms (72 and 127). All are examples of his exceptional wisdom.

During his reign, Solomon established a strong central monarchy, his kingdom experienced its greatest prosperity, and he completed the temple at Jerusalem. His reign was unusually peaceful. This was due in part to his skillful formation of political alliances; peace mostly came, however, through treaties sealed by marriages to foreign princesses. To placate his foreign wives, he allowed them to worship their pagan deities, which sowed seeds for future problems.

but completed by Solomon, it was a large structure noted for its beauty (1 Ki 6–7; 2 Ch 3–4).

SOLOMON'S POOLS—Three pools that provided Jerusalem with water via an aqueduct system (Ecc 2:6).

SON OF MAN

In the Old Testament, "son of man" meant a human being (Ps 8:4) or the coming Messiah (Da 7:13). In the New Testament, it was a title for Jesus (Mk 10:45).

Jesus' favorite expression to describe himself was the Son of Man. He called himself this 78 times in the New Testament. Many believe Jesus chose to use the name for practical rather than religious reasons. He did not use the title to claim he was the brother of all humans nor that he was only human and not divine. In this way he was less apt to receive criticism and possible blasphemy charges.

It is likely that Jesus did see himself in two roles. He was at once the "earthly" Son of Man whose mission was to bring new hope to the outcast—and the future Son of Man, referring to the "One Who Has Been Living Forever" in Daniel's vision of the coming Messiah (Da 7:9–13).

SON—A male child and a father's immediate descendant (Gen 27:1). Also, a guild member (2Ki 2:3); an adopted son (Ex 2:10); a term used by an older man when addressing a younger one (Jos 7:19); a native of a town or group of people (Lam 4:2); or a person with special qualities (1Sa 25:17).

SON OF GOD—A phrase in Hebrew tradition meaning "God" or "equal to God." In the Old Testament, a divine being (Da 3:25). In the New Testament, it refers to Jesus (Jn 5:18).

SONG OF ASCENT—Psalms 120–134, whose titles include this phrase. It is believed they were sung by those making a pilgrimage to Jerusalem to worship.

SONG OF SOLOMON—A collection of poetry about marriage and love. While bearing Solomon's name, many question that he is the author. The poems speak of the wonders of human love and the essential goodness of physical love.

SONS *(Children) of God*—In the Old Testament, heavenly beings who are God-like (Ps 29:1); those who are given the responsibility of exercising God's judgment, such as the judges (Ex 21:6); those related to God through the covenant (Ex 4:22). In the New Testament, those who act in ways that please God (Mt 5:9; Lk 6:35).

SONS OF THUNDER—A name Jesus gave to James and John because of their fiery tempers (Mk 3:17).

SOP *(SAHP)*—A piece of bread used to dip food from a common platter (Jn 13:26).

SOPATER, SOSIPATER *(SOH pat uhr, so SIP uh tuhr)*—A Christian who accompanied the Apostle Paul on his last journey from Corinth to Jerusalem, when he brought his offering for the poor (Ac 20:4).

SORCERY—Magic and occult arts, widespread in ancient times. Sorcery was considered evil by Israel. In the New Testament, sorcerers claimed to have supernatural powers (Isa 47:9; Ac 8:9–13).

SOREK, VALLEY OF *(SOH rek; "vine")*—A valley between the Mediterranean Sea and Jerusalem that served as an inland route. It was the home of Delilah (Jdg 16:4).

SOSIPATER *(soh SIP uh tuhr)*—See **SOPATER.**

SOSTHENES *(SAHS thuh neez)*—A synagogue official before whom charges

449

against Paul were brought. When Sosthenes acquitted Paul, an angry crowd beat him (Ac 18:17). Also, Paul's companion when he wrote the first letter to the Corinthians. Some believe the two are the same man.

SOUL—An Old Testament term for a living being (Gen 2:7). In the New Testament, the term describes the nonphysical part of human beings that is believed to be immortal (Mt 10:28).

SPAIN—Conquered by the Romans during the time of Augustus. Paul had planned to visit Spain, but it is unknown whether he did (Ro 15:24, 28).

SPARROW—Several varieties of small birds. House sparrows were most common in Palestine. Some were sold for food. Jesus assured that if God cared for the sparrows, which cost a penny for two, God would surely care for us (Mt 10:29).

SPEAR—A wooden shaft with a sharp metal head that was the favorite weapon of the infantry (1Sa 13:19).

SPICES—Fragrant plants used in ancient times as cosmetics, perfumes, incense, burial preparations, and for flavoring food.

SPIKENARD (SPIKE nard)—An expensive ointment made from the spikenard plant from India. Jesus was anointed with it when he ate at the homes of Simon the leper and Lazarus in Bethany (Mk 14:3; Jn 12:3).

SPIRIT—Wind, breath, or having life (Ex 10:13; 1Ki 19:11; Gen 6:17). Relating to God, it describes his awesome power. In the New Testament, it is the spiritual level at which humankind and God can have a relationship (Ro 8:16).

SPIRIT OF GOD—God's creative power that gives

SPEAKING IN TONGUES

This spiritual gift was first given by the outpouring of the Holy Spirit during the Jewish holiday of Pentecost. Those who received this gift spoke in languages they did not know.

In the early Church, speaking in tongues was proof of the Spirit's presence and a sign that the person had been converted. While there are accounts of conversions without the presence of speaking in tongues (Ac 2:41–42, 4:4, 8:35–38), the ability to do so became standard among some Christian groups.

Paul spoke in tongues, but became concerned about its common use in worship, especially in the church in Corinth. He feared the ecstatic speaking and the resulting scenes would be offensive to outsiders. His recommendation was to use it in private devotions (1 Co 14:2–19) and to see it as a gift of the Spirit, and thereby subordinate to the gift of love (1 Co 13:8). In this way the gift would benefit the whole Church.

life and continually re-creates life. Like breath and wind, God's divine energy cannot be seen but can be experienced (Gen 2:7; Eze 37:9).

SPIRITS IN PRISON—Those in Hades who refused to listen to Noah's message. According to 1 Peter, Jesus, after his death, preached to them, sharing his victory over sin and death (1 Pe 3: 18–20).

SPIRITUAL GIFTS—Particular gifts given to individuals by God. They were to be used to help build the Christian community (1 Co 14:1–6, 26).

SPIRIT, HOLY SPIRIT

In the Old Testament, the term Holy Spirit occurs only a few times and identifies the presence of God's power. At creation, the Spirit of God was "moving over the waters" (Gen 1:2). The Spirit empowered individuals for service. Joshua was filled "with the spirit of wisdom" (Dt 34:9).

Through the Spirit, creation is continually renewed. Isaiah says Israel will be cleansed "by a spirit of judgment and burning" (Isa 4:4), and the promised Messiah will be anointed and empowered by the Spirit (Isa 61:1). In the Old Testament, the Spirit is the agent by which God accomplishes his intentions.

In the New Testament, the term occurs nearly one hundred times. Jesus calls it the source of his ability to cast out demons and do miracles (Lk 4:1–2). By the power of the Holy Spirit, Jesus performed miracles that were signs of the coming of God's kingdom (Lk 4:18–20).

In the New Testament, the Holy Spirit's purpose is to create the new community of Jesus known as the Church by giving believers spiritual gifts. All these gifts are expressed through the most important one, love (Gal 5:22), and are not for the individual alone but for the common good of the Church.

SPIRITS, EVIL—In the Old Testament, instruments of God used to cause dissension between people, leading to political unrest (Jdg 9:23; 1Sa 16:14–23, 18:10–11; 1Ki 22:19–23). In the New Testament, demons caused some physical disabilities. Freeing these individuals from demons was an important part of Jesus' ministry (Mk 1:23, 9:25–26).

SPIT—Both Jews and Gentiles thought that human saliva had healing powers (Mk 7:33).

SPITTING—Spitting on or at another was a sign of deep-seated hatred (Job 17:6; Mk 10:34).

STACHYS (STAY kis; "ear of corn")—A Christian in Rome greeted by Paul and called his "dear friend" (Ro 16:9).

STADIA (STAY dee uh)—A unit of measurement equal to about 200 yards. Nine stadia convert to a little more than a mile.

STAR OF BETHLEHEM—The eastern star seen by the Magi. They believed it was a sign of the birth of a new king of the Jews (Mt 2:1–10). Some believe it was the appearance of some natural phenomena like a comet or comets rather than the unique appearance of a single star.

STARS—Called God's handiwork (Gen 1:16; Ps 8:3), stars were believed to be under God's control (Isa 13:10; Jer 31:35).

STEPHANAS (STEF uh nuhs)—A Corinthian baptized by Paul, along with his household (1Co 1:16), and commended by Paul for his service to the Church (1Co 16:15).

STEWARD—In the Old and New Testaments, one who manages another's property and goods (Isa 22:15; Lk 16:1).

STOCKS—A device made of two large blocks of wood, between which a prisoner's feet, neck, and hands were placed for punishment (Jer 20:2; Ac 16:24).

STOICS—The Greek school of philosophy founded by Zeno; they believed salvation would come by being at one with nature, expressed through virtuous living. They emphasized reason above emotions

STEPHEN

The first Christian martyr, this Greek-speaking Jew converted to Christianity and was stoned to death as a blasphemer (Ac 7:58). Described as a man "full of faith and the Holy Spirit," Stephen was one of seven to be elected by the early Church as a deacon. His election came about when the small band of Greek-speaking Jewish Christians like himself complained to the Hebrews that they were not taking care of their widows.

Of course, Stephen is better known for his martyrdom. It was his conviction that the gospel should be made available to non-Jews. In arguing his case, he claimed that from the time of Moses the Hebrews had not been faithful to God's call for them to be a nation that would lead people to God. He also spoke out against the temple since he believed communion with God was no longer limited to the temple. The charges against him were considered blasphemy against God, Moses, and the temple. He was convicted and executed by stoning.

Stephen's death resulted in persecution of the Christians but also the spread of the Gospel beyond Jerusalem. Those who fled persecution took Christianity with them. Paul was likely first introduced to the Gospel at Stephen's trial and, while he agreed with the outcome at the time, he later became the "Apostle to the Gentiles" (Ro 11:13).

and had the reputation of being indifferent to pain or pleasure.

STOMACHER (STUHM uhk ur; "rich robe")—A highly decorated piece of clothing worn by women that covered the upper part of the body (Isa 3:24).

STONE—In Palestine, limestone was in great abundance and was used to make numerous everyday implements. Its most important use was for building, since it was considered superior to brick (Isa 9:10). Its hardness, weight, and strength also led to many symbolic meanings (Ex 15:5; 1Sa 25:37; Mt 21:42).

STONING—A means of execution for crimes punishable by death according to Hebrew law (Lev 20:27; Ac 7:58).

STORE-CITIES—Frontier cities where reserve supplies were stored to maintain a strong defense (1Ki 9:15–19; 2Ch 8:4–6).

STRAIGHT, STREET CALLED—Address of a Jew named Judas whose home Paul was taken to after being blinded on the road to Damascus (Ac 9:11).

STRIPES—Marks left on the body from being whipped , a common form of ancient punishment. The severity of punishment was determined by the number of stripes (Dt 25:2).

STUMBLING BLOCK/STONE—Anything that caused another to unexpectedly fall or trip. Symbolically, anything (such as greed) that caused people to turn from God (Eze 14:3; Jer 18:15). Jesus was characterized as a stumbling block to the Jews (1Co 1:23).

SUCCOTH (*SUHK ahth; "tents"*)—A city in the Jordan Valley where Jacob settled (Gen 33:17). Also, the first place the Israelites stopped as they fled from Egypt (Ex 12:37).

SUCCOTH-BENOTH (*BEE noth; "tents of daughters"*)—A pagan god worshiped in Samaria after the Assyrians captured it (2Ki 17:24–30). Also, tents put up by the Babylonians to house cultic prostitutes.

SUFFERING—Conflict, pain, and drudgery thought to be brought on by evil and sin (Gen 1:31). Both the Old and New Testaments see God allowing suffering as a consequence of people's choices (Gal 6:8; Jdg 6). God will abolish suffering in the new heaven and Earth (Rev 21:4). Suffering for one's faith is a way Christians share in Christ's suffering (2Co 1:5–7).

SUKKIIM (*SUHK ihm*)—Libyan warriors who joined Shishak of Egypt in his invasion of Judah (2Ch 12:3). They were also called Sukkites.

SUKKOTH (*SUHK uhth; "booths"*)—Another name for the Feast of Tabernacles, the tradition of living in small huts or booths to recall how the Israelites lived in tents during their time of wanderings. *See* **SUCCOTH.**

SUMER, SUMERIANS (*SOO mehr, soo MEHR ee uhns*)—The land at the head of the Persian Gulf, later called Babylon. Its first inhabitants formed what is believed to be the first highly developed human civilization.

SUN—God created the sun to give light to day (Gen 1:16). Since it was responsible for life and growth and was a means of determining direction, the sun became an object of worship, which was against Hebrew law (2Ki 23:5). It was a symbol of God's constancy and power (Ps 72:5, 104:19).

SUPERSCRIPTION—Words painted on the board nailed to Jesus' cross (Mk 15:26). It was Roman custom to force criminals to carry such a board naming the crime for which they were being punished. Also, inscriptions on coins.

SUPH (*SOOF*)—Unknown place where Moses first read the law to the Israelites (Dt 1:1).

BOOK OF SUSANNA

This short book appears in the Apocrypha. It is about a Jewish woman accused of adultery but proved innocent by Daniel.

Susanna was the beautiful and faithful wife of Joakim, a leader in the Jewish community. Two Jewish elders desired her and plotted to seduce her. Waiting in her garden as she came to bathe, they tried to bribe her into having intercourse by threatening to accuse her of adultery if she refused. After she rejected them, they fulfilled their threat and she was accused of adultery with a young man.

Despite her claims of innocence, she was found guilty and sentenced to death. Daniel, inspired by God, protested her conviction because it was made by taking the word of the elders rather than through a fair trial. He was given the right to cross-examine the elders separately. He asked each the same question: "Where were you standing when you saw Susanna committing adultery?" One said, "Under a mastic tree." The other said, "Under an evergreen oak." Since their stories differed, Daniel proved they were lying. Susanna was acquitted, and the elders were executed according to Jewish law (Dt 19:16–19).

SUSA (*SOO suh*)—A Babylonian city and capital in the Persian Empire during the reign of Darius the Great (Ne 1:1). Daniel had a vision there about the end of the world (Da 8:2).

SUSANNA (*soo ZAN uh; "a lily"*)—A woman healed by Jesus who then accompanied him on his preaching journeys and provided for him and the disciples from her own means (Lk 8:1–3).

SYNAGOGUE

In New Testament times, Jews met to worship and be instructed in the law in synagogues. No factual evidence exists about when the synagogue came about. It is believed to be tied to the Exile, when the Jews were without a temple. They were far from Jerusalem and in need of a place to worship and receive instruction in the law.

The synagogue became the focal point for Jewish life, serving a cross-section of functions as a place of worship, a school to teach the law, a hub for local government, and a social gathering place for the community.

By the first century A.D., a synagogue existed wherever Jews lived. For worship to take place, there had to be a minimum of ten adult males. Worship was divided into five sections: reading the Shema (Dt 6:4–9); prayers, including 18 petitions and benedictions; a reading from the law; a reading from the prophets; and an interpretation of the Scripture followed by a benediction.

There was no altar in the synagogue, since sacrifice was replaced by the reading of the Scriptures as the primary focus of worship. A chest in which scrolls of the law were kept was the one indispensable piece of furniture. During his ministry, Jesus regularly attended the synagogue.

SWINE—Pigs. They were considered unclean by the Israelites because they scavenged food (Lev 11:7). Swine were also a symbol for anything that was despised or hated (Pr 11:22; Lk 15:15).

SYCAMORE *(SIK uh mor)*—A sturdy tree with spreading branches and figlike fruit.

SYCHAR *(SY kahr)*—A Samarian city where Jacob's well was located (Jn 4:5).

SYENE *(sy EEN)*—A town on the east bank of the Nile that served as a marketplace between Africa and Egypt. Some Jews sought refuge there after the fall of Jerusalem (Isa 49:12).

SYMBOL—The use of persons, objects, or actions to relay a deeper spiritual meaning than normally would be suggested by the item's literal meaning.

SYNOPTIC GOSPELS *(sih NAHP tihk)*—The first three gospels, so named because they give a similar view of Jesus' life, ministry, and teaching.

SYNTYCHE *(SIN tih chee)*—A Christian woman in Philippi. Paul encouraged her to settle her dispute with Euodia, another Christian woman (Php 4:2).

SYNZYGUS *(SIN zih guhs)*—A term of affection Paul used, meaning "yoke fellow" (Phm 4:3).

SYRACUSE *(SEER uh kyoos)*—A prosperous and important harbor city on the east coast of Sicily. Paul stayed there for three days en route to Rome (Ac 28:12).

SYRIA, SYRIANS *(SEER ee uh, SEER ee uhns)*—An area north of Canaan and west of the Mediterranean coast. It was conquered by David, became independent during Solomon's reign, and was often in conflict with the Jews (1Ki 15: 18–20).

SYROPHOENICIAN *(SY ro fuh NEESH uhn)*—A Phoenician from Syria. Jesus expelled a demon from the daughter of a Syrophoenician woman near Tyre (Mk 7:26).

TAANACH *(TAY uh nak; "sandy")*—A city near Megiddo. Located along important trade routes, it was captured by Joshua and occupied by the Israelites (Jdg 1:27, 5:19).

TABERNACLES, FEAST OF—A pilgrimage feast celebrated to remind the Jews of how God provided for them during their wanderings. During the celebration, the people stayed in small shelters made from tree and palm branches (Ex 25–40). *See* **SUCCOTH.**

TABITHA *(TAB ih thuh; "gazelle")*—A Christian woman in Joppa whom Peter raised from the dead. She was noted for her good works.(Ac 9:36–43).

TABLETS OF THE LAW—Slabs of stone upon which the Ten Commandments were written (Ex 24:12, 34:1–4). Moses placed them in the ark of the covenant, where they stayed until the reign of Solomon (Dt 10:5; 1Ki 8:9).

TABOR, MT.—A mountain located on the Plain of Jezreel. It was used for Baal worship during Hosea's time (Hos 5:1).

TADMOR *(TAD mohr)*—A city in the wilderness north of Palestine. Solomon built Tadmor to serve as a trade route with the East.

TAHPANHES *(TAH puhn heez)*—An Egyptian city where a small group of Jews fled after the fall of Jerusalem. They took Jeremiah with them against his will, and he prophesied Nebuchadnezzar's defeat of Egypt (Jer 43:5–13).

TAHPENES *(TAH peh neez)*—An Egyptian queen who reared Genubath, the

TABERNACLE

A large tent supported by a wood frame of acacia, the tabernacle was used as a place of worship by the nomadic Hebrews. Its side walls were made of cloth covered with goat hair. Ram skin (which was dyed red) was used for the roof. The interior was decorated with violet, purple, and scarlet tapestries sewn together into large curtains.

The tabernacle consisted of two rooms separated by a large embroidered curtain. The larger of these rooms—called the Holy Place—was where the people gathered to worship. The smaller room—the Holy of Holies—held the ark of the covenant and was considered the most sacred place. Only the high priest was allowed to enter the Holy of Holies (once a year, during the Day of Atonement).

During the Israelites' journey, those tending the ark of the covenant would go ahead of the group and find a suitable place to camp. Once a camp was set up, the tabernacle would be built in the center, followed by the priests' tents, and then the tents of the Twelve Tribes. After the wilderness journeys, the tabernacle was set up at Shiloh. It was moved from there twice (first to Nob and then to Gibeon). Solomon had its remains delivered to the site of his temple.

son of her sister and King Hadad (1Ki 11:14–22).

TAHTIM-HODSHI *(tah tim HAHD shy)*—An unknown area where Joab, a census taker, visited while working for David (2Sa 24:6).

TALE BEARING, SLANDER—The sharing of slanderous gossip. This activity was forbidden by Hebrew law (Lev 19:16).

TALITHA CUM *(TAL ih thuh KOOM; "little girl arise")*—Jesus spoke these two Aramaic words when he raised Jairus' daughter from the dead (Mk 5:41).

TALMAI *(TAL may eye)*—A king of Geshur. His daughter, Maacah, was one of David's wives and the mother of Absalom (2Sa 3:3, 13:37).

TAMAR *(TAY mahr)*—**1.** Absalom's daughter (2Sa 14:27). **2.** Absalom's half-sister, whom Amnon raped (2Sa 13). **3.** The wife of Er. When Er died, Tamar's father-in-law, Judah, or-dered Er's brother, Onan, to impregnate her. When he refused, God put Onan to death. Later, Tamar posed as a prostitute to become pregnant by Judah. She gave birth to twins, one of whom was an ancestor of David and Jesus (Gen 38).

TAMARISK *(TAM uh risk)*—A 10- to 20-foot tree with strong wood and small needlelike leaves. It pro-vided shade in bleak areas and was a popular choice for burial spots.

TAMMUZ *(TAM uhz; "sprout")*—A Babylonian fertility god associated with spring vegetation. He was believed to have the power to create new life in the spring. When plant life died, women performed ritual mourning for Tam-muz (Eze 8:14).

TANNING—The preparation of animal hides for use as leather. It was held in low esteem by the Hebrews since it involved working

TALMUD AND MIDRASH

The Talmud (*TAL muhd*) is a large collection of Jewish writings that discuss law, legends, and wisdom. The Palestinian (Jerusalem) Talmud was collected before the fifth century A.D.; the 12-volume Babylonian Talmud was assembled during the fifth century.

Handed down through oral tradition before it was first written, the Talmud is considered the most important Jewish document for giving instruction on how to live as a Jew. It is divided into two parts. The *Mishnah* ("learning by repetition") deals with feasts, agriculture, women, holiness, purity, and damages. The *Gemera* ("learning from the heart") is a commentary on the Mishnah.

Since there is room for much interpretation, discussion was required for students of the Talmud. One form of biblical interpretation, which was found in ancient rabbinical writings, is called midrash (*MID rash*). Mostly philosophical in nature, midrashes were popular during the early centuries A.D. They often contained commentary, morality stories, and ethical sayings.

with dead animals and unclean substances (such as urine).

TAPPUAH (*ta PYOO uh*)—1. A town in the lowlands of Judah, west of Bethlehem (Jos 15:34). 2. A town near the boundary of Ephraim, west of Shechem (Jos 16:8).

TARAH (*TEAR uh*)—One of the sites where the Israelites camped on the journey from Egypt to the plains of Moab (Nu 33:27–28).

TARE (TAR)—An ancient weed. It was indistinguishable from wheat until harvest, when it could be easily separated (Mt 13:29–30).

TARGUMS (TAHR guhmz)—Aramaic translations (or paraphrases) of most Old Testament books. These were written when Aramaic began to replace Hebrew as the language of the Jews (c. 250 B.C.–A.D. 300).

¹TARSHISH (TAHR shish)—The grandson of Noah.

²TARSHISH—The land where the descendants of Tarshish lived. It is believed to have been located along the western coast of the Mediterranean Sea.

TARSUS (TAHR suhs)—A Roman city in the province of Cilicia, near the Mediterranean Sea. It was the birthplace and early residence of the Apostle Paul (Ac 9:11).

TARTAK (TAHR tak)—A pagan god worshiped by the Avvites in Samaria (2Ki 17:31).

TARTAN—A high military rank, likely commander-in-chief, in the Assyrian army (2Ki 18:17; Isa 20:1).

TASSEL—An ornament of white woolen threads and blue cord that hung from the four corners of an Israelite's garment. They reminded the wearer of God's deliverance from Egypt and the need to keep the law (Nu 15:37–41).

TATTENAI (TAT uh nigh)—A Persian governor of territory west of the Euphrates who opposed rebuilding the temple (Ezr 5:3, 6:6).

TAURUS MOUNTAINS—A mountain range near Tarsus rich with lead and silver. Melting snow created a harbor lake that made the Mediterranean accessible for shipping and gave Tarsus a thriving maritime trade.

TAVERNS, THREE—A camp on the Appian Way, 30

TAX COLLECTOR

In biblical times, those who enjoyed the right to collect taxes (called "tax farmers") usually didn't live in their tax area. Instead, they hired local tax collectors—who knew the area and the people—to collect the money. The tax farmer worked for Roman or local Jewish rulers (such as Herod Antipas) and had to pay a predetermined amount to the Romans in advance. In this way, the Romans received their taxes immediately.

This system was open to abuse at every level. For the tax farmer to make a profit, he had to charge the people more than he was paying both Rome and his tax collectors. The local tax collector was paid little and often extorted money from the taxpayer.

Tax officials were never popular, but the system used in Palestine made them even more despised. Jews especially hated them, not only because they extorted from people, but also because they worked on the Sabbath and were in continual contact with Gentiles, which was considered unclean.

miles south of Rome. Paul was met there by Roman Christians who encouraged him as he came to stand trial (Ac 28:15).

TAX—Charges imposed upon citizens of a country by its officials. Hebrews at first paid taxes only to maintain the tabernacle (Dt 18:1). During the monarchy, the demand for taxes increased (1Sa 8:15). All who lived in Roman provinces paid regular taxes to Caesar (Mt 22:17).

TEKOA (teh KOH ah; "fort")—A Judean town,

home to Amos and the "wise woman" who worked to reconcile David and his son Absalom (2Sa 14:1).

TELAIM (teh LAY im; "lambs")—The site where Saul assembled his army in preparation for battle with the Amalekites (1Sa 15).

TELASSAR (teh LAS ur; "Assyrian hill")—A city in Mesopotamia inhabited by children of Eden. Their gods could not protect them from the Assyrians (Isa 37:12).

TELL—A mound formed by a town being built upon the remains of another. Archaeological excavations of tells have provided much information about ancient cultures.

TEMA (TEE muh)—The son of Ishmael. A place where Ishmael's descendants lived, an oasis on an important caravan route (Isa 21:13–14).

TEMAN (TEE muhn)—Esau's grandson. His descendants,

noted for their wisdom, lived in a region in Edom called Teman (Jer 49:7).

TEMPLE SERVANTS—Workers who performed everyday menial tasks and duties in the temple. They were the lowest in status of the five groups who performed temple work.

TEMPTATION—Pressure to do wrong, sin, or turn away from God. Some temptations were believed to be a form of testing by God (Dt 8:2–3).

TENT—Ancient tents were made of cloths or animal skins stretched on poles and held firm with ropes tied to ground stakes. Tents were used by nomads, shepherds, and soldiers.

TENT OF MEETING—A temporary shelter that Moses built outside the Hebrew camp for those wanting to seek God. After the Israelites made the golden calf, God refused to dwell in their midst (Ex 33:7–11).

TEMPLE

A temple was considered a sign of stability. It proved the power of the deity that was worshiped there.

During the Israelites' journey from Egypt to the Promised Land, they worshiped God in the tabernacle, a portable temple. After the Hebrews settled, King David proposed the construction of a permanent temple in Jerusalem that would be the center for worship, sacrifice, and instruction. David's dream became reality under the reign of Solomon. It took seven years for the work to be completed. The temple was lavishly adorned with the finest wood, bronze, and gold.

There were two main rooms in a Hebrew temple: the Holy Place, where the people gathered for sacrifice; and the Holy of Holies, a sacred inner room that housed the ark of the covenant. Only the high priest could enter the Holy of Holies, during the Day of Atonement. Side chambers all around the temple provided living space for the priests and storage for articles used in worship.

Solomon's Temple was destroyed by the Babylonians. Later, returning Jewish exiles (under Zerubbabel) built a second temple on the site of the first. It lasted for 500 years. Herod the Great restored and enlarged the temple during his reign.

TERAH *(TEAR uh)*—The father of Abraham, Nahor, and Haran. Terah lived in Ur and worshiped pagan gods. Later, he moved to the city of Haran, where he died at age 205 (Gen 11: 25–32).

TEN COMMANDMENTS

In ancient times, relationships between nations and rulers were based upon covenants, formal agreements of promise. The people were expected to maintain loyalty to the ruler offering the covenant. Those who were loyal experienced the blessing of the relationship.

The Ten Commandments were the obligations that the Hebrews were expected to follow in order to experience the blessing of a relationship with God. The commandments were spoken by God to Moses on Mt. Sinai so that all the people could hear them. Later, they were written down (twice) by God on two stone tablets (Ex 19:16–20).

The intent of the commandments was not to condemn human behavior or to place a burden upon people. Rather they were a summons for human behavior to imitate the holiness and purity of God. The first four commandments focus on people's relationship with God; the other six deal with people's relationship with one another.

TERAPHIM (*TEAR uh fim*)— Small household idols in human form (Gen 31:19, 32–35). Associated with pagan practices and the occult, they were condemned by Israelite law.

TERTIUS (*TUHR shee uhs*)— Paul's secretary, who took dictation for his letter to the Romans (Ro 16:22).

TERTULLUS (*tuhr TUL uhs*)—The prosecuting lawyer for the Jews against Paul before Felix (Ac 24: 2–8). He spoke in flowery language typical of that time.

TESTIMONY—Affirmation or giving of evidence. In the Old Testament, the Ten Commandments and the Law of Moses were considered the testimony of God (Is 8:16, 20; Dt 17:6; Rev 1:9). The term also referred to a witness in a trial (Ru 4:7; Dt 19:15; Mt 18:16–19). The ninth commandment forbade false testimony against one's neighbor (Ex 20:16).

TETRARCH (*TEH trark; "a ruler of a fourth"*)—A Roman title for a regional ruler (Mt 14:1, Lk 3:1).

TEXTS AND VERSIONS—Raw material from Hebrew, Greek, and Syriac translations of Scripture. Scholars try to get close to the original meaning by comparing documents and identifying errors. The oldest surviving manuscript fragments are the Dead Sea Scrolls.

THADDEUS (*THA day uhs*)—One of the 12 disciples, possibly listed elsewhere as Judas, the son of James (Mt 10:3; Ac 1:13).

THANK OFFERING—A voluntary offering to God in appreciation for unexpected gifts, help, or blessings (Ps 56:12–13; Lev 7:12–14).

Theater at Beth-Shan

THEATER—Biblical theaters were outdoor cultural centers cut into naturally concave hillsides. Seats circled a raised stage (Ac 19:29).

THEBES (*THEEBZ*)—The capital of Egypt. It was located on the Nile. Once a great city, it was plundered by the Assyrians in 663 B.C. Prophets compared its fall to what awaited Nineveh (Na 3:8; Jer 46:25).

THEBEZ (*THEE beez*)—A fortified city on Mt.

469

Ephraim where Abimelech was killed by a millstone thrown from a window (Jdg 9:50).

THEFT—In biblical times, theft was punishable by restitution—often at many times the original value (Ex 20:15; 2Sa 12:6; Pr 6:31). Thieves who couldn't make restitution were sold into slavery. Jesus was crucified between two thieves (Lk 23:41).

THEOPHANY (*thee AH fuh nee*)—The manifestation of God in a physical form. In the Old Testament, God appeared in human form and took the shape of clouds and fire (Gen 3:8; Ex 3:2–6, 13:21; Isa 30:27–28).

THEOPHILUS (*thee AH fuh luhs; "dear to God"*)—The person to whom Luke dedicated his gospel and the Acts of the Apostles (Lk 1:3; Ac 1:1). He was likely a Gentile who wanted to obtain a readable document.

THESSALONIANS, LETTERS TO THE (*thes uh LO nee uhnz*)—The earliest of Paul's letters, written to the church in Thessalonica, which was founded on his second journey. The letters focus on Christ's return and how to behave as a Christian.

THEUDAS (*THYOO duhs*)—A Jewish rebel who claimed to be the Messiah. He won 400 converts (Ac 5:36).

THIGH—Placing a hand on each other's thigh when swearing an oath signified the importance of the oath. Hitting the thigh meant amazement or shame (Gen 24:2; Eze 21:12).

THOMAS—One of Jesus' 12 disciples. Courageous and practical, he later became well known as "doubting Thomas" because of his skeptical questions about Jesus' resurrection (Ac 1:13; Jn 20:24–25). When Jesus showed him the scars of crucifixion, Thomas was convinced (Jn 20:26–27).

THORNS, CROWN OF—A crude crown that was placed mockingly on Christ's head at his crucifixion (Mt 27:29). It was likely made from thorny burnet, a common Palestinian plant.

Threshing floor

THRESHING FLOOR—A flat outdoor area where grain was threshed. It was usually located on a hill, so that wind could blow away the chaff. Grain was trampled by animals pulling a sled (Dt 25:4; 1Co 9:9). David built his temple at the site of a threshing floor (2Sa 24:15–25). It was used as a symbol for divine judgment (Isa 21:10, 27:12).

THRONE—A symbol of authority (1Ki 10:18–20; Lk 1:32). In the Bible, God was portrayed as looking upon creation from a throne (Ps 103:19).

THUMMIM—*See* **URIM AND THUMMIM**.

THUNDER—The Bible often used thunder to describe God's voice expressing power, displeasure, or judgment (Ex 19:16, 20:18; Rev 4:5; 1Sa 7:10).

THYATIRA *(thigh uh TYE ruh)*—An ancient city northeast of the Aegean Sea. It was famous for purple dyes and metal crafts. The Apostle John wrote to Christians there (Rev 2:18–19).

TIBERIAS *(tye BEER ee uhs)*—A city on the western shore of the Sea of Galilee (Jn 6:23). It was a center of Gentile culture and learning and therefore unclean for Jews.

TIBERIAS, SEA OF—*See* **GALILEE, SEA OF**.

TIBHATH *(TIB hath)*—An unknown place in Syria

471

where David celebrated a great victory (1Ch 18:8).

TIDAL *(TYE duhl)*—King of Goiim. An ally of King Chedorlaomer of Elam, Tidal helped subdue unidentified kings of the plains (Gen 14:1, 9).

TIGLATH-PILESER *(TIG lath pih LEE zuhr)*—An expansionist king of Assyria who conquered northern Palestine and deported many people from Naphtali (2Ki 15:29).

TIGRIS *(TYE gris)*—The easternmost major river in Mesopotamia. It flowed from the Garden of Eden (Gen 2:14). Daniel had a vision along its bank (Da 10:4).

TILE—A clay block inscribed with a stylus (Eze 4:1–8). Tiles were often baked for permanent records. Tile roofs were rare and are mentioned only once in the Bible (Lk 5:19).

TIMAEUS *(tih MAY uhs; "honorable")*—The father of Bartimaeus, a blind beggar whom Jesus cured at Jericho (Mk 10:46).

TIMBREL *(TIM bruhl)*—A small hand drum or tambourine (Ex 15:20; Isa 5:12).

TIMNA *(TIM nuh; "holding in check")*—**1.** A concubine of Esau's son Eliphaz. She was the mother of Amalek (Gen 36:12). **2.** A chief of Edom (Gen 36:40); Esau's descendant.

TIMNAH *(TIM nah; "allotted territory")*—**1.** A border town of Judah assigned to Dan (Jos 15:10, 19:43). **2.** Delilah's hometown (Jdg 14:1–2).

TIMOTHY *("honoring God")*—A converted Christian who was Paul's co-worker during missionary journeys. He was the son of a Jewish mother and a Greek father. Two of Paul's New Testament letters were written to Timothy (1Th 3:1–2; Ac 16:1, 18:5, 19:22; 1Co 4:17).

TIMOTHY, LETTERS TO

These two New Testament letters, considered to be from the Apostle Paul to his coworker Timothy, offer words of encouragement and directions for faithful Church life. They are included with Titus in the Pastoral Epistles because of their similar styles and themes.

In his first letter (written sometime between A.D. 60 and 65), Paul instructs the young Church leader in practical and spiritual problems confronting members of the congregation. The importance of Church leadership is stressed.

In his second letter (written during the same period), Paul cautions that tough times are ahead. Paul uses his own life as an example to encourage Timothy to remain steadfast and faithful to God and Jesus, to avoid false teachings, and to persevere in the face of hardships and challenges in the fledgling Church.

TIPHSAH *(TIF suh)*—A city near the Euphrates River (1Ki 4:24).

TIRAS *(TYE ruhs; "longing")*—Son of Japheth (Gen 10:2). His descendants were "sea peoples"— or pirates—who invaded Egypt during the thirteenth century B.C.

TIRHAKAH *(tuhr HAY kuh)*—Son of Piankhy, an Ethiopian king who conquered northern Egypt (2Ki 19:9).

TIRSHATHA *(tuhr SHAY thuh; "governor")*—A title given to post-Exile governors of Judah (Ezr 2:63).

TIRZAH *(TUHR zuh)*—A Canaanite royal city known for its beauty (SS 6:4). It was conquered by Joshua (Jos 12:24).

TITHES—Giving one-tenth of all one's goods to God. The Levites received the tithes and used them to operate the temple (Gen 14:18–20, 28:22; Ne 13:5).

TITIUS JUSTUS (*TISH ee uhs JUS tuhs*)—A Corinthian citizen whose house was next to the synagogue (Ac 18:7). He welcomed Paul and the Corinthian Christians after they were rebuffed in the synagogue.

TITTLE—*See* **JOT AND TITTLE.**

TITUS (*TYE tuhs*)—A Gentile coworker of Paul. He accompanied Paul and Barnabas to the Apostolic Council of Jerusalem in A.D. 49 (Gal 2:1, 3). Paul sent him to Corinth and Crete (2Co 2:13, 7:6; Titus 1:4).

TITUS, LETTER TO—A New Testament epistle (written between A.D. 60 and 65) from Paul to his coworker Titus in Crete. Similar in style and theme to his letters to Timothy, Paul advised Titus how to guide believers.

TOBIAH (*toh BYE uh; "Yahweh is good"*)—**1.** A Levite who taught the law under King Jehoshaphat (2Ch 17:8). **2.** An ancestor of exiled Jews who returned to Judah (Ezr 2:60). **3.** An opponent of rebuilding the Jerusalem walls (Ne 2:10).

TOGARMAH (*toh GAHR muh; "bony, strong"*)—The son of Gomer. He was a descendant of Japheth (Gen 10:3). His name is related to the region Beth-Togarmah.

TOLA (*TOH luh*)—**1.** The eldest son of Issachar (Gen 46:13). His descendants were warriors and heads of households during David's reign (Nu 26:23). **2.** A minor judge who ruled Israel for 23 years (Jdg 10:1).

TOMB—Biblical tombs were often natural caves. A family tomb prepared

TOBIT, BOOK OF

Written sometime around 200 B.C., this apocryphal book contains the story of Tobit, a devout man from the tribe of Naphtali. Set in the eighth century B.C., this morality tale portrays Tobit as a hero of faith.

After coming into contact with bird droppings, Tobit was struck blind. Despite this calamity—and the temptation to succumb to Assyrian ways while in exile—he remained faithful to God and Jewish law, including strict dietary and burial practices.

Tobit wondered why such tragedy had befallen him. Wasn't God supposed to reward the just and punish the wicked? Feeling abandoned and betrayed, he still remained faithful. During this time, he sent his son, Tobias, to reclaim some valuable property. In the process, Tobias found a wife, cured her of a demon, and met the angel Raphael (present in human form). Through Raphael, Tobias learned how to cure his father's blindness.

before death showed honor. Joseph of Arimathea provided his tomb for Jesus (Mt 27:57–60).

TOMB, JESUS'—Joseph of Arimathea's tomb, in which Jesus was buried. The Church of the Holy Sepulchre, located in the Old City of Jerusalem (the Christian Quarter), is the traditional site of the tomb (Mt 27:57–60).

TONGUES, GIFT OF—*See* **GLOSSOLALIA; SPEAKING WITH TONGUES.**

TOPHEL *(TOH fel)*—An unknown place in the wilderness where Moses addressed the Israelites after the defeat of the Amorites (Dt 1:1).

TOPHETH *(TOH feth)*—A high place in the Hinnom Valley where child sacrifices were made to the god Molech (Jer 7:31). It was condemned by the prophet Isaiah, and the site was later destroyed by King Josiah (Isa 30:33).

TOWER—A tall defensive structure located on ancient city walls (2Ch 14:7; Mt 21:33). Smaller towers guarded vineyards and fields (Mt 21:33).

TOWN CLERK—The highest city official in biblical times. The town clerk of Ephesus settled a riot with his speech to an unruly crowd (Ac 19:35–41).

TRACHONITIS *(trak o NYE tiss)*—A volcanic area southeast of Damascus. Today, it is known to Arabs as the Fortress of Allah (Lk 3:1).

TRADE AND COMMERCE—Palestine, a world crossroads, exported grain, oil, wine, and iron. The control of trade routes was strategically important. Solomon arranged partnerships with mercantile cities (1Ki 9:27, 28, 10:11).

TRADITION—The passing of information—in either oral or written form—between people or generations. Oral tradition was the basis of biblical literature (Mt 15:2–6; Col 2:8; 2Co 11:2).

TRANSGRESSION—The violation of God's law through sin or rebellion against God (Ps 19:13; Ro 4:15; Mk 7:21–22).

TRANSJORDAN—A large plateau east of the Jordan River. It was associated with Moses, Joshua, and the tribes of Reuben, Gad, and Manasseh. In Old Testament times, the region included Moab and Gilead; in the New Testament, it included Perea and Decapolis.

TRAVAIL—Hard or painful work (Isa 53:11). It was

TORAH

The Law of Moses—or Torah—is the Hebrew name for the first five books of the Bible: Genesis, Exodus, Leviticus, Numbers, and Deuteronomy. (The Greek name for these group of books is the *Pentateuch*.) Mentioned more than 200 times in the Old Testament, the Torah contains God's laws, which were revealed to Moses at Mt. Sinai.

The Hebrew verb related to the Torah is *yarah* ("to shoot an arrow"). To study the Torah is to point in the right direction for having a relationship with God. Rabbi Hillel, a great Jewish teacher who lived before Christ, was once asked by a skeptic to teach the whole Torah while standing on one leg. The rabbi replied, "What is hateful to yourself, do not do to another. This is the whole Torah. Go and study it. The rest is commentary."

The Torah is written on large, ornamental scrolls and carried in a special cabinet built for that purpose. Today, the scrolls are kept in a curtained area of the synagogue and brought out by the rabbi to read during services.

often linked to childbirth (Gen 35:16; 1Sa 4:19), trouble (Isa 23:4), weakness (Jer 4:31), and weariness (Ex 18:8).

TRAVEL—In biblical times, people made journeys for trade, colonization, exploration, pilgrimages, migration, preaching, and exile. Travels are recorded from earliest times in the Old Testament. Because travel was hazardous, it was not undertaken for pleasure (2 Co 11:25–27; Ac 27, 28). In the New Testament, the

TRANSFIGURATION

Three of the four gospels record this miraculous event, in which Jesus' physical body was filled with an inner light and Moses and Elijah appeared (Mt 17:1–8; Mk 9:2–8; Lk 9:28–36). Peter, James, and John each witnessed the transfiguration and described it in great detail. As Jesus prayed, his face and his clothes glimmered and glowed. At the same time, they saw Jesus talking to Moses and Elijah about his coming "departure."

The purpose of this divine event was to show the disciples Jesus' true nature as God's son and the Messiah. It also hinted at his coming glory. The conversation with Moses and Elijah brought full circle their Old Testament prophecy concerning a coming messiah. Although not all of the details are completely clear, historians believe the transfiguration occurred on or near Mt. Hermon, a large mountain near Caesarea Philippi.

Romans built many excellent roads, many of which are still in use.

TRAYS—Gold vessels used with the seven-branched lampstand in the tabernacle, perhaps to carry ashes (Ex 25:38; Nu 4:9).

TREASURE—A royal or sacred collection of valuables, including provisions. So-called "treasure cities" were often arsenals (Ex 1:11; Eze 28:4). The term "treasure" was also used to describe the preservation of precious items in sealed clay jars, as happened with the Dead Sea Scrolls (Lk 12:33; 2Co 4:7).

TREE—More than 25 varieties of trees—including cedar, acacia, olive, apple, fir, and elm—grew in ancient Palestine. Trees often identified locations (Gen 12:6). In his preaching, Jesus used trees as symbols of faith (Mt 3:10, 7:16–19).

TREE OF LIFE—A fruit-bearing tree in the Garden of Eden that held the power of eternal life. Because of sin, Adam and Eve (and all of humanity) lost access to the tree. It was a popular ancient symbol on pottery, seals, and in literature (Gen 2:9). The New Testament used the tree as a symbol for the everlasting life promised by Jesus (Rev 22:2).

TRESPASSES—Violations of another's rights, or against God. Jewish law required a trespass offering. Jesus suggested forgiving others' trespasses as ours are forgiven (Mt 6:9–13).

TRIAL OF JESUS—After his betrayal by Judas, Jesus stood trial several times. He appeared before Annas, the Sanhedrin, Pilate, and Herod before being condemned (Jn 18:13, 33–38; Mk 14:60–65).

TRIBULATION—Trouble or anguish, especially of a spiritual or emotional nature (Job 28:33). Tribulation was considered a natural part of life, but sometimes it was seen as punishment by God (Ro 2:9). At the end of time, God will send great tribulation (Rev 7:14; Mt 24:21).

TRIBUNAL—A public platform with a high official's seat, located in cities of the Roman Empire where cases were heard. Paul appeared before Gallio at a tribunal in Corinth (Ac 18:12–17).

TRIBUTE—A tax forced upon a defeated country by its conqueror (Ex 5; 1Ki 20:1–7). King Hoshea's refusal to pay the annual tribute to Assyria resulted in Israel's downfall (2Ki 17:3–6).

TRIBES OF ISRAEL

The 12 sons of Jacob each gave their name to a Jewish tribe (Gen 32:28). They consisted of Reuben, Simeon, Levi, Judah, Zebulun, Issachar, Dan, Gad, Asher, Naphtali, Joseph (later divided into Ephraim and Manasseh), and Benjamin. When the Israelites were grouped together in Egypt, the tribes were known by these names, but during the Exodus the Hebrews were known collectively as the Tribes of Israel.

God assigned the tribe of Levi as caretakers of the tabernacle. Before entering the Promised Land, the tribes of Reuben and Gad (and half of Manasseh) chose to settle east of the Jordan (Gen 32:33). After Canaan was overtaken, the conquered territory was divided among the remaining tribes (Jos 15–19), which were self-ruled by judges.

During David's reign, the entire kingdom of Israel was divided and united twice (2Sa 2:4, 5:3). After Solomon's death, Judah and Benjamin permanently separated from the kingdom and became one nation, Judah. All of the area north of them became Israel (1Ki 12:20). This division lasted until both nations fell into foreign captivity (Israel by Assyria in 721 B.C.; Judah by Babylon in 586 B.C.). The Exile dissolved all tribal distinctions (Jos 13–19).

TRINITY—The three ways that God's nature is revealed: as Father, Son, and Holy Spirit (Dt 6:4–5; 1Co 8:5–6). The trinity is the classic Christian foundation of God's personhood.

TROAS (*TROH us*)—A principal Aegean seaport

on the northwest corner of Asia Minor. Its artificial harbors protected against strong winds.

TROGYLLIUM (*tro JIL ee uhm*)—A strip of land jutting from the Asian mainland and overlapping eastern Samos. Paul's ship was forced there by navigational problems (Ac 20:15).

TROPHIMUS (*TROF ih muhs; "nourishing"*)—A Gentile Christian from Ephesus who accompanied Paul on part of his third missionary journey (Ac 21:29; 2Ti 4:20). He inadvertently caused an incident at the Jerusalem temple, leading to Paul's imprisonment (Ac 21:29).

TRUMPET—Made from antelope or ram's horn, ancient trumpets were used to signal battles, alarms, assemblies, feasts, and religious ceremonies. The ram's horn—or shofar—is still used today for Jewish ceremonies (Jdg 3:27; Nu 10:2; Ne 4:18, 12:35).

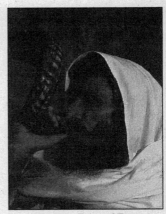

Beginning the Feast of Trumpets

TRUMPETS, FEAST OF—Celebrated on the first day of the seventh month of the Hebrew calendar (Tishri; September-October), the Feast of Trumpets marked the beginning of the new year. All work was stopped, meetings were held, and sacrifices were made (Nu 29:2–6). After the Exile, the day became the religious festival Rosh Hashanah.

TUBAL-CAIN (*TOO bahl CAYN*)—Son of Lamech and Zillah. A descendant of Cain, he was the first cold-forger of brass and iron, a skill that he taught (Gen 4:20–22).

TURBAN—A cloth headdress worn for protection against the sun. Turban styles varied with one's nationality, sex, and social rank. High priests wore special turbans with engraved plates (Ex 28:4).

TURTLEDOVE—A grey and tan pigeon that was the herald of spring in Palestine (Jer 8:7). It was considered clean for sacrifice.

TWELVE, THE—The 12 apostles whom Jesus chose early in his ministry to learn, teach, preach, and heal in his name and be with him after the resurrection (Mt 10:2–4; Mk 3:14–19; Lk 6:13–16; Ac 1:13). The number recalls the Twelve Tribes of Israel.

TYCHICUS (*TIK ih cuhs; "child of fortune"*)—An Asian Christian who was Paul's valued friend and helper (Ac 20:4; Tit 3:12).

He was with Paul during imprisonments and carried his letters to the Ephesians and Colossians (Eph 6:21; 2Ti 4:12; Col 4:7–9).

TYRANNUS (*tih RAN uhs*)—A Greek teacher. After being kicked out of the synagogue, Paul taught in Tyrannus' school (Ac 19:9).

TYRE (*TIRE*)—A Phoenician port north of Carmel. It was famous for dyes, glassware, and metalwork (Isa 23:2, 8). Jesus was well received there (Mk 7:24–31); Paul stayed a week in Tyre (Ac 21:3–7).

TYROPOEON VALLEY (*tye ro PEE ahn; "valley of cheesemakers"*)—A valley that bisects Jerusalem into an "upper" and "lower" city. Herod built bridges across the valley to the temple. When the temple was destroyed in A.D. 70, its debris was tossed into the valley. Its shape is visible today while walking from the Temple Mount to the Old City.

UGARIT (*oo GAR it*)—A Syrian coastal city famous for ancient texts discovered there in 1929. Written between 1550–1220 B.C., these texts provide important background of the Old Testament.

ULAI (*OO lye*)—A river in Elam near the Persian capital of Susa. Daniel saw himself along the river's bank in his vision of the ram and goat (Da 8:2, 16).

UNBELIEF—In the New Testament, doubt was associated with disobedience, making it a major sin and an affront to God (Jn 16:9; 1Jn 5:10).

UNCTION—Anointment with oil after bathing. Seen as a sign of respect, kings and priests were anointed, and Jesus was called "Messiah" ("anointed one"). Unction was also associated with healing and used for ancient medicinal purposes (1Jn 2:20; Mk 6:13; Jas 5:14). Later, it was used as a rite for the dying.

UNFORGIVABLE SIN—Condemning the religious leaders of his day, Jesus said that blasphemy against the Holy Spirit was unpardonable (Mk 3:28–30). This type of sin may also include deliberately and repeatedly rejecting God's grace (Heb 6:4–6).

UNITED MONARCHY—After an earlier split, the Twelve Tribes of Israel were united during David's reign (2Sa 2:4, 5:3). Following Solomon's death, the kingdom divided into two nations (1Ki 12:20). *See* **TRIBES OF ISRAEL.**

UNKNOWN GOD—An altar inscription that Paul saw in Athens. He mentioned it in a speech to tell the people about the true "Lord of heaven and earth" (Ac 17:22–31).

UNLEAVENED BREAD, FEAST OF—*See* **PASSOVER.**

UPHAZ (*YOO faz*)—An unknown site where gold was found (Jer 10:9). It may be the same place as Ophir.

UPPER ROOM—A guest room in a flat-roofed Palestinian home; sometimes a tent (2Sa 16:22). Jesus and his disciples held their last meal in such a room (Mk 14:15), and he appeared in one after his resurrection (Lk 24:33).

UR OF THE CHALDEES (*UR, KAL deez*)—A Mesopotamian city; home of Abraham's father, Terah (Gen 11:28). It was Abraham's point of departure for Canaan (Gen 11:31, 15:7).

URBANUS (*uhr BAY nuhs; "belonging to a city"*)—A Christian believer whom Paul greeted, perhaps one of Caesar's household slaves at Rome (Ro 16:9; Php 4:22).

URIAH (*yoo RYE uh; "Yahweh is my light"*)—The husband of Bathsheba. A Hittite believer, he was one of David's mighty men. When David had an affair with Bathsheba and she conceived a son, he arranged for Uriah to be killed in battle (2Sa 11:1–27).

URIEL (*YOO ree el*)—**1.** A chief of Koathite Levites who helped King David bring the ark of the covenant to Jerusalem (1Ch 15:5, 11–12). He was likely also Uzziah's father (1Ch 6:24). **2.** An angel named in extrabiblical writings.

URIM AND THUMMIM (*YOO rim, THUM im*)—A pair of small objects (such as stones) used by the Hebrew high priest to decide God's will. Carried in the breastpiece (Ex 28:29–30), they were either drawn from a pouch or cast like lots (1Sa 28:6).

¹Uz *(UHZ)*—The son of Aram; grandson of Shem (Gen 10:23; 1Ch 1:17).

²Uz—The homeland of Job. Its location is unknown (Job 1:1).

¹Uzal *(OO zuhl; "wanderer")*—Son of Joktan; a descendant of Shem (Gen 10:27). His descendants were an Arabian tribe.

²Uzal—An ancient Syrian city that was a great source of wine (Eze 27:19).

¹Uzza *(UHZ uh; "strength")*—**1.** A person who touched the ark of the covenant and was struck dead (2Sa 6:3). **2.** An ancestor of temple servants who returned to Jerusalem from Babylonian exile (Ezr 2:49).

²Uzza—A palace garden where the Judahite kings Manasseh and Amon were buried (2Ki 21:18, 26).

Uzzi *(UHZ eye; "my strength")*—**1.** A priest descended from Eleazar; an ancestor of Ezra (Ezr 7:4). **2.** The father of Elah, one of the first Benjaminites to resettle the land after Babylonian exile (1Ch 9:8). **3.** A priest who participated in dedicating the repaired temple in Jerusalem (Ne 12:42).

Uzziah *(uh ZYE uh; "Yahweh is my strength")*—Another name for Azariah, the ninth king of Judah (2Ki 14:13). During his reign, he extended Judah's borders, fortified Jerusalem, and maintained godliness. But as his achievements grew, he became proud, and he contracted leprosy (2Ch 19).

Uzziel *(uh ZYE uhl; "God is my strength")*—Levi's grandson. He was the founder of a Levitical family who helped bring the ark of the covenant to Jerusalem (Nu 3:19, 30; 1Ch 23:12, 20).

VANITY—Vanity is used in the Bible to indicate pointlessness and futility. Vanity is the theme for the Book of Ecclesiastes (Ecc 1:2). The word "vain" has several biblical meanings: false (Eze 12:24); empty (Mt 6:7); conceited (Gal 5:26); and without effect (Php 2:16). To take God's name "in vain" (Ex 20:7) means to use it in an improper manner.

VEGETABLES—In biblical times, many people tended small gardens near their homes. Beans and lentils were the primary source of protein for those who had little meat (2Sa 17:28). Other vegetables eaten by the Israelites in Egypt were cucumbers, leeks, onions, and garlic (Nu 11:5).

VESPASIAN *(ves PAY zee uhn)*—A Roman emperor (A.D. 69–79). As a soldier, he led a siege against Jews in Jerusalem. Though he is not named, he is referred to in the apocryphal Book of Esdras (2Esd 12:26).

VESSELS—Hollow containers (such as pots, bottles, bowls, vases, or cups) for holding liquids. Ancient vessels were made from metal, wood, stone, and pottery (Jer 18:4).

VESTURE—An antiquated word for clothing. It is also translated as robes, garment, cloak, or covering (Gen 41:42; Dt 22:12).

VIA DOLOROSA *(VEE uh dol uh ROH suh; "the sorrowful way")*—The route Christ traveled on the way to his crucifixion at Golgotha. It began at Pilate's judgment hall (Jn 19:13–17).

VIAL—A small flask or container for holding

VEIL

When Abraham's servant brought Rebekah home to become Isaac's bride, Rebekah saw Isaac walking in the field. As he approached, she quickly covered herself with her veil (Gen 24:65).

Throughout biblical times, it was the custom for most women to wear veils during prayer or worship and in the presence of strangers. Servants and prostitutes went unveiled. At home, the veil could be put aside or thrown back in the presence of servants, but it had to be replaced before speaking to guests.

The veil was typically made of white linen. It was often elaborately patterned or embroidered (but a widow's veil was black and unadorned). In Ruth's time, veils were made of cloth sturdy enough to be used for carrying food and other goods. Boaz measured out a generous amount of barley, and Ruth carried it home in her veil (Ru 3:15). In the New Testament, Paul acknowledged the tradition of head-covering for women and urged the continued use of the veil, particularly in church (1Co 11:5).

liquid. Samuel anointed Saul with a vial of oil to proclaim him ruler over Israel (1Sa 10:1).

VICTORY—In the Old Testament, God often delivered the Israelites victory over their oppo-

VINE, VINEYARD

Grapes were an important part of the Hebrew diet because the hilly country and climate around Palestine was particularly well suited to the growing of vines. Noah was the first man in the Bible to plant a vineyard (Gen 9:20), but grapevines had been cultivated in ancient Egypt (Gen 40:9–11).

Before planting, the hills were terraced with stones to prevent the loss of soil. A fence or wall was built around the vineyard to keep out animals and thieves. Large boulders were removed, and the ground was hoed and spaded. A watchtower was erected for added protection, on a high spot of ground where the watchman could view the entire vineyard.

Vines were planted up to 12 feet apart, and carefully pruned so the healthiest branches could bear fruit. The vines blossomed in April and May. Harvesting took place during September and October and was a time of joy and celebration. Each vineyard had its own winepress where a portion of the grapes were stomped and the juice collected for making wine. The grapes that couldn't be eaten fresh were dried, and the raisins stored for later use.

Vines and vineyards were used in a number of Jesus' parables to symbolize prosperity. The grapevine was also a metaphor for the Israelites, God's Chosen People. Jesus called himself "the true vine" whose branches (Israel) could not bear fruit without him (Jn 15:1).

nents in battle. In the New Testament, God gave believers victory over death through the resurrection of Christ (1Co 15:54–57).

VILLAGE—Biblical villages were often located near a fortified town, where the people could take refuge in times of invasion or attack (2Ch 28:18).

VINEGAR—A sour liquid produced by fermentation of wine. Jesus was offered

VIRGIN BIRTH

Mary was a humble peasant girl. While she was engaged to be married, she was visited by the angel Gabriel, who told her that she was to conceive a child who would be called the Son of God. The conception would not be caused by human intercourse, but by the power of God through the Holy Spirit (Lk 1:26–38).

Joseph, a carpenter in Nazareth and a descendant of David, was Mary's husband-to-be. By law, he had the right to accuse her of adultery and terminate the betrothal. Instead, he chose to obey the angel's command and continue with the marriage. The couple traveled to Bethlehem to register for a census. While there, the baby Jesus—God in human flesh—was born.

This miraculous birth was predicted by the prophet Isaiah (Isa 7:14). The event was reported in two separate biblical accounts, each from a different perspective. Matthew is believed to have received his story from Joseph (Mt 1:18–25). Luke's version is said to have come directly from Mary (Lk 1:26–2:7). The virgin birth is one of the major doctrines of the Christian Church, confessed by believers in the Apostles' Creed.

vinegar on a sponge while he was on the cross (Mk 15:36). The word may also have described "sour wine," a cheap drink used by the lower classes and soldiers.

VIPER—A poisonous snake commonly found in the Negev desert (Isa 30:6). It was used as a metaphor for wicked people. Jesus called the scribes and Pharisees "a brood of vipers" (Mt 23:33). A viper bit Paul's hand when he was on Malta. Because no harm came to him, the natives thought he was a god (Ac 28:3).

VIRGIN—A young girl or unmarried woman who has not had sexual intercourse (Gen 24:16). The word also referred to chaste males (Rev 14:4). Figuratively, it has been used to denote a city (Isa 23:12).

VIRTUE—Moral strength or excellence. Boaz called Ruth a virtuous woman (Ru 3:11), which was considered more precious than rubies (Pr 31:10).

VISION—A supernatural appearance; something seen by means other than ordinary sight. Visions often came in dreams and were considered revelations from God. God came to Abraham and to Jacob in visions (Gen 15, 46). Biblical visions concerning the kingdom of God were reported by the prophets.

VOW—A solemn promise or commitment. Advice concerning vows to the Lord is found in Deuteronomy 23:23. Jacob vowed that if God would be with him, he would make Bethel a house of God and give a tenth of all he received to the Lord (Gen 28:18–22).

WADI (*WAH dee*)—A stream bed that contains rushing water during the rainy season but dries up in summer. Though the word does not appear in the Bible, hundreds of wadis are found in Palestine.

WAFER—A thin, crisp cake or biscuit made from flour. Used as baked offerings to God (Ex 16:31), wafers were unleavened (1Ch 23:29) and spread with oil (Ex 29:2).

WAGES—According to the Law of Moses, wages for work were to be paid daily (Dt 24:14–15). In the New Testament, a *denarius* was the usual daily wage (Mt 20:2). The word is also used in the sense of consequences: "the wages of sin is death" (Ro 6:23).

WALK—Often used as a symbol for the pattern of one's life and conduct. Isaiah spoke of "the people who walked in darkness" (Isa 9:2). Paul urged believers to "walk in love," "walk as children of light," and "walk wisely" (Eph 5:2, 8, 15).

WALLS—Stone walls were often built around ancient fields and vineyards (Isa 5:5). Paths or highways through vineyards had walls on either side (Nu 22:24). Walls were built around cities for protection and defense (1Ki 3:1).

WAR—In the Old Testament, the Israelites sought God's approval before battles (Jdg 20:23, 27, 28; 1Sa 14:37). Their victories were attributed to God. War in the New Testament was often spiritual, with good seeking victory over evil (Eph 6:10–17).

WARS OF THE LORD, BOOK OF THE—An unknown text referred to in Numbers 21:14. It was a collection of folk poems and battle songs, one of which was quoted in the verse.

WASHBASIN—A shallow bowl to hold water for washing. A bronze basin was used by the priests to wash their hands and feet in the tabernacle or temple before approaching the altar (Ex 30:18–20). Jesus used a basin to wash the disciples' feet as a sign of love and servanthood (Jn 13:5).

WATCH—A division of the night during which a military guard remained on duty. Instead of hours, the night was divided into four watches: Evening (9 P.M.); Midnight; Cockcrow (3 A.M.); and Morning (6 A.M.).

WATCHMAN—**1.** One who guarded the walls and gates of a city, or an army camp, against attack (1Sa 14:16; 2Sa 18:24–27). **2.** One

Watchtower in Israeli countryside

who was hired to guard a vineyard from thieves or animals. The vineyard watchtower (Isa 5:2) became the watchman's home for the summer, and often his family lived there with him. **3.** A man stationed at one of the watchtowers built in the wilderness to guard the herds (2Ch 26:10).

WATER—Water was scarce in Palestine. Rivers were small and contained almost no water in summer. The only continuously flowing source of water, the Jordan River, was

WEALTH

Among the Old Testament nomads, wealth was measured in flocks and herds, silver and gold, and the number of servants one had. God seemed to have no quarrel with the amassing of wealth. He saw to it that his people prospered and continually reminded them that he was the source of their wealth (Dt 8:12–18). When Solomon asked for wisdom rather than wealth, God was so pleased he gave him both.

As humans began to put their trust in silver and gold—rather than in God—wealth became a stumbling block. In the New Testament, Jesus urged his followers not to store up treasures on Earth, because material wealth was not lasting. Instead, he advised them to be concerned with the treasures of heaven (Mt 6:19–33).

A number of Christ's parables dealt with the subject of wealth. In the parable of the rich fool (Lk 12:13–21), Jesus lamented those who stored up treasures for themselves and left God out of the picture. Two other parables likened the kingdom of God to a hidden treasure (Mt 13:44–45).

far from Israel's main cities. People depended on rainwater collected in cisterns for their water supply. A heavy dew helped to water vegetation in summer.

WATER SHAFT—A vertical passageway that enabled residents within a walled city to draw water from an underground source.

WAVE OFFERING—A ceremonial rite in which peace offerings were waved back and forth before the Lord. These offerings included

WEIGHTS AND MEASURES

In the early days of the Old Testament, goods were bought and sold through barter. Silver and gold eventually became the standards of exchange. A system of weights also developed, with the *shekel* as the basic unit.

Biblical merchants used simple balance scales to weigh their products and the precious metals. Hebrew law called for the honest use of weights and measures (Dt 25:13–16). Stones were cut in various denominations to help weigh both the goods and the payment. Merchants and customers each carried a set of these stone weights in a small purse to keep check on one another.

Liquid and dry measures were based on the size of household pots, jars, and baskets. The *omer* (about a tenth of a bushel), *ephah* (about a bushel), and *homer* (10 bushels, or a donkey load) were common dry measures. Liquid measures included the *kab* (more than a quart), *hin* (just under a gallon), *bath* (nearly six gallons), and *homer* (ten baths, or about 60 gallons). Distance was measured by the time it took to travel it. (For example, one could make a "three days' journey" or a "five days' journey.") Parts of the body were commonly used to measure length. A *finger* was approximately three quarters of an inch, a *palm* was four fingers (3 inches), a *span* was three palms (9 inches), and a *cubit* was two spans (18 inches).

the breast of a sacrificed animal, the sheaf of first-ripe grain, and loaves made from the new grain harvest (Ex 29:24–28).

WAY—In addition to indicating a physical direction, the word described a manner of living. In the Old Testament, parents were advised to train their children in "the right way" (Pr 22:6). Jesus said he was "the way" to God (Jn 14:6). "The Way" was an early name for the Christian faith (Ac 9:2).

WAYMARK—A road marker or guidepost made of a stone or a heap of stones (Jer 31:21). The Israelites heading for exile were told to place markers along the route so they could find their way back to Judah.

WEAVING—The weaving of cloth was an ancient art, necessary for making clothing and tents. It was first mentioned in the Book of Exodus (Ex 28:39).

WEDDING—While weddings in biblical times did not involve a religious ceremony, marriage was the culmination of a contract drawn up at the time of betrothal. The celebration included a procession and a wedding feast, at which one or more guests would give a benediction (Ru 4:11). Jesus performed his first miracle at a wedding in Cana (Jn 2:1–11).

WEEDS—In one of his parables, Jesus likened the weeds to children of the devil who will be burned up with fire (Mt 13:24–43).

WEEKS, FEAST OF—An annual harvest festival occurring seven weeks after the wave offering of the first-ripe grain sheaf (Dt 16:9–12). Later it became known as Pentecost. The feast took on new meaning when the Holy Spirit came to believers on that day (Ac 2:1).

WHALE—A translation of the Greek word *ketes,* which

495

means a large fish or sea animal. The Book of Jonah called it "a great fish" (Jnh 1:17), but Matthew used the word "whale" (Mt 12:40).

WHEAT—A principal grain crop in Palestine, wheat was planted in winter after the rains began. Wheat flour was used to make bread (Ex 29:2). A common variety was grown by the Israelites, but the Egyptian wheat described in Pharaoh's dream had seven ears on one stalk (Gen 41:22).

WHEEL—Early wheels were made of solid wood, but later chariot wheels were well developed, with axles, rims, spokes, and hubs (1Ki 7:33). Potters used a wheel to work their clay (Jer 18:3), and wheels were sometimes used to pull up the ropes of a deep well.

WHIRLWIND—This word may have signified any violent windstorm, rather than a whirling wind. God answered Job out of a whirlwind (Job 38:1), and Elijah went up to heaven in a whirlwind (2Ki 2:11). A familiar proverb warned of the danger of doing evil: "They sow the wind and reap the whirlwind" (Hos 8:7).

WHITE—A symbol of purity, white was used in the Bible to describe the garments of angels (Jn 20:12) and the color of Jesus' clothing at his transfiguration (Mt 17:2).

WHITEWASH—A preparation made of lime and water. It was used during biblical times for whitening the walls of houses (Eze 13:10–15) and burial tombs (Mt 23:27).

WICKEDNESS—The state of being sinful or evil; living contrary to God's law. It was the wickedness of humankind that prompted God to send a great flood to destroy the people of the Earth (Gen 6:5–7). Christ and his disciples warned people to repent of their wickedness (Ac 8:22).

WIDOW—A biblical widow was expected to act appropriately and wear special garments. In the Old Testament, widows were to be shown special consideration (Dt 24:19). In the New Testament, they were cared for by the Church (1Ti 5:3–10).

WILDERNESS—A general term that referred variously to a desolate, uncultivated plain, suitable as pasture land (Nu 14:33); an arid, rocky desert (Dt 32:10); and the plain of the Jordan River and Dead Sea (2Sa 2:29).

WILDERNESS OF WANDERING—The 22,000 square miles of sandy, barren land where the Israelites wandered for 40 years after escaping from slavery in Egypt (Dt 1:31). The area was bounded by the Mediterranean Sea, lower Palestine, the Gulf of Suez, and the Gulf of Akabah.

WIND—The most frequent mention of wind in the Bible referred to the destructive east wind (Job 27:21). The north wind was considered cold (Sir 43:20); the south wind was dry and hot (Job 37:17); and the west wind brought rain (1Ki 18:45). Wind was often a biblical symbol of God's power. The first mention of wind occurred when God created it to stop the waters of the Flood (Gen 8:1).

WINE AND STRONG DRINK—The fermented juice of grapes and other intoxicating liquor, such as barley beer (Isa 5:11). These drinks were forbidden to priests and Nazirites (Lev 10:9; Nu 6:3). Jesus called wine "the fruit of the vine" (Mt 26:29) and turned water into wine at Cana (Jn 2:1–11).

WINE PRESS—A stone trough in which grapes were pressed for wine. The juice flowed through a hole

WISDOM LITERATURE

The sacred literature of the Jews was arranged into three groups: the Law, the Prophets, and the Writings. Wisdom literature, a part of the latter group, consisted of wise sayings, proverbs, fables, riddles, songs, and discussions of everyday subjects. The Jews continually sought wisdom through observation, experience, and reflection, because they believed "the price of wisdom is above pearls" (Job 28:18).

In the Old Testament, most wisdom literature is found in the books of Job, Ecclesiastes, and Proverbs. Job is a poetic treatment of the problem of suffering; Ecclesiastes ponders the meaning of life; and Proverbs deals with the moral conduct of everyday life at home, in business, and in social relationships. Though each of these books is quite different from the others, they are all concerned with morality in daily life. They point to the importance of God in every facet of human existence and the need to respect him and follow his laws in order to find wisdom.

Some of the Psalms are also included among the wisdom books. This collection of poems, songs, and prayers covers the entire range of human experience and acknowledges the presence of God in every area of life.

and into a vat. Men stomped on the grapes while holding onto ropes hanging above them (Mt 21:33).

WINNOWING FORK—A large wooden fork used for tossing grain into the air so the wind could blow away the chaff.

WISDOM—The perfect understanding, judgment, and knowledge of all things. Supreme wisdom ascribed only to God (Ro 11:33–36). For humans, wisdom is a combination of knowledge and good judgment. The Old Testament states that "the fear of the Lord is the beginning of wisdom" (Ps 111:10).

WISDOM OF SOLOMON—1. King Solomon was known as a wise and understanding man, well versed in botany and zoology (1Ki 4:29–34). His wisdom was a gift from God and has been described as exceeding "all the kings of the Earth" (1Ki 10:23). 2. The fourth book of the Apocrypha. Its purpose was to strengthen the flagging Jewish faith by showing how God's wisdom directed the history of the nation of Israel.

WITCHCRAFT—Occult practices involving the use of sorcery, magic, and evil spirits to gain secret knowledge. Among the abhorrent practices condemned by God were child sacrifice, divination, soothsaying, augury, casting spells, and consulting ghosts or spirits (Dt 18:10).

WITNESS—A person who testified to an event that took place in his or her presence. At the Ascension, the followers of Jesus were called his witnesses (Ac 1:22). Stones, pillars, and altars were also erected as "witnesses" to events in the Old Testament (Gen 18:10; Isa 19:20).

WOE—Terrible trouble or affliction. Declarations of woe were common in prophetic writings. They were directed toward wicked cities, rebellious children, scribes and Pharisees, and those who betrayed Jesus (Lk 22:22).

WOMAN—The first woman was created as a partner to man (Gen 2:18–24). Though most women in

WISE MEN

Though the term "wise men" could refer to any men of knowledge and skill, it is popularly used to represent the Magi, who came to Bethlehem from the East in search of the baby Jesus (Mt 2:11). Like the Levites in Israel, these men held a special religious position. The Magi interpreted dreams and omens and were astrologers. It is possible  they were familiar with the Old Testament prophecy of a coming messiah: "A star shall come out of Jacob" (Nu 24:17). They followed a star that led them directly to the holy child.

The fact that these men were received by Herod in Jerusalem indicates that they had some stature. Traditionally, they have been called the "Three Kings" or the "Three Wise Men" and had been given names of Gaspar, Melchior, and Balthasar, but the Scripture does not specify their names or number.

After the wise men visited the baby (Mt 2:11–12) and presented their gifts (gold, frankincense, and myrrh), they returned home by another route to avoid Herod's men, who were ordered to kill Jesus.

biblical times took subordinate roles, there were notable exceptions, such as Sarah, Rebekah, Rachel,

Hannah, Ruth, and Esther. In the New Testament, women were active in the early Church, and Mary became the most revered of all women.

WOMB—Several times in the Bible, God took pity on barren or unloved wives and "opened their wombs" so they could have children. Among these were Hannah (1Sa 1:20), Leah (Gen 29:31), and Rachel (Gen 30:22).

WOOL—The fleece of sheep was used to make cloth for warm outer garments. The first fleece of the flock was to be given to the Levitical priests (Dt 18:4).

WORD—The Hebrew word *davar* ("a thing said") refers to God's word, which created the world (Ps 33:9). The Bible is also known as "God's word," through which he reveals himself to all people. The Greek word *logos* refers to Jesus, the word of God in fleshly form (Jn 1:14).

WORKS—Good or righteous deeds. David sang of God's wonderful works (1Ch 16:9). Paul said a person is not justified by works, but by faith in Christ (Gal 2:16).

WORMWOOD—A plant found in Palestine, known for its bitter taste (Pr 5:4). Mentioned many times in the Bible, wormwood was used as a symbol for bitterness and sorrow (La 3:15).

WORSHIP—The Bible teaches that worship was to be given to God alone (Mt 4:10). The Israelites worshiped God by offering sacrifices (Gen 4:3). In the New Testament, Jesus emphasized the spiritual nature of worship (Jn 4:22–24).

WRATH—Great anger, particularly of God. God's wrath is followed by punishment for sin (Heb 10:26–31). In the Book of Revelation, the wrath of God brought seven terrible plagues (Rev 16).

WRITING—Much of the writing in biblical times was done by professional scribes (Ps 45:1). The act of writing was first mentioned in the Bible when God instructed Moses to write a historic document of Israel's victory over the Amalekites (Ex 17:14). On Mt. Sinai, Moses received two stone tablets that were written "with the finger of God" (Ex 31:18).

XERXES (*ZURK seez*)—A Greek name for Ahasuerus, a Persian king who chose Esther as his wife after Queen Vashti refused to obey him (Est 2:17). He was mostly known as a cruel despot who ruled from 486–465 B.C.

YARMUK (*yar MOOK*)—One of three important rivers southeast of the Sea of Galilee. Though not mentioned in the Bible by name, the Yarmuk empties into the Jordan River, contributing vast quantities of water.

YOKE—A device that joins together a pair of work animals. The word was used as a symbol for a burden or obedience. Jesus said, "My yoke is easy" (Mt 11:30).

YOM KIPPUR (*yahm kih POOR*)—A Jewish holy day described in Leviticus 16 that includes fasting, prayer, repentance, and forgiveness of sins. *See* **DAY OF ATONEMENT**.

YAHWEH

Yahweh (*YAH weh*), the personal name for the God of Israel, is mentioned more than 6,000 times in the Hebrew Bible. It was first revealed when God appeared in the burning bush and chose Moses to lead the Israelites out of Egypt (Ex 3:11–15). The Lord identified himself as the God of Moses' ancestors and promised to be with his people throughout the Exodus.

Before the Hebrew language had a vowel system, the name was represented by four consonants, YHWH. The Israelites considered the name to be too sacred to pronounce and used it only in written form. Another name, *Adonai* ("my Lord"), was substituted when reading aloud. When the vowels from Adonai were combined with the consonants YHWH, the name "Jehovah" was invented. (Sometimes YHWH is pronounced "Jehovah" for convenience.)

In the Bible, YHWH was also used in combination with other words to indicate the presence and goodness of God. *YHWH-jireh* ("Yahweh will provide") was the name given by Abraham to the spot where God provided a ram to be sacrificed in place of Isaac (Gen 22:14). In observance of a victory at Rephidim, Moses named a memorial altar *YHWH-nissi* ("Yahweh is my banner") (Ex 17:15–16). Another altar, *YHWH-shalom* ("Yahweh is peace") was built by Gideon to commemorate a visit by God's angel who called him to deliver Israel (Jdg 6:23–24). *YHWH-shammah* ("Yahweh is there") was the name given to Jerusalem in Ezekiel's vision (Eze 48:35).

ZAANAN (*ZAY uh nan*)—A town in the low country of Judah. It was the home territory of the prophet Micah, who prophesied the fall of Judah and the destruction of Zaanan at the hands of the Assyrians (Mic 1:11).

ZAANANNIM, ZAANAIM (*zay uh NAN im; zay uh NAY im*)—A place that was part of the land of the tribe of Naphtali (Jos 19:33). The encampment of Heber the Kenite, whose wife Jael killed the Canaanite General Sisera with a tent peg, was located there (Jdg 4:11).

ZABAD (*ZAY bad*)—**1.** The son of Nathan (1Ch 2:36). **2.** An Ephraimite; the son of Tahath (1Ch 7:21). **3.** The name of three men who gave up their foreign wives (Ezr 10:27–44). **4.** One of two conspirators who killed King Joash (2Ch 24:23–26).

ZABBAI (*ZAB ay eye*)—**1.** The father of Baruch, who helped repair the walls of Jerusalem (Ne 3:20). **2.** A man who gave up his foreign wife at the urging of Ezra (Ezr 10:28).

ZABDI (*ZAB dye*)—**1.** The grandfather of Achan (Jos 7:1). **2.** One of the sons of Shimei. He was a member of the tribe of Benjamin (1Ch 8:19). **3.** An administrator of the produce for King David's wine cellars (1Ch 27:27). **4.** A Levite who aided in worship at Jerusalem (Ne 11:17).

ZADOK (*ZAY dahk*)—One of the Levite priests that King David selected to bring the ark of the covenant to Jerusalem (1Ch 15:11–13). Zadok's loyalty to David prompted King

ZACCHEUS

As a chief tax collector for the Romans in Jericho, Zaccheus (*ZA kee uhs*) was not only rich; he was re-garded by the Jews as a traitor to his people. One day,  Jesus traveled through the town. Curious to get a look at the teacher, but unable to see over the heads of the crowd because he was so short, Zaccheus climbed a sycamore tree. As Jesus passed nearby, he singled out Zaccheus, telling the little man to come down from the tree. Jesus then expressed his inten-tion to visit the tax collector's house.

Like others who did not understand Christ's mis-sion to seek and to save lost souls, the crowd became angry. The self-righteous among them complained because Jesus was inviting himself to be the guest of this detested tax collector—a known sinner.

When Zaccheus pledged to give half of his posses-sions to the poor and to pay back fourfold anyone he had cheated, Jesus declared that salvation had come to the house that day. He had accomplished his purpose and pronounced Zaccheus a son of Abraham, a redeemed Israelite (Lk 19:10).

Solomon to make him high priest after David's death (1Ki 2:26–35).

ZAIR *(ZAY ir)*—A village near Edom where King Joram of Israel attacked the revolting Edomites at night (2Ki 8:21). Its exact location is unknown.

ZALMON (*ZAL mon*)—**1.** An Ahohite, also called Ilai, who was one of David's elite warriors (2Sa 23:28; 1Ch 11:29). **2.** A mountain where Abimelech and his troops cut the brushwood that was used to set fire to Shechem (Jdg 9:48–49).

ZAMZUMMIM (*zam ZUM im*)—A name that conquering Ammonites used for a strong, tall Canaanite tribe. *See* **REPHAIM.**

ZANOAH (*zuh NO uh*)—**1.** A hillside settlement of exiles who helped rebuild Jerusalem's wall (Ne 3:13, 11:30). **2.** A town in western Canaan inherited by the tribe of Judah (Jos 15:55).

ZAPHENATH-PANEAH (*ZAF ee nath peh NEE eh*)—The Hebrew form of a name that Pharoah gave to Joseph after the young Jew interpreted the ruler's dreams (Gen 41:45).

ZAPHON (*ZAY fon; "north"*)—A Gadite town east of the Jordan River where Jephthah the Gileadite and his men defeated 42,000 Ephraimites. Using the word "Shibboleth" (which the Ephraimites mispronounced as "Sibboleth") as a test, the Gildeadites were able to identify and kill their enemies (Jdg 12:1–7).

ZAREPHATH (*ZAR eh fath; "dye"*)—A Phoenician coastal city, south of Sidon, that was famous for its glassware. During a time of famine, Elijah stayed there and was miraculously fed (1Ki 17:8–24; Ob 1:20).

ZARETHAN (*ZAR eh thon*)—A city in the Jordan Valley (Jos 3:16). It was there that Hiram the Phoenician cast bronze vessels for Solomon's Temple (1Ki 7:46).

ZEALOT—A member of a political party that was dedicated to the liberation of Israel from foreign dominion. The Zealot movement originated during the time of Herod the Great (Lk 6:15; Ac 1:13).

ZEBAH *(ZEH bah)*—One of two Midianite kings whom Gideon pursued and killed near Penuel, the place where Jacob wrestled with an angel (Jdg 6–8; Ps 83:11).

ZEBEDEE *(ZEB eh dee)*—The husband of Salome. A resident of Bethsaida (near the Sea of Galilee), he was the father of James and John, with whom he mended fishing nets (Mk 1:19–20).

ZEBOIIM, ZEBOYIM *(zee BOY im)*—A land in south Canaan that was ruled by Shemeber, one of five kings defeated in the Valley of Siddim by an alliance of four kings (Gen 10:19, 14:2, 8).

ZEBOIM *(zee BOH im; "hyena")*—**1.** A valley near Michmash overlooked by a landmark mountain used by Philistines pursuing King Saul of Israel (1Sa 13:15). **2.** A Benjaminite village settled by returning exiles (Ne 11:34).

ZEBUL *(ZEE buhl; "lofty place" or "dominion")*—A ruling officer over the Canaanite city of Shechem. Zebul was appointed by Abimelech (Jdg 9:22).

ZEBULUN *(ZEB yoo luhn)*—The tenth son of Jacob (Gen 30:20). His descendants, the Zebulunites, were participants in the Maccabean revolt. Nazareth was located in the abundant land of Zebulun (Mt 4:13–16).

ZECHARIAH, ZACHARIAS *(ZEK uh rye uh, ZAK uh rye us)*—**1.** An Old Testament priest-prophet; author of the Book of Zechariah (Zec 1:1). **2.** The name of several men in the Old Testament, including clan leaders, Levites, singers, priests, a king, a counselor, a witness, and a martyr. **3.** The father of John the Baptist (Lk 3:2).

ZECHARIAH, BOOK OF (*ZEK uh rye uh*)—The eleventh of 12 short Old Testament prophetic books delivered to exiled Jews. Zechariah encouraged the rebuilding of Jerusalem's temple and predicted a coming messianic kingdom.

ZEDAD (*ZE dad*)—The "outer limit" of the northern boundary of Israel's land inherited from Yahweh (Nu 34:8; Eze 47:15).

ZEDEKIAH (*zed eh KYE uh; "Yahweh is righteous"*)—1. One of 400 false prophets who opposed Micaiah. He predicted that King Ahab would defeat the Syrians (1Ki 22:11). 2. Judah's last king (597–586 B.C.); the youngest son of Josiah (2Ki 24:18).

ZELOPHEHAD (*zee LOH feh had*)—A man from the tribe of Manassah who had five daughters but no sons. The situation of women inheriting land necessitated a law concerning heiresses (Nu 27:1–11).

ZELZAH (*ZEL zuh*)—A town of Benjamin near Jerusalem. Samuel prophetically referred to Zelzah when he anointed Saul the first king of Israel (1Sa 10:2).

ZEMARAIM (*ZEM uh RAY ihm*)—1. A Benjaminite town north of Jericho. 2. A mountain in Ephraim upon which King Abijah of Judah stood to judge Israel's rebellion (2Ch 13:4).

ZEMARITES (*ZEM uh rytes*)—Descendants of Noah's son Ham. They apparently settled along the Mediterranean coast near Tripolis (Gen 10:15–17).

ZENAS (*ZEE nuss; "gift of Zeus"*)—An expert in Jewish law. After a grueling confrontation with local experts, Paul sent for Zenas (Titus 3:8–13).

ZEPHANIAH (*ZEF uh nye uh; "He whom Yahweh has protected"*)—A prophet of

Jerusalem at a time when Assyrian power diminished and Babylonian power increased. He was probably a prince descended from King Hezekiah (Zep 1:1).

ZEPHANIAH, BOOK OF—The ninth of 12 Old Testament books of minor prophets. Believed to have been written during the reign of King Josiah of Judah (640–609 B.C.), the book warned of God's universal, national, and local judgment.

ZEPHATHAH (*ZEF uh thuh*)—A valley near Mareshah in western Judah. Warriors of King Asa met and defeated an overwhelmingly large and well-equipped Ethiopian army there (2Ch 14:1–12).

ZER (*ZUR*)—A fortified town northwest of the Sea of Galilee. It was given to the tribe of Naphtali by the casting of lots (Jos 19:35).

ZERAH (*ZEE rah*)—**1.** A son of Judah; grandson of Jacob. A twin brother of Perez, Zerah was the ancestral father of the Zerites (Gen 38:30). **2.** Zerah "the Ethiopian," a Cushite king who led a powerful army against King Asa at Zephathah (2Ch 14:9). **3.** An ancestor of Jesus (Mt 1:3).

ZERED (*ZEE red*)—A brook that formed the natural border between Moab and Edom in Transjordan. Just north of major mountains of Edom, it drained into the Dead Sea. The Israelites camped at the Wadi Zered on their journey to Moab (Nu 21:12).

ZERUBBABEL (*zeh ROOB uh bel; "shoot of Babylon"*)—The successor to Sheshbazzar as governor of Jerusalem. He led exiles from Babylon in rebuilding the temple (Ezr 2:2–5:2; Hag 1:1).

ZERUIAH (*zeh ROO yuh*)—A sister or half-sister to David (1Ch 2:16). Her three sons were all generals or chief officers for King David (2Sa 2:18, 17:25).

ZEUS—The supreme Greek deity; known to the Romans as Jupiter. In Lystra, Barnabas was mistaken for Zeus (Ac 14:12).

ZIBA (*ZY buh*)—A servant of King Saul. He was charged with caring for Saul's crippled son Mephibosheth. After David assumed the throne, Ziba tried to gain Saul's inheritance by claiming that Mephibosheth was disloyal to the new king. Later, when Mephibosheth pleaded innocent, David divided Saul's estate between Ziba and Mephibosheth (2Sa 9, 16, 19).

ZIGGURAT (*ZIG uh raht*)—Any massive Mesopotamian shrine dedicated to rites of a local god. They are not specifically mentioned in the Bible.

ZIKLAG (*ZIK lag*)—A place of sanctuary located across the Judean mountains from the King's Highway. It was given by Achish, Philistine King of Gath, to David, who was escaping Saul's violence (1Sa 27).

ZILPAH (*ZIL puh*)—A female slave of Jacob who became his second wife when Leah no longer bore children. She was the mother of Gad and Asher (Gen 30:9–13).

ZIMRAN (*ZIM ran*)—The first of six sons of Keturah, Abraham's concubine wife after the death of Sarah (Gen 25:2; 1Ch 1:32).

ZIMRI (*ZIM ree*)—1. An Israelite who was killed for taking a Midianite wife (Nu 25). 2. A Judahite elder (1Ch 2:6). 3. A descendant of Saul (1Ch 8:36). 4. A conspirator against Israel's king Elah (1Ki 16:9).

ZIN, WILDERNESS OF—An arid, rock-strewn region of the Negev Highlands. It was bordered on the east by Edom and on the west

ZION

Another name for Jerusalem, Zion was originally an ancient fortress that occupied a plateau 2,500 feet above the Mediterranean Sea. Its inhabitants safely drew water from the nearby Gihon Spring through a rock-cut passage within the walls. The fortress itself was protected by massive natural rock, formidable walls, gates, and towers.

Well into the reign of David, Jebusites held the fortress. Zion was considered so secure that they mocked all attempts to conquer it. Finally, Israel triumphed over the plateau and renamed it the City of David (2Sa 5:6–7). King Solomon built his temple on the adjoining Mt. Moriah, which was often called Zion. The prophet Isaiah spoke of God's love for Zion (Isa 31:4). The Apostle John referred to the heavenly city as Mt. Zion (Rev 14:1).

by the Sinai Desert. Much of early Hebrew history took place there (Nu 20:1).

ZIOR (ZYE or; "smallness")— A Canaanite town located somewhere north of the wilderness of Zin. It was inherited by the tribe of Judah (Jos 15:53).

ZIPH (zif)—1. A Judean town (Jos 15:24, 55). 2. A hilly wilderness located a few miles southeast of Hebron. Saul and David encountered one another there (1Sa 23, 26; 1Ch 2:42).

ZIPPOR (*ZIP or*)—The father of Balak, king of Moab (Nu 22:2, 10).

ZIPPORAH (*ZIH por uh; "bird"*)—One of seven daughters of Jethro, a priest of Midian. The first wife of Moses, she obeyed God by circumcising her sons (Ex 4:18–31).

ZIZ (*zihz*)—An ascending slope near the wilderness of Tekoa, 12 miles from Jerusalem. The Ammonites and Moabites traveled along this pass in an attack against King Jehoshaphat (2Ch 20:16).

ZOAN (*ZOH ehn*)—An Egyptian city on the Nile Delta. A home to pharaohs, it was the seat of worship of the deity Seth. Moses appeared in the fields of Zoan (Ps 78:12, 43).

ZOBAH, ZOBA (*ZOH buh*)—A kingdom near Syria. Ruled by King Hadadezer, it was rich in precious metals and chariot weaponry. Chariotless, David defeated Zobah and netted a booty of gold and copper (2Sa 8:3–8).

ZOPHAR (*ZOH far*)—The last of Job's three friends; a Naamathite. He concluded that Job's wickedness deserved more suffering (Job 2:11, 11:1, 20:1, 42:9).

ZOPHIM (*ZOH fim*)—A field atop Mt. Pisgah, near the northeast shore of the Dead Sea. In an attempt to curse Israel, Balak built seven altars there (Nu 23:14).

ZORAH (*ZOR uh*)—A town located about 15 miles west of Jerusalem. It was the home of Samson's father, and Samson was raised there.